The Speedy Extinction of Evil and Misery

The Speedy Extinction of Evil and Misery

Selected Prose

of James Thomson (B.V.)

EDITED BY

WILLIAM DAVID SCHAEFER

University of California Press

Berkeley and Los Angeles 1967

University of California Press
Berkeley and Los Angeles, California

Cambridge University Press
London, England

Library of Congress Catalog Card Number: 67-11799
Printed in the United States of America
Designed by Theo Jung

Contents

Introduction

The most recent edition of Thomson's prose works, a collection of thirteen of his less attractive essays, was compiled by Bertram Dobell more than seventy years ago (*Biographical and Critical Studies,* London, 1896). Dobell, who for two decades had been attempting to establish Thomson as a major author, could not have done greater harm to his friend's reputation than he did in publishing this volume, the first 240 pages of which are devoted to three "biographical essays" Thomson had written for *Cope's Tobacco Plant,* a literary journal published to advertise tobacco. These three essays on Rabelais, Saint-Amant, and Ben Jonson, with their repeated references to the smoking habits and tobacco interests of the subjects (eighty pages alone are concerned with a survey of tobacco references in Jonson's plays), sound more like the work of a nicotine fanatic than that of a serious author. Dobell expressed the hope that, if reader response so dictated, *Biographical and Critical Studies* would be only the first of a five-volume collected edition of Thomson's prose. Reader response was, to say the least, limited.

Twelve years earlier another friend of Thomson's, the freethought author and editor, G. W. Foote, had brought out an edition equally limited in its appeal (*Satires and Profanities,* London, 1884), a collection of twenty-three at times blasphemous essays that Thomson had published in the *National Reformer* and the *Secularist.* Even in secularist circles the volume does not seem to have sold very well, for although a second, greatly abridged, edition appeared in 1890, this occurred only after most of the 3,000 copies originally printed had been destroyed in a warehouse fire. Today, even in the best of libraries, one rarely finds a copy of *Satires and Profanities.*

The third and only other "selected prose of James Thomson" was compiled by "B.V." himself and published the year before his death (*Essays and Phantasies,* London, 1881). Although by far the best of the three, this collection is really no more representative than the other two because Thomson, in attempting to attract as wide an audience as possible, included all four of his phantasies, omitted all "profanities," and reprinted very little in way of literary criticism. Moreover, roughly half of the 1,000 copies printed were destroyed in the same warehouse fire, making *Essays and Phantasies* as difficult to obtain as *Satires and Profanities.* I doubt if there are a dozen libraries in the world fortunate enough to own copies of both.

Several other editions are worthy of mention. In 1892 J. M. Robertson brought out *Poems, Essays, and Fragments* in which he published five essays not previously collected; two of these, however, are minor secularist articles Foote had wisely omitted from *Satires and Profanities,* and the other three are early essays written when Thomson was still in his twenties. In 1884 Dobell collected everything Thomson had ever published on Shelley and had it printed for private circulation; in 1909 the same thing was done with the essays on Meredith. Both volumes are now collector's items. More easily available (but still rare) are Dobell's 1905 edition of Thomson's essays on and translations from Leopardi (*Essays, Dialogues and Thoughts of Giacomo Leopardi*) and his 1910 edition of the articles on Whitman (*Walt Whitman: The Man and the Poet*).

In short, then, although more than sixty of Thomson's essays, phantasies, articles, and reviews have been reprinted in various editions, these works are not only difficult to obtain, but represent only a quarter of his total prose writings—unfortunately, neither the best nor, for the twentieth-century reader, the most interesting portion. To read Thomson's published prose in its entirety necessitates going to the periodicals in which his work originally appeared, and these periodicals are even more difficult to locate than the collected editions. In America, I know of only two complete sets of the *National Reformer,* the periodical in which Thomson published almost exclusively from 1862 to 1875 (the Library of Congress owns one set; the other is in California at the Claremont School of Theology). The *Secularist* is equally hard to find (Yale apparently has the only complete set in America), and although copies of *Cope's Tobacco Plant* are not uncommon in American libraries, particularly in the tobacco-growing states, few authors, major or minor, have published in periodicals as obscure as the *London Investigator, The Liberal, Progress,* and the *Jersey Independent.*

Consequently, the present edition, which contains sixteen

previously uncollected works along with sixteen of the most important pieces reprinted in earlier editions (including nine of the nineteen Thomson himself selected for *Essays and Phantasies*), makes available some of the best of "B.V.'s" prose in what is, for the first time, a representative selection of his work. The arrangement is both generic and thematic, so that the section containing "satires and profanities" is dominated by Thomson's religious writings, "essays and articles" by his social and political criticism, "critical studies and reviews" by just that, and "phantasies," the final section, by two of his "prose poems." Because the edition includes works covering a twenty-year period, the generic-thematic arrangement at times gives a false impression of inconsistency or even contradiction in Thomson's ideas and beliefs. To minimize confusion, introductory notes preface each selection, and, within the major divisions, the selections are usually arranged by date of composition; it also seems advisable, however, without going into the complexities of Thomson's biography, to sketch his career as a prose writer and to summarize the important phases in his intellectual development.

Thomson was born in Port Glasgow, Scotland, in 1834. Having lost his parents as a child, he was educated at the Royal Caledonian Asylum, a school for the children of poor Scottish soldiers and sailors, where he proved to be a precocious, imaginative student. At the age of sixteen he entered the Royal Military Asylum in Chelsea and, after four years of training, enlisted as an army schoolmaster, a profession he followed until 1862 when he left the army and settled permanently in London. While stationed in Ireland in 1852–53, he became intimate with Charles Bradlaugh, and it was with Bradlaugh's aid that his first essay was published, significantly, in a free-thought periodical (the *London Investigator*, December 1, 1858). In the early 1860's, Thomson published a few articles in the *Jersey Independent* and the *Daily Telegraph*, but from 1862 to 1875 most of his poetry and virtually all his prose works, more than a hundred articles and reviews in addition to translations from Heine, Goethe, and Leopardi, appeared in Bradlaugh's "Atheist-Republican-Malthusian" *National Reformer*.

During these years Thomson held a number of minor clerical jobs, and his writing was done either after work or during his not infrequent periods of unemployment, the result, at least in part, of the chronic alcoholism from which he suffered throughout his adult life. Only once during this period, in 1873 when he worked briefly as a war correspondent for the New York *World,* did he have steady employment as a professional writer, but beginning in 1874, when he worked full time as a staff writer for Bradlaugh, and continuing until his death in 1882, Thomson earned his living entirely through his pen and primarily through his prose writings. In 1876, after an argument with Bradlaugh had ended their long friendship, he published some fifty articles and reviews in G. W. Foote's *Secularist,* and from 1876 until the magazine ceased publication in 1881, he wrote voluminously for *Cope's Tobacco Plant.* I estimate, in fact, that over the five-year period roughly 25 percent of all the material published in *Cope's* was written by Thomson, work that included literary reviews, phantasies, informal essays, and long biographical studies, in addition to such things as a thirteen-part article on "Tobacco Legislation in the Three Kingdoms" and a seven-part study of "Tobacco Smuggling in the Last Generation." Not until 1881, however, did Thomson attain the goal he had long been seeking, publication in the "respectable periodicals." In the last years of his life, after more than two decades of hiding behind pseudonyms—"Bysshe Vanolis" or the famous "B.V.," "X.," "Crepusculus," "Sigvat," "T.J.," and "J.S.T."—he finally had the satisfaction of seeing "James Thomson" printed at the end of articles in the *Athenaeum* and *Gentleman's Magazine.* Had he lived even another few years, continuing to publish in such periodicals, it is unlikely that his prose works would have been so completely ignored by both his generation and ours.

During a literary career that spanned nearly a quarter of a century, Thomson naturally altered a good many of his beliefs. He was raised as an orthodox Christian, and, although in the 1850's his Christianity was tempered by his reading of Carlyle, Emerson, and Shelley, as late as 1863 his world view, as indicated in his attitude toward Frederic Harrison's *Meaning of History,* was still Christian-oriented. But by 1864, after a few years of life in London with Bradlaugh and the National Reformers, he completely rejected Christianity and became a pantheist; as he explains in his "Introductory Note" to "A Lady of Sorrow," he "believed in the soul's immortality as a Materialist believes in the immortality of matter; he believed that the universal soul subsists for ever, just as a Materialist believes that universal matter subsists for ever." Inextricably involved with this new pantheistic faith was a new philosophy of life, an optimistic sort of *carpe diem* in which he implored his fellowmen, as he states it in the "sermon" that concludes "A Lady of Sorrow," to "really live, knowing, and gladly accepting, and bravely working out your little part in the sublime economy of the universe." Becoming convinced that Christianity was a major stumbling block to "really living life," he also at this time began to write the blasphemous antichristian satires that during the next decade were to earn him, in the eyes of National Reformers, the prose-laureateship of free thought. But although the attacks upon religion continued well into the 1870's, both the "live life" philosophy and the pantheism that gave rise to it had faded out by the end of the 1860's, to be replaced by a bleak atheism; thus by 1873 and the completion of "The City of Dreadful Night," Thomson was able to bring "authentic word" that "there is no God," that

> The world rolls round for ever like a mill;
> It grinds out death and life and good and ill;
> It has no purpose, heart or mind or will.

In spite of his long association with the *National Reformer,* Thomson never became actively involved in reform movements, believing with Carlyle that reform must begin—and end—with the individual. Although a Republican "in principle," he never actively participated in the Republican movement, his major contribution to the cause being his attacks upon despotism and imperialism as revealed in such essays as "A Commission of Inquiry on Royalty" and the bitterly biased criticism of Disraeli ("In the Valley of Humiliation"). Thomson's social criticism centered, for the most part, simply upon a denunciation of what he called "Bumbleism"—in effect, the dullness, dishonesty, conservatism, and complacency of his century. And it was only when he came to realize that Bumble was impervious to change, that there was in fact a natural savagery in the human heart, that his atheism became combined with a pessimism as to any hope for improvement in mankind. "The City of Dreadful Night" is a pessimist's manifesto for a select group, those "whose faith and hope are dead, and who would die," but in his

"Proposals for the Speedy Extinction of Evil and Misery" Thomson involves the entire human race, ridiculing the prospect of progress, laughing at man's dreams of perfectibility.

As a literary critic, Thomson discovered different values to accord with his changing views on God and man. While a Christian, and later as a pantheist, he was strongly attracted to the English Romantic poets and to the idea that the "inspired" poet was God's messenger, a divine hierophant sent to reveal the beauty and harmony of the visible universe. But as he gradually moved toward the position of atheist and pessimist, he became increasingly convinced that the great works were those that depicted life realistically, the great authors those who were not afraid to show the "bitter old and wrinkled truth / Stripped naked of all vesture that beguiles." Thus, in his many reviews and biographical essays of the 1870's, Thomson was attracted to men like Swift, Burns, Browning, and Meredith; his early interest in Novalis was replaced by admiration for Heine; and it was Leopardi, not Dante; Epictetus, not Plato; Whitman and Melville, not Emerson, whose works he attempted to learn and to propagate. For Thomson, always retaining a touch of the army schoolmaster, was at heart a moralist and humanist who, even after he had lost faith in both God and man, paradoxically attempted to enlighten and to teach, however unpleasant the lesson for the day.

It is no longer necessary to make apologies for the subject matter of the satires Thomson wrote for the secularists, and it is most unlikely that anyone today will write to the publisher of this edition, as did one Victorian gentleman after reading a Thomson "profanity," and suggest that "your paper, yourself, and all your supporters ought to be burned." Indeed, many of the ideas expressed in Thomson's "profanities" are now commonplace, and the modern reader will probably be less shocked by the content than by the freshness of expression, whether Thomson is writing about Jehovah, Son, and Company as "The Story of a Famous Old Jewish Firm," or describing Jesus as a "poor sexless Jew with a noble feminine heart, and a magnificent though uncultivated and crazy brain," or proudly proclaiming that "the man is a fool who in his heart says there is no God, and has not the courageous wisdom to publish it abroad with tongue or pen." Such views are, of course, no more cheerful today, or any less blasphemous to Christians, than they were in the 1860's and 1870's, but, if we are to judge by the continued interest in "The City of Dreadful Night," there is considerable attraction even in repulsion, and few modern readers (attracted or not) would agree with an early reviewer that a work such as "Proposals for the Speedy Extinction of Evil and Misery" is "deplorably vulgar." Readers of "The City," first approaching Thomson's prose with expectations of gloom and melancholy, will, in fact, be pleasantly surprised by the wealth and variety of his humor. In the "Proposals," for instance, Thomson wisely harnessed his talents to the genius of Jonathan Swift, and, if the satire lacks the delightful morbidity of Swift's baby eating, the moral to be drawn from Thomson's modest proposal—that universal suicide is the key to eliminating evil and misery—has all the black charm of the conclusion of *Gulliver's Travels*. There is surely nothing "funny" about his attack on Bishop Alford or about his analysis of "Jesus Christ Our Great Exemplar," but Thomson's sense of the absurd stood him in good stead when he picked up the monthly paper of the Association for Intercessory Prayer and playfully pointed out the ludicrousness of two or three hundred subscribers praying that N. be cured of gluttony and drunkenness. Which "N.," Thomson asks, of all the hundreds of Englishmen who are gluttons and drunkards? "Why, the particular N. meant by the anonymous individual who sent a certain communication to the secretary of the Association for Intercessory Prayer before the 24th of one month, so that the case was inserted in the next monthly paper." God must surely be omniscient, Thomson points out, "not to be quite puzzled with such prayers," and "good-natured indeed not to fly into a passion with such outrageous stupidity."

Many of these free-thought articles from the *National Reformer* and the *Secularist*, as well as the tobacco articles written for *Cope's Tobacco Plant*, were, of course, little more than hack-work. Not even Ruskin or Huxley could have written for more than five years on the subject of tobacco without staining their reputations, and Thomson's long association with tobacco and free thought has undoubtedly hurt his position as a serious author. He once admitted, referring to the *National Reformer*, that "I am an author thoroughly unknown, and writing for a periodical of the deepest disrepute," and, as he well knew, most of the readers of these "disreputable" journals cared "nothing for literature as literature, but only as a club to hit parsons and lords on the head with." By and large, these articles were expected to do little more than feed the apparently insatiable freethought appetites of men long since "unconverted" from religion, and it must have been somewhat discouraging to attempt to write sophisticated satire for such an audience (on at least one occasion the editor had to publish a note explaining to a confused if freethinking reader that "B.V.'s" recent reference to "merciful providence" had been ironic). But it is a tribute to both his sincerity and his skill that Thomson succeeds as consistently as he does, even when merely "hacking out" another article to amuse and edify secularist iconoclasts who, for the most part, were too busily engaged in hurling bricks at a God no longer there to recognize Thomson's true value.

Of course not all of Thomson's prose is in this vein. His social criticism — to Thomson, at least, the more important aspect of his work — is in the great tradition of Victorian prose. This work reminds us somewhat of Matthew Arnold's, lacking Arnold's range and urbane sophistication, no doubt, but at one with Arnold in expressing the belief that Hebraism was definitely not the *unum necessarium* for the nineteenth century (as Thomson put it, the "continual cry of Work! Work! Work! is simply the Imperative mood of a doctrine which, couched in the quiet Indicative, reads, 'Mankind is a damned rascal' "). Thomson's attack upon Bumbledom was partly inspired by Arnold's comments on the Philistines, and, like Arnold, Thomson devoted much of his career to writing "biographical essays" and "introductory reviews" that were intended to propagate some of the best "known and thought in the world." Thomson, however, distrusting what he considered to be Arnold's kid-glove aloofness, offered a more down-to-earth "message" than Arnold's plea for "sweetness and light" Hellenism, calling for a sort of workingman's realism, encouraging men to live their lives fully and honestly while facing up to harsh reality. The message is neither original nor profound, but there is a clean masculinity and directness in Thomson's statement which avoid both the sentimental "robust optimism" of Browning or Henley and the limp-wristed hedonism of the later aesthetes.

Thomson's essays and articles also provide fresh insight into "Victorianism," and contain some lively portraits of the age. His prediction at the outbreak of the Franco-Prussian War makes interesting reading even a century later ("The time is not very distant when France will be glad to have in the center of Europe, between herself and Russia, a solid German Fatherland"), and his warning about the dangers of rushing into a democratic republic before England is "taught and trained into something like fitness for it," reminds us again that even liberals in the 1880's still had fears about "shooting Niagara." His attack upon Disraeli has a white-hot intensity seldom encountered in today's political debate, and although his playful criticism of a "Saturday Reviewer," his anecdotal musings on pipe smoking, or his impressions of a French border town on the eve of a Spanish revolution, may move too slowly for modern tastes, students of literature will surely appreciate a snapshot such as that in which we see Thomson at the concert looking down from his one-shilling seat to study the face, beaming with rapture, of Robert Browning ("I have seen him throw up his hands and let them fall helpless, made womanish for the moment with wonder"). In these general essays, students of literature will also find Thomson's style to be of interest, a style that reminds us, in turn (and sometimes simultaneously), of Lamb, Carlyle, Ruskin, Arnold, Huxley, and even Newman. If eclecticism in prose style is sinful, then Thomson is indeed the chief of sinners, and his stylistic "faults," shared at least in part by most of his more famous contemporaries, are easily detected (a tendency to overwrite, occasional "cuteness," a maddening pride in "correctness," incredibly bad dialogue, and overdrawn analogies). The odd thing, however, is that Thomson's style—in spite of the bits and pieces of which it is composed—has a certain charm and flavor distinctly its own, and I suspect that anyone familiar with his prose could, as I have done, turn to the hundreds of unsigned articles in the periodicals for which he wrote and recognize his work at a glance.

Thomson's achievement as a literary critic and reviewer is the most remarkable, and least known, aspect of his work, remarkable particularly when we remember that he lacked the advantages of intimacy with a literary circle, or even of a university background. He was at one with his age in admiring Carlyle, Ruskin, Mill, and George Eliot (and Dante and Goethe for that matter); he was outrageously wrong in his early championing of Garth Wilkinson and in his failure to recognize Dickens' genius. But Thomson was far in advance of his age in his other evaluations—in his virtual worship of Shelley as early as the 1840's; in his early disillusionment with Tennyson and recognition of Browning as the greatest poet of the age, and this at a time when most of his contemporaries were still considering the author of *Men and Women* to be Mrs. Browning's lesser half ("Tennyson is a rare 'literary luxury' for us all, and especially for our youths and maidens; but Robert Browning is indeed the poet of Men and Women"); in his appreciation of Blake, his essay on Blake's poems anticipating even Swinburne's famous early study; and in his praise of Meredith, whom, long before most Victorians were aware of his work, Thomson was proclaiming as "the Robert Browning of our novelists." Thomson was one of the first to appreciate and to translate Leopardi; he was one of few Victorians to read Swift and Burns for the right reasons; at a time when "Rabelais," "Flaubert," "Baudelaire," and "Whitman" were dirty words to most Englishmen, Thomson was extolling these men's works; and decades before twentieth-century criticism was to launch its attack upon Victorian literature, Thomson recognized that "it is astonishing what a large part of even a good modern book has been written without any exercise of the faculty of thought," had praised works by Pope and Swift because "nearly every sentence has required a distinct intellectual effort [that shames] by their powerful virility our effeminate modern books."

The phantasies, on the other hand—although Thomson himself probably considered "A Lady of Sorrow" to be his finest work in prose—may not prove very exciting to the modern reader. This is unfortunate because "A Lady of Sorrow," in spite of its excessive length and the flimsiness of the pseudo-Darwinian pantheism preached by the Shadow woman in Part III, does have passages at least equaling the best of De Quincey. From the terse opening line ("I lived in London, and alone"), through the nightmare journey into labyrinthic caverns with the culminating carnival orgy ("the maddest and most lawless in a world all mad and lawless"), right up to the conclusion when, after the dolorous march of death, the "gloom grows deeper still and yet more awful," Thomson reaches toward a terrible beauty seldom attained even in the best passages of "The City." And even more emphatically than "The City" or the "Proposals for the Speedy Extinction of Evil and Misery," the phantasy titled "In Our Forest of the Past," where the moanings of all the wasted and frustrated lives echo back from the past and blend with the swelling storm, could serve as Thomson's final and most pessimistic statement as to the futility of life.

I do not know whether Thomson's prose is better than his poetry; I suspect that it is. That his collected prose would fill ten or twelve volumes, while his poetry could be collected in one, is no indication as to quality; but it is unfortunate that in the five books, some twenty articles, and seven doctoral dissertations devoted to Thomson in the past quarter century, so little attention has been paid to his prose. It would be absurd to suggest that he deserves the same recognition afforded to men like Carlyle, Ruskin, or Arnold; his prose exerted absolutely no influence, stylistically or intellectually, upon his age or ours. But Thomson is perhaps our finest example of a "middle-class," self-educated Victorian author, and his works provide a fascinating portrait of one man's struggle to come to terms with the new ideas and shifting values of a dynamic century. We can hardly say that in Thomson's prose we have found God's plenty; but we can say that his prose is of greater value and of considerably greater interest than has yet been recognized.

A word on the text of this edition. My text is based on the original periodical publications except for works that Thomson himself had reprinted and (in a few instances) revised. For these works, mainly involving the selections from *Essays and Phantasies,* I have used the later text. All Thomson's footnotes are included, and his spelling and punctuation are left unchanged, except for obvious misprints which I have silently corrected. In my own footnotes I have indicated the sources of Thomson's quotations; the few passages without notes are those I was unable to identify. In four instances I have reprinted only part of a longer work: the essay titled "Mill on Religion" is the first installment of a long and cumbersome review; from the essay on Heine, I have omitted the first two sections which review William Stigand's book on Heine; from the long "Indolence: A Moral Essay" I have omitted Thomson's rather tedious classification of the indolent; and from "Proposals for the Speedy Extinction of Evil and Misery" I have printed only four of the nine sections, for reasons explained in the prefatory note to that essay. All the selections have brief introductions giving the publication background and supplemental information about the work and its author, but a complete checklist of Thomson's prose may be found in my recent study, *James Thomson (B.V.): Beyond "The City"* (University of California Press, 1965).

This edition evolved from that study, for which I had occasion to read everything that Thomson ever published. Consequently, acknowledgments as expressed in my earlier book would largely apply here also, but in addition I should like to express my thanks to the University of California for several grants that enabled me to bring this material together sooner than I could have without financial assistance; to Mr. W. R. Denton, acquisitions librarian at the Claremont School of Theology, who kindly allowed me to xerox the library's previously unmolested copies of the *National Reformer*; and to librarians at the University of California in Berkeley, the Wisconsin State Historical Society, Yale University, the Bodleian Library, and the British Museum for assistance in locating and photocopying additional material.

W. D. S.

I. Satires and Profanities

Proposals for the Speedy Extinction of Evil and Misery

[*Thomson began writing his "Proposals" in 1868, but did not complete the work until 1871; it appeared in nine installments in the* National Reformer *(August 27–November 12, 1871). Although Thomson included it in its entirety in* Essays and Phantasies, *a shortened version is reprinted herein. The omitted sections are mainly digressive and, unlike Swift's digressions in* A Tale of a Tub, *are not integral to the total work. Moreover, most of the ideas covered in the omitted sections — satire on reform committees, on a triune God, on Jesus as man versus Christ as divinity — are treated more effectively in other works included in this volume. As Thomson's frequent references to Swift indicate, Swift was very much on his mind when he wrote the satire, and obviously provided the pattern for the reformer who makes these modest proposals.*]

I

"Your promised Reformation is so indispensable; yet it comes not: who will begin it — with himself?" — CARLYLE: French Revolution, vol. i. book 2, chap. 8.

"But the lofty spirits of my century discovered a new, and as it were divine counsel: for not being able to make happy on earth any one person, they ignored the individual, and gave themselves to seek universal felicity; and having easily found this, of a multitude singly sad and wretched they make a joyous and happy people." — LEOPARDI: Palinodia.

"Whether the human race is progressing is a strange unanswerable philosophical question. Why is it not asked, Does the human race alter? This question is higher. Only from alteration can we draw any inference as to improvement or the opposite." — NOVALIS: vol. ii. p. 268.

IN THE OLD YOUNG years, when I could still wonder at things which are human, I now and then wondered how it came to pass that while so many learned and subtle treatises had been written to solve the question of the origin of evil; treatises doubtless of great value if only the question would kindly condescend to be soluble; there had yet been so few essays towards the extinction of the said evil. It seemed to me that the doctors were letting the sick man perish before their eyes, while they discussed at length the remote origin of his maladies, instead of the present condition and the treatment instantly required. And it seemed to me that even those who did concern themselves with the present condition of the patient, the charitable associations and philanthropists generally, acted not as doctors who hoped to cure, but were rather as kind nurses who tried to soothe the sufferer and lessen the pangs of his certain perishing; they moistened his parched lips and wiped his damp brow, smoothed his pillow, tidied up his room, gave him narcotics and anodynes, humoured his sick caprices, spoke cheering words, and smiled vain hopes; but with the horrible, devouring, mortal cancer they did not even try to contend. I have since heard that in recent times, say within the last hundred years, projects for the universal reform and beatification of mankind have begun to abound; but as none of these (to the best of my knowledge) has been thoroughly realised, it follows that even if any of them are theoretically perfect they still remain practically imperfect, and that, therefore, the spacious ground is still to-let for system-building purposes. And I may modestly add that the said projects, in so far as I know anything of them, appear to derive from what I cannot but think a wrong principle; so that in my own poor judgment (which naturally is for me the one best judgment in the world) I am bound to prefer my own proposals, which derive from what I must esteem the true principle.

But here I bethink me that some one may deny the need or use of any such project; affirming (for what is there that some people will not affirm?) that mankind and the condition of mankind are as near perfection now as they ever will or can be, and that for the extinction of what we call evil and misery the human race and the world in which it dwells must be extinguished. To such a one I will only reply, before entering tranquilly on the exposition of my proposals, that he is far in the rear of our most advanced thinkers, and has but small share in the present glorious aspirations of Humanity; that if he does not take heed to himself he is in danger of becoming a cynic, an odious, yelping, snappish animal that lives in a tub, and pulls to pieces even this house, in order to fling the staves at decent people and trip up passers-by with the hoops; that if he feels no necessity, or has no hope, of becoming much better himself, the majority of us feel such want for ourselves, and have good hope that it shall be satisfied, if not in ourselves, yet in our more or less distant posterity, in which hope we find great and reasonable comfort; and lastly, that it is quite plain that myself and others would never weave projects and build systems for catching and caging the said evil and misery, if these did not actually exist, and were not to be caught and caged, just as there would never have been bird-traps and fishing-nets were there not birds and fish not only in being but liable to capture.

To me it seems clear that there are two radical universal reforms essential to the real triumph of any and every reform ever attempted or proposed, and that these two reforms once accomplished, all others will be found included in them; and I therefore consider them as solely entitled to our study and exertions. For who wishing to fell a tree, would bring it down leaf by leaf and chip by chip, if it could be effectually axed from the ground? and who, wanting to purify a river, would filter it by bucketsful, if he could dam off the polluting drain higher up? The two reforms, to which I have reduced this vast problem, are simply a universal change to perfection of nature and human nature: of which I think that we as men should enterprise the latter first. The radical reform of human nature consists merely in this, that every human being shall put off the seven cardinal with all the minor sins, follies and defects, and shall at once in lieu thereof put on the seven cardinal with all the minor virtues, wisdoms and graces; or, in other words, that each shall annihilate in self the imperfect human nature, and create in self a perfect divine nature. When every human being has performed this easy double operation (of which the second part follows as naturally on the first as a step of the right foot one of the left), I am inclined to believe that the great work of the extinction of evil and misery, and the establishment of universal good and felicity, will be more than half accomplished. The radical reform of nature consists merely in this, that the universe shall be made altogether and exactly such as the perfect men shall require. With this second reform, I am further inclined to believe that the pilgrimage of man from hell on earth to heaven on earth will be completed; that evil and misery, both as suffering and vice, will be extinct beyond resurrection; that everybody will be good and happy everywhere evermore.

Some people, who have not bestowed upon this problem such long and painful thought as the writer, may at first sight deem that the radical universal reform of human nature, though of the utmost simplicity (being, indeed, but as putting off one suit of clothes and putting on another), will not be very easy to effect. But a little candid thought will prove to them that it must certainly be much less difficult than any of the merely partial and superficial reforms which have been and are now being attempted; all of which this supersedes amicably by inclusion. For hitherto nearly all plans of reform have been trying to get plentiful fruit from a barren tree, and clean water from a foul stream; while this would first make the tree fruitful and the fountain pure. And hitherto nearly every reformer, whether social or political, moral or religious, has endeavoured to make a large number of men and women (not to speak of children), and has usually hoped to make in the course of time all other men and women (of whom no two can be quite like each other and no one quite like the reformer; and of whose various characters and temperaments, minds, bodies and circumstances he could know little or nothing), think and believe and act in precisely the same way as himself. But in the scheme I venture to propose, every man will modestly limit himself to the reform of one person only; which person he knows and loves infinitely better than any one else; and which person is of exactly the same character, temperament, mind and body, and always situated in exactly the same circumstances, as himself, the reformer.

II

As this point is of capital importance, I think it well to bring to my assistance against all previous and other reformers (for whom, however, my feelings are of the most benevolent nature), two or three passages from writers of authority. And first I will quote from one of the most solid and useful sections of one of the greatest works of perhaps the greatest of our divines; Section ix. of "A Tale of a Tub": being "A dissertation concerning the original, the use, and improvement of Madness in a Commonwealth." And I may remark that this subject has been strangely neglected by other philosophers, considering how much every Commonwealth, whatever its form of government, has been and still is indebted to this noble condition of mind. "For what man, in the natural state or course of thinking, did ever conceive it in his power to reduce the notions of all mankind exactly to the same length and breadth and height of his own? Yet this is the first humble and civil design of all innovators in the empire of reason. . . . Now I would gladly be informed how it is possible to account for such imaginations as these in particular men, without recourse to my phenomenon of vapours ascending from the lower faculties to overshadow the brain, and there distilling into conceptions for which the narrowness of our mother-tongue has not yet assigned any other name besides that of madness or phrenzy." Montaigne also, who is usually so temperate in his language, cries out in a great passion of contemptuous indignation (book ii. chap. 32, "Defence of Seneca and Plutarch"): "It appears to each that the model form of human nature is in him; all others should be regulated in accordance with him: the ways which are not as his ways are feigned or wrong. What beastly stupidity! . . . Oh, the dangerous and insupportable donkeyishness! *Quelle bestiale stupidité! . . . O l'asnerie dangereuse et insupportable!*" And the great Italian writer already quoted, Leopardi, says ("Dialogue between Tristan and a Friend"): "*The individuals have given way to the masses*, say elegantly the modern thinkers. . . . Let the masses do all; though what they are to do without the individuals, being composed of individuals, I desire and hope to have explained to me by some of those now illuminating the world who understand individuals and masses." The careful reader will remark that the sarcasm here hinted does not touch me, while it wounds nearly all other reformers; they would reform by masses, I would reform by individuals; and my plan, in brief, is the flourishing modern plan of division of labour carried to its utmost perfection in the moral world.

To make the distinction yet more clear, if possible, and more clear the inestimable superiority of my principle over any other, let me call attention to the very peculiar and almost incredible fashion in which great practical problems are worked out by the reforms and reformers still in vogue. As a very fair type of the reforms I will take the recent Electoral Reform Bill, whose logical outcome is universal suffrage, for greater stake in the country can no one have than dear life. The problem is: Given a vast number of timbers, nearly all more or less rotten, it is required to build a seaworthy ship. To which our Reform Bill answers in triumph: Let us use the whole lot indiscriminately! Or in other terms: Given a foul and deformed body politic, full of all manner of diseases, required to make it pure, handsome and healthy. To which our Reform Bill answers cheerfully: Let us clothe it in fine new constitutional garments, with splints, bandages, padding, a good wig, a glass eye, a few false teeth, and so forth, and a complete cure will doubtless be effected! Now I beg the candid reader to lay his hand upon his heart, and declare upon his honour whether he really can consider these enterprises very hopeful. The ship may turn out a very Great Eastern for hugeness, but she will be at least as unseaworthy as her timbers are rotten, however deftly put together; and the more timbers the less cohesion. The diseased monster may be dressed out to look tolerably well as a dummy, but there will be even less life and health in him than before when he is strangled with ligaments and smothered with padding. The idea of working such stupendous marvels dwelleth not in me. My proposal modestly says: Let us get some sound timbers, and it will not be very hard to build with them a sound ship; let us get the pure, handsome, healthy body, and the question of clothes will not give us much trouble.

Not many readers will, I think, deny that when every human being has become perfect, the whole human race or society will be perfect also. But even with such perfection attained, there would probably still exist among mankind a large amount of suffering if the universe remained as it is. For not only man, but also the world in which man lives (or supposes himself to live), is at present very imperfect. I do not inquire into the origin of this mundane imperfection, any more than I inquired into the origin of human evil; I am content to propound a certain cure for both. How natural theologians manage to survey the world and find it all alive with divinity, find everywhere clear marks of a Creator infinite in goodness, wisdom and power, would certainly surprise me, if I were now capable of being surprised by any enormity of human folly or frenzy. For while in order to explain man's evil condition they have the excellent absurdities of Freewill and the Fall, even they do not pretend that the world has freewill, that it sinned and thus grew corrupt;

yet surely the world is about as badly off, as far from perfection, as man. Let me note a few of its maladies and defects. This poor earth of ours suffers dreadfully with colics, heartburns, violent vomitings, convulsions, paroxysms; she has burning fire in her belly and heart; and some of us always suffer directly or indirectly from the throes of her suffering. She has but one moon, while Jupiter has four, Uranus six, Saturn seven; and her domains are much smaller than those of the majority of the other planets. She has been roughly crushed in at top and bottom, and these extremities are paralysed with cold; and uncouthly swollen about the middle, where she burns with a fierce inflammation. Her beauty has been thus seriously damaged, and she is moreover blotched with nasty boils and ulcers of geysers and volcanos. Her axis has been shamefully jarred from rectitude; and her land and water are so unequally and irregularly arranged that she looks altogether lop-sided. Heat and light, with all things flowing from them, are very unfairly distributed over her body, and therefore among us who live upon her body. For such light and heat as she gets, she has to keep whirling and spinning round the sun in the most undignified and wearisome manner. The animals she brings forth (not to speak of the plants and the minerals) are in many cases ugly, unamiable, ferocious, and tormented with monstrous appetites, which can only be satisfied by devouring their fellow-creatures; nearly all of them are quite selfish and immoral; and the few of them that are philanthropic (such as surly old lions, tigers, wolves, sharks, vultures and other sweet carrion fowl; all genuine lovers of man) are almost as disagreeably so as our human philanthropists themselves. She has no moral character at all, and her moods are most capricious and violent. In her dealings with man she is seldom fair, and the unfairness is nearly always against man: thus she hardly ever grants him what he has not worked for, while she very often withholds from him what he has worked for. The ignorant creature knows nothing of the wise doctrines of Malthus, but spawns forth as many children of all sorts as ever she can, without the least prudential restraint. She has consequently far more than she can properly feed and rear; so that a large part perishes in infancy (and we are told that none of these except the human sucklings will rise to another life; poor bereaved monkey and donkey mothers, for instance, being altogether without the precious consolations of immortality); a considerable part is eaten up by mankind and other hungry animals, and the remainder can seldom get food enough. And with regard to man in particular; as the human race grows ever more numerous, while the means of Mother Earth do not increase in proportion, she must age after age starve and half-starve more and more of us; and thus in a few thousand years, if she and we exist so long (and unless, of course, these my beneficent proposals be carried out), she will prove to us the stingiest old hag ever known. And looking beyond our own frigate the earth (of whose tender, the moon, I could say a good deal), and regarding our little fleet of the Solar System, we find that there is an absurd and perilous want of communication between the various vessels; that we not only cannot pass or signal to any of the others, but in fact know next to nothing of them, and absolutely nothing of their crews; so that in case of a threatened attack by corsair comet or shooting star we could concert no plan of common defence or evasion. Moreover, it is very doubtful whether the fleet is in a good position in the Sea of Space; and whether our flag-ship the Sun, who leads us cruising whithersoever he likes, is taking a judicious course for a prosperous voyage, or is but hurrying on recklessly, and likely to lead us to "eternal smash" among breakers; for not only are we never consulted as to the course, but we are never told anything about it when it has been settled, and so go drifting on for ever in a most ignominiously blindfolded fashion. And I might go farther still, and note many things in the universe beyond our system which probably need improvement or abolition; but I really have not spare time just now. I can only add a few short notes on things requiring amendment in the relation of Nature to Man. She treats our intelligence with profound disdain, never giving us the slightest trustworthy hint of her origin, character, business, processes, objects, and final causes, if indeed she really has any final causes or cause. She manifestly carries on her large business (whatever it really is) without any special care for our convenience or profit, being wont to ignore us with our plans and wishes in the most exasperating way. She turns us out into the world without giving us any choice in the matter; though all other suffrages and freedoms are perfectly insignificant in comparison with that of which we are thus deprived, an effective and enlightened vote on the question: Shall I, or shall I not, be born? She only keeps us alive by a complicated system of the most shameful illusions, falsifying beyond rectification life, death, and after-death. Having made us take part in this poor puzzling game of life, she has taken care that all the rules shall be unfavourable to us: the cards are marked, the dice are loaded, we are always swindled. Thus years of hard work and self-denial are frequently lost by a slip or chance, but seldom or never saved by a chance. Our health may be ruined by a pin-prick, but never doubled by an accident. We fall seriously ill in a moment, and take weeks or months to recover; lose a limb by some sudden mishap, but never by a good hap regain it. We cannot reach even a low degree of wisdom or knowledge without long hard study, while to be ignorant and foolish is the easiest and most natural thing in the world for us. Our sorrows are real and enduring; our joys deceptive and transient; our prizes of victory are not to be compared with our forfeits of defeat. And so I might go on through an indefinite number of items in which we are unfairly dealt with; but these scanty hints must suffice for the present. Scanty as they are, I think they show conclusively that nature needs improving and perfecting no less than does human nature; and, in particular, that nature will have to be radically reformed in order to suit precisely our new perfect men.

[*In the sections omitted here, "B.V." proposes that three virtuous and intelligent National Reformers should perfect themselves, and then form a provisional committee to start the Universal Perfection Company, Unlimited. Once formed, this company will at once be joined by members of all other reform societies, since "every one who has faith that his own doctrine is true and his own plan of life good, must have faith that the better and wiser men become, the more will they believe his doctrine and adopt his plan of life." Thus, the "very flower of humanity will certainly join the Universal Perfection Company, Unlimited."*]

VI

Strengthened in the very beginning of its career by accessions so numerous and powerful, and wielding irresistible might by the perfection of each of its members in contrast with the enormous imperfection of unregenerate men, the Universal Perfection Company, Unlimited, will certainly in the course of a very few years predominate in all the regions of the earth, not only among the tribes termed barbarous, but also among the nations we pleasantly call civilised. When it is thus become more potent in itself than all the rest of mankind, it will probably feel bound to decide at once which of two courses of conduct it ought to adopt as the better for the true interests of the world and the human race: whether the Company shall bear with the stolid and stubborn imperfect men, hoping to win them and their children gradually to self-perfection, or at worst leaving them to die out gradually as an inferior race; or whether the Company shall promptly exterminate them. If this latter course be chosen, we may anticipate that a plain and kindly warning to the following effect, will be brought to the notice of all the recusants: — "Whereas, in despite of the example and counsel of the members of this Company, certain obdurate human creatures persist in their imperfection; and whereas the existence of such creatures is necessarily a misery to themselves and others, and those of them who do not feel this misery must be the most wretched of all, as debased to the level of their actual lot; and whereas such diseased and foul creatures cannot but poison our atmosphere, polluting our young purity and infecting our scarcely established health; and whereas, moreover, the existence of such creatures doth not only afflict with sore affliction and shame the souls of the perfect who must witness their obscene vileness, but doth degrade Humanity now first rising and in part risen to its due eminence: We the members of this Company, both jointly and severally, being overfilled with love and compassion for these poor worthless creatures who were lately our fellowmen, and yearning continually with fraternal yearnings for their salvation, do hereby most tenderly and earnestly entreat them to leave forthwith their loathsome sin and misery, and unite with us in the beatitude of perfection: And furthermore, notice is hereby given unto all whom it may concern, that this Company, moved by profound pity for such of these creatures as are incurable, and constrained by its solemn duty to the Universe and Humanity, hath resolved and will with unfailing exactitude execute the resolution (and therefore all those to whom it shall apply); That whoever of human kind hath not ere the expiration of (say) one year from this date performed upon himself either the simple perfecting process, which is incomparably the best *hari-kari* or happy despatch, or else that other happy despatch known as honourable suicide, which is incomparably better than continuance of base life, shall be then happily despatched by this Company, in order that the world in general and himself in particular may be promptly and thoroughly delivered from his evil and misery." One would fain trust that a pleading and warning conceived in a spirit so affectionate, and embodied in the consummate eloquence which will characterise everything spoken or written in the name of the Company, must persuade even the most obdurate to self-reform: as it would certainly persuade all those who in pure modesty shrank from becoming perfect, to depart uncompelled from a world in which their life was shown to be noxious. And one can safely affirm beforehand that it would indeed be a good riddance of bad rubbish to put speedily out of existence all wretches to whom such an appeal proved ineffectual. It is moreover quite clear that a minority composed of similar wretches, or even a large majority, could only offer the most puny resistance to a majority, or even a very small minority, of men all perfect. It is to be remarked that I do not venture to suggest that the Company is likely to choose the one course rather than the other, to exterminate rather than tolerate, or tolerate rather than exterminate the incorrigible. If it has to make the choice, it will doubtless select that which is really preferable, and which will the sooner secure the universal perfection of humanity.

When every human being on the earth is thus perfect, evil in the senses of vice, sin, crime, error, folly, impurity, disease, deformity, ugliness, will be extinguished or nearly extinguished from among mankind; and with evil a large part of misery in the sense of pain or suffering will no doubt disappear. The immaculate goodness and infallible wisdom of the new men will likewise, beyond doubt, remedy or avoid many of the sufferings to which nature now subjects us, and which we account inevitable and incurable. But, so far as we can see, so long as the present laws and constitution of nature continue there must still remain a vast amount of really inevitable suffering for mankind, without reckoning beastkind, birdkind, fishkind, insectkind, reptilekind, plantkind, and leaving quite out of discussion, stonekind. Storm and earthquake, landslip and flood, lightning and volcanic eruption will probably injure or slay these perfect men, though not so frequently as us. Their exquisite sense of justice will be keenly outraged, I fancy, by those iniquitous inequalities in the universe which I have touched upon in the second section of this wonderful treatise. Child-bearing may continue painful to mothers and discommodious to fathers; teething may still be a troublesome process alike to infants and parents. These new men, naturally enjoying life much more than we can, may demand either to live forever or to live at any rate as long as they please; for it is ignominious to be pushed forcibly out of the world at an uncertain moment, whether one would like to stay longer or not. I think, too, that the decay from the grand climacteric into old age, with its weakness, torpor, senility, and general Struldbrugism, will by no means suit them, and that they will prefer to live out their life to the last minute (in case they are content to have a last minute) in full vigour of mind and body. They will scarcely brook confinement to this petty earth of ours, but will want to roam at pleasure through the limitless universe. I think that their generous souls will be wrought to indignation by the condition and prospects of the inferior creatures. In the complex relations between nature and human nature, there are innumerable other matters with regard to which the perfect men will probably require more or less important change, as the meditative reader will easily discover for himself.

Let me here touch upon but one more point, which is rather interesting at the present time. When all social, political, religious, moral, intellectual, and other distinctions have been done away with, is it probable that these perfect human beings will allow nature to violate decency and thorough equality by perpetuating the gross distinctions of sex? Imperfect as we still are, our most advanced thinkers have already arrived at the doctrine of the absolute equality of man and woman, tempered perhaps by some vague superiority on the female side; and already our cultivated moral delicacy, our refined spirituality, our exquisite modesty, our ethereal chastity, are ashamed of things so coarse and carnal and obscene as these sexual distinctions. We dare not allude to them publicly, except in the most distant and evasive fashion; society placidly ignores them, men and women alike being supposed utterly ignorant of each other's bodily form, and extremely unwilling to learn anything on the subject; legislation puts a triple bandage on the eyes of justice (completely blindfolded, if not blind, already) whenever they are in question; religion fears and hates them as the chief organs of the filthy and damnable lusts of the flesh. As in the meanwhile, under all this veiling and ignoring in the world of pretences, the said distinctions are as vigorous and influential as ever in the world of facts (nature with reckless immodesty continuing to produce them now just as she did in the old licentious times, ere nude statues were made decent with figleaves and the naked truth presentable with cant), the actual results may be summed up in that great sad word of William Blake, which sums up so much of our actual life: "Prisons are built with stones of law; brothels with bricks of religion." In order to ensure absolute equality (which perchance cannot co-exist with essential distinctions) the new race may demand either that sex be abolished, or that every human being be of both sexes. Perhaps the very perfecting process will either unsex or androgynise its subject, so that all alike shall be regenerated either neutral or epicene. But if in their new birth they remain and consent to continue respectively male and female, they will doubtless openly and honourably recognise these distinctions of sex; so that what is now in public ignored, and in private spoken of basely and obscenely, shall be then both in public and private spoken of with joyous and noble frankness; and what is now in great part prostituted to ignoble emotions and degrading companionship, shall be then hallowed by the ardent chastity of free and natural love.

VII

But will change of the laws and constitution of the world be feasible? Can even perfect men persuade or compel nature to improve and perfect herself into thorough unison with their requirements? I am not only convinced that they can, but I am able to show that the change is quite practicable even to our poor understandings; and everybody will surely allow that what is proved practicable to us must be mere child's play to the new men.

The first question is, To whom or what should reformed Humanity address the summons for the instant reformation of the universe? to Fate, Law, Chance, the Gods, or Nature herself?

Not to Fate, for it is blind, dumb, deaf, inexorable; and moreover all our modern philosophy ignores or contemns it, and the palatial edifice of this my system is built upon the foundation of its tomb.

Not to Law, for it is impotent, being the mere creature of the things that seem to obey it. Nor can it change, for it perishes in mutation; and change of it must come from what is above or beyond it. And yet though it cannot alter, it always manages to range itself on the side which has proved victorious, graciously sanctioning all that has been done, and which by the leagued universe cannot be undone. It may be disregarded altogether with perfect safety.

Not to Chance, for it cannot be relied upon; its caprices confound all the mathematics of probabilities and baffle the wildest hazards of guess. It is altogether too frivolous for the serious consideration of wise men who deal with cause and effect or steady-going unphilosophical sequence, and march firmly through logical premises booted with because and therefore.

Not to the Gods, though at first one might think there would be hope in them, for their devotees assure us that they are all-good and all-powerful, and that they love to grant the prayers of the righteous. But there are so many of them and so diverse, and they hate each other so intensely, that no plan of world-reformation could ever be agreed upon, much less carried out, by them. And, besides, it is possible, and perchance even probable, that the new perfect men will have no Gods or God at all.

It seems likely, therefore, that the momentous appeal will have to be made direct to Nature herself, still known to a few as the mighty mother, but to more as the cruel and stingy stepmother, while the vast majority see in her but the lowly fostermother or menial nurse of our royal selves the glorious children of mankind; conceited and thankless little brats, who defame the womb which bore us and the breasts which gave us suck. The new men will know well in what character to regard her. To Her the living reality, and not to the gods or other shadowy supreme powers, will the summons be addressed; for as the sage poet chants ("Faerie Queene"; Mutabilitie, vii. 5): —

> Then forth issew'd (great goddess) great Dame Nature,
> With goodly port and gracious majesty,
> Being far greater and more tall of stature
> Than any of the gods or powers on high.

If she accords at once with a good grace all that the perfect men demand, all will at once be well both for them and for herself. But if she resolves to continue in her old ways, and will not be persuaded by their filial pleadings, they can resort to affectionate constraint, as in the case of their incorrigible human brothers, delicately discussed in Section VI. And as these perfect men will be perfect in unanimity and resolution, there can be no rational doubt of their speedy triumph, as I will now triumphantly prove.

Uncertain as are most things about which we freely dogmatise, it is quite certain, and indeed an axiomatic truth well known and understood by all civilised people, that man (including of course woman and the children) is the very crown and head of nature; that he is so at present, whether or not destined so to continue for ever. I need not dwell on a proposition so obvious to the clear and impartial human intelligence. Buzzard and ass may be unaware of it, each fondly fancying itself the supreme model form of life, the true final cause and object of the world's existence; but we men know better. We know that all the other offspring of nature aspire and point to man, and are in him alone fully developed; though it is true that he cannot swim like frog or grampus, nor fly like midge or wildgoose. We know that all her other works are consecrated with the celestial stamp of use solely in relation to him and his flourishing life; the chief end of sun, moon, stars, air, ocean, and earth, being to serve man and glorify him, perhaps for ever. Without him, nature would be a fruitless stem, an arch wanting its key-stone, a palace untenanted (we don't count as tenants the rats and mice and such small deer), a discrowned queen, a headless trunk. All this is well known to civilised people, but the most important inferences to be drawn from it are very little known, for man has been hitherto, and still remains, an animal timid and inconsequent in ratiocination.

In the first place, it is clear that since man is the head of nature, to cut off him would be to decapitate her. It may be true that she is a sort of hydra, having had several successive heads; and that unless man perfects himself, as I here urge and implore him, he will be eventually superseded by a better, or at least a stronger head: but the one head has not fallen off suddenly, and the next suddenly sprung up in its place; each change has occupied a vast period of time, the one head slowly giving way while the other as slowly came to the front, as in the case of children's first and second teeth, as in the sloughing of snakes and the moulting of birds. On the other hand, it may be true, as nearly all of us modestly assume, that man is the last if not the only head of nature, so that in losing him she would be as an adult losing a tooth, who finds no other grow to replace it. The adult, indeed, may procure an artificial tooth; but who ever heard of an artificial head effectively fulfilling the functions of a natural one? And, moreover, the essential character of nature renders it impossible for her to be in anything artificial. We are therefore entitled to conclude that cutting off the human race suddenly would kill nature by beheading her; for either she would have absolutely no other head, even in germ, or the head meant to supply its place would as yet exist only in embryo and be quite unfit for duty; and we cannot conceive a being so highly organised as nature continuing to live without a head, either for ever or during a period of interregnum between the premature fall of the one and the arrival at maturity of the other.

But the one ruling passion and principle of nature is surely her love of life; as the true proverb runs, Self-preservation is the first law of nature. Supreme is she in philoprogenitiveness, that is to say, in the love not so much of progeny as of generating. She spawns perpetually, and by millions and billions, producing unscrupulously myriads of imperfect types for one that is perfect, devouring indifferently and wholesale the perfect and the imperfect in order to produce faster and more abundantly; all that we term death being but her swift process of securing material to be worked up into ever fresh forms of life. So limitless and, from our point of view, improvident is her lust of procreation, that we may well deem it rather a fierce monomania than a ruling principle. The one thing, therefore, which she most abhors and shrinks from must be death absolute, the death of herself, the termination of the continually active quasi-birth and quasi-death which constitute her continually active life, her eternal being which is eternal becoming.

Seeing, therefore, that the sudden destruction of mankind would kill nature, and that she intensely and monomaniacally loves her own life, the conclusion is manifest that she would do anything and everything short of self-murder, in order to avoid the premature extinction of our species. And from this inexpugnable proposition I draw the fateful practical corollary, *That the human race, so long as no other is ready to supersede it, can compel nature to do what it pleases, by resolving on instant universal suicide in case of her refusal.* In all modesty, and without the slightest disrespect for preceding and contemporary sages (who if they have taught us but little, have at anyrate taught all they knew, and in fact a good deal more), I believe myself justified in affirming that this is beyond measure the most important law of nature discoverable by man; and that its discovery, which gives him the simplest and easiest of formulas for working instantaneously the perfection of the universe, must ever remain unique in eternal and infinite beneficence. And I must not omit to add that this formula is not only unique, by the unlimited good results of its (infallibly) successful application, but is characterised by such prodigal superabundance of goodness, that even in case of failure (which our sovereign human intelligence declares impossible) its application would benefit mankind immensely more than they ever have been or are ever likely to be benefited by anything else. It is a medicine which if it could fail in working the perfect cure, must yet do more good to the patient than all the rest of the pharmacopœia. For suppose that we resolve on instant wholesale suicide if nature refuses to perfect herself, and (the impossible case) that nature does refuse, and we have forthwith to carry out our resolution: can any thoughtful and conscientious man, candidly considering our state and that of the world (perfection being supposed unattainable), doubt that such universal suicide would be the one best and most beatific action we could perform for ourselves and our (potential) posterity and our world in general? Lest the fascinated reader should make away with himself hurriedly and for inappropriate reasons (while appropriate ones too surely abound), as Cleombrotus in a fine frenzy threw himself to death in the sea after studying the *Phœdo,* I call special attention to the fact that it is only our *universal* suicide which would prove a panacea for all the ills our flesh is heir to; individual suicides can do little or no good, save to the individuals themselves. Thus true philosophers may rationally and generously deny themselves the luxury of self-murder, because their death must leave the human average still worse than it is; and, besides, death's coming is so certain and (at farthest) so near, that it is scarcely worth while to put one's self out of breath hastening to meet him.

Men have been hitherto so imperfect in intelligence, that they have not been fully aware of this, their immense reserve of compelling power; and so imperfect in will, that even if fully aware thereof, they could not unanimously have carried and carried out the requisite resolution. Yet there seems always to have existed some obscure and confused consciousness of such really miraculous power over nature; while (in the blessed order of Providence) it was reserved for the present luminous writer, in the present illustrious age, to discover and formulate with comprehensive precision the sublime law of this power. All the old traditions of supernatural magic and miracles; the loftiest rhapsodies of mysticism in all climes and ages, the trances of seers, the ecstasies of philosophers, the rapturous influxes and effluxes of saints; the nirvana of Buddhism, the faith of Jesus which could move mountains, and to which nothing was impossible (faith being the favourite abracadabra of Jesus, just as perfection is mine); the celibacy, self-mortification, self-mutilation, rage for martyrdom, common to Brahminism, Buddhism, and Christianity, and probably to all religions; the austere Stoicism of Greece and Rome; the much-decried bloodthirstiness of famous conquerors, who magnanimously took upon themselves the useful and onerous task of extinguishing by myriads their ignoble fellow-men; all these point to some dim intuition of the supreme truth I have just demonstrated, as in all the mode of subduing nature is by suppression and destruction of humanity. But nature could not and cannot ever be constrained into self-improvement by sporadic or even endemic or epidemic cases of slow or swift suicide and slaughter, so long as the premature extinction of the whole human race was not and is not seriously threatened. Threaten this seriously, and she will forthwith become our most obedient humble servant. This is the forcible plan of "strikes" by labour against capital, applied in its utmost extension by man against nature; as you have already mere trades'-unions, organise a universal Man-union, and threaten, if all your demands are not immediately granted, to "strike" living, to "turn out" of human existence, and you will at once bring the everlasting employer to reason.

And if man even in his present state is the very crown and head of nature, think what a crown and head he will be when perfect, when divine! I can scarcely imagine that she will then have the heart to refuse him anything. Should she, however, prove obdurate to the first courteous and affectionate appeal of the new men, they can deliver to her the dreadful *ultimatum:* Immediate compliance with all we ask (which we ask for your good no less than for our own), or we immediately all kill ourselves, thus beheading you. And she, knowing their inexorable resolution, must straightway yield, and perfect herself as they require; and in the maternal and general feminine fashion love them all the more for thus absolutely dominating her.

And thus in the course of not many years (let us make a liberal allowance for mischances and unforeseen obstacles, and say by the beginning of the twentieth century, which is nearly thirty years hence), evil will be extinct by the perfection of man, and misery by the perfection of nature, and everybody will be thoroughly good and happy everywhere for evermore.

[*In the section that follows, "B.V." comments again on his reasons for ignoring the origins and concerning himself only with the extinction of evil and misery. In the ninth and final section, he explains that he lacks the requisite health, energy, and ambition to become the first member of the committee for establishing the Universal Perfection Company, Unlimited, but adds that as soon as the committee is formed, he will qualify himself for membership. If no one will take the initiative, he at least will be free from blame, and the responsibility for the damnation of Man and Nature will not rest on him.*]

A Commission of Inquiry on Royalty

[*Thomson's attacks upon royalty were frequent, and seldom as good-natured as in this satire. For instance, his 1867 poem "L'Ancien Régime" suggests that servility, war, harlotry, and lies are the "gifts" most desired by kings, but that the best "gift" for "our lord the king" would be death. Thomson did not, however, consider England's "gingerbread monarchy" to be a serious threat to society, and elsewhere expressed the opinion that "the whole thing will be pitched to Limbo if ever the people get mature enough to put away childish things." This satire, which, like "Proposals for the Speedy Extinction of Evil and Misery," owes a good deal to Swift, was originally published in the "Jottings" column of the* National Reformer *(September 18, 1870) under the title, "Commission of Inquiry as to Complaints against Royalty." In 1876 Thomson republished it as a twopenny pamphlet under the shorter title, "A Commission of Inquiry on Royalty," and at that time added the "P.S." and made a few minor revisions. G. W. Foote reprinted this later version in* Satires and Profanities, *from which the present text is taken.*]

THE SUBJECTS for our solemn consideration are the seclusion of her Most Gracious Majesty, and the complaints thereanent published in several respectable journals. In order to investigate the matter thoroughly, we constituted ourselves (the unknow number x) into a special Commission of Inquiry. We are happy to state that the said Commission has concluded its arduous labors, and now presents its report within a week of its appointment; surely the most prompt and rapid of commissions. The cause of this celerity we take to be the fact that the Commissioners were unsalaried; we being unanimously of opinion that had we received good pay for the inquiry throughout the period of our session, we could have prolonged it with certain benefit, if not to the public yet to ourselves, for a great number of years. If, therefore, you want a Commission to do its work rapidly vote no money for it. And do not fear that the most headlong haste in gathering evidence and composing the report will diminish the value of such report; for when a Commission has lasted for years or months it generally rises in a quite different state of the subject matter from that in which it first sat, and the report must be partly obsolete, partly a jumble of anachronisms. In brief, it may be fairly affirmed as a general rule that no Commission of Inquiry is of any value at all; the appointment of one being merely a dodge by which people who don't want to act on what they and everybody else see quite well with their naked eyes, set a number of elderly gentlemen to pore upon it with spectacles and magnifying glasses until dazed and stupid with poring, in the hope that this process will last so long that ere it is finished the public will have forgotten the matter altogether. And now for the result of our inquiries on this subject, which is not only immensely important, but is even sacred to our loyal hearts.

A West-end tradesman complains bitterly that through the absence of the Court from Buckingham Palace, and the diminished number and splendor of royal pomps and entertainments, the "Season" is for him a very poor season indeed. The Commissioners find that the said tradesman (whose knowledge seems limited to a knowledge of his business, supposing he knows that) is remarkably well off; and consider that West-end tradesmen have no valid vested interest in Royalty and the Civil List, that at the worst they do a capital trade with the aristocracy and wealthy classes (taking good care that the punctual and honest shall amply overpay their losses by the unpunctual and dishonest); that if they are not satisfied with the West-end, they had better try the East-end, and see how that will suit them; and, in short, that this tradesman is not worth listening to.

Numerous fashionable and noble people (principally ladies) complain that they have no Court to shine in. The Commissioners think that they shine a great deal too much already, and in the most wasteful manner, gathered together by hundreds, light glittering on light; and that if they really want to shine beneficially in a court there are very many very dark courts in London where the light of their presence would be most welcome.

It is complained on behalf of their Royal Highnesses the Prince and Princess of Wales that they have to perform many of the duties of royalty without getting a share of the royal allowance. The Commissioners think that if the necessary expenses of the heir to the throne are really too heavy for his modest income, and are increased by the performance of royal duties, he had better send in yearly a bill to his Mamma for expenses incurred on her account, and a duplicate of the same to the Chancellor to the Exchequer; so that in every Budget the amount of the Civil List shall be equitably divided between her Majesty and her Majesty's eldest son, doubtless to their common satisfaction.

It is complained on behalf of various foreign royal or ruling personages that while they in their homes treat generously the visiting members of our royal family, they are treated very shabbily when visiting here. The Commissioners think that Buckingham Palace, being seldom or never wanted by the Queen, and very seldom wanted for the reception of the English Court, should be at all times open for such royal or ruling visitors; that a Lord Chamberlain, or other such noble domestic servant should be detailed to attend on them, and see to their hospitable treatment in all respects; and that to cover the expenditure on their account a fair deduction should be made from her Majesty's share of the Civil List, which deduction, being equitable, her Majesty would no doubt view with extreme pleasure.

It is complained on the part of her Majesty's Ministers, that when they want the royal assent and signature to important Acts of Parliament, they have to lose a day or two and undergo great fatigue (which is peculiarly hard on men who are mostly aged, and all overworked) in travelling to and from Osborne or Balmoral. The Commissioners think the remedy plain and easy, as in the two preceding cases. Let a law be passed assuming that absence, like silence, gives consent; so that whenever her Majesty is not in town, the Speaker of the Commons or the Lord Chancellor, or other great officer of State, be empowered to seal and sign in her name, and generally to perform any of her real and royal duties, on the formal demand of the Ministry, who always (and not the Queen) are responsible to Parliament and the country for all public acts.

A taxpayer complains that for fourteen years her Majesty has been punctually drawing all moneys allotted to support the royal dignity, while studiously abstaining from all, or nearly all, the hospitalities and other expensive functions incident to the support of the said dignity. The Commissioners consider that her Majesty is perchance benefiting the country more (and may be well aware of the fact) by taking her money for doing nothing than if she did something for it; that if she didn't take the said money, somebody else would (as for instance, were she to abdicate, the Prince of Wales, become King, would want and get at least as much); so that while our Government remains as it is, the complaint of the said taxpayer is foolish.

Another Taxpayer, who must be a most mean-minded fellow, a stranger to all sacred sympathies and hallowed emotions, says: "If a washerwoman, being stupified by the death of her husband, neglected her business for more than a week or two, she would certainly lose her custom or employment, and not all the sanctity of conjugal grief (about which reverential journalists gush) would make people go on paying her for doing nothing; and if this washerwoman had money enough of her own to live on comfortably, people would call her shameless and miserly if she asked for or accepted payment while doing nothing; and if this washerwoman had a large family of boys and girls around her, and shut herself up to brood upon her husband's death for even three or four months, people would reckon her mad with selfish misery. The Commissioners (as soon as they recover from the stupefaction of horror into which this blasphemy has thrown them) consider and reply that there can be no proper comparison of a Queen and a washerwoman, and that nobody would think of instituting one, except a brute, a Republican, an Atheist, a Communist, a fiend in human form; that anyhow if, as this wretch says, a washerwoman would be paid for a week or two without working, in consideration of her conjugal affliction, it is plain that a Queen, who (it will be universally allowed) is at least a hundred thousand times as good as a washerwoman, is therefore entitled to at least a hundred thousand times the "week or two" of salary without performance of duty—that is, to at least 1,923 or 3,846 years, whereas this heartless and ribald reprobate himself only complains that our beloved Sovereign has done nothing for her wage throughout "fourteen years." The Commissioners therefore eject this complainant with ineffable scorn; and only wish they knew his name and address, that they might denounce him for prosecution to the Attorney-General.

A Malthusian (whatever kind of creature that may be) complains that her Majesty has set an example of uncontrolled fecundity to the nation and the royal family, which, besides being generally immoral, is likely, at the modest estimate of £6,000 per annum per royal baby, to lead to the utter ruin of the realm in a few generations. The Commissioners, after profound and prolonged consideration, can only remark that they do not understand the complaint any better than the name (which they do not understand at all) of the "Malthusian;" that they have always been led to believe that a large family is a great honor to a legitimately united man and woman; and that, finally, they beg to refer the Malthusian to the late Prince Consort.

A devotedly loyal Royalist (who unfortunately does not give the name and address of his curator) complains that her Majesty, by doing nothing except receive her Civil List, is teaching the country that it can get on quite as well without a monarch as with one, and might therefore just as well, and indeed very much better, put the amount of the Civil List into its own pocket and call itself a Republic. The Commissioners remark that this person seems the most rational of the whole lot of complainants (most rational, not for his loyalty, but most rational as to the grounds of his complaint, from his own point of view; in accordance with the dictum, "A madman reasons rightly from wrong premises; a fool wrongly from right ones"); and that his surmise is very probably correct—namely, that her Majesty is really a Republican in principle, but not liking (as is perfectly natural in her position) to publicly profess and advocate opinions so opposed to the worldly interest of all her friends and relatives, has been content to further these opinions practically for fourteen years past by her conduct, without saying a word on the subject. The Commissioners, however, find one serious objection to this surmise in the fact that if her Majesty is really a Republican at heart, she must wish to exclude the Prince of Wales from the Throne; while it seems to them that the intimate knowledge she must have of his wisdom and virtues (not to speak of her motherly affection) cannot but make her feel that no greater blessing could come to the nation after her death than his reigning over it. As this is the only complaint which the Commissioners find at once well-founded and not easy to remedy, they are happy to know that it is confined to the very insignificant class of persons who are "devotedly loyal Royalists."

The Commissioners thus feel themselves bound to report that all the complaints they have heard against our beloved and gracious Sovereign (except the one last cited, which is of no importance) are without foundation, or frivolous, or easily remedied, and that our beloved and gracious Sovereign (whom may Heaven long preserve!) could not do better than she is now doing, in doing nothing.

But in order to obviate such complaints, which do much harm, whether ill or well founded, and which especially pain the delicate susceptibilities of all respectable men and women, the Commissioners have thought it their duty to draw up the following project of a Constitution, not to come into force until the death of our present beloved and gracious Sovereign (which may God, if so it please Him, long avert!), and to be modified in its details according to the best wisdom of our national House of Palaver.

DRAFT

Whereas it is treasonable to talk of dethroning a monarch, but there can be no disloyalty in preventing a person not yet a monarch from becoming one:

And whereas it is considered by very many, and seems proved by the experience of the last........years that the country can do quite well without a monarch, and may therefore save the extra expense of monarchy:

And whereas it is calculated that from the accession of George I. of blessed memory until the decease of the most beloved of Queens, Victoria, a period of upwards of a century and a half, the Royal Family of the House of Guelph have received full and fair payment in every respect for their generous and heroic conduct in coming to occupy the throne and other high places of this kingdom, and in saving us from the unconstitutional Stuarts:

And whereas the said Stuarts may now be considered extinct, and thus no longer dangerous to this realm:

And whereas the said Royal Family of the House of Guelph is so prolific that the nation cannot hope to support all the members thereof for a long period to come in a royal manner:

And whereas the Dukes of this realm are accounted liberal and courteous gentlemen:

And whereas the constitution of our country is so far Venetian that it cannot but be improved in harmony and consistency by being made more Venetian still:

Be it enacted, etc., That the Throne now vacant through the

ever-to-be-deplored death of her late most gracious Majesty shall remain vacant. That the members of what has been hitherto the Royal Family keep all the property they have accumulated, the nation resuming from them all grants of sinecures and other salaried appointments. That no member of the said Family be eligible for any public appointment whatever for at least one hundred years. That the Dukes in the order of their seniority shall act as Doges (with whatever title be considered the best) year and year about, under penalty of large fines in cases of refusal, save when such refusal is supported by clear proof of poverty (being revenue under a settled minimum), imbecility, brutality, or other serious disqualification. That no members of a ducal family within a certain degree of relationship to the head of the house be eligible for any public appointment whatever; the head of the house being eligible for the Dogeship only. That the duties of the Doge be simply to seal and sign Acts of Parliament, proclamations, etc., when requested to do so by the Ministry; and to exercise hospitality to royal or ruling and other representatives of foreign countries, as well as to distinguished natives. That a fair and even excessive allowance be made to the Doge for the expenses of his year of office. That the royal palaces be official residences of the Doge. That the Doge be free from all political responsibility as from all political power; but be responsible for performing liberally and courteously the duties of hospitality, so that Buckingham Palace shall not contrast painfully with the Mansion House. Etc., etc.

God preserve the Doge!

The Commission of Inquiry having thus triumphantly vindicated our beloved and gracious Sovereign against the cruel aspersions of people in general, and having moreover drafted a plan for obviating such aspersions against any British King or Queen in future, ends its Report, and dissolves itself, with humble thankfulness to God Almighty whose grace alone has empowered it to conclude its arduous labors so speedily, and with results so incalculably beneficial.

P.S.—Since the above report was drawn up, that ardent English patriot and loyalist, Benjamin Disraeli being by the grace of God and the late Earl of Derby Prime Minister of this realm, has proposed that Parliament shall enable her Most Gracious Majesty to assume the additional title of Empress of India, and Parliament has so far humbly assented. Being sore pressed by many cantankerous persons to give valid reasons for this change, he has given reasons many and weighty; such as the earnest desire of the princes and people of India, which desire has been so abundantly expressed that the expressions thereof cannot be produced lest they should overwhelm Parliament and destroy the balance of the world in general; then the imposing authority of "Whitaker's Almanack," a dissenting minister and a schoolgirl aged twelve: and lastly the necessity of such a title for scaring all the Russians from India. But I believe that in deference to the well-known modesty of her Most Gracious Majesty he has not produced the most cogent reason of all, which is that for her wonderful and continual goodness during the past fourteen years in abstaining from the active functions of royalty, thus not only doing no mischief but preparing us for a Republic *de jure* by habituating us to a Republic *de facto*, she merits a great reward; and that, as she has already more money than she knows what to do with, this reward of royal virtue can most fittingly be rendered by her grateful subjects promoting her to the rank of Empress. And it should be noted that whereas the old title of Queen has a certain strength and stability in the habitudes if not in the affections of the people, the new fangled title of Empress has no such support, so that in assuming it our beloved monarch is but working consistently and resolutely toward the great end of her reign, the speedy abolition of monarchy and establishment of a Republic.

The Story of a Famous Old Jewish Firm

[*This allegory, one of Thomson's earliest antichristian satires, became a minor "classic" in Victorian free-thought circles. It was originally published in two installments in the* National Reformer *(December 24, 31, 1865) under the title, "The Story of a Famous Old Firm." In 1876 Thomson made minor revisions and republished the satire as a twopenny pamphlet; the title was first advertised in the* Secularist *as "Jehovah, Son, and Company, or The Story of a Famous Old Firm," but after a reader objected to this title as being vulgar and flippant, Thomson dropped the "Jehovah, Son and Company" and the pamphlet finally appeared as "The Story of a Famous Old Jewish Firm." This version was reprinted in 1883 and again in the 1884* Satires and Profanities, *from which the present text is taken.*]

MANY thousand years ago, when the Jews first started in business, the chief of their merchants was a venerable and irascible old gentleman named Jah. The Jews have always been excellent traders, keen to scent wealth, subtle to track it, unweary to pursue it, strong to seize it, tenacious to hold it; and the most keen, subtle, untiring, strong, tenacious of them all, was this Jah. The patriarchs of his people paid him full measure of the homage which Jews have always eagerly paid to wealth and power, and all their most important transactions were carried out through him. In those antique times people lived to a very great age, and Jah is supposed to have lived so many thousands of years that one may as well not try to count them. Perhaps it was not one Jah that existed all this while, but the house of Jah: the family, both for pride and profit, preserving through successive generations the name of its founder. Certain books have been treasured by the Jews as containing exact records of the dealings of this lordly merchant (or house) both with the Jews themselves and with strangers. Many people in our times, however, have ventured to doubt the accuracy of these records, arguing that some of the transactions therein recorded it would have been impossible to transact, that others must have totally ruined the richest of merchants, that the accounts often contradict each other, and that the system of book-keeping generally is quite unworthy of a dealer so truthful and clear-headed as Jah is affirmed to have been. The records are so ancient in themselves, and they treat of matters so much more ancient still, that it is not easy to find other records of any sort with which to check their accounts. Strangely enough the most recent researches have impugned the accuracy of the most ancient of these records; certain leaves of a volume called the "Great Stone Book," having been brought forward to contradict the very first folio of the ledger in which the dealings of Jah have been posted up according to the Jews. It may be that the first few folios, like the early pages of most annals, are somewhat mythical; and the present humble compiler (who is not deep in the affairs of the primæval world, and who, like the late lamented Captain Cuttle with *his* large volume,* is utterly knocked up at any time by four or five lines of the "Great Stone Book") will prudently not begin at the beginning, but skip it with great comfort and pleasure, especially as many and learned men are now earnest students of this beginning. We will, therefore, if you please, take for granted the facts that at some time, in some manner, Jah created his wonderful business, and that early in his career he met with a great misfortune, being compelled, by the villainy of all those with whom he had dealings, to resort to a wholesale liquidation, which left him so poor, that for some time he had not a house in the world, and his establishment was reduced to four male and as many female servants.

He must have pretty well recovered from this severe shock when he entered into the famous covenant or contract with Abraham and his heirs, by which he bound himself to deliver over to them at a certain, then distant, period, the whole of the valuable landed property called Canaan, on condition that they should appoint him the sole agent for the management of their affairs. In pursuance of this contract, he conducted that little business of the flocks and herds for Jacob against one Laban; and afterwards, when the children of Abraham were grown very

*In Dickens' *Dombey and Son,* Captain Cuttle quotes garbled scripture with the advice to "overhaul your catechism" and "when found, make a note of."

numerous, he managed for them that other little affair, by which they spoiled the Egyptians of jewels of silver and jewels of gold; and it is even asserted that he fed and clothed the family for no less than forty years in a country where the commissariat was a service of extreme difficulty.

At length the time came when he was to make over to them the Land of Canaan, for this purpose evicting the several families then in possession thereof. The whole of the covenanted estate he never did make over to them, but the Jews freely admit that this was through their own fault. They held this land as mortgaged to him, he pledging himself not to foreclose while they dealt with him faithfully and fulfilled all the conditions of the covenant. They were to pay him ten per cent. per annum interest, with sundry other charges, to put all their affairs into his hands, to have no dealings whatsoever with any rival merchants, etc., etc. Under this covenant the Jews continued in possession of the fine little property of Canaan for several hundred years, and they assert that this same Jah lived and conducted his business throughout the whole period. But, as I have ventured to suggest, the long existence of the house of Jah may have been the sum total of the lives of a series of individual Jahs. The Jews could not have distinguished the one from the other; for it is a strange fact that Jah himself, they admit, was never seen. Perhaps he did not affect close contact with Jews. Perhaps he calculated that his power over them would be increased by mystery; this is certain, that he kept himself wholly apart from them in his private office, so that no one was admitted even on business. It is indeed related that one Moses (the witness to the execution of the covenant) caught a glimpse of him from behind, but this glimpse could scarcely have sufficed for identification; and it is said, also, that at certain periods the chief of the priesthood was admitted to consultation with him; but although his voice was then heard, he did not appear in person—only the shadow of him was seen, and everyone will allow that a shadow is not the best means of identification. And in further support of my humble suggestion it may be noted that in many and important respects the later proceedings attributed to Jah differ extremely in character from the earlier; and this difference cannot be explained as the common difference between the youth and maturity and senility of one and the same man, for we are expressly assured that Jah was without change—by which we are not to understand that either through thoughtlessness or parsimony he never had small cash in his pocket for the minor occasions of life; but that he was stubborn in his will, unalterable in his ideas, persistent in his projects and plans.

The records of his dealings at home with the Jews, and abroad with the Egyptians, the Assyrians, the Philistines, the Babylonians, the Persians, the Edomites, and other nations, as kept by the Jews themselves, are among the strangest accounts of a large general business which have ever been put down in black on white. And in nothing are they more strange than in the unsullied candor with which the Jews always admit and proclaim that it was their fault, and by no means the fault of Jah, whenever the joint business went badly, and narrate against themselves the most astonishing series of frauds and falsehoods, showing how they broke the covenant, and attempted to cheat the other party in every imaginable way, and, in order to ruin his credit, conspired with foreign adventurers of the worst character—such as MM. Baal, Ashtaroth, and Moloch. Jah, who gave many proofs of a violent and jealous temper, and who was wont to sell up other debtors in the most heartless way, appears to have been very patient and lenient with these flagitious Jews. Yet with all his kindness and long-suffering he was again and again forced to put executions into their houses, and throw themselves into prison; and at length, before our year One, having, as it would seem, given up all hope of making them deal honestly with him, he had put certain strict Romans in possession of the property to enforce his mortgage and other rights.

And now comes a sudden and wonderful change in the history of this mysterious Jah. Whether it was the original Jah, who felt himself too old to conduct the immense business alone, or whether it was some successor of his, who had not the same self-reliance and imperious will, one cannot venture to decide; but we all know that it was publicly announced, and soon came to be extensively believed, that Jah had taken unto himself two partners, and that the business was thenceforth to be carried on by a firm, under the style of Father, Son, and Co. It is commonly thought that history has more of certainty as it becomes more recent; but unfortunately in the life of Jah, uncertainty grows ten times more uncertain when we attain the period of this alleged partnership, for the Jews deny it altogether; and of those who believe in it not one is able to define its character, or even to state its possibility in intelligible language. The Jews assert roundly that the alleged partners are a couple of vile impostors, that Jah still conducts his world-wide business alone, that he has good reasons (known only to himself) for delaying the exposure of these pretenders; and that, however sternly he has been dealing with the Jews for a long time past, and however little they may seem to have improved so as to deserve better treatment, he will yet be reconciled to them, and restore them to possession of their old land, and exalt them above all their rivals and enemies, and of his own free will and absolute pleasure burn and destroy every bond of their indebtedness now in his hands. And in support of these modest expectations they can produce a bundle of documents which they assert to be his promissory notes, undoubtedly for very large amounts; but which, being carefully examined, turn out to be all framed on this model: "I, the above-mentioned A. B." (an obscure or utterly unknown Jew, supposed to have lived about three thousand years ago), "hereby promise in the name of Jah, that the said Jah shall in some future year unknown, pay unto the house of Israel the following amount, that is to say, etc." If we ask, Where is the power of attorney authorising this dubious A. B. to promise this amount in the name of Jah? the Jews retort: "If you believe in the partnership, you must believe in such power, for you have accepted all the obligations of the old house, and have never refused to discount its paper: if you believe neither in Jah nor in the partnership, you are a wretch utterly without faith, a commercial outlaw." In addition, however, to these remarkable promissory notes, the Jews rely upon the fact that Jah, in the midst of his terrible anger, has still preserved some kindness for them. He threatened many pains and penalties upon them for breach of the covenant, and many of these threats he has carried out; but the most cruel and horrific of all he has not had the heart to fulfil: they have been oppressed and crushed, strangers have come into their landed property, they have been scattered among all peoples, a proverb and a by-word of scorn among the nations, their religion has been accursed, their holy places are defiled, but the crowning woe has been spared them (Deut. xxviii. 44); never yet has it come to pass that the stranger should lend to them, and they should not lend to the stranger. There is yet balm in Gilead, a rose of beauty in Sharon, and a cedar of majesty on Lebanon; the Jew still lends to the stranger, and does not borrow from him, except as he "borrowed" from the Egyptian—and the interest on money lent is still capable, with judicious treatment, of surpassing the noble standard of "shent per shent."

And even among the Gentiles there are some who believe that Jah is still the sole head of the house, and that the pair who are commonly accounted junior partners are in fact only superior servants, the one a sort of manager, the other general superintendent and agent, though Jah may allow them a liberal commission on the profits, as well as a fixed salary.

But the commercial world of Europe, in general, professes to believe that there is a *bona fide* partnership, and that the three partners have exactly equal authority and interest in the concern; that, in fact, there is such thorough identity in every respect that the three may, and ought to be, for all purposes of business, considered as one. The second partner, they say, is really the son of Jah; though Jah, with that eccentricity which has ever abundantly characterised his proceedings, had this son brought up as a poor Jewish youth, apparently the child of a carpenter called Joseph, and his wife Mary. Joseph has little or no influence with the firm, and we scarcely hear of a transaction done through him, but Mary has made the most profitable use of her old *liaison* with Jah, and the majority of those who do business with the firm seek her good offices, and pay her very liberal commissions. Those who do not think so highly of her influence, deal with the house chiefly through the son, and thus it has come to pass that poor Jah is virtually ousted from his own business. He and the third partner are little more than sleeping partners, while his mistress and her son manage every affair of importance.

This state of things seems somewhat unfair to Jah; yet one must own that there are good reasons for it. Jah was a most haughty and humorous gentleman, extremely difficult to deal with, liable to sudden fits of rage, wherein he maltreated friends and foes alike, implacable when once offended, a desperately sharp shaver in the bargain, a terrible fellow for going to law. The son was a much more kindly personage, very affable and pleasant in conversation, willing and eager to do a favor to any one, liberal in promises even beyond his powers of performance, fond of strangers, and good to the poor; and his mother, with or without reason, is credited with a similar character. Moreover, Jah always kept himself invisible, while the son and mother were possibly seen, during some years, by a large number of persons; and among those who have never seen them their portraits are almost as popular as photographs of the Prince and Princess of Wales.

With the real or pretended establishment of the Firm, a great change took place in the business of Jah. This business had been chiefly with the Jews, and even when it extended to foreign transactions, these were all subordinate to the Jewish trade. But the Firm lost no time in proclaiming that it would deal with the whole world on equal terms: no wonder the Jews abhor the alleged partners! And the nature of the contracts, the principal articles of trade, the mode of keeping the accounts, the commission and interest charged and allowed, the salaries of the agents and clerks, the advantages offered to clients, were all changed too. The head establishment was removed from Jerusalem to Rome, and branch establishments were gradually opened in nearly all the towns and villages of Europe, besides many in Asia and Africa, and afterwards in America and Australia. It is worth noting that in Asia and Africa (although the firm arose in the former) the business has never been carried on very successfully; Messrs. Brahma, Vishnu, Seeva, and Co., the great houses of Buddha and Mumbo Jumbo, various Parsee firms, and other opposition houses, having among them almost monopolised the trade.

The novel, distinctive, and most useful article which the Firm engaged to supply was a bread called *par excellence* the Bread of Life. The Prospectus (which was first drafted, apparently in perfect good faith, by the Son; but which has since been so altered and expanded by successive agents that we cannot learn what the original, no longer extant, exactly stated) sets forth that the House of Jah, Son and Co. has sole possession of the districts yielding the corn whereof this bread is made, the sole patents of the mills for grinding and ovens for baking, and that it alone has the secret of the proper process for kneading. The Firm admits that many other houses have pretended to supply this invaluable bread, but accuses them all of imposture or poisonous adulteration. For itself, it commands the genuine supply in such quantities that it can undertake to feed the whole world, and at so cheap a rate that the poorest will be able to purchase as much as he needs; and, moreover, as the firm differs essentially from all other firms in having no object in view save the benefit of its customers, the partners being already so rich that no profits could add to their wealth, it will supply the bread for mere love to those who have not money!

This fair and beautiful prospectus, you will easily believe, brought vast multitudes eager to deal with the firm, and especially large multitudes of the poor, ravished with the announcement that love should be henceforth current coin of the realm; and the business spread amazingly. But at the very outset a sad mischance occurred. The Son, by far the best of the partners, was suddenly seized and murdered and buried by certain agents of the old Jewish business (furious at the prospect of losing all their rich trade), with the connivance of the Roman installed as inspector. At least, these wretches thought they had murdered the poor man, and it is admitted on every side that they buried him: but the dependants of the Firm have a strange story that he was not really killed, but arose out of his tomb after lying there for three days, and slipped away to keep company with his father, the invisible Jah, in his exceedingly private office; and they assert that he is still alive along with Jah, mollifying the old man when he gets into one of his furious passions, pleading for insolvent debtors, and in all things by act and counsel doing good for all the clients of the house. They, moreover, assert that the third partner, who as the consoling substitute for the absent Son is commonly called the Comforter, and who is very energetic, though mysteriously invisible in his operations, superintends all the details of the business in every one of the establishments. But this third partner is so difficult to catch, that, as stated before, the majority of the customers deal with the venerable mother, as the most accessible and humane personage belonging to the house.

Despite the death or disappearance of the Son, the firm prospered for a considerable time. After severe competition, in which neither side showed itself very scrupulous, the great firm of Jupiter and Co., the old Greek house, which had been strengthened by the amalgamation of the wealthiest Roman firms, was utterly beaten from the field, sold up and extinguished. In the sale of the effects many of the properties in most demand were bought in by the new firm, which also took many of the clerks and agents into its employment, and it is even said adopted in several important respects the mode of carrying on business and the system of book-keeping. But while the firm was thus conquering its most formidable competitor, innumerable dissensions were arising between its own branch establishments; every one accusing every other of dealing on principles quite hostile to the regulations instituted by the head of the house, of falsifying the accounts, and of selling an article which was anything but the genuine unadulterated bread. There were also interminable quarrels among them as to relative rank and importance.

And whether the wheat, as delivered to the various establishments, was or was not the genuine article which the firm had contracted to supply, it was soon discovered that it issued from the licensed shops adulterated in the most audacious manner. And, although the prospectus had stated most positively that the bread should be delivered to the poor customers of the firm without money and without price (and such seems really to have been the good Son's intention), it was found, in fact, that the loaves, when they reached the consumer, were at least as costly as ever loaves of any kind of bread had been. It mattered little that the wheat was not reckoned in the price, when agents', commissioners', messengers' fees, bakers' charges, and a hundred items, made the price total so enormous. When, at length, the business was flourishing all over Europe, it was the most bewildering confusion of contradictions that, perhaps, was ever known in the commercial world. For in all the establishments the agents professed and very solemnly swore that they dealt on principles opposed and infinitely superior to the old principles of trade; yet their proceedings (save that they christened old things with new names) were identical with those which had brought to shameful ruin the most villainous old firms. The sub-managers, who were specially ordered to remain poor while in the business, and for obedience were promised the most splendid pensions when superannuated, all became rich as princes by their exactions from the clients of the house; the agents, who were especially commanded to keep the peace, were ever stirring up quarrels and fighting ferociously, not only with opposition agents but with one another. The accounts, which were to be regulated by the most honest and simple rules, were complicated in a lawless system, which no man could understand, and falsified to incredible amounts, to the loss of the customers, without being to the gain of the firm. In brief, each establishment was like one of those Chinese shops where the most beautiful and noble maxims of justice and generosity are painted in gilt letters outside, while the most unblushing fraud and extortion are practised inside. When poor customers complained of these things, they were told that the system was perfect, that the evils were all from the evil men who conducted the business! but the good people did not further explain how the perfection of the system could ever be realised, since it must always be worked by imperfect men. Complainants thus mildly and vaguely answered were very fortunate; others, in places where the firm was very powerful, were answered by imprisonment or false accusations, or by being pelted and even murdered by mobs. Many who thought the bread badly baked were themselves thrust into the fire.

Yet so intense is the need of poor men for some bread of life, so willing are simple men to believe fair promises, that, in spite of the monstrous injustice and falsehood and cruelty and licentiousness of the managers and sub-managers and agents of the firm, the business continued to flourish, and all the wealth of Europe flowed into its coffers. And generations passed ere some persons bethought them to think seriously of the original Deed of Partnership and the fundamental principles of the Firm. These documents, which had been carefully confined in certain old dead languages which few of the customers could read, were translated into vulgar tongues, which all could read or understand when read, and everyone began studying them for himself. This thinking of essentials, which is so rare a thought among mankind, has already produced remarkable effects, and promises to produce effects yet more remarkable in a short time.

Behold a few of the questions which this study of the first documents has raised. — The Father, whom no one has seen, is there indeed such a personage? The Son, whom certainly no one has seen for eighteen hundred years, did he really come to life again after being brutally murdered? The junior partner, whom no one has ever seen, the Comforter, is he a comforter made of the wool of a sheep that never was fleeced? The business, as we see it, merely uses the names, and would be precisely the same business if these names covered no personages. Do the managers and sub-managers really carry it on for their own profit, using these high names to give dignity to their rascality, and to make poor people believe that they have unbounded capital at their back? One is punished for defamation of character if he denies the existence of the partners, yet not the very chief of all the managers pretends to have seen any of the three!

And the vaunted Bread of Life, wherein does it differ from the old corn-of-Ceres bread, from the baking of the wheat of Mother Hertha? Chiefly in this, that it creates much more wind on the stomach. It is not more wholesome, nor more nourishing, and certainly not more cheap: and it does us little good to be told that it would be if the accredited agents were honest and supplied it pure, when we are told, at the same time, that we must get it through these agents. It is indeed affirmed that, in an utterly unknown region beyond the Black Sea, the genuine wheat may be seen growing by any one who discovers the place; but, as no one who ever crossed the sea on a voyage of discovery ever returned, the assertion rests on the bare word of people who have never seen the corn-land any more than they have seen the partners of the firm; and their word is bare indeed, for it has been stripped to shame in a thousand affairs wherein it could be brought to the test. They tell us also that we shall all in time cross the Black Sea, and if we have been good customers shall dwell evermore in that delightful land, with unlimited supplies of the bread gratis. This may be true, but how do they know? It may be true that in the sea we shall all get drowned for ever.

These and similar doubts which, in many minds, have hardened into positive disbelief, are beginning to affect seriously the trade of the firm. But its interests are now so inextricably bound up with the interests of thousands and millions of well-todo and respectable people, and on its solvency or apparent solvency depends that of so large a number of esteemed merchants, that we may expect the most desperate struggles to postpone its final bankruptcy. In the great Roman establishment the manager has been supported for many years by charitable contributions from every one whom he could persuade to give or lend, and now he wants to borrow much more. The superintendent of the shops in London is in these days begging for ten hundred thousand pounds to assist the poor firm in its difficulties. It seems a good sum of money; but, bless you, it is but a drop in the sea compared with what the business has already absorbed, and is still absorbing. Scattered shops in the most distant countries have only been sustained for many years by alms from customers here. The barbarians won't eat the bread, but the bakers sent out must have their salaries. A million of pounds are being begged here; and people (who would prosecute a mendicant of halfpence) will give it no doubt! Yet, O worthy manager of the London Shops, one proved loaf of the real Bread would be infinitely more valuable, and would infinitely more benefit your firm! The villainy of the agents was monstrous, generation after generation, the cost of that which was promised without money and without price was ruinous for centuries; but not all the villainy and extortion multiplied a hundred-fold could drive away the poor hungry customers while they had faith in the genuineness of the bread. It was the emptiness and the wind on the stomach after much eating, which raised the fatal doubts as to the *bona fides* of the whole concern. The great English managers had better ponder this; for at present they grope in the dark delusion that more and better bakers salaried with alms, and new shops opened with eleemosynary funds will bring customers to buy their bran cakes as wheaten loaves. A very dark delusion, indeed! If the pure promised bread cannot be supplied, no amount of money will keep the business going very long. Consider what millions on millions of pounds have been subscribed already, what royal revenues are pouring in still; all meant for investment in wholesome and nourishing food, but nearly all realised in hunger and emptiness, heartburn and flatulence. The old Roman shrewdly calculated that the House of Olympus would prove miserably insolvent if its affairs were wound up, if it tried honestly to pay back all the deposits of its customers. As for this more modern firm, one suspects that, in like case, it would prove so insolvent that it could not pay a farthing in the pound. For Olympus was a house that dealt largely in common worldly goods, and of these things really did give a considerable quantity to its clients for their money; but the new firm professed to sell things infinitely more valuable, and of these it cannot prove the delivery of a single parcel during the eighteen hundred years it has been receiving purchase-money unlimited.

The humble compiler of this rapid and imperfect summary ought, perhaps, to give his own opinion of the firm and the partners, although he suffers under the disadvantage of caring very little for the business, and thinks that far too much time is wasted by both the friends and the enemies of the house in investigation of every line and figure in its books. He believes that Jah, the grand Jewish dealer, was a succession of several distinct personages; and will probably continue to believe thus until he learns that there was but one Pharaoh King of Egypt, but one Bourbon King of France, and that the House of Rothschild has always been one and the same man. He believes that the Son was by no means the child of the Father, that he was a much better character than the Father, that he was really and truly murdered, that his prospectus and business plans were very much more wise and honest and good than the prospectus as we have it now, and the system as it has actually been worked. He believes that the Comforter has really had a share in this as in every other business not wholly bad in the world, that he has never identified his interests with those of any firm, that specially he never committed himself to a partnership of unlimited liability with the Hebrew Jah, that he undoubtedly had extensive dealings with the Son, and placed implicit confidence in him while a living man, and that he will continue to deal profitably and bountifully with men long after the firm has become bankrupt and extinct. He believes that the corn of the true bread of life is sown and grown, reaped, ground, kneaded, baked and eaten on this side of the Black Sea. He believes that no firm or company whatever, with limited or unlimited liability, has the monopoly for the purveyance of this bread, that no charters can confer such monopoly, that the bread is only to be got pure by each individual for himself, and that no two individuals of judgment really like it prepared in exactly the same fashion, but that unfortunately (as his experience compels him to believe) the bulk of mankind will always in the future no less than in the past persist in endeavouring to procure it through great chartered companies. Finally, he believes that the worthy chief baker in London with his million of money is extremely like the worthy Mrs. Partington with her mop against the Atlantic.*

*In 1832 Sydney Smith compared attempts by the House of Lords to reject the Reform Bill with the efforts of Mrs. Partington, who, during an 1824 flood in Sidmouth, had tried to protect her home by keeping back the Atlantic with her mop.

Christmas Eve in the Upper Circles

[*This satire was published in the* National Reformer *on January 7, 1866, immediately after the appearance of "The Story of a Famous Old Firm"; it was later reprinted in* Satires and Profanities. *Thomson and Bradlaugh were well aware that publication could lead to prosecution under the blasphemy laws, but Thomson, who at the time was almost as dedicated an iconoclast as Bradlaugh himself, agreed to take full responsibility. As he expressed it in a later* National Reformer *essay: "For the Atheist, God is a figment, nothing; in blaspheming God he therefore blasphemes nothing." Thomson had, moreover, a precedent for such blasphemy in the works of Heinrich Heine, from whose* De l'Allemagne *he had recently been translating similar satires. Perhaps the more interesting relationship, however, is with Rabelais, whom Thomson, as he put it in his 1876* Cope's *essay, considered to be "the greatest genius in French literature." Thomson frequently alluded to or quoted from Rabelais in his essays (notably in the 1875 "Great Christ is Dead!"), but "Christmas Eve in the Upper Circles," in which Rabelais actually makes an "appearance," is Thomson's most ambitious attempt to capture Rabelaisian humor—"a frank, jolly laughter, unrestrained, diluvian, immense, inextinguishable as the laughter of the gods."*]

POOR DEAR GOD sat alone in his private chamber, moody, melancholy, miserable, sulky, sullen, weary, dejected, supernally hipped. It was the evening of Sunday, the 24th of December, 1865. Waters continually dripping wear away the hardest stone; year falling after year will at length overcome the strongest god: an oak-tree outlasts many generations of men; a mountain or a river outlasts many celestial dynasties. A cold like a thick fog in his head, rheum in his eyes, and rheumatism in his limbs and shoulders, his back bent, his chin peaked, his poll bald, his teeth decayed, his body all shivering, his brain all muddle, his heart all black care; no wonder the old gentleman looked poorly as he cowered there, dolefully sipping his Lachryma Christi. "I wish the other party would lend me some of his fire," he muttered, "for it is horribly frigid up here." The table was crowded and the floor littered with books and documents, all most unreadable reading: missionary reports, controversial divinity, bishops' charges, religious periodicals, papal allocutions and encyclical letters, minutes of Exeter Hall meetings, ponderous blue books from the angelic bureaus — dreary as the humour of *Punch*, silly as the critiques of the *Times*, idiotic as the poetry of *All the Year Round*. When now and then he eyed them askance he shuddered more shockingly, and looked at his desk with loathing despair. For he had gone through a hard day's work, with extra services appropriate to the sacred season; and for the ten-thousandth time he had been utterly knocked up and bewildered by the Athanasian Creed.

While he sat thus, came a formal tap at the door, and his son entered, looking sublimely good and respectable, pensive with a pensiveness on which one grows comfortably fat. "Ah, my boy," said the old gentleman, "you seem to get on well enough in these sad times: come to ask my blessing for your birthday *fête*?" "I fear that you are not well, my dear father; do not give way to dejection, there was once a man — " "O, dash your parables! keep them for your disciples; they are not too amusing. Alack for the good old times!" "The wicked old times you mean, my father; the times when we were poor, and scorned, and oppressed; the times when heathenism and vain philosophy ruled everywhere in the world. Now, all civilised realms are subject to us, and worship us." "And disobey us. You are very wise, much wiser than your old worn-out father; yet perchance a truth or two comes to me in solitude, when it can't reach you through the press of your saints, and the noise of your everlasting preaching and singing and glorification. You know how I began life, the petty chief of a villainous tribe. But I was passionate and ambitious, subtle and strong-willed, and, in spite of itself, I made my tribe a nation; and I fought desperately against all the surrounding chiefs, and with pith of arm and wile of brain I managed to keep my head above water. But I lived all alone, a stern and solitary existence. None other of the gods was so friendless as I; and it is hard to live alone when memory is a sea of blood. I hated and despised the Greek Zeus and his shameless court; yet I could not but envy him, for a joyous life the rogue led. So I, like an old fool, must have my amour; and a pretty intrigue I got into with the prim damsel Mary! Then a great thought arose in me: men cannot be loyal to utter aliens; their gods must be human on one side, divine on the other; my own people were always deserting me to pay homage to bastard deities. I would adopt you as my own son (between ourselves, I have never been sure of the paternity), and admit you to a share in the government. Those infernal Jews killed you, but the son of a God could not die; you came up hither to dwell with me; I the old absolute king, you the modern tribune of the people. Here you have been ever since; and I don't mind telling you that you were a much more loveable character below there as the man Jesus than you have proved above here as the Lord Christ. As some one was needed on earth to superintend the executive, we created the Comforter, prince royal and plenipotentiary; and behold us a divine triumvirate! The new blood was, I must own, beneficial. We lost Jerusalem, but we won Rome; Jove, Neptune, Apollo, Bacchus, and the rest, were conquered and slain; our leader of the opposition ejected Pluto and Pan. Only I did not bargain that my mistress should more than succeed to Juno, who was, at any rate, a lawful wife. You announced that our empire was peace; you announced likewise that it was war; both have served us. Our power extended, our glory rose; the chief of a miserable tribe has become emperor of Europe. But our empire was to be the whole world; yet instead of signs of more dominion, I see signs that what we have is falling to pieces. From my youth up I have been a man of war; and now that I am old and weary and wealthy, and want peace, peace flies from me. Have we not shed enough blood? Have we not caused enough tears? Have we not kindled enough fires? And in my empire what am I? Yourself and my mistress share all the power between you; I am but a name at the head of our proclamations. I have been a man of war, I am getting old and worn out, evil days are at hand, and I have never enjoyed life; therefore is my soul vexed within me. And my own subjects are as strangers. Your darling saints I cannot bear. The whimpering, simpering, canting, chanting blockheads! You were always happy in a pious miserableness, and you do not foresee the end. Do you know that in spite of our vast possessions we are as near bankruptcy as Spain or Austria? Do you know that our innumerable armies are a Chinese rabble of cowards and traitors? Do you know that our legitimacy (even if yours were certain) will soon avail us as little as that of the Bourbons has availed them? Of these things you are ignorant: you are so deafened with shouts and songs in your own praise that you never catch a whisper of doom. I would not quail if I had youth to cope with circumstance; none can say honestly that I ever feared a foe; but I am so weak that often I could not walk without leaning on you. Why did I draw out my life to this ignominious end? Why did I not fall fighting like the enemies I overcame? Why the devil did you get born at all, and then murdered by those rascally Jews, that I who was a warrior should turn into a snivelling saint? The heroes of Asgard have sunk into a deeper twilight than they foresaw; but their sunset, fervent and crimson with blood and with wine, made splendid that dawnless gloaming. The joyous Olympians have perished, but they all had lived and loved. For me, I have subsisted and hated. What of time is left to me I will spend in another fashion. Let us eat and drink, for to-morrow we die." And he swallowed hastily a bumper of the wine, which threw him into convulsions of coughing.

Serene and superior the son had let the old man run on. "Do not, I entreat you, take to drink in your old age, dear father. You say that our enemies lived and loved; but think how unworthy of divine rulers was their mode of life, how immoral, how imprudent, how disreputable, how savage, how lustful, how un-Christian! What a bad example for poor human souls!" "Human souls be blessed! Are they so much improved now? . . . Would that at least I had conserved Jove's barmaid; the prettiest, pleasantest girl they say (we know you are a Joseph, though you always had three or four women dangling about you); fair-ankled was the wench, bright-limbed; she might be unto me even as was Abishag, the Shunammite, unto my old friend David." "Let us speak seriously, my father, of the great celebration to-morrow." "And suppose I *am* speaking very seriously, you solemn prig; not a drop of my blood is there in you."

Here came a hurried knocking at the door, and the angelic ministers of state crawled in, with super-elaborate oriental cringings, to deliver their daily reports. "Messages from Brahma, Ormuzd, etc., to congratulate on the son's birthday." "The infidels! the mockers!" muttered the son. "Good words," said the father; "they belong to older families than ours, my lad, and were once much more powerful. You are always trying to win over the parvenus." "A riot in the holy city. The black angels organised to look after the souls of converted negroes having a free fight with some of the white ones." "My poor lambs!" sighed the son. "Black sheep," growled the father; "what is the row?" "They have plumed themselves brighter than peacocks, and scream louder than parrots; claim precedence over the angels of the mean whites; insist on having some of their own hymns and tunes in the programme of to-morrow's concert." "Lock'em all up, white and black, especially the black, till Tuesday morning; they can fight it out then—it's Boxing Day. We'll have quite enough noise to-morrow without 'em. Never understood the nigger question, for my part: was a slave-holder myself, and cursed Ham as much as pork." "New saints grumbling about lack of civilised accommodation: want underground railways, steamers for the crystal sea, telegraph wires to every mansion, morning and evening newspapers, etc. etc.; have had a public meeting with a Yankee saint in the chair, and resolved that heaven is altogether behind the age." "Confound it, my son, have I not charged you again and again to get some saints of ability up here? For years past every batch has been full of good-for-nothing noodles. Have we no engineers, no editors at all?" "One or two engineers, we believe, sire, but we can't find a single editor." "Give one of the *Record* fellows the measles, and an old *l'Univers* hand the cholera, and bring them up into glory at once, and we'll have two daily papers. And while you are about it, see whether you can discover three or four pious engineers—not muffs, mind—and blow them up hither with their own boilers, or in any other handy way. Haste, haste, post haste!" "Deplorable catastrophe in the temple of the New Jerusalem: a large part of the foundation given way, main wall fallen, several hundred workmen bruised." "Stop that fellow who just left; countermand the measles, the cholera will be enough; we will only have one journal, and that must be strictly official. If we have two, one will be opposition. Hush up the accident. It is strange that Pandemonium was built so much better and more quickly than our New Jerusalem!" "All our best architects and other artists have deserted into Elysium, my lord; so fond of the company of the old Greeks."

When these and many other sad reports had been heard, and the various ministers and secretaries savagely dismissed, the father turned to the son and said: "Did I not tell you of the evil state we are in?" "By hope and faith and charity, and the sublime doctrine of self-renunciation, all will yet come right, my father." "Humph! let hope fill my treasury, and faith finish the New Jerusalem, and charity give us peace and quietness, and self-renunciation lead three-quarters of your new-fangled saints out of heaven; and then I shall look to have a little comfort." "Will you settle to-morrow's programme, sire? or shall I do my best to spare you the trouble?" "You do your best to spare me the trouble of reigning altogether, I think. What programme can there be but the old rehearsal for the eternal life (I wish you may get it)? O, that horrible slippery sea of glass, that bedevilled throne vomiting thunders and lightning, those stupid senile elders in white nightgowns, those four hideous beasts full of eyes, that impossible lamb with seven horns and one eye to each horn! O, the terrific shoutings and harpings and stifling incense! A pretty set-out for my time of life! And to think that you hope some time or other to begin this sort of thing as a daily amusement, and to carry it on for ever and ever! Not much appearance of its beginning soon, thank goodness—that is to say, thank badness. Why can't you have a play of Aristophanes, or Shakespeare, or Molière? Why should I meddle with the programme? I had nothing to do with first framing it. Besides, it is all in your honour, not in mine. You like playing the part of the Lamb; I'm much more like an old wolf. You are ravished when those beasts give glory and honour and thanks; as for me, I am utterly sick of them. Behold what I will do; I must countenance the affair, but I can do so without disturbing myself. I'll not go thundering and roaring in my state-carriage of the whirlwind; I'll slip there in a quiet cloud. You can't do without my glory, but it really is too heavy for my aged shoulders; you may lay it upon the throne; it will look just as well. As for my speech, here it is all ready written out; let Mercury, I mean Raphael or Uriel, read it; I can't speak plainly since I lost so many teeth. And now I consider the matter, what need is there for my actual presence at all? Have me there in effigy; a noble and handsome dummy can wear the glory with grace. Mind you have a handsome one; I wish all the artists had not deserted us. Your pious fellows make sad work of us, my son. But then their usual models are so ugly; your saints have good reason to speak of their vile bodies. How is it that all the pretty girls slip away to the other place, poor darlings? By the bye, who are going on this occasion to represent the twelve times twelve thousand of the tribes of Israel? Is the boy Mortara dead yet?* He will make one real Jew." "We are converting them, sire." "Not the whole gross of thousands yet, I trust? Faugh! what a greasy stench there would be—what a blazing of Jew jewelry! Hand me the latest bluebook, with the reports. . . . Ah, I see; great success! Power of the Lord Christ! (always *you*, of course). Society flourishing. Eighty-two thousand pounds four shillings and twopence three-farthings last year from Christians aroused to the claims of the lost sheep of the House of Israel. (Very good.) Five conversions! ! Three others have already been persuaded to eat pork sausages. (Better and better.) One, who drank most fervently of the communion wine suffered himself to be treated to an oyster supper. Another, being greatly moved, was heard to ejaculate, 'O, Christ!' . . . Hum, who are the five? Moses Isaacs: wasn't he a Christian ten years ago in Italy, and afterwards a Mahommedan in Salonica, and afterwards a Jew in Marseilles? This Mussulman is your oyster-man, I presume? You will soon get the one hundred and forty-four thousand at this rate, my son! and cheap too!"

He chuckled, and poured out another glass of Lachryma Christi; drank it, made a wry face, and then began coughing furiously. "Poor drink this for a god in his old age. Odin and Jupiter fared better. Though decent for a human tipple, for a divinity it is but *ambrosie stygiale*, as my dear old favorite chaplain would call it. I have his devotional works under lock and key there in my desk. *Apropos*, where is he? Left us again for a scurry through the more jovial regions? I have not seen him for a long time." "My father, really, the words he used, the life he led; so corrupting for the young saints! We were forced to invite him to travel a little for the benefit of his health. The court *must* be kept pure, you know." "Send for him instantly, sir. He is out of favor because he likes the old man and laughs at your saints, because he can't cant and loves to humbug the humbugs. Many a fit of the blues has he cured for me, while you only make them bluer. Have him fetched at once. O, I know you never liked him; you always thought him laughing

*Edgar Mortara (1852–1940), Italian Jew, principal in the famous "Mortara case," as a child was allegedly abducted by his nurse after she had arranged for his baptism into the Roman Catholic church. In spite of his parents' attempts to recover him, the pope refused to intervene and the boy was held in Rome; he was discovered during the occupation of Rome in 1870, but chose to remain a Roman Catholic.

at your sweet pale face and woebegone airs, laughing '*en horrible sarcasm et sanglante derision*' (what a style the rogue has! what makes that of your favorite parsons and holy ones so flaccid and flabby and hectic?) 'Physician, heal thyself!' So, in plain words, you have banished him; the only jolly soul left amongst us, my pearl and diamond and red ruby of Chaplains, abstracter of the quintessence of pantagruelism! The words he used! I mustn't speak freely myself now, and the old books I wrote are a great deal too coarse for you! Michael and Gabriel told me the other day that they had just been severely lectured on the earnestness of life by one of your new *protegés*; they had to kick him howling into limbo. A fine set of solemn prigs we are getting!" "My father, the holiness of sorrow, the infiniteness of suffering!" "Yes, yes, I know all about it. That long-winded poet of yours (he does an ode for you to-morrow?) began to sermonise me thereon. By Jupiter, he wanted to arouse me to a sense of my inner being and responsibilities and so forth. I very soon packed him off to the infant school where he teaches the alphabet and catechism to the babies and sucklings. Have you sent for my jovial, joyous, jolly Curé of Meudon?" "I have; but I deeply regret that your Majesty thinks it fitting to be intimate with such a free-liver, such a glutton and wine-bibber and mocker and buffoon." "Bah! you patronised the publicans and sinners yourself in your younger and better days. The strict ones blamed you for going about eating and drinking so much. I hear that some of your newest favourites object to the wine in your last supper, and are going to insist on vinegar-and-water in future."

Whereupon entered a man of a noble and courtly presence, lively-eyed and golden bearded, ruddy complexioned, clear-browed, thoughtful, yet joyous, serene and unabashed. "Welcome, thrice welcome, my beloved Alcofribas!" cried the old monarch; "very long is it since last I saw you." "I have been exiled since then, your Majesty." "And I knew nothing of it!" "And thought nothing of it or of me until you wanted me. No one expects the King to have knowledge of what is passing under his eyes." "And how did you manage to exist in exile, my poor chaplain?" "Much better than here at court, sire. If your Majesty wants a little pleasure, I advise you to get banished yourself. Your parasites and sycophants and courtiers are a most morose, miserable, ugly, detestable, intolerable swarm of blind beetles and wasps; the devils are beyond comparison better company." "What! you have been mixing with traitors?" "Oh, I spent a few years in Elysium, but didn't this time go into the lower circles. But while I sojourned as a country gentleman on the heavenly borders, I met a few contrabandists. I need not tell you that large, yea, enormous quantities of beatitude are smuggled out of your dominions." "But what is smuggled in?" "Sire, I am not an informer; I never received anything out of the secret-service money. The poor angels are glad to run a venture at odd times, to relieve the tedium of everlasting Te Deum. By the bye, I saw *the* Devil himself." "The Devil in my kingdom! What is Uriel about? he'll have to be super-annuated." "Bah! your Majesty knows very well that Satan comes in and returns as and when he likes. The passport system never stops the really dangerous fellows. When he honoured me with a call he looked the demurest young saint, and I laughed till I got the lockjaw at his earnest and spiritual discourse. He would have taken yourself in, much more Uriel. You really ought to get him on the list of court chaplains. He and I were always good friends, so if anything happens. . . . It may be well for you if you can disguise yourself as cleverly as he. A revolution is not quite impossible, you know." The Son threw up his hands in pious horror; the old King, in one of his spasms of rage, hurled the blue-book at the speaker's head, which it missed, but knocked down and broke his favourite crucifix. "Jewcy fiction *versus* crucifixion, sire; *magna est veritas et prevalebit!* Thank Heaven, all that folly is *out*side my brains; it is not the first book full of cant and lies and stupidity that has been flung at me. Why did you not let me finish? The Devil is no fonder than your sacred self of the new opinions; in spite of the proverb, he loves and dotes upon holy water. If you cease to be head of the ministry, he ceases to be head of the opposition; he wouldn't mind a change, an innings for him and an outings for you; but these latest radicals want to crush both Whigs and Tories. He was on his way to confer with some of your Privy Council, to organise joint action for the suppression of new ideas. You had better be frank and friendly with him. Public opposition and private amity are perfectly consistent and praiseworthy. He has done you good service before now; and you and your Son have always been of the greatest assistance to him." "By the temptation of Job! I must see to it. And now no more business. I am hipped, my Rabelais; we must have a spree. The cestus of Venus, the lute of Apollo, we never could find; but there was sweeter loot in the sack of Olympus, and our cellars are not yet quite empty. We will have a *petit souper* of ambrosia and nectar." "My father! my father! did you not sign the pledge to abstain from these heathen stimulants?" "My beloved Son, with whom I am not at all well pleased, go and swill water till you get the dropsy, and permit me to do as I like. No wonder people think that I am failing when my child and my mistress rule for me!"

The Son went out, shaking his head, beating his breast, scrubbing his eyes, wringing his hands, sobbing and murmuring piteously. "The poor old God! my dear old father! Ah, how he is breaking! Alack, he will not last long! Verily, his wits are leaving him! Many misfortunes and disasters would be spared us were he to abdicate prudently at once. Or a regency might do. But the evil speakers and slanderers would say that I am ambitious. I must get the matter judiciously insinuated to the Privy Council. Alack! alack!"

"Let him go and try on his suit of lamb's wool for to-morrow," said the old monarch. "I have got out of the rehearsal, my friend; I shall be conspicuous by my absence; there will be a dummy in my stead." "Rather perilous innovation, my Lord; the people may think that the dummy does just as well, that there is no need to support the original." "Shut up, shut up, O, my Curé; no more politics, confound our politics! It is Sunday, so we must have none but chaplains here. You may fetch Friar John and sweet Dean Swift and the amiable parson Sterne, and any other godly and devout and spiritual ministers you can lay hold of; but don't bring more than a pleiad." "With Swift for the lost one; he is cooling his 'sæva indignatio' in the Devil's kitchen-furnace just now, comforting poor Addison, who hasn't got quit for his death-bed brandy yet." "A night of devotion will we have, and of inextinguishable laughter; and with the old liquor we will pour out the old libations. Yea, Gargantuan shall be the feast; and this night, and to-morrow, and all next week, and twelve days into the new year the hours shall reel and roar with Pantagruelism. Quick, for the guests, and I will order the banquet!" "With all my heart, sire, will I do this very thing. Parsons and pastors, pious and devout, will I lead back, choice and most elect souls worthy of the old drink delectable. And I will lock and double bolt the door, and first warm the chamber by burning all these devilish books; and will leave word with the angel on guard that we are not to be called for three times seven days, when all these Christmas fooleries and mummeries are long over. Amen. Selah. *Au revoir.* Tarry till I come."

Religion in the Rocky Mountains

[*This colorful but very uneven satire is notable for two reasons; it is the one work known to have been written by Thomson as the result of his 1872 visit to America, when he was working in Colorado as secretary for a mining company; and it is the only essay of Thomson's that Bradlaugh refused to print in its entirety. The first installment appeared in the* National Reformer *on March 30, 1873, the second on April 13, with a note that the work would be concluded in the next issue. The concluding section, however, with its "Western" jokes about Christ cheating at poker and a drunken Joseph being locked out of heaven, was found to be "too wicked for publication," as Thomson later expressed it; the entire work appears only in Foote's* Satires and Profanities, *from which the present text is taken.*]

Top of Pike's Peak, March 4th, 1873.

HONOURED with your special commission, I at once hurried across to Denver, and thence still westward until I found myself among the big vertebrae of this longish backbone of America. I have wandered to and fro among the new cities, the advanced camps of civilisation, always carefully reticent as to my mission, always carefully inquiring into the state of religion both in doctrine and practice. You were so hopeful that high Freethought would be found revelling triumphant in these high free regions, that I fear you will be acutely pained by this my true report. Churches and chapels of all kinds abound—Episcopalian, Methodist Episcopal (for the Methodists here have bishops), Presbyterian, Baptist, Congregational, Roman Catholic, etc. Zeal inflaming my courage, three and even four times have I ventured into a church, each time enduring the whole service; and if I have not ventured oftener, certainly I had more than sufficient cause to abstain. For as I suffered in my few visits to churches in your England, so I suffered here; and such sufferings are too dreadful to be frequently encountered, even by the bravest of the brave. Whether my sensations in church are similar to those of others, or are peculiar to myself, I cannot be sure; but I am quite sure that they are excruciating. On first entering I may feel calm, wakeful, sane, and not uncomfortable, except that here I rather regret being shut in from the pure air and splendid sky, and in England rather regret having come out through the raw, damp murk, and in both regret that civilisation has not yet established smoking pews; but the Church is always behind the age. It is pleasant for awhile to note the well-dressed people seated or entering; the men with unctuous hair and somewhat wooden decorum; the women floating more at ease, suavely conscious of their fine inward and outward adornments. It is pleasant to keep a hopeful look-out for some one of more than common beauty or grace, and to watch such a one if discovered. As the service begins, and the old, old words and phrases come floating around me, I am lulled into quaint dream-memories of childhood; the long unthought-of school-mates, the surreptitious sweetstuff, the manifold tricks and smothered laughter, by whose aid (together with total inattention to the service, except to mark and learn the text) one managed to survive the ordeal. The singing also is pleasant, and lulls me into vaguer dreams. Gradually, as the service proceeds, I become more drowsy; my small faculties are drugged into quiet slumber, they feel themselves off duty, there is nothing for which they need keep awake. But, with the commencement of the sermon, new and alarming symptoms arise within me, growing ever worse and worse until the close. Pleasure departs with tranquility, the irritation of revolt and passive helplessness is acute. I cannot find relief in toffy, or in fun with my neighbours, as when I was a happy child. The old stereotyped phrases, the immemorial platitudes, the often-killed sophistries that never die, come buzzing and droning about me like a sluggish swarm of wasps, whose slow deliberate stinging is more hard to bear than the quick keen stinging of anger. Then the wasps, penetrating through my ears, swarm inside me; there is a horrid buzzing in my brain, a portentous humming in my breast; my small faculties are speedily routed, and disperse in blind anguish, the implacable wasps droning out and away after them, and I am left void, void; with hollow skull, empty heart, and a mortal sinking of stomach; my whole being is but a thin shell charged with vacuity and desperate craving; I expect every instant to collapse or explode. It is but too certain that if anyone should then come to lead me off to an asylum for idiots, or a Young Men's Christian Association, or any similar institution, I could not utter a single rational word to save myself. And though all my faculties have left me, I cannot attempt to leave the church; decorum, rigid and frigid, freezes me to my seat; I stare stonily in unimaginable torture, feebly wondering whether the sermon will outlast my sanity, or my sanity outlast the sermon. When at length released, I am so utterly demoralised that I can but smoke furiously, pour much beer and cram much dinner into my hollowness, and so with swinish dozing hope to feel better by tea-time. Now, though in order to fulfil the great duties you entrust to me, I have cheerfully dared the Atlantic, and spent long days and perilous nights in railroad cars, and would of course (were it indeed necessary) face unappalled mere physical death and destruction, I really could not go on risking, with the certainty of ere long losing, my whole small stock of brains; especially as the loss of these would probably rather hinder than further the performance of the said duties. For suppose me reduced to permanent idiocy by church-going, become a mere brazen hollowness with a riotous tongue like Cowper's church-going bell;* is it not most likely that I would then turn true believer, renouncing and denouncing your noble commission, even as you would renounce and denounce your imbecile commissioner?

Finding that I could not pursue my inquiries in the churches and chapels, I was much grieved and perplexed, until one of those thoughts occurred to me which are always welcome and persuasive, because in exact agreement with our own desires or necessities. I thought of what I had remarked when visiting your England: how the churches and chapels and lecture-halls, each sect thundering more or less terribly against all the others, made one guess that the people were more disputatious than pious; how one became convinced, in spite of his infidel reluctance, that the people were indeed, as a rule, thoroughly and genuinely religious, by mingling freely with them in their common daily and nightly life. I asked myself, What really proved to me the pervading Christianity of England? the sermons, the tracts, the clerical lectures, the missionary meetings? the cathedrals and other theatres and music-halls crowded with worshippers on Sunday, while the museums and other public-houses

*See page 123n.

were empty and shut? No, scarcely these things; but the grand princeliness of the princes, the true nobleness of the nobles, the lowliness of the bishops, the sanctity of the clergy, the honesty of the merchants, the veracity of the shopkeepers, the sobriety and thrift of the artisans, the independence and intelligence of the rustics; the general faith and hope and love which brightened the sunless days, the general temperance and chastity which made beautiful the sombre nights; the almost universal abhorrence of the world, the flesh, and the Devil; the almost universal devotion to heaven, the spirit, and God.

I thereupon determined to study the religion out here, even as I had studied it in England, in the ordinary public and private life of the people; and you will doubtless be sorely afflicted to learn that I have found everywhere much the same signs of genuine, practical Christianity as are so common and patent in the old country. The ranchmen have sown the good seed, and shall reap the harvest of heavenly felicity; the stockmen will surely be corraled with the sheep, and not among the goats, at the last day; not to gain the whole world would the storekeepers lose their own souls; the pioneers have found the narrow way which leadeth unto life; the fishermen are true disciples, the trappers catch Satan in his own snares, the hunters are mighty before the Lord; bright are the celestial prospects of the prospectors, and the miners are all stoping-out that hidden treasure which is richer than silver and much fine gold. As compared with the English, these Western men are perchance inferior in two important points of Christian sentiment: they probably do not fear God, being little given to fear anyone; they certainly do not honour the king, perhaps because they unfortunately have none to honour. On the other hand, as I have been assured by many persons from the States and the old country, they are even superior to the English in one important point of Christian conduct. Christ has promised that in discharging the damned to hell at the day of judgment, he will fling at them this among other reproaches, "I was a stranger, and ye took me not in"; and this particular rebuke seems to have wrought a peculiarly deep impression in these men, perhaps because they have much more to do with strangers than have people in old settled countries, so much, indeed, that the word "stranger" is continually in their mouths. The result is (as the said persons from England and the States have often solemnly assured me) that any and every stranger arriving in these regions is most thoroughly, most beautifully, most religiously taken in. So that should any of these fine fellows by evil hap be among the accursed multitude whom Christ thus addresses, they will undoubtedly retort in their frank fashion of speech: "Wall, boss, it may be right to give us hell on other counts, but you say you was a stranger and we didn't take you in. What we want to know is, Did you ever come to our parts to trade in mines or stock or sich? If you *didn't*, how the Devil *could* we take you in? if you *did*, it's a darned lie, and an insult to our understanding to say we *didn't*."

But though the practical life out here is so veritably Christian, you still hope that at any rate the creeds and doctrines are considerably heterodox. I am sincerely sorry to be obliged to destroy this hope. In the ordinary talk of the men continually recur the same or almost the same expressions and implications of orthodox belief, as are so common in your England, and throughout Christendom. Why such formulas are generally used by men only, I have often been puzzled to explain: it may be that the women, who in all lands attend divine service much more than do the men, find ample expression of their faith in the set times and places of public worship and private prayer; while the men, less methodical, and demanding liberal scope, give it robust utterance whenever and wherever they choose. These formulas, as you must have often remarked, are most weighty and energetic; they avouch and avow the supreme personages and mysteries and dogmas of their religion; they are usually but brief ejaculations, in strong contrast to those long prayers of the Pharisees which Jesus laughed to scorn; and they are often so superfluous as regards the mere worldly meaning of the sentences in which they appear, that it is evident they have been interjected simply to satisfy the pious ardor of the speaker, burning to proclaim in season and out of season the cardinal principles of his faith. I say speaker, and not writer, because writing, being comparatively cold and deliberate, seldom flames out in these sharp swift flashes, that leap from living lips touched with coals of fire from the altar.

I am aware that these fervid ejaculations are apt to be regarded by the light-minded as trivial, by the cold-hearted as indecorous, by the sanctimonious as even profane; but to the true philosopher, whether he be religious or not, they are pregnant with grave significance. For do not these irrepressible utterances burst forth from the very depths of the profound heart of the people? Are they not just as spontaneous and universal as is the belief in God itself? Are they not among the most genuine and impassioned words of mankind? Have they not a primordial vigour and vitality? Are they not supremely of that voice of the people which has been well called the voice of God? Thus when your Englishman instead of "Strange!" says "The Devil!" instead of "Wonderful!" cries "Good Heavens!" instead of "How startling!" exclaims "O Christ!" he does more than merely express his emotions, his surprise, his wonder, his amaze; he hallows it to the assertion of his belief in Satan, in the good kingdom of God, in Jesus; and, moreover, by the emotional gradation ranks with perfect accuracy the Devil lowest in the scale, the heavens higher, Christ the loftiest. When another shouts "God damn you!"* he not only condemns the evil of the person addressed; he also takes occasion to avow his own strong faith in God and God's judgment of sinners. Similarly "God bless you!" implies that there is a God, and that from him all blessings flow. How vividly does the vulgar hyperbole "Infernally hot," prove the general belief in hell-fire! And the phrase "God knows!" not merely declares that the subject is beyond human knowledge, but also that an all-wise God exists. Here in the West, as before stated, such brief expressions of faith, which are so much more sincere than long formularies repeated by rote in church, are quite as common as in your England. When one has sharply rebuked or punished another, he says "I gave him hell." And that this belief in future punishment pervades all classes is proved by the fact that even a profane editor speaks of it as a matter of course. For the thermometer having been stolen from his sanctum, the said worthy editor announced that the mean cuss who took it might as well bring or send it back (no questions asked) for it could not be of any use to him in the place he was going to, as it only registered up to 212 degrees. The old notion that hell or Hades is located in the middle of the earth (which may have a scientific solution in the

*Is it not time that we wrote such words as this damn at full length, as did Emily Brontë, the Titaness, whom Charlotte justly vindicates in this as in other respects; instead of putting only initial and final letters, with a hypocritical fig-leaf dash in the middle, drawing particular attention to what it affects to conceal? These words are in all men's mouths, and many of them are emphatically the leading words of the Bible. (Thomson's note.)

Plutonic theory that we dwell on the crust of a baked dumpling full of fusion and confusion) is obviously tallied by the miner's assertion that his vein was true-fissure, reaching from the grass-roots down to hell. The frequent phrase "A God-damned liar," "A God-damned thief," recognise God as the punisher of the wicked. I have heard a man complain of an ungodly headache, implying first, the existence of God, and secondly, the fact that the Godhead does not ache, or in other words is perfect. Countless other phrases of this kind might be alleged, a few of them astonishingly vigorous and racy, for new countries breed lusty new forms of speech; but the few already given suffice for my present purpose. One remarkable comparison, however, I cannot pass over without a word: it is common to say of a man who has too much self-esteem, He thinks himself a little tin Jesus on wheels. It is clear that some profound suggestion, some sacrosanct mystery, must underlie this bold locution; but what I have been hitherto unable to find out. The connexion between Jesus and tin may seem obvious to such as know anything of bishops and pluralists, pious bankers and traders. But what about the wheels? Have they any relation to the opening chapter of Ezekiel? It is much to be wished that Max Müller,* and all other such great scholars, who (as I am informed, for it's not I that would presume to study them myself) manage to extract whatever noble mythological meanings they want, from unintelligible Oriental metaphors and broken phrases many thousand years old, would give a few years of their superfluous time to the interpretation of this holy riddle. Do not, gentleman, do not by all that is mysterious, leave it to the scholars of millenniums to come; proceed to probe and analyse and turn it inside out at once, while it is still young and flourishing, while the genius who invented it is still probably alive, if he deceased not in his boots, as decease so many gallant pioneers.

And here, before afflicting you further, O much-enduring editor, let me soothe you a little by stating that some particles of heresy, some few heretics, are to be found even here. I have learned that into a very good and respectable bookstore in a city of these regions, certain copies of Taylor's "Diegesis" have pene-

*Friedrich Max Müller (1823–1900), Anglo-German orientalist and philologist, whose *Introduction to the Science of Religion* appeared in 1873, the date of Thomson's essay.

trated, who can say how? and that some of these have been sold. A living judge has been heard to declare that he couldn't believe at all in the Holy Ghost outfit. It has also been told me of a man who must have held strange opinions as to the offspring of God the Father, though certainly this man was not a representative pioneer, being but a German miner, fresh from the States. This Dutchman (all Germans here are Dutch, doubtless from *Deutsche,* the special claims of the Hollanders being ignored) was asked solemnly by a clergyman, "Who died to save sinners?" and answered "Gott." "What," said the pained and pious pastor, "don't you know that it was Jesus the *Son* of God?" "Ah," returned placidly the Dutchman, "it vass one of te boys, vass it? I always dought it vass te olt man himselben." This good German may have been misled by the mention of the sons of God early in Genesis, yet it is strange that he knew not that Jesus is the only son of God, and our saviour. A story is moreover told of two persons, of whom the one boasted rather too often that he was a self-made man, and the other at length quietly remarked that he was quite glad to hear it, as it cleared God from the responsibility of a darned mean bit of work. Whence some have inferred the heresy that God is the creator of only a part of the universe; but I frankly confess that in my own opinion the reply was merely a playful sarcasm.

The most decided heresy which has come under my own observation was developed in the course of a chat between two miners in a lager-beer saloon and billiard-hall; into the which, it need scarcely be remarked, I was myself solely driven by the fierce determination to carry out my inquiries thoroughly. Bill was smoking, Dick was chewing; and they stood up together, at rather rapidly decreasing intervals, for drinks of such "fine old Bourbon" rye whiskey as bears the honourable popular title of rot-gut. The frequency with which the drinking of alcoholic liquors leads to impassioned and elevated discussion of great problems in politics, history, dog-breeding, horse-racing, moral philosophy, religion, and kindred important subjects, seems to furnish a strong and hitherto neglected argument against teetotalism. There are countless men who can only be stimulated to a lively and outspoken interest in intellectual questions by a series of convivial glasses and meditative whiffs. If such men really take any interest in such questions at other times, it remains deplorably latent, not exercising its legitimate influence on the public opinion of the world. Our two boys were discussing theology; and having had many drinks, grappled with the doctrine of the triune God. "Wall," said Bill, "I can't make out that trinity consarn, that three's one and one's three outfit." Whereto Dick: "Is that so? Then you warn't rigged out for a philosopher, Bill. Look here," pulling forth his revolver, an action which caused a slight stir in the saloon, till the other boys saw that he didn't mean business; "look here, I'll soon fix it up for you. Here's six chambers, but it's only one pistol, with one heft and one barrel; the heft for us to catch hold of, the barrel to kill our enemy. Wall, God a'mighty's jest made hisself a three-shooter, while he remains one God; but the Devil, he's only a single-shot deringer: so God can have three fires at the Devil for one the Devil can have at him. Now can't you figure it out?" "Wall," said Bill, evidently staggered by the revolver, and feeling, if possible, increased respect for that instrument on finding it could be brought to bear toward settlement of even such a difficulty as the present; "Wall, that pans out better than I thought it could: but to come down to the bed-rock, either God's a poor mean shot or his piece carries darned light; for I reckon the Devil makes better play with his one chamber than God with his three." "Maybe," replied Dick, with calm candor, strangely indifferent to the appalling prospects this theory held out for our universe; "some of them pesky little things jest shoot peas that rile the other fellow without much hurting him, and then, by thunder, he lets daylight through you with one good ball. Besides, it's likely enough the Devil's the best shot, for he's been consarned in a devilish heap of shooting more than God has; at any rate" — perchance vaguely remembering to have heard of such things as "religious wars" — "of late years between here and 'Frisco. Wall, I guess I don't run the creation. Let's liquor"; manifestly deriving much comfort from the consciousness that he had no hand in conducting this world. Bill acquiesced with a brief "Ja," and they stood up for another drink. I am bound to attest that, in spite or because of the drinks, they had argued throughout with the utmost deliberation and gravity, with a dignified demeanour which Bishops and D.D.s might envy, and ought to emulate.

Having thus comforted you with what little of heresy and infidelity I have been able to gather, it is now my painful duty to advance another class of proofs of the general religiousness here; a class of which you have very few current specimens in England, unless it be among the Roman Catholics. All comparative mythologists—indeed, all students of history—are said to agree that the popular legends and myths of any race at any time are of the utmost value, as showing what the race then believed, and thus determining its moral and intellectual condition at that period; this value being quite irrespective of the truth or untruth to fact of the said legends. Hence in modern times collections of old traditions and fairy tales have been excellently well received, whether from the infantile literature of ancient peoples, as the Oriental and Norse, or from the senile and anile lips of secluded members of tribes whose nationality is fast dying out, as the Gaelic and Welsh. And truly such collections commend themselves alike to the grave and the frivolous for the scientific scholar finds in them rich materials for serious study, and the mere novel-reader can flatter himself that he is studying while simply enjoying strange stories become new by extreme old age. All primitive peoples, who read and write little, have their most popular beliefs fluidly embodied in oral legends and myths; and in this respect the settlers of a new region, though they may come from the oldest countries, resemble the primitive peoples. They are too busy with the tough work of subduing the earth to give much time to writing or reading anything beyond their local newspapers; they love to chat together when not working, and chat, much more than writing, runs into stories. Thus religious legends in great numbers circulate out here, all charged and surcharged with faith in the mythology of the Bible. Of these it has been my sad privilege to listen to not a few. As this letter is already too long for your paper, though very brief for the importance of its theme, I will subjoin but a couple of them, which I doubt not will be quite enough to indicate what measureless superstition prevails in these youngest territories of the free and enlightened Republic.

It is told—on what authority no one asks, the legend being universally accepted on its intrinsic merits, as Protestants would have us accept the Bible, and Papists their copious hagiology—that St. Joseph, the putative father of our Lord, fell into bad habits, slipping almost daily out of Heaven into evil society, coming home very late at night and always more or less intoxicated. It is suggested that he may have been driven into these courses by unhappiness in his connubial and parental relations, his wife and her child being ranked so much above himself by the Christian world, and the latter being quite openly attributed to another father. Peter, though very irascible, put up with his misconduct for a long time, not liking to be harsh to one of the Royal Family; and it is believed that God the Father sympathised with this poor old Joseph, and protected him, being himself jealous of the vastly superior popularity of Mary and Jesus. But at length, after catching a violent cold through getting out of bed at a preposterous hour to let the staggering Joseph in, Peter told him roundly that if he didn't come home sober and in good time, he must just stay out all night. Joseph, feeling sick and having lost his pile, promised amendment, and for a time kept his word. Then he relapsed; the heavenly life proved too slow for him, the continual howling of "all the menagerie of the Apocalypse" shattered his nerves, he was disgusted at his own insignificance, the memory of the *liaison* between his betrothed and the Holy Ghost filled him with gall and wormwood, and perhaps he suspected that it was still kept up. So, late one night or early one morning Peter was roused from sleep by an irregular knocking and fumbling at the gate, as if some stupid dumb animal were seeking admittance. "Who's there?" growled Peter. "It's me—Joseph," hiccoughed the unfortunate. "You're drunk," said Peter, savagely. "You're on the tear again; you're having another bender." "Yes," answered Joseph, meekly. "Wall," said Peter, "you jest go back to where you come from, and spend the night there; get." "I can't," said Joseph. "They're all shut up; they've turned me out." "Then sleep outside in the open air; it's wholesome, and will bring you round," said Peter. After much vain coaxing and supplicating, old Joe got quite mad, and roared out, "If you don't get up and let me in at once, by God I'll take my son out of the outfit and bust up the whole consarn!" Peter, terrified by this threat, which, if carried out, would ruin his prospects in eternal life by abolishing his office of celestial porter, caved in, getting up and admitting Joseph, who ever since has had a latch-key that he may go and come when he pleases. It is to be hoped that he will never when tight let this latch-key be stolen by one of the little devils who are always lurking about the haunts of dissipation he frequents; for in that case the consequences might be awful, as can be readily imagined.

Again it is told that a certain miner, a tough cuss, who could whip his weight in wild cats and give points to a grizzly, seemed uncommonly moody and low-spirited one morning, and on being questioned by his chum, at length confessed that he was bothered by a very queer dream. "I dreamt that I was dead," he explained; "and a smart spry pretty little angel took me up to heaven." "Dreams go by contraries," suggested the chum, by way of comfort. "Let that slide," answered the dreamer; "the point isn't there. Wall, St. Peter wasn't at the gate, and the angel critter led me on to pay my respects to the boss, and after travelling considerable we found him as thus. God the Father, God the Son, God the Holy Ghost and Peter, all as large as life, were playing a high-toned game of poker, and there was four heavy piles on the table—gold, not shinplasters, you bet. I was kinder glad to see that they played poker up in heaven, so as to make life there not onbearable; for it would be but poor fun singing psalms all day; I was never much of a hand at singing, more particularly when the songs is psalms. Wall, we waited, not liking to disturb their game, and I watched the play. I soon found that Jesus Christ was going through the rest, cheating worse than the heathen Chinee at euchre; but of course I didn't say nothing, not being in the game. After a while Peter showed that he began to guess it too, if he wasn't quite sure; or p'r'aps he was skeared at up and telling Christ to his face. At last, however, what does Christ do, after a bully bluff which ran Pete almost to his bottom dollar, but up and show five aces to Pete's call; and 'What's that for high?' says he, quite cool. 'Now look you, Christ,' shouts Pete, jumping up as mad as thunder, and not caring a cent or a continental what he said to anybody: 'look you, Christ, that's too thin; we don't want any of your darned miracles here!' and with that he grabbed up his pile and all his stakes, and went off in a mighty huff. Christ looked pretty mean, I tell you, and the game was up. Now you see," said the dreamer, sadly and thoughtfully, "it's a hard rock to drill and darned poor pay at that, if when you have a quiet hand at poker up there, the bosses are allowed to cheat and a man can't use his deringer or put a head on 'em; I don't know but I'd rather go to the other place on those terms."

Not yet to be read in books, as I have intimated, but circulating orally, and in versions that vary with the various rhapsodists, such are the legends you may hear when a ring is formed round the hotel-office stove at night, in shanties and shebangs of ranchmen and miners, in the shingled offices of judge and doctor, in railroad cars and steamboats, or when bumming around the stores; whenever and wherever, in short, men are gathered with nothing particular to do. The very *naïveté* of such stories surely testifies to the child-like sincerity of the faith they express and nourish. It is the simple unbounded faith of the Middle Ages, such as we find in the old European legends and poems and mysteries, such as your poetess Mrs. Browning well marks in Chaucer—

> the infantine
> Familiar clasp of things divine.

Many of the so-called liberal clergy complain of the gulf which yawns in this age of materialistic science between religion and every-day life, this world and the next, heaven and earth, God and man. The higher things are treated as mere thin abstractions, they say; and only the lower things are recognised as real. These pious pioneers, in the freshness and wonderfulness of their new life, overleap this gulf without an effort, realising heaven as thoroughly as earth. How could the communion and the human nature of saints be better exhibited than in St. Joseph falling into dissipation and St. Peter playing poker? How could the manhood as well as the Godhead of Jesus Christ be more familiarly brought home to us than by his taking a hand at this game and then miraculously cheating? When generations have passed away, if not earlier, such legends as these will assuredly be gathered by earnest and reverent students as quite invaluable historical relics. They must fill the Christian soul with delight; they must harrow the heart of him who hath said in his heart, There is no God.

In conclusion, I must again express my deep regret at being forced by the spirit of truth to give you so favourable an account of the state of religion out here, both in creed and practice. I trust that you will lose no time and spare no exertion in attacking and, if possible, routing out the Christianity now entrenched in these great natural fortresses. Be your war-cry that of the first pioneers, "Pike's Peak or bust"; and be not like unto him found teamless half-way across the plains, with the confession on his waggon-tilt, "Busted, by thunder." For you can come right out here by railroad now. As for myself, I climbed wearily and with mortal pantings unto the top of this great mountain, thinking it one of the best coigns of vantage whence to command a comprehensive view of the sphere of my inquiries, and also a spot where one might write without being interrupted or overlooked by loafers. Unfortunately I have not been able to discover any special religious or irreligious phænomena; for, though the prospect is indeed ample where not intercepted by clouds or mist, very few of the people and still fewer of their characteristics can be made out distinctly even with a good glass. How I am to get down and post this letter puzzles me. The descent will be difficult, dangerous, perhaps deadly. Would that I had not come up. After all there is some truth in the Gospel narrative of the Temptation: for by studying the general course of ecclesiastical promotion and the characters of the most eminent churchmen, I was long since led to recognise that it is indeed Satan who sets people on pinnacles of the temple; and I am now moreover thoroughly convinced that it is the Devil and the Devil only that takes any one to the top of an exceeding high mountain.

Mr. Kingsley's Convertites

[*As Thomson admits in this 1865 essay, he had read all Kingsley's novels (except for* Hereward the Wake, *which was then appearing in installments in* Good Words*) with considerable interest and admiration. Even a decade later, when writing an obituary notice on Kingsley, he still had high praise for* Yeast *and* Alton Locke, *and noted that Kingsley had possessed "the gift of seeing and picturing clearly, in words very simple and pregnant, all features and aspects of earth and sea and sky." But "Canon Kingsley" was another matter: "A man of any genius does not in our days become a Canon and a Royal Chaplain for nothing; much money shall he have, and much honor in respectable society, and his praises shall be chanted in full choir by all the newspapers of Bumbledom; but for these sweet things he must pay a great price, even that most precious jewel which he calls a soul." Thomson's main thesis here—that Christianity is a religion to die with, not to live with—owes a good deal to Heine, whose works he had been translating at that time (see p. 256 of this edition where Thomson summarizes Heine's views on religion: "When health is used up, money used up, and sound human sense used up, Christianity begins"). "Mr. Kingsley's Convertites" first appeared on September 24, 1865, in the* National Reformer, *from which this text is taken; it was later reprinted in* Satires and Profanities.]

READERS can scarcely have forgotten the amusing "turn-up" between the Rev. Mr. Kingsley and the Rev. Dr. Newman, in which the latter got the former "into Chancery," and punished him so pitilessly. While reading the *Apologia pro Vitâ Suâ,* one naturally reflected now and then upon the opinions, as stated in the books, of Dr. Newman's antagonist; and the fight grew more and more comically exquisite as one gradually learnt the thorough agreement at bottom of the two who were struggling so fiercely at top. When I speak of Mr. Kingsley's books, I mean his novels and romances, all of which (except the one not yet completely published) I have duly read and enjoyed. As for certain collections of sermons, a dialogue for loose thinkers, a *jeu d'esprit* on the Pentateuch, together with various trifles by way of lectures on History and Philosophy, I confess that none of these have I ever even attempted to peruse. To palliate this sin of omission, I can only urge the high probability that a man of Mr. Kingsley's character must find much more vigorous and ample expression in a free and easy novel than in any didactic or argumentative treatise, with its wearisome requirements of consecutiveness and cramping limitations of logic. I now ask the readers of the *National Reformer* to accompany me in a general review of his romances, because I think that such a review will develop two or three facts seldom noticed in the critiques—whether friendly or adverse—that abound upon his writings. Especially, I think that it will be found that the popular phrases, *Muscular Christianity* and *Broad Church*, by no means sufficiently characterise his religious tendency; and that, with all the superficial unlikeness, almost amounting to perfect contrast between him and Dr. Newman, the opponents as religious men are fundamentally alike in this—that their respective creeds satisfy, or appear to satisfy, in the same manner the same peculiarly intense want in their several natures.

In every one of Mr. Kingsley's romances there is a chief personage, more or less naturally good but decidedly godless at the beginning, god-fearing and saintly at the end. Some of the romances have each two or three of these convertites, the throes of whose regeneration are the principal "motives" of the most striking scenes, and may be thus fairly said to furnish the plot and passion of the book. My present object is not Aesthetic, and I, therefore, need not argue the question whether narratives thus constructed can have any claim to rank as genuine works of art. With the melancholy Jaques in *As You Like It*, I believe

—Out of these Convertites
There is much matter to be heard and learned:

so will stay "to see no pastime, I," but run through the stories of these conversions, touching only the most salient points.

Alton Locke, when adolescent, is a very poor tailor, a poet whose verses are far more vigorous than his character, a chartist, a sceptic. He madly falls in love with a Dean's daughter, and through the patronage of the Dean himself, gets a volume of poems published. As the fiercest of the rhymes have been soothed out of this volume by the decorous Dean, radical friends forward to young Locke a pair of plush-breeches—fitting testimonial to the flunkeyism conspicuous in the omissions. He is imprisoned for inciting a rustic mob to a chartist outbreak, confounds the prison chaplain by sporting the latest novelties in heresy direct from Germany, shares when released in the delirium of the memorable tenth of April, finds that the lady of his love is to be married to his cousin, and consummates the long orgy of excitement with a desperate fever. The Dean had directed his attention to the study of natural history; hence the frenzy of the fever takes a zoological turn, and he undergoes therein marvellous transmigrations through a series of antediluvian monsters; awaking at last to sane consciousness (*sane* comparatively, he is never quite in his right senses, poor fellow) to find himself nursed by a young widow, the Dean's elder daughter, who soothes him with readings from Tennyson. She has very recently lost her husband, who was merely a brilliant nobleman, and she herself a Convertite; in a few days the modest Alton is hinting at a declaration to her. She will not marry him, nor indeed any other man, but she sends him out to South America on a special poetical mission. On the voyage thither he dies, a believer, regenerate, leaving as legacy to his friends and the world at large a war-song of the Church (ferociously) Militant. What has converted him?—the plush-breeches? the crash of the tenth of April? the loss of his first lady love? the reading of the *Lotus-eaters*? the delirious Fugue of Fossils? Some or all of these it must be supposed; for weak though he was, he surely could not have been seriously influenced by the comical caricatures of Socratic dialectics, which the Dean sometimes played with him in lieu of chess or backgammon.

Next comes *Yeast*, whose great convertite is Lancelot Smith. He is introduced to us as fresh from Cambridge, a stalwart gallant fellow of great abilities, rather debauched, but discontented with his debauchery, and utterly without fixed creed. An accident confines him long to the house of the Squire whom he is visiting, during his convalescence he becomes the lover of one of the Squire's daughters—a young lady whose vernacular name is Argemone, and who is herself rapidly growing a perfect saint. He also becomes the friend of a gamekeeper, who reads Carlyle, writes poetry, and has experienced special religious illumination. Lancelot then loses all his fortune by the failure of his uncle's bank, and loses his sweetheart by the sulphuretted-hydrogen fever; turns street-porter for the nonce to earn a bit of bread; and finally goes off one knows not whither, an excellent fervid Christian, after playing through several bewildering pages a wild burlesque of the Platonic dialogue with a personage so mysterious that I prefer not to attempt a description of him. What has converted Lancelot? The loss of his money and the death of his sweetheart seem to have been the main influences. For, although he was stunned with calamity, I will not deem him so stupified as to think that he was made a believer by the unintelligible dialogue.

Then follows *Hypatia.* And here I may remark that I am unable to concur in what seems the general opinion—namely, that Mr. Kingsley intended his heroine to represent the character of the Hypatia of history. Although living in the same city at the same period, both lecturing on philosophy, and both ultimately murdered by Christian mobs; it appears to me that, as women, the two Hypatias differed so much from each other that no one having heard them talk for five minutes could have the slightest doubt as to which was which. History and Mr. Kingsley have each composed an acrostic on this lovely name, and with the same *bouts rimés*; but the body (and the spirit) of the one poem is extremely unlike the body (and the spirit) of the other. Mr. Kingsley proffers us an ancient cup and a flask, Greek-lettered "Wine of Cyprus"; we commence to drink solemnly and devoutly, but—O most miserable mockery! it is indubitable brandy and water. Well may he call this an old foe with a new face! The Kingsley Hypatia is not altogether, but is very nearly a convertite; so nearly that he would certainly have made her altogether one, had not the *bouts rimés* been too well known for alteration. Her best pupil (of whom more anon) abandons her, she begins to love a beautiful young Greek monk, and yet (that philosophy may have the help of worldly power in its mortal duel with Christianity) consents to marry the Prefect of Alexandria, whom she very justly despises. While miserable with the consciousness of how low she is stooping to conquer, she is fascinated or mesmerised by an old Jewish hag, and crouches in a sort of fetish worship to what she thinks a statue of Apollo, said statue being represented by the handsome monk. In the agony of shame which follows her discovery of this cheat, she performs a short parody of the Socratic dialogue in concert with the pupil, who had left her and who has returned a Christian, and, at last, when going to the lecture hall (where murder shall prevent her from ever lecturing more) she confesses to a certain longing for Christianity. Why? She was wretched, humiliated, defeated, weary; she had staked all on the red, and had lost, — what more natural than a yearning to try the black? And this character is published and generally received for the Hypatia of history?

But the great convertite of this romance is the pupil already mentioned, the renegade Jew Raphael Ben Ezra. In the prime of life, wealthy, the favourite comrade of the Prefect, superlatively gifted with that subtle Hebrew clearness, which, swayed by a strong will and intense self-love, can scarcely be distinguished from genius, we find him in the opening chapters already as used-up as the old King Solomon of *Ecclesiastes*, having exhausted all excitements of wine, women, and philosophy, all voluptuousness, physical and intellectual. Desperate with *ennui*, he abandons Hypatia, casts away his wealth (how many Jews do the same!), barters clothes with a beggar, and sets out to wander the world with an amiable British bull-bitch (afterwards the happy mother of nine sweet infants) for his sole guide, philosopher, and friend. The chapter, wherein his Pyrrhonism disported itself "on the floor of the bottomless," seems to have been, in great measure, borrowed from the talk of one Babbalanja in Herman Melville's *Mardi*; perhaps, however, both were borrowed direct from Jean Paul's gigantic grotesque, *Titan*. Becoming involved in the meshes of the great war in Africa — that revolt of Heraclian against Honorius which Gibbon treats with such contemptuous brevity in his thirty-first chapter — he is nearly killed himself, saves an old officer from death, and soon falls in love with this officer's daughter. He reads about this time certain epistles, and infers therefrom that Saul of Tarsus was one of the finest gentlemen that ever lived. Also, while the guest of good Bishop Synesius, he hears Saint Augustine preach, and engages with him in long discussions, fortunately unreported. Returning to Alexandria, he almost converts Hypatia, sees her murdered, sharpens his tongue on Cyril the primate, and leaves again to marry his saintly sweetheart, and end his life as quite a model Christian. What has converted him? His love for the young Christian? the gentlemanly character of Paul's Epistles? the bull-bitch with her ninefold litter, like Shakespeare's nightmare? the murder of Hypatia by the Christians, who rent, and tore, and shred her living body to fragments? Or was it mere satiety and weariness of thinking, — the weariness which leads so many, who thought freely when young, to find a resting place in the bosom of the Church as they get old?

In *Westward, Ho!* the great conversion is of Ayacanorah. But as this is a conversion not merely religious but also moral, social, and intellectual, a conversion from barbarism to civilisation, it does not come fairly into the class I am describing. Two incidents in the romance, however, must not be passed over. The first occurs in the Lotus-eating chapter: — Will Paracombe, tired, as well he may be, of wandering about savage America in search of El Dorado, blindly refuses to see that it is his chief end as man to continue wandering until El Dorado is found, and the captain has glutted his heart with vengeance on the Spaniards; and Will gives such excellent reasons for staying in the beautiful spot where he is, with the beautiful and affectionate native woman whom he is willing and anxious to marry in the most legal mode attainable, that Captain Amyas Leigh, who has been urging him onward with true Kingsleyan diffidence and mildness, finds himself dumbfounded. But valuable logical assistance is at hand. A jaguar like a bar of iron plunges on poor Will, and he and his arguments are settled on the spot. Amyas thanks God for this special interposition of providence in his favour: and the man who wrote the adventures of Amyas can sneer at the faith of a Catholic like Dr. Newman! The other incident is the conversion of Amyas from his diabolical hatred of the Spaniards in general, and of the Don with whom Rose had eloped in particular. A lightning-flash strikes him blind, and he thereupon repents him of his hatred and desire of revenge, and, moreover, has a vision of the Don drowned with his sunken galleon, who assures him that his hatred was without just cause. These are the true Kingsleyan dialectics; these, and not those burlesques of what Plato wrote and Socrates spoke, and Mr. Kingsley is no more able to conduct than I am to lead on the violin like Herr Joachim, a great concerted composition of Beethoven. Let a jaguar loose into your opponent's syllogistic premises, blind him with a lightning-flash that he may see the truth, and have clear vision of the right way. Yet Mr. Kingsley has undoubtedly read about a tower in Siloam that fell, and what Joshua Bar-Joseph said of the people killed by this accident.

Lastly, we have *Two Years Ago*, whose great Convertite is Tom Thurnal. Tom is one of the jolliest of characters, true as steel, tough as oak, quick and deft for all emergencies, a compact mass of common sense, and courage, and energy, living in the most godless state. He is not a heathen, he is more godless yet; for a heathen has something of wood or stone which serves him for a Deity. In the Saga of Saint Olaf (in that great and glorious work *The Heimskringla*) we read how this pious and terrible King going to his last battle was asked by two brothers, who were freebooters, for permission to fight in his ranks. But although these and their followers were "tall" men, and the King was in sore need of recruits, he would not accept their services unless they believed in Christ. Whereupon they answered that they saw no special need of the help of the "White Christ"; that they had been hitherto wont to believe in themselves and their own luck, and with this belief had managed to pull through very well, and thought they could do the same for the future. Ultimately, these excellent fellows did consent to be baptised and called Christians—not from any religious motive, alas! but only because of a "sthrong wakeness" they had for taking part in a set battle. Tom Thurnal has just as much, and as little, religion as these had. After wandering all over the world in all sorts of capacities, he comes back to be shipwrecked on the Cornish Coast, and is the only one on board saved. While he is being dragged up the beach senseless, his belt of money—the fruit of a season at the Australian diggings—disappears; and he resolves to settle in the village, in order to discover it or the thief. Here he falls in love with the village schoolmistress, a sweet mystical devotee, whom he rather suspects of stealing his gold, and whom he defends from one ruffian in order to grossly insult her himself. In the village Tom is doctor, and, when the cholera comes, he is assisted in bringing the village through it by this saintly schoolmistress, and a pious Major, and a fervid High Church parson. At the breaking out of the Crimean War, Tom gets charged with a secret mission to the East. Somewhere in Turkey, in Asia, an imbecile Sheikh or Pasha whom he is endeavouring to serve, mistakes his manœuvres, and keeps him in captivity for a year or two. From this imprisonment he comes home crushed and abject, "afraid in passing a house that it would fall and smother him," etc., marries his sweetheart, and ends a model Christian. What has converted him? Simply, it appears, the year or two of solitary confinement—which took all the pith and manhood out of him. This last case, the work of Mr. Kingsley in the full maturity of his powers, is the most flagrant of all.

If I have not summed up these cases fairly, the novels and romances in question are in everybody's hands to convict me of the unfairness. I have simply sketched the leading points as they remain in my memory, not referring to the books again to pick out what would best serve my purpose. It is not my fault if the personages, who looked so great and grandiose in the flowing and ample draperies of romance, do not strip well for anatomy.

Now, what is common to all these cases of conversion? This: that the characters become religious, not when healthy, but when diseased; the religion in every case is exhibited as a drug for the sick, not as wholesome food for the healthy. While you are sane, well, and hearty, doing your work in the world deftly, sound in mind, and wind, and limb, and fairly prosperous, you have no need of this religion, you can get through the world very well without it. But when your fortune is lost, your sweetheart dead or married to another, your courage cowed, your heart broken, your mind diseased, your self-respect humiliated, then you long for and embrace Christianity (or whatever religion is dominant around you): it is a soft pillow for the aching head, a tender couch for the bruised body, a flattering nurse for the desolate invalid. I can scarcely add that it is a medicine for the sickness, for its medicinal virtues are hardly shown; but it is, at any rate, as we read of its effects in these books, a narcotic and an anodyne for restlessness and pain. It is a religion to die with, not to live with. All these things, so soothing and beneficial to the invalid, are nauseous and noxious to the healthy. A man could no more live vigorous life on such a religion, than he could live vigorous life couched tenderly, pillowed softly, nursed assiduously, and drugged with narcotics and anodyne all the days of his life.

Is the religious world willing to accept this view of religion? It would seem so by the remarkable popularity of these books. This view may be correct or incorrect, wise or foolish; at any rate, it is strangely at variance with the view commonly ascribed to *Muscular Christians,* and strangely identical with that which Dr. Newman explicitly avows in the most eloquent pages of his *Apologia.* People generally consider *Muscular Christianity* as a clever and cheerful improvement on the old solemn ascetic Christianity, as a doctrine which fully recognises the goodness of the common world and common worldly life, as a liberal cultus which does not sacrifice body to soul any more than soul to body, but is at once gymnastic and spiritualistic in its "exercises"; a vague notion is abroad that, whereas the early religion of Christ and his apostles was of sorrow and suffering, this, its latest development, is a religion of happiness and health; in short, it is believed that *Muscular Christianity* has added the Gospel* of the body and this life to the primitive Gospel of the soul and the next life: and yet the most popular and vigorous writer of this new school, after exhausting a very fertile imagination in the suggestion of methods and modes by which godless sinners may be converted to godliness, has absolutely found no other process effectual than this of showering upon them misfortunes, humiliations, afflictions, calamities (such as do not in real life fall upon one human being in a thousand, and working results such as they would not work in one real human being out of ten thousand); until health and hope, self-respect, and the capacity for sane joy, are altogether destroyed in them, the manhood and womanhood overwhelmed and crushed out of

*The Gospel of the body and this life has been powerfully preached in the most explicit terms on the continent. In England, we have been too prudish to advocate it so clearly, although it is, of course, essential to the most enlightened Positivism and Secularism. That much-abused book the *Elements of Social Science*, preaches it with more thoroughness, knowledge, and ability, than any other English work I have met with. I do not pretend to be wise enough to judge this book, and so far as I can judge it, I differ from it in many respects; but on the broad question of the spirit in which it is written, I do not fear to assert that no honest and intelligent man can find pruriency and impurity in it, without he brings the pruriency and impurity in his own heart and mind to the study of it. I can understand ascetic Christians abhorring it, I can understand timid Freethinkers being frightened by it because they *are* timid; but I cannot understand men who claim to be bold and honest Freethinkers, avoiding it as an unholy thing merely because of the subjects it treats, without reference to the mode of treatment, and without sympathy for the admirable motives which manifestly incited the author. He may well say with the most brilliant and daring of all who have preached this gospel of the body in our age (this gospel which is so sorely needed to complement and modify the exclusive gospel of the soul, this gospel which Plato preached along with the other while Jesus preached the other only), he may well say with Heine: —

Doch die Castraten Klagten,
Als ich meine Stimm' erhob;
Sie Klagten und sie sagten:
Ich sange viel zu grob.
(Thomson's note.)

them; after which he brings in these miserable wrecks and relics of what were once men and women as all that he can contribute to the extension of the Church, which ought to be the cheerful congregation of wholesome men and women throughout the world, the richest flower and ripest fruit of humanity. If the Church of the future is to be composed of creatures like Mr. Kingsley's convertites, Westminster Abbey must be turned into a Grand Chartreuse, and St. Paul's into an Hospital for Incurables, and the metropolitan Cathedral of England must be Bedlam.

Hints for Freethought Novels

[*This essay is one of the numerous "Jottings" that Thomson did for the* National Reformer *in 1870–71, usually under the signature "X." Although most of his work was written for free-thought periodicals and was read by men and women actively engaged in reform, Thomson himself did not take reform movements seriously, feeling that even were mankind to be dragged out of one pitfall, it would "immediately stumble into another as deep and dangerous." Not infrequently, then, Thomson's essays and satires in the* National Reformer *quietly ridiculed secularist reform, and this particular "Jotting," although primarily a satire against Christian novels, makes free-thought propaganda appear equally ridiculous. The essay was published on November 20, 1870, and is reprinted here for the first time.*]

A CERTAIN philosopher, after profound studies in sociology and elaborate calculations of probabilities, has arrived at the conclusion that in less than a hundred years the whole or nearly the whole of the instruction of our nation in things in general will be carried on by means of the divine trinity, novels, journals, and lectures. A few peculiar people, he thinks, will go on writing solid and heavy works, and a few other peculiar people go on reading the same; but in the course of another hundred years both these classes will dwindle away as surely as alchemists and astrologers have dwindled away already. Then no ponderous books will be produced any more, except perhaps those compilations called works of reference. He points out that quarterly reviews which half a century back were considered quite volatile, are now found to be bulky and heavy as mastodons, and as certainly behind the age. That monthly magazines find serious essays too heavy to carry, and can only float buoyed up by three or four strings of bladders called serial novels, with the addition of one or two small bladders called short tales for each number. That weekly periodicals are already too slow, so that by the time they appear much of their information and philosophy is out of date. And he even doubts whether journals are fast enough, since many of them issue several editions a day; and opines that we shall soon have horals, each with the latest telegrams and leading articles of a few sentences; the more elaborate essays and correspondence, whose wisdom and news may be thought fit to last the whole day, being given in a series of instalments from morning to night for the easier digestion of readers.

The said philosopher does not seem to rejoice in what he thus forecasts; perhaps because he has been used to read solid and heavy books, and even means to write two or three such himself. But for our part, we think the prospect decidedly cheerful. Ponderous books were very well suited to the old times when the world moved so sluggishly that scarcely any change could be perceived in the course of fifty or a hundred years. But with the world's present rapid rate of progress we must have our philosophy and information fresh daily (if not hourly) in order not to be left far behind in the flying march. A man who writes a thoroughly ponderous work, "a book which no gentleman's library should be without," must devote several years to it; so that the earlier portions thereof, instead of being inspired with the most advanced ideas and rich in the latest knowledge, must be dim and mouldering with hoar antiquity. And the reader has to give the leisure of months to master such a work, so that when he lifts his eyes from it and looks around him he will learn that the van of progress is hundreds of leagues in advance, that the main body is far far beyond sight, that he is among the extreme joints of the long tail of the rear. Who lays in a stock of eggs, milk, bread, meat, fish, for three months to come, when he can get them fresh day by day as wanted? And moreover solid books, demanding long and laborious study from the writer and reader (or readers, should there be more than one), are very injurious to the health of both, and when finished leave both with a sad sense of ignorance. But novels, and journals, and lectures, being written and spoken fluently and with scarcely any study, by persons who need know little more of the subjects than the reader or hearer who knows not anything, do not fatigue the brain, yet leave all concerned with the pleasant impression that they know all worth knowing of the matter. And who can doubt that tongue and pen run the better the less weight they carry? Besides, if this novel fails it is only the luck of the season, if this article or lecture is unsatisfactory it is only the chance of the day; next season or to-morrow the luck may alter; but the failure of a solid book (whose solidity is heavy against it) means the loss of many years, perhaps the best part of a lifetime.

The said philosopher has further calculated that this trinity of novels and journals (or horals) and lectures will be pretty equally divided between the sexes; woman having the novels, man the journals, and the lectures going half to one and half to the other. As to the novels he points out that woman is already making them her own; and he ventures to predict that ere long no woman will think of having a baby until she has given birth to at least one novel, while those who have no babies at all will give birth to all the more novels; and he even expects that short works of fiction will soon take the place of themes at boarding schools for girls. Indeed he avows his astonishment that women did not long ago monopolise and thenceforth retain the monopoly of novel writing, and that men, real masculine men, can still be found struggling to compete with them in a branch of industry so truly feminine. For, as he remarks, you cannot hear two women, however poor and uneducated, talking in the street, without hearing a bit of a novel; the narrative being exact and ample, with full details of dress, place, time, gestures, and countless circumstances relevant and irrelevant; and the style being rather more picturesque and vigorous, and not more faulty and diffuse than that of a fairly written novel of the season by a lady of title. Whereas a man telling by word of mouth some little bit of his autobiography, stupidly goes at once to what he calls the point, leaves out all picturesque circumstances and dramatic incidents, gives the mere dead skeleton of the affair instead of the living flesh and blood story.

Now our mind has been much exercised by these announcements of our philosopher, for should his scientific predictions prove correct it deeply concerns us how the new state of things may be turned to the profit of Freethought. Lectures we have already, and lecturers both male and female, and these lecturers already get considerable audiences; so that this department seems able to take care of itself for the present. As for journals, this vigorous hebdomadal will doubtless in due time plant succulent shoots of journals and horals, and like a flourishing Indian figtree become a very forest of leaves. But so little has hitherto been done by the party in the way of novel writing, that this subject should have at once our most anxious consideration. For if the party goes on increasing as at present, and the philosopher's calculations be verified, think what a multitude of Freethinking ladies must soon be engaged in the manufacture of works of fiction! In these they will of course vehemently preach and teach their own opinions; and as they are still without experience in their art, we venture very humbly to proffer a few hints on the best way of advocating Freethought in novels. In order to qualify ourselves a little for this important task, we have looked into and sometimes even tried to peruse a large number of "novels with a purpose," as they are called, written by very earnest and eloquent ladies belonging to the various and widely varying sects of the one indivisible Church. The experience we have thus acquired as to the modes of advocacy, good, bad, and just tolerable, ought to be of use if the contagion of the said novels has left us intellect enough to use it.

It is well known, and is admitted by even the most stubborn of men, that ladies usually, we may probably write always, get the best of it in any argument with the opposite sex, and this not by reason, but in spite of reason. Men being stupid and loving logic (with a love which is seldom reciprocated) generally seem to think that these female victories are unfair because won thus in spite of reason. For ourselves, however, we esteem them the more on this very account; for any dullard ought to prevail in argument with reason on his side, but to conquer against reason, shows a splendid genius in the victor, as to fight and conquer without arms is more glorious than well-armed to fight and conquer. Since, then, the goddess of reason (naturally enough) prefers the opposite sex to her own, we advise our ladies to avoid reasoning in their books. We have noted that the arguments are the weak points in all the "novels with a purpose" read by us, and that in fact they usually nullify all the rest of the work. The author of that infidel novel, "The Pilgrim and the Shrine,"* does indeed copiously argue, but he is a man and a very clever one, and even in his case we would prefer the story by itself and the arguments by themselves. Let the ladies trust wholly to the story for recommending and inculcating their opinions, and let them make this story as interesting as they can. A few sharp sentences or short passages from classical Freethink-

*Edward Maitland (1824–1897), whose autobiographical novel, *The Pilgrim and the Shrine; or, Passages from the Life and Correspondence of Herbert Ainslie*, was published anonymously in 1868 and praised for its outspoken treatment of religious doubt.

ers may be introduced when a little argument or exposition seems much needed, but this will be very seldom if the story be well managed and kept moving briskly. Make all your good characters Infidels and Republicans, all your bad characters orthodox and conservative; lavish talents and virtues on the poor and mean, follies and vices on the wealthy and noble. The effect of this in a good story will be really wonderful. Readers will learn to associate vice with religion, virtue with Infidelity; and abstract arguments will not be required. If you allow a single good character in the upper ranks, be careful to show in the third volume that he or she was really born of poor parents, just as the dear old snobbish novels used to show at last that the hero or heroine in humble life was a stray scion of nobility. A murderous aristocrat, a rector who commits forgery, an archdeaconess eloping with a High-Church curate, a bigamous bishop (was there not one once said to have been a buccaneer?) these and the like characters well worked up in a "sensational" story will be very effective against rank and religion. Nor need it be feared that such personages would be at all more unnatural than most of those who now flourish in our successful novels. All depends upon making the story interesting; probability and even possibility may be freely dispensed with, so long as the plot keeps the reader excited. The one deadly sin is slowness or dulness.

While avoiding argument, which is double-edged and dangerous to handle, be prodigal of sentiment, which is a safe cordial and much enjoyed by the candid reader. Your Infidel characters cannot utter too many noble sentiments, nor your orthodox characters too many base ones. But apart from sentiment do not let your personages talk much except talk which is "business"; for it is disappointing to open a bottle labelled champagne and find it full of ginger-beer.

A most important point, as we have been taught by countless pious fictions, is the death-scene. Make your religious characters die despairing and raving of Hell and the Devil, except here and there a very imbecile one whose talk of Heaven shall be contemptible and ludicrous; and let your Infidels expire placidly content with the life they have lived, and assured that it cannot be otherwise than well with them hereafter. There is here a very large and fertile field to be laboured by your genius.

Don't forget that in Scripture-readers, tract-distributors, Sunday-school teachers, members of Young Men's Christian Associations, and so on, you have an inexhaustible stock of those useful characters the zanies and butts; and be sure that with all your efforts you will not be able to caricature such species, to draw them more fatuous than they are.

Parsons have been bountifully served up in fictions already, and you may study bad types of them with great advantage in various religious novels. Each party in the Church has been more pitiless for those of the other parties than you as outsiders will like to be for any. For vilification of the pious, clerical and lay, we might also refer you to the religious periodicals, but their language is so bad, their malignancy so intense, their rage so furious, their logic so vile, their spirit so untruthful, that even in the interest of the good cause we cannot recommend you as ladies to glance at them at all.

While carefully avoiding argument you may here and there throw in as it were negligently some of those inconsistencies which abound in the Bible, and between the doctrine and practice of the pious. Don't use any of the doubtful or petty ones, as you will not easily exhaust the stock of those which are immense, flagrant, astounding. And remember that while you eschew arguments and discourses in favour of your own side, you may give as many in favour of the orthodox side as you please, so that they be comic and do not hinder the progress of the story too much. In this case also it will be impossible for you to caricature the originals; for imagine the most stupid and grotesque you can, there are yet real ones much more so.

Humbly hoping that this advice will be received in good part, and prove not less profitable than most good advice, especially as we have hastened to give it while the sexes are still commonly accounted equal, we beg to assure our fair readers that we shall never be guilty of such an impertinence after a few years, when their decided superiority will be established.

Association for Intercessory Prayer

[*This article appeared in the* National Reformer *for February 26, 1871, and is reprinted here for the first time. It is one of many such articles that Thomson wrote for secularist editors, who apparently collected material from Christian periodicals and turned it over to Thomson for comment. Usually such hackwork was uninspired and heavy-handed, but on occasion, as in this article, Thomson could and did produce sparkling satire.*]

WE WONDER whether this Association is still in existence. It may have dissolved ere now, or at least limited its action to prayers for heretics and unbelievers, for Christendom has been in so heavenly a state recently that intercession for any of its inhabitants would have been quite absurd. Two years ago the Association was in full working order, for we have chanced upon its *Monthly Paper*, dated Oxford, January, 1869. The secretary was then the Rev. R. M. Benson, of Cowley, Oxford; the Manual of the Association could be had, price 1s. and 1s. 6d., postage 2d. extra, of him and of Messrs. Bell and Daldy, 186, Fleet Street, London; persons desirous of obtaining the papers of the Association were requested to forward one shilling annually to the secretary for postage, and also solicited to make occasional contributions to cover the cost of printing; and cases for insertion in the monthly papers were to be sent in before the 24th day of each month. Considering the smallness of the expenses one thinks that vast numbers of the innumerable believers in the efficacy of prayer must have joined the Association.

The monthly paper before us opens with these words: — "The prayers of the associates are desired for the subjoined objects. The figures in brackets denote the collects in the Manual." Two, three, and even four of such numbers follow some of the names. The first section is for conversion from sin in general, and the cases are rather numerous, comprising an ungodly and negligent priest, a brother in penal servitude, one who has committed sacrilege and threatened murder, 122 prisoners and discharged.

The second section is for conversion from the Seven Deadly Sins: anger, pride, gluttony and drunkenness (these two count one, being branches of intemperance), lust, avarice, envy, sloth, each of which forms a subdivision. Gluttony and drunkenness have the longest list, including, besides several initials, a nobleman, two sisters, other two sisters, a priest, a woman. Under lust we find Edmund and Katherine, Fanny, Watson, a guilty priest, four couples living in sin, H. We are glad to see that avarice has no followers, and envy only two, of whom one is termed jealous.

The third section is for conversion from unbelief, heresy, and schism, and the list is unfortunately very long. Among others we note a Socinian, an Unitarian, an unbelieving authoress, a denier of infant baptism (this wretch's initial is H.; would we could denounce him or her by the full name!), a priest who has seceded to Rome, a family of Dissenters several of whom are inclined to the church. There is also an officer of rationalistic views, whom doubtless it is wished to convert to irrationalistic views; and lastly one A. H. a rationalist, whom of course the association wants converted into an irrationalist. Perhaps A. H. here stand for Austin Holyoake, and the volley of prayers on his behalf two years ago may have procured his conversion; but if so, he has been uncommonly successful in keeping his regeneration a secret.

There are other sections for persons neglecting the sacraments (among which is confession), for deliverance out of temptation and peril, for sanctification of sickness and recovery, and so forth. Likewise for missions and parochial needs, for religious works, for increase of spiritual grace, etc. The last is for spiritual mercies, and includes a newly married couple (who perhaps want a baby in due season, only that would be a mercy common and not special), John trying for an appointment, "that a spiritual director may resume the guidance of a soul," and W. W. for a peaceful end if it be the will of God.

Finally there is a section of thanksgivings, though these seem scarcely included in the professed object of the Association.

To really believe in the efficacy of intercessory prayer, one must believe two things; first, that God with all his goodness does not take such a loving interest in certain of his creatures as is taken by some of their fellow creatures; and secondly, that the prayers of pious creatures can induce him to favour and change the destiny of other creatures. We do not say that all the believers are conscious of holding these two doctrines as thus sharply expressed, but these doctrines are essential to the maintenance of the belief. The God of such believers is the old God of the Jews, the absolute despotic king of the East, with a character grown somewhat milder than in his fierce youth. He is mutable and even capricious, a will to be moved by prayers, not a steadfast and impartial law. Nor is he even thought of as all-wise; for if he were, the petitioners would not ask any special boons of him, being sure that their true wants are better known to him than to themselves. In the really touching petition which we have quoted among the cases for special mercies, "W. W. for a peaceful end if it be the will of God," we have the contradiction between old and new conceptions; W. W. modifies his prayer for a peaceful end by the condition "if it be the will of God," which condition makes manifest the uselessness of the prayer; for if it be the will of God, W. W. will certainly have a peaceful end without praying for it, and even if praying against it. On the whole such prayer as we are considering, seems to us far less logical and reasonable than that which we have seen recorded of certain savages. These do not pray to the Good Spirit; there is no need to pray to him, for he naturally wishes them well and does the best he can for them; but they shrewdly direct all their prayers and offerings to the Evil Spirit, for he is the one to propitiate, as all harm done is done by him.

While, however, we deem our civilised Christian suppliants less advanced than the rudest savages in the science of prayer, we freely admit that it is very natural for any believer in a God to pray yearningly for any person or any thing in which he is deeply interested; it is quite logical for the heart, however senseless to the brain. But what shall we say of an Association like this? A joint-stock company, limited, based on the equitable commercial principle of "I will pray for what you want, if you will pray for what I want?" A person can pray heartily for dear self and dear friends; and might even manage to pray with a certain warmth for a nobleman given up to intemperance (indeed, what good Briton could not pray warmly for any nobleman!), for Fanny, for a guilty priest, for a newly married couple, for W. W. who begs a peaceful end if it be the will of God, though all these were unknown to him. But who could pray with any real fervour of heart for three pages full of such instances, including an immense number of mere capital letters without any characterisation at all save the heading of the section under which they are marshalled? Think of a person honestly trying to supplicate, and in many of the cases trying to repeat, not simply with the lips but also with the heart, collects specially pointed out, for N., A., B., gluttony and drunkenness; H., lust; W. G. S., W. H. W., A. H., E. L. L., A., A., unbelief, heresy, and schism; and so on through numerous variations of single, double, and triple capital letters and two dozen sections of sins and temptations! One might as well try to pray with fervour for number after number of a column of logarithms. God need be omniscient not to be quite puzzled with such prayers. Among the many millions of supplications in various languages demanding his attention at a certain time, two or three hundred in English beseech him to cure N. of gluttony or drunkenness. Which N. of all the hundreds in this blessed island of the free who are gluttons or drunkards? Why, the particular N. meant by the anonymous individual who sent a certain communication to the secretary of the Association for Intercessory Prayer before the 24th of one month, so that the case was inserted in the next monthly paper. A pretty sort of riddle this to propound to one's heavenly father, who must be good-natured indeed not to fly into a passion with such outrageous stupidity.

We have said that the cases to be prayed for fill three pages. Now if an associate properly prayed for each case, and recited all the collects of the Manual which are indicated, he or she would have little or no time for doing anything else in the day. And we should not be surprised if such an Association numbered ten times or even a hundred times as many members, and published monthly papers of thirty or three hundred pages; for the pious are plentiful and foolish enough, and surely the sinners do no less abound. Some one might suggest that all the cases should be brought under the simple heading of conversion from sin in general; but on the same principle the utmost brevity might be obtained, and the Association with its Manual and Monthly Paper rendered quite superfluous, by all Christians adopting the uniform comprehensive supplication, God bless everybody and everything. This, however, would deprive many good weak-minded creatures of the comfort of pottering a long while over their spiritual work, which is about as useful and bracing as the bodily exercise of tatting, but like it is excellent for killing time which the patient has not vitality enough to employ. This Association, in fact, is a notable symptom of a tendency which we have remarked as continually increasing in many departments of thought and action, we mean the tendency to live as it were by algebra, avoiding the rough and multitudinously varied concrete, and dealing with a few bare abstract signs. It is a tendency which marks impoverishment and decrepitude of life and intellect. When God has become a mere phantom, what more fitting supplications can be addressed to him than prayers for a lot of capital letters which denote the Lord knows whom?

By the bye, we must not forget to point out that such an Association can be made to do excellent worldly service as a sacred school for scandal, and the Monthly Papers turned into pious counterparts of profane scurrilous journals which are no longer tolerated, such as the *Age* and the *Satirist,* or have only a sort of underground circulation like their great colleague the main drainage system. For living in a circle of which many are members of such a society, you have only to send such notices as we find in this paper, and the unfortunates to be prayed for shall be clearly indicated to all their neighbours, while you the delator are concealed beyond discovery. We find here a priest and his wife at variance, Edmund and Katherine, Watson, a father quarrelling with his clergyman, B. B. causing much dissension at home, and similar instances which could at once be identified by dear friends and neighbours conversant with the proceedings of the Association. The system thus combines the two capital merits of impotence for good and efficiency for harm; an associate, or the neighbour of an associate, has his initials vaguely prayed for by a lot of utter strangers, and his real or supposed faults distinctly denounced to a knot of acquaintances. We cannot think that an Association so beautifully adapted to human nature both unregenerate and regenerate, has ceased to exist, although as we acknowledged in the beginning of this article the present celestial beatitude of Christendom renders intercession for any of its inhabitants (except the few heretics and unbelievers) quite a work of supererogation.

Bishop Alford on Professor Tyndall

[*Like the "Association for Intercessory Prayer," this article is an example (in a more serious vein) of the religious attacks Thomson based upon Christian material provided by secularist editors. It appeared in the* National Reformer *on September 27, 1874, just four months after "The City of Dreadful Night" had been published in the same periodical. The concluding statement on atheism is, therefore, of interest to readers of "The City," as well as to critics who have questioned the sincerity of Thomson's atheism. Thomson himself apparently thought highly of the essay, for he chose to publish it under his famous pseudonym "B.V." rather than the "X" with which he usually signed such articles. This is the first time the essay has been reprinted.*]

THE *Birkenhead and Cheshire Advertiser* gives three columns to the report of a sermon by the Right Rev. Bishop Alford, in Christ Church, Claughton, in reply to the Belfast address of Professor Tyndall. As the newspaper highly praised the sermon, I began to read the report with some slight hope of at length encountering a little real argument on the Christian side, not altogether unworthy of the great question in discussion. But he who looks for real arguments from Christians struggling with Science, is doomed to perpetual disappointment. I cannot in equity treat this sermon as of any value in relation to the subject; nor as of any value at all, save as an index of the ordinary state of mind of the people who term themselves Christians. A combat *à outrance* is proceeding between theology and philosophy, mythology and science; here are samples of the weapons in which the main body of Bibliolaters trust. The sight is ludicrous, yet pitiful; these men have rummaged in mediæval armouries, and come forth gallantly with the old coats of mail, the old swords and bucklers, bows and arrows, and musketoons, against trained soldiers whose arms of precision are the rifles and artillery of to-day. It is Chinese junk against British ironclad; it is worse than Ashantee or Abyssinian against European, for those barbarians had the sense to get hold of the most modern weapons they could. It is thus intellectually; morally, I am sorry to say that the Christians, like the mediævalists and barbarians, are too ready to resort to poisoning when legitimate weapons fail. One can take but little interest in so absurdly unequal a fight.

The preacher commences with equal wisdom and charity by explaining why it has been the favourite and studious effort of Infidelity to throw discredit upon the first chapter of Genesis. "It is to be traced not so much, I believe, to any special difficulties the narrative presents, but rather to the fact that if the story of creation be admitted, the existence of a Creator cannot be denied! Then, if man has a Creator, man is subject to his law, which, like God himself, is holy, just, and good! And this vain man, proud man, sinful man, cannot endure! . . . There lies the root of Infidelity! It is not for want of evidence, but for want of the will to love God, and obey God, that men affect Atheism! The cause is moral rather than intellectual; as our Saviour himself has taught us, 'Men love darkness rather than light because (in various degrees of enormity) their deeds are evil.' Thus Infidelity *in varied forms* is indigenous in the heart of fallen man!"

It will be seen that the Bishop, like the semi-barbarous warriors with whom I have been forced to compare himself and his fellows, believeth greatly in the efficacy of shouting for affrighting the foe and heartening the friend. Nearly every sentence is a spasmodic exclamation; one might fancy he had put on hysterics with his preaching-gown. Could anything be more ingenuous than his belief that the attacks on the first chapter of Genesis are not traceable to any special difficulties the narrative presents? Could anything be more false and insolent than his charge that men "affect Atheism" through loving darkness rather than light because their deeds are evil? What possible excuse has this Bishop Alford for asserting that such a man as Tyndall is vain, proud, sinful; that he rejects the law of God because that law is holy, just, and good; that he "affects Atheism" not for want of evidence of God's existence, but because he loves darkness rather than light? Where are the Christians who morally and intellectually are superior or equal to the champions of science? What British names can they, without exciting a storm of contemptuous laughter throughout cultivated Europe and America, set against such names as Darwin, Huxley, Tyndall, Spencer, Mill? I know but two places in which such monstrous and shameless calumny as that above quoted finds fitting utterance, where it is regarded as natural—the religious press and the pulpit. To the subscribers and congregations it is sweet as honey, to outsiders it is nauseous as assafœtida, but they have come to be no more surprised at its emission from those quarters than at the mode of defence of the pole-cat and the skunk: what would you have? it is disgusting, but it is the nature of the animals; you must just keep them as far from you as possible. Of a truth, this Bishop Alford condemning Tyndall, this dwarf attempting to lynch that giant, the Insignificant availing himself of the freedom of the pulpit and the press to defile the Illustrious, makes one remember that sentence of Carlyle: "When your lowest blockhead and scoundrel (usually one entity) shall have perfect freedom to spit in the face of your highest sage and hero, what a remarkably free world we shall be!" I do not say that Bishop Alford is a blockhead and scoundrel, much less that he is the lowest blockhead and scoundrel the religious press and pulpit can produce; but I fear that in this instance every grain abated from the "scoundrel" must be carefully added to the "blockhead."

Proceeding to the special subject of his sermon, "The Consistency and Reasonableness of the Record of Creation as Revealed in the Holy Scriptures," the Bishop, incredible as it appears, absolutely seems to think that he has reconciled the irreconcilable antagonisms of Geology and Genesis, by stating that any period of time, however vast, may have elapsed between the "beginning" when God created the Heaven and the Earth, and the commencement of the six days' work! So far as I can see he accepts the work of preparing the earth for man, as literally the work of six days! He goes from verse to verse, from stage to stage, with the calm and confident fatuity of some Sunday-school teacher of the pre-scientific epochs, whose ignorance was bliss; who had no doubt, having no knowledge. Here is a short specimen of his exegesis. "'And God said let us make man in our image, after our likeness' . . . 'Let us make man *in our image*'! That must be the image of His Holiness." Why, in the name of common sense, must it? Why not simply the image, the form, shape, substantial frame and outline, of the anthropomorphic God, who is the God of the early books of the Bible? To confirm the account in Genesis, he quotes from Job, from Exodus, from Proverbs, from the Gospel called of St. John, from Epistles attributed to Peter and to Paul; and he absolutely seems to think that any and every repetition or echo of the early myth is a proof of its accuracy! In brief, his notion of logic in the discussion allows him to assume throughout the certainty in his favour of the chief point in dispute—*i.e.*, the historical and scientific accuracy of the Bible narratives, and with this modest assumption to prove that Genesis should be preferred to all philosophic theories whatever. One might as well try to beat a feather-bed flat as to impress with arguments a soft and downy unintelligence of this sort. Strike it low here, it bulges up there, having no backbone or organism or sensibility to be hurt or disturbed by the infliction.

I am not going to track him from verse to verse through his beloved opening chapter of Genesis. That has been too frequently and thoroughly dissected to need another cutting-up here. I can give no stronger proof of the Bishop's utter ignorance or ignoring of modern science, of his perfect incompetence to deal with the subject, than this: "The record of creation, properly expounded, is entirely consistent with facts around us, physical and moral, and as far as it goes, and in all that we can comprehend, it is perfect and complete." Now, even if the words "properly expounded," be taken to mean (as they so often have meant in the writings of Biblical apologists), twisted and wrested, slurred and stretched, with the most unscrupulous pettifogging cunning, this assertion is now notoriously and ridiculously untrue.

I have not treated Bishop Alford with respect, because I cannot see that he deserves it. How can I respect a man who begins his sermon with the impudent slander that all unbelievers in his nonsense are immoral, and that their unbelief is the mere consequence of their immorality? If ever he learns to esteem honest Atheists and treat them courteously, and to recognise the immeasurable inferiority of a Christian Bishop like himself to a Natural Philosopher like Tyndall, he may look for respectful treatment in these columns,—should we ever think it worth while to mention him again.

Need I add, in finishing, that a controversialist of this calibre quotes the words of the Psalmist, The fool hath said in his heart there is no God? Now, it is a golden rule in criticism to attribute the best, and not any inferior, meaning to what you are examining. Wherefore, being anxious to believe that the Psalmist spoke good sense, and being encouraged to an essay in exegesis by the brilliant success of Bishop Alford, I venture to infer that the Psalmist meant that the man is a fool who in his heart says there is no God, and has not the courageous wisdom to publish it abroad with tongue or pen. He don't declare the man a fool who proclaims aloud that there is no God; but the man who limits himself to saying in his heart. What a lot of such fools we have in England! What myriads say in their hearts (not to speak of the millions who say it in their lives), There is no God; but are afraid even to whisper the fact except to their nearest friends! Fools, indeed, as cowards always are; for if all the unbelievers freely proclaimed themselves, if all the scribes and pharisees, who now miserably cant, spoke out, it would be found that already "There is no God" is the true creed of the mass of the intelligence and energy of this very Christian country.

Jesus Christ Our Great Exemplar

[*This essay appeared in the* National Reformer *(October 25, 1874) and is reprinted here for the first time. Although in earlier essays on Jesus, such as "Christmas Eve in the Upper Circles," Thomson had ridiculed the divinity of Jesus (a "sham sacrifice of a God"), he had always defended Jesus as a man. In 1866, for instance, in "Jesus: As God; As a Man," he had written that "His words, as reported by the Evangelists, are everflowing fountains of spiritual refreshments; and I feel that he was in himself even far more wise and good than he appears in the gospel." By 1874, however, when writing on Jesus as "Our Great Exemplar," Thomson had obviously had second thoughts about Jesus' life and teachings.*]

THE PEOPLE who fancy themselves Christians are continually holding up to us Jesus as the Great Exemplar, the perfect pattern, whom all humankind should seek to resemble. It is true they also tell us that he differed essentially in nature from humanity, being at once God and man, incapable of sin; so that it is hopeless to try to reach his standard. However, we should all strive to approximate to it as closely as possible. Thus the "Imitation of Christ" has been probably the most frequently printed and the most influential Christian book ever written; more influential than the New Testament itself, having been devoutly studied by countless thousands who never saw the Bible in their own language, and were unable to read it in the original or in the Vulgate.

Now, surely the Exemplar for the whole human race ought to have lived a life covering immense fields of experience, in order that his example could be of practical use to the greater number of the diversified classes of mankind. His biography, too, or biographies, ought surely to be very clear, exact, and full of details, in order to furnish as much instruction as possible for the guidance of those expected and commanded to tread in his steps. But the life of Jesus covered a very small field of experience, and was intensely singular instead of typical. We have four biographies, or reputed biographies of him, three probably copied, with variations, from the first, all very brief and vague; and the fourth giving a totally different spirit and meaning to his life from those prevailing in the others. These are strange guide-books for a subject of supreme and infinite importance.

Let me note briefly a few of the main defects in the experience of Jesus. There is no record, though there is tradition, that he ever worked for his living, or engaged in trade of any kind, and if he really did in his youth, he abandoned it in his manhood; so that all who have to labour can find nothing in his conduct to assist them in withstanding the trials and temptations of business, and in the hard attempt to earn an honest livelihood. If they followed his example, they would all strike work and go wandering about the country, preaching to one another and denouncing the respectable classes.

He was not a husband and father, and seems to have thought all sexual relations sinful, or at least inimical to holiness (Matt. xix. 12). If the world had followed his example in this respect, it would indeed have come to an end almost as soon as he thought it would. In all the cares and troubles of married life no guidance or good inspiration is afforded by him. Having had no children he furnishes no example to parents. He did indeed once say, Suffer little children to come unto me, for of such is the Kingdom of Heaven; but it is easy to have a sentimental moment for young ones when you haven't to feed, clothe, tend, nurse, and rear them; and if the Kingdom of Heaven is full of mere innocent little babes, it is no place for virtuous men and women, who have grown wise and strong in struggling with the tremendous difficulties of life.

As a son and a brother he furnishes very dangerous example and doctrine, publicly disowning his mother and brothers (Matt. xii. 46–50); teaching that all relatives the nearest and dearest should be forsaken for him (Matt. x. 37, xix. 39); and proclaiming that he was not come to send peace on earth, but a sword, to set a man at variance against his father, daughter against mother, daughter-in-law against mother-in-law. (Matt. x. 34–36).

He counselled to take no thought for the morrow (Matt. vi. 25–34); so that all prudent Christians who save up for a rainy day, who insure their property or assure their lives, are disobeying him. He told a young man that if he would be perfect he must sell all that he had and give to the poor (Matt. xix. 21). So in a world of perfect Christians, the rich would sell all they had and give to the poor; this would make the rich poor and the poor rich; the poor grown rich would at once return their newly-acquired property to the rich grown poor; there would thus be a continual giving and returning, wasting time and property, only made impossible (as most specially Christian precepts are seen to be when one looks at them practically) by the fact that there would be no one left to buy when all the rich wanted to sell. It was of course easy for Jesus, who had nothing because he took care to earn nothing, to preach this absurd doctrine.

He taught, Resist not evil (Matt. v. 39); Render unto Cæsar the things which are Cæsar's (Matt. xxii. 21); which his great apostle carried out quite logically into the doctrine, The powers that be are ordained of God, whosoever therefore resisteth the power, resisteth the ordinance of God: and they that resist shall receive unto themselves damnation (Romans xiii. 1, 2). So that all political striving, all patriotism, and championship of liberty, have been against Christian teaching; which declares that such men as Wallace, Eliot, Pym, Vane, Milton, Cromwell, Washington, Kosciusko, Mazzini, Garibaldi, shall receive to themselves damnation for resisting the ordinance of God. In the same spirit he taught, The Scribes and the Pharisees sit in Moses' seat: all therefore whatsoever they bid you observe, that observe and do: but do not ye after their works; for they say and do not (Matt. xxiii. 2, 3). By the bye, this is a clear injunction to his followers to observe the whole Mosaic ceremonial law; and the Jews, in this respect, always are and have been the only orthodox Christians.

It must be noted that a great deal of his moral teaching is based upon a delusion, in which he and his disciples firmly believed, and which he most explicitly proclaimed (though with characteristic honesty, Christian advocates refuse to read his plain meaning in his plain words); the delusion that the end of the world was close at hand. He tells his disciples that the Son of man shall be seen coming in the clouds of heaven with power and great glory, that he shall send his angels with a great sound of a trumpet, and they shall gather together his elect from the four winds; and he adds, Verily, I say unto you, This generation shall not pass till all these things be fulfilled (Matt. xxiv. 34). Can words be plainer? Compare 1 Thessalonians iv. 15–17, to see that the great apostle believed this just as firmly. As above remarked, had every one followed the example of Jesus in remaining childless, and the doctrine already alluded to of Matt. xix. 12 (see also 1 Cor. vii.), the world would have come to an end, for the human race at least, with the passing away of the then living generations. Cherishing this delusion, it is no wonder that Jesus and his immediate followers had no care for thought of the morrow, for marriage and posterity, for patriotism; the wonder is how modern professing Christians dare to pretend that the delusion is not to be read clearly in the Gospels and Epistles. Well may Prof. Newman observe (in his "Phases of Faith," I think) that if any classes of men had an interest in disputing the accuracy of the Fifth Proposition of the first Book of Euclid, they would find some means of doing it, and unblushingly employ them.

Had the biographies of Jesus shown that he worked hard, and got an honest livelihood as a carpenter; that he proved himself, under great difficulties, a good sweetheart, husband, father, citizen, patriot, making the best of the world as he found it; that he was modest and sensible, while enthusiastic for the good of his fellows; that the sordid and wearing circumstances of a life of toil and trouble left his mind serene and his heart noble, so that he was ever preaching lofty and liberal truth; that he died bravely as he had lived; then he would indeed have been a Great Exemplar for millions of poor men and women struggling to be good and true in all the natural and common relations of life.

To sum up: This poor sexless Jew, with a noble feminine heart, and a magnificent though uncultivated and crazy brain, did no work to earn his bread; evaded all social and political responsibilities, took no wife and contemned his own family; lived a vagabond, fed and housed by charity (if by miracle, it is clear that we cannot imitate him: would that we could!); uttered many beautiful and even sublime moral truths and more impracticable precepts; preached continually himself, and faith in himself alone as the one thing necessary; and died with the lamentable cry of womanish desperation, perhaps the most significant confession in history of a life of supreme self-illusion laid bare to itself at the point of death, My God, my God, why hast thou forsaken me? He founded a sect which holds him up as the Great Exemplar of mankind, and scarcely one member of which even tries to tread in his footsteps. I have much love and reverence for him as a man; but am quite certain that if every one really set about following his example, the world (which is surely mad enough already) would soon be one vast Bedlam broken loose.

Most of these things have been often said before, but they must be repeated again and again while a spurious Christianity not only corrupts the honesty and softens the brains of its adherents, and absorbs the wealth which should educate the people, but opposes science and progress at every step.

II. Essays and Articles

Bumble, Bumbledom, Bumbleism

[*Although most of Thomson's work in the* National Reformer *was in line with Bradlaugh's editorial policy ("in religious matters, Atheistical; in politics, Republican; on social questions, Malthusian"), he also published essays of a more general nature. This essay on Bumbleism, which should be compared with Arnold's essays on the Philistines, is one of the earliest, and best. It appeared in the* National Reformer *in two installments on October 29 and November 5, 1865, thus predating Arnold's* Culture and Anarchy *by some four years, his "Culture and Its Enemies," as published in* Cornhill, *by almost two years. Thomson reprinted the essay in* Essays and Phantasies.]

I

WE WERE ALL, I think, very much pleased when Mr. Matthew Arnold, not long ago, in his Essay on "Heinrich Heine," in the *Cornhill Magazine*, took occasion to tell us that we English are the most inaccessible to ideas of any people in Christendom. We were so pleased, not because of any novelty in the information, but because it was charming to be spoken to with such frankness by a scholar, a poet, a gentleman, and above all, an Oxford Professor, and because we all in our hearts detest and chafe at our universal submission to routine, just as we all hate the chimney-pot hat which yet we all wear. This essay of Mr. Arnold's, though admirable in spirit, does not render complete justice to Heine (and still less does another by the same author in the same *Magazine*, in which Heine is served up along with Theocritus and Saint Francis); but it certainly renders complete justice to our abjectness under the yoke of the commonplace. The essence of this inert commonplace and monotonous routine, Mr. Arnold recommends us to call by its German name, *Philistinism*, and its slave *Philistines*.* He remarks, fairly enough, that *respectable* is too valuable a word to be perverted into the

*By the bye, Will Watch, the bold smuggler, in the song which is now well up in years, cries "The *Philistines* are down on us!" and Hogg, in his "Life of Shelley" (Vol. I. p. xxviii), quotes a letter written in 1824, wherein Sir Timothy is branded as *the old Philistine*. So Mr. Arnold is not correct in stating that we have not the term in English. (Thomson's note.)

scornful meaning with which Mr. Carlyle uses it; and that the common French term, *épicier,* is less apt and expressive than *Philistine,* while it also casts a slur upon a respectable class composed of living and susceptible members. I may add that the words *Snob* and *Snobbery,* which Thackeray pushed out into such broad significance, have too much of a sneer in them, imply too much of *conscious* hypocrisy, subserviency, and meanness; and that *Mrs. Grundy* is not general enough, being too closely related with the tea-table and mere scandal.

But Mr. Arnold seems to have quite forgotten that we have already denominations of our own — concrete singular and general, as well as abstract — better for us than the French, the Carlylese, or the German. These denominations head this paper: *Bumble, Bumbledom, Bumbleism.** In the first place, their very sound (and *sound* is of immense importance in a nickname), heavy, obese, rotund, a genuine John Bull mouthful of awkwardness, is far more consonant with their meaning than the sound of *respectable, épicier, snob,* or *Philistine* (the German word *Philister* is in this respect superior to *Philistine*): and *Bumble,* moreover, is intimately allied with those most respectable and ancient English words, *grumble, stumble, mumble, jumble, fumble, rumble, crumble, tumble,* all heads of families of the very choicest middle-class blood in the language.

Secondly, and this consideration is decisive; we do not want the same word as the Germans, because we have not the same thing. Essentially "the humdrum people, slaves to routine, enemies to the light, stupid and oppressive, but at the same time very strong," are of the same nature in all countries; but circumstances materially alter existence and character — above all, humdrum existence and character — so that their weapons, their modes of warfare, the things for which they fight, the objects of their devotion and detestation, their watchwords and battle-cries, are not the same in any two countries, and are very different indeed in England and on the continent. (I mean the *continent* generally, as represented by France, Prussia, Austria, Russia, and until lately Italy: the term continent is convenient,

*The *O.E.D.* reveals that Dickens' Mr. Bumble had already been adopted into common usage by the time Thomson wrote this essay. As early as 1856 in the *Saturday Review* there are references to the "collective Bumbledom of Westminster" and to the "great Bumble mind." Similarly, the *Spectator* (April 22, 1865) had used the phrase, "the true spirit of parish Bumbledom."

and quite accurate enough, for broad contrast with England.) There is as great unlikeness between a Philister and a Bumble, as between a continental *mouchard* and one of our detectives.

The Philistines, well so named on the continent, uphold the despotism of absolute governments, oppress the children of the light by brute force of armies and the yet more merciless machinery of bureaucracy and *espionnage*, imprison them in fortresses which disgrace our century, thrust them out into life-long exile, shoot or bayonet or strangle them in critical emergencies. I say that the Philistines do all these things, although many of them may be disapproved of by thousands of decent Philistines; but without the Philistines these things could not be done; the Philistines, by their selfish and stupid and cowardly passivity, empower the immediate agents to perpetrate these atrocities; the Philistines are the great dull block without which for a fulcrum the devil's lever could not act, the coiled worm by which the screw bites. Opposed to these, the continental children of the light, the men of ideas and aspirations, playing desperately for an enormous stake, — for liberty of speech, liberty of the press, and civil freedom, with imprisonment or exile or death as the forfeit if they lose — work by conspiracies, secret societies, insurrections, bloody revolutions, sometimes even by assassinations.

But here in Britain the warfare is not the same, the positions of the opponents and the stakes they contest being so different. Our enemies of the light no longer withhold from us the extreme necessaries, they withhold merely some of the comforts and many of the luxuries of intellectual and moral freedom. Liberty of speech, liberty of the press, and civic independence, we have. The great men who fronted Charles I. with the sword, and at last beheaded him with the axe, the small men who got William of Orange to shoulder James II. out of his palace, and then finessed his flight into an abdication; these fought and won for us the last really desperate and dangerous national battles with Philistinism, abased the strength of Goliath, broke his spear and shattered his armour, and left but a Bumble to bother us; Bumble who is by no means terrible, except as a "terrible bore." Our children of the light triumph by a Reform Bill (such triumph as it is! but the smaller the stakes the better for the players) or a repeal of the Corn Laws, not by a bloody Revolution. When they wish to rouse the people, they don't think of barricades, but write to and in the journals, have public dinners or public meetings without dinners, where they spout away to their hearts' content, get up petitions—to which, let us hope, the majority of the signatures are genuine, and, at length, push a Bill through Parliament. They are liable to the calumnies and contempt of "good society," but need have no fear of the fortress, the bullet, or the scaffold: and the hatred or contempt of society in general does not hurt them much, the fear of it is far worse than the reality; for their own particular society, the people among whom they live day and night, are full of admiration and enthusiasm.* Our *carbonari* are Freemasons who chiefly meet to eat and think to drink, or Benefit Society Odd Fellows and Foresters. Our *gendarmerie* are the county constabulary. Our *prêtraille* and *ultramontains* are rural clergy who vote against Jowett and Gladstone, Sabbatarians who shut up the Crystal Palace and the Museum on Sundays, Archdeacons who attack Colenso in Convocation, Oratorians with a mania for luring pretty girls to confession. The commonplace is really an immense burden on our backs in ordinary social and domestic life, and a heavier burden still in the more elevated intellectual and moral life; but it is not terrible, nor malignant, nor sanguinary; it is simply a very great bother and bore, and each man knows quite well that he can throw off its yoke whenever he has the necessary courage. In brief, it is Bumble and not Goliath who oppresses us. It would be easy to pursue the contrast through a multitude of details, but I think that these are sufficient for a clear understanding. One is surprised that it never seems to have occurred to a writer so thoughtful and careful as Mr. Matthew Arnold.

*A man's *world* consists simply of those people in whose society he spends most of his time. Very few feel acutely the opinions of classes outside these. One is apt to think that a *Mouravieff* should sink overwhelmed under the execrations of Christendom: not at all; he is naturally surrounded by a staff of officials likeminded with himself, and their talk is for him the expression of public opinion. I once saw two poor women enter a public-house, clad in those thin colourless bits of stuff that our poor elderly women wear, and with such flowers in their shapeless bonnets as showed that even flowers can be unlovely. The one had agreed to "stand" a quartern or half-quartern of gin, but had to borrow a penny from the other for the accomplishment of this generous act. In their talk they happened to discuss the plans and prospects of a son of the liberal lady, and I heard her answer some suggestion of her companion with an "Ah, it *might* be better: *but then what would the world say!*" Poor old dame, with thy world of a back-court! to thee of more account (nor to the Universe of less) than court of greatest king or kaiser. (Thomson's note.)

In his public official capacity we all know Bumble, with the great gold-laced hat, the ample scarlet cloak, the wand of awful power. He is portly and of good stature; a little weazened Bumble is an abomination, an imposture. His fat face is dignified by the repose of a solemn disdain of thought, though the ruddiness of his complexion and the likeness of his nose to an overmature strawberry reveal that he can be jolly in private life. He hath an immense genius of inertia (quite the most useful genius in this troubled world); so that the weariness of the immeasurable hours, by which so many weaklings are driven desperate into all sorts of dissipation and mischief, cannot prevail over him; stolidly patient and firm as a pyramid—whose head is so narrow and whose base is so broad—he endureth and repulseth the long assaults of time. His carriage is erect, and he moves with slow pomp, for well he knoweth that he is a chief pillar of the state, and that there is not an institution in the realm more ancient and honourable than he. For he is more truly essential to the sanctity of the cathedral than the Dean himself, more necessary to the stability of the bank than are the chairman and all the other directors. His reverence for the rich and powerful is in exact ratio to his scorn for the poor and mean. His low bows and elaborate subservience to the Alderman are gracefully rounded off by the smart tap which he letteth fall upon the head of the charity urchin; in the former, he signeth himself in large letters "Bumble," in the latter he putteth a fair flourish to this signature. He reverences the rich because they *are* rich; and because people get rich by leading model lives, by being through many years frugal, industrious, sober, discreet, and orthodox. He scorns the poor because they *are* poor, because poverty is odious in itself; and because, if indeed it is not a crime in itself, it is at any rate the fruit and symbol of vice, the outward and visible sign of an inward and spiritual disgrace; for people get poor by being reckless, improvident, lazy, dissolute, enthusiastic, heterodox, and generally by flying in the face of the world.

Bumble as Beadle is Bumble in his most perfect official manifestation, but he is by no means limited to this office so ancient and honourable and useful. He has filled, and he now fills, and for years and generations to come he will fill, a large proportion of the highest and best-paid offices in the State, the Army, the Navy, and a large majority of those in the Court, the Press, and the Church. What, indeed, is the union of Church and State — glorious and happy union, on which we can never enough felicitate our noble selves! — but a grand national homage and tribute to Bumbleism? a wise provision of cosy stalls, lawn sleeves, shovel-hats, gaiters, benefices, pluralities, princely sees, for multitudes of deserving little Bumbles?

And while Bumble is pre-eminently Beadle in his public incapacity; in private life he is more richly developed and more easily studied when of the standing of a Churchwarden (the French *Marguillier*). It is the same Bumble, one and indivisible, with the same plenary inspiration of Bumbleism, in both aspects; and the discrimination is but a matter of convenience, furnishing us with two consummate types, the one for social, the other for political study. The *Imitation of Christ* is supposed to have wrought some good in Europe: he will be England's chief saint and sage who can give us a masterly *Imitation of Bumble.* In the meantime we cannot do better than read, mark, learn, and inwardly digest, out of doors the ensample of Bumble the Beadle, at home the ensample of Bumble the Churchwarden. This Bumble at home can be most jolly and hospitable, can display the most excellent common-sense, is often what we term well-educated, and is in the enjoyment of an easy competence if not absolutely wealthy. For Bumble at home is at home with the middle classes. "The nobles have their traditions, the poor have their aspirations, the middle classes have nothing but their money." The nobles look backward to their Creator, the poor look forward to their Redeemer, the middle classes look neither to the past nor to the future, but enjoy the present whose Holy Ghost is Bumbleism. And the middle classes, as everybody knows, now rule England; and their Bible is the *Times,* of late, like other Bibles, losing much of its authority, and over which may soon be written the epitaph: "Here still lies the *Times,* once a great power; singular among despots and demagogues for this, that it never, during many years of supreme sway, had one moment of magnanimity."

Holy is the spirit of Bumbleism, glorious is the constitution of Bumbledom, great in rank and wealth and power is Bumble, in this our happy Island of the Free! We have not a King Stork, as so many continental miserables have; Bumble is our King Log, a good quiet king, though he beareth somewhat heavily upon our shoulders. He ruleth England far more than do Queen,

Lords, and Commons, with the noble Fourth Estate into the bargain. Little hindereth that his sway be carried out into its ideal perfection; as Dryden hath pictured it with rapture in *Macflecknoe*, and Pope with ecstasy in the *Dunciad*. These men, who were rhymers, clever, but vagabonds of restless, unstable, and foolishly excitable temperament, could not appreciate the worth of the character whose lineaments they saw clearly and drew well: this profound and godlike tranquillity, this equally godlike subsistence without need of thought and speculation, without possibility of development, this magnificent eupepsy of the world and life, they termed *Dulness*, and used this grand word (which involves the loftiest sublimities of immutable inertia) in a base sense of *stupidity* or *duncehood*—just as the lovely word *simple* has been perverted to convey the meaning of *silly*. However, as the word *Dulness* is now by usage established, we may as well boldly adopt it (using it reverentially, not with the evil intention of those who sit in the seats of the scornful), and admit that the essence of the potency of Bumbleism is Dulness; dulness placid and content, dulness of the highest respectability, dulness infallible and impeccable; dulness which preacheth and heareth sermons,—the force of dulness can no further go. The abysses of this dulness no plummet can ever fathom; philosophy may be very profound, yet remain but a shallow pool when compared with these divine depths; the noblest alacrity in sinking will not enable the deepest philosopher to arrive at the "floor of the bottomless." Peter Bell may give some faint idea of this dulness; and by *Peter Bell*, I mean either the poem itself of Wordsworth or the hero of the poem of Shelley; for Peter Bell, like Bumble, is duplicate—nay, the best authority* says that he is triplicate, and so is Bumble, but we are not concerned with Bumble in his beatitude of Bumbleism beyond the tomb:—

> His sister, wife, and children yawned
> With a long slow and drear *ennui*
> All human patience far beyond;
> Their hopes of Heaven they would have pawned
> Anywhere else to be.

*Shelley himself, who in his dedication to "Peter Bell the Third," explains that Peter Bells "are not one, but three; not three, but one." The quoted passage occurs in Part VII, stanzas 13 and 14 of the poem.

But in his verse, and in his prose,
 The essence of his dulness was
Concentered and compressed so close,
'Twould have made Guatimozin doze
 Upon his red gridiron of brass.

(And what better service, I should like to know, *could* have been rendered to Guatimozin in his exceedingly uncomfortable predicament than this of making him doze?)

These two stanzas—by a vagabond yet more restless and unstable and foolishly excitable than those two other vagabonds I have mentioned—relate to the dulness of *Peter Bell*; were their intensity exalted to the hundredth power, they would relate equally well (with reverence be it written) to the dulness of Bumble.

Bumble is not malignant; he is King Log. But one thing he does hate—if an ecstasy of blind wrath and terror can be called hatred: this thing is a new idea, or even the semblance of a new idea such as a novel opinion. He abhors it as a bull or a quaker abhors scarlet, or a Calvinist the Scarlet Lady. And I hold that he is thoroughly justified in his abhorrence. Every new idea is a reproach and insult cast upon our old doctrines and institutions; and the sacred spirit of our old doctrines is Bumbleism; the most venerable of our old institutions is Bumbledom. Bumble is the very bull's-eye of the target against which new ideas rain bullets: and would you expect a living bull's-eye to love marksmen? If things as they immemorially have been and as they now are—our holy Church and noble State, as by law and the wisdom of our ancestors established—be worthy of the most reverent conservation; what pretence can there be for changing them by the application of new ideas? If you want variety (and were you a regular, consistent, well-principled character, you would not want variety), content yourself with dressing up the old ideas in new fashions, as you are fain to content yourself with dressing your own old body in occasionally new garments; do not sap the foundations of our prosperity and undermine the constitution of Bumbledom with new-fangled ideas. For ideas are most perilous things to handle; suddenly explosive as gunpowder and gun-cotton, no one is safe from being blown up by them, and Bumble is safe to be blown up by them: Guy Fawkes *may* go in fragments through the air, the Parliament Houses with king, bishops and nobles are sure to, if once the confounded train catches.

II

I have said that the Fourth Estate itself is not nearly so powerful as Bumble; and as much ludicrous misunderstanding appears to prevail regarding the subject, it may be as well to amplify the assertion. We know that the Press is continually boasting that it leads public opinion, and we are pleasantly called upon to pretend or even endeavour to think that this leading is away from Bumbleism into the Promised Land of New Ideas. It is a good joke; and Bumble can afford to buy the journals in thousands and tens of thousands, and chuckle over it with happy equanimity. What fun that the journalists, of whom about ninety-nine of every hundred are born Bumbles, but weakly and afflicted with incontinency of their dulness, and of whom about ten times ten of every hundred mainly or wholly depend for their livelihood upon the favour of their stronger brother Bumbles, should affect freedom from and enmity to Bumbleism! The joke is enormously useful to Bumbledom. We poor people, for instance, are getting more and more dissatisfied with things as they are, and resolve to emigrate for the Promised Land of New Ideas: forthwith half the Bumble trumpeters of the Press open their throats of brass, and put themselves in our van, blaring: "We, and we only, can and will lead you out of this stupid old Bumbledom into the Canaan flowing with milk and honey!" And in case we should doubt these fair promises, the opposition moiety of the trumpeters open *their* throats of brass, screaming dolorous, wrathful, desperate: "The poor dear ignorant people are being led away from the venerable sanctuary of Bumbleism, from the paternal care of Bumbledom, to perish in the Wilderness of Sin and New Ideas!" This testimony, wrung from the rage of the antagonists, kills our last doubt, and we throng multitudinously after those first trumpeters, who straining their throats of brass lead us forth gallantly, round, and round, and round, through interminable dreary tracts, and at last bring us, all bewildered and exhausted, to the old flesh-pots again, to the cucumbers, and the melons, and the leeks, and the onions, and the garlic, and, with a joyous final flourish, proclaim: "Lo, the true Promised Land! lo, the real milk and honey! — the only milk and honey in this life attainable!" Wearied and disheartened, we perforce rest discontentedly contented for another period. Now, were there none of these clever leaders of public opinion, we poor stupid people might really emigrate by marching stupidly right forward; and so Bumbleism and Bumbledom get actually abandoned.

Of course, the Press, while thus continually boasting of its freedom, knows quite well, and has a comfortable understanding with Bumbledom, that it is, in fact, only free to glorify Bumble. It truckles to him more abjectly than does any commonplace man in private life. For this commonplace man makes boots or hats or coats, sells bread or meat or beer, things which Bumble cannot help liking and must have; while the journalist manufactures and sells only opinions, which are things that Bumble can do very well without, and won't buy if they are not manufactured to please him. A journalist could no more live by producing opinions too large for Bumble, than a tailor by making coats to the size of Daniel Lambert, or a bootmaker by proportioning boots from the ground plan of Adam's foot in Ceylon.* Journalist, tailor, and bootmaker, must all manufacture their articles to the size of their customers: luckily for tailor and bootmaker, it is not ignominious and demoralising to manufacture *their* articles thus. The Press truckles to Bumble, and beslavers him with flattery, and when it ventures to rally him, it does so in the self-same spirit with which a Court-jester used now and then to rally his royal master; and it always apologises to him for any chance glimmer of new light that may manage to penetrate its close columns, by immediately proving that the said glimmer must have come from Bumble's own parlour-fire or one of his church-tapers.

And not only the Press but the mass of our contemporary literature is thus slavishly subservient to Bumble. He cares little for abstract politics, and less for science and art: therefore on politics, science, and art, bookmakers may almost express what

*Daniel Lambert (1770–1809) weighed 739 pounds; his waistcoat, preserved in the Leicester Museum, measures 102 inches around the waist. On Adam's Peak in Ceylon there is a hollow 5 feet 4 inches by 2 feet 6 inches which resembles the form of a human foot; it is held in veneration by Muslims who ascribe the "footprint" to Adam.

they please. But Bumble is the virtuous husband of one virtuous wife, and the father of a thriving legitimate family, and as "church-going" as Cowper's bell* (when did *it* go to church, I wonder, after the visit in which it was hung?); and woe be to any one who shall have the audacity to shock his cherished, his sacred convictions, on any social or moral or religious matter!

Freedom (that is to say, practical freedom) of the Press and of publication generally, is greater in England than on the continent only in certain respects; it is far less in other respects, which certainly are not so important to comfortable animal life, but which are very much more important to the higher intellectual and moral life. We can write freely of the acts of our government and of the public acts of our public men, we can freely discuss our political questions (or, more precisely, questions in the sphere of political expediency), as no writers in Germany or France dare to discuss and write about their home-politics and statesmen. But, on the other hand, a writer in France or Germany can freely discuss questions of religion, of casuistry in morals, of sociology, as no English writer who lives by his writings dare discuss. If the French paper or book ventures beyond the bounds of governmental restrictions in politics, it is warned or suppressed by the Government. If the English paper or book ventures beyond the bounds of Bumbledom's restrictions in religion or morals, it is effectually suppressed by Bumble, — he won't buy it, however brilliant and thoughtful and honest it may be. Imperialism imposes fines, imprisonment, banishment; Bumble simply imposes death by starvation. For the one man-in-black who visits the editors of Paris, we have ten thousand men-in-black. We are free to print what we will; but we must be very rich in courage and money, or independence of money, to afford the free exercise of our freedom. We are also free to become candidates for Parliament, "to enter the London Tavern,"† to seek equity in the Court of Chancery, to attempt arson and murder and suicide.

Our present literature is so devotedly subservient to Bumble, that I think it may be safely asserted that there are not half-a-dozen thoughtful and powerful writers now in England, writers

*Cowper's "Verses Supposed To Be Written by Alexander Selkirk," l. 29, mentions "the sound of the church-going bell."

†The London Tavern was a very popular establishment, famous for its dinners, and greatly in demand for public meetings.

able to earn a good livelihood with the pen, who have ever attempted since they were mature frankly to publish their thoughts and feelings on subjects interdicted by Bumble; that is to say, on precisely the most important and urgent problems in religion and sociology. For all thought bearing on the future of our race, and not physico-scientific or artistic, we are nearly in a state of sterile impotence. Pick up a popular French or German book, and note how many problems in morality and religion are touched upon, how much free and healthy scepticism is carelessly implied or explicitly stated; problems with which no English writer whose book is meant to sell would dare to grapple, scepticism which he dare not avow any more than a Gallic writer dare openly attack the Empire. And then ponder what warm interest in these questions, what freedom in their discussion, what wholesome love of originality, what toleration of honest doubt, what devotion to the pursuit of truth, must have existed for long years among the French and Germans, ere light popular literature could make good use of such problems and flourish on such scepticism. How many English writers of repute, earning good incomes by their writings, would have the courage, however pure and lofty their intent, to treat with the same freedom the same subjects we find treated in a work of Balzac or Heine? Bumble scareth from such essays: our professional bookmakers suppress their own most vigorous and honest thoughts; and the vast majority do much worse, lubricating Bumbledom with oily cant inexpressibly and revoltingly nauseous. For Bumble is pitiless in his rage. Quiet as King Log when undisturbed, patient, slow, and mighty of digestion for all the "good things" of this life, as Carlyle's Oxen of the Gods (each of which, indeed, is a very Apis of the Bumble-worship of John Bull); he is furious when roused; like the Enceladus of Keats—

> Once tame and mild
> As grazing ox unworried in the meads;
> Now tiger-passioned, lion-thoughted, wroth.*

Bumble will permit no one in England to write against the sanctities of Bumbleism or the decorums of Bumbledom, under penalty of being an outcast, despised of men and rejected of women,

***Hyperion*, Book II, ll. 66–68.

who must starve if he has learnt no better trade than bookmaking. But in the matter of reading, Bumble is more tolerant. The continental languages are very useful, and to keep up one's knowledge of those languages, one must occasionally read in their books. Fortunately for Bumble, it happeneth that, as a rule, the very people who know continental languages and can afford to purchase their literature, are the rich and powerful, are Society with a capital S; Society, which Bumble holds in equal reverence with the Golden Calf, and with whose pleasures and privileges he would never willingly interfere; for in his private churchwarden capacity, the chief object of his ambition is to become part and parcel of this Society. Hence, while good Mrs. Bumble and the angelic Miss Bumbles distribute and recommend pious tracts to the poor as the only profitable reading in addition to the Bible and the Book of Common Prayer, they never dream of thrusting these tracts into the hands of the rich: the rich may import any number of books in all the colours of the rainbow full of *livres* and lechery from France, any weight of slab-like tomes ponderous with Rationalism and erudite Infidelity from Germany. One condition, however, is perfectly understood: in any review of these books, all the narrative pieces which specially tickled and enthralled must be overwhelmed with the fiercest of virtuous indignation; all the argumentative passages which really threw light upon vexed questions, must be sternly denounced, the illumination being clearly traced to the Nether Fire. This condition faithfully observed, the poor and uneducated scared from corruption, Society may read without stint. Thou dear respectable Churchwarden-Bumble, it is pleasant to think how thy Vicar and Archdeacon and Bishop have laughed with inextinguishable laughter over Aristophanes and Lucian and Rabelais and Heine; how all thy decorous sons would get full marks in a competitive examination based on Paul de Kock; how thy daughters Angelina and Seraphina, who distribute the tracts, have thrilled over the pages of Soulié* and epicene Sand.

Nay, Bumble in his adoration of Society, will even allow the wealthy and noble to laugh and sneer at his most cherished convictions, so long as the laugh and the sneer circulate exclusively in the higher circles, and are not put into books for the perdition

*Charles Paul de Kock (1793–1871) and Melchior-Frederic Soulié (1800–1847), French novelists and dramatists whose works were considered sensational, if not actually licentious.

of the lower classes, of the ignorant rabble, who, massed and levelled, make such a broad firm floor for his feet, that he may walk through life eminent and unsoiled. And now and then he goes further yet, half awaking to the perception that he himself, and many of his dearest brother Bumbles, of the glorious dynasty of Bumbledom, have secret doubts as to the infallibility of Bumbleism, and venture at whiles to fancy that their heads would be more light and comfortable if relieved from the enormous cocked hats, and their limbs more free were the ample scarlet cloaks thrown off. Yet he and they continue to wear the old garments solemnly, keeping each other in countenance and overawing the vulgar. For good habits are the ideal of Bumble's morality; never mind from what motives and for what purposes they are worn.

Yet, let no one accuse Bumble of conscious insincerity; dissimulation he detests, though a discreet simulation he may patronise. When he seems to the irreverent observer to be playing the hypocrite in concert with his brother Bumbles, be assured that he is doing what he is doing with the very best intentions, and the saintliest anxiety for the continuation of the stability and prosperity of that Bumbledom which he honestly loves and venerates.

Bumble is not thus mightiest of the mighty altogether by his own innate strength, supernal as is the power of inertia and masterly inactivity, unconquerable as is that aboriginal dulness, "against which the gods themselves fight in vain." He is permanently strengthened by nearly the whole deadweight of the men who are not Bumbles, but who lavish all their living momentum to push the progress each of his particular art, science, or profession, and in all matters beyond passively side with Bumble. By a tribute of nine-tenths to Bumble, they obtain permission to devote one-tenth to individuality. Thus eminent sailors, soldiers, engineers, painters, bankers, merchants, whose work is their worship, use all their vital energy in their work, and thus, as a rule, can care very little, and do very little, for anything else, except, perhaps, some harmless hobby. So, for the most part, they are ready to acquiesce quietly in whatever creed they find predominant about them: to take up with a heresy would injure their special work in two ways — by lowering them in public opinion, and by making large demands upon the energy which can scarcely in the present age be more than adequate for their special work. And the creed predominant around them is naturally always the creed of Bumbleism; so that, although they contribute to Bumbledom none of the thought and ability which have made them eminent, they add to it the whole power of their general reputation; and if any audacious wight, who *has* bestowed thought upon the creed, ventures to impugn it, he is at once overwhelmed by the authority of these certainly distinguished men. In other words, Bumbleism is the bed in which great activities and intelligences sleep; when they awake, they leave it for the bank, the ship, the railroad, the factory, the studio: yet Bumble complacently brags of them as if all their great works had been wrought while in the bed of Bumbleism they reposed. Very few men indeed have enough individuality to animate the whole circle of their being.

The irreverent, and the giddy, and the vagabond, have laughed much at Bumble as beadle; they do not find it so easy to laugh at him in domestic life as the churchwarden. These irreverent scholars and thinkers are very bold and scornful creatures in their libraries; Aristophanes, Lucian, Rabelais, Montaigne, Shakespeare, Swift, Voltaire, Lessing, Goethe, Leopardi, Heine, Burns, Shelley, Carlyle, and the like pestilent authors ranged around them; but when in the dining-room, or the railway carriage, they meet a respectable churchwarden Bumble, rich, self-complacent with health and prosperity, clear-headed for all ordinary business, conspicuously excellent in all the common relations of life, self-reliant (that is to say, reliant on the whole of Bumbledom which backs him); where then is the courageous and scornful criticism of the scholars and thinkers? The thinker feels as if he had no firm standing-ground; "sicklied o'er with the pale cast of thought," he seems to himself thin and unsubstantial; his ideas of the study have kept in the study and won't come at his command, or if they do come, sneak in with an air of utopian silliness: he is crushed by the broad firm-planted weight, by the flourishing suave and rotund completeness, of this excellent, cheerful, comfortable, prosperous, moral Bumble; and is far more inclined to envy than disdain. Is this, the poor thinker asks himself, one of those dead barren rock-cliffs against which the restless and luminous waves of the living sea, tide after tide, year after year, century after century, fling themselves so gallantly and so vainly, ever flung back in ragged foam? Why, this is a fat and smiling river valley, rich in corn and wine and oil, full of all manner of pleasantness, the sheltered abode of prosperity and peace; and the sea itself is barrenness and desolation and everlasting unrest. Thus, the law of compensation works: abstract thought triumpheth throughout the millenniums over abstract Bumbleism; but the concrete Bumble triumpheth in his generation over the concrete thinker.

Here should follow a rhapsody on the primordial generation and the final cause of the sacred existence of universal Bumbledom, including Bumble proper, and *Epicier* and *Philister*, and all other species of the sublime genus. What magnificent themes for dithyrambic! but lack of space, not to speak of the writer's modesty, forbids the attempt to do justice to them. There is room, however, for one little confession. Were I a well-known author, flourishing on authorship, and writing for a respectable periodical, I should never dream of exposing, even so slightly as I have here exposed, the solemn mysteries of Bumbleism. Luckily I am an author thoroughly unknown, and writing for a periodical of the deepest disrepute. One is very free, with no name to lose; and one is freer still, with such a name that it cannot possibly be lost for a worse; and, between us, we possess both these happy freedoms. It is really remarkable that authors and periodicals can bear to be cabined, cribbed, confined, within the gilded bars of a good reputation! Bumble is generally attacked, as revolutions are stirred up, by young fellows and old fellows not yet arrived at years of discretion, who have little or nothing to lose, save their heads, which (as in my own case) being of quite inconsiderable value, they quite inconsiderately venture. In revolutions there are always two or three wealthy nobles, who, transported by an insanely generous enthusiasm, fight for the people more valiantly than the people fight for themselves. And just so in literature, there are always two or three really great writers living, who fling assured wealth and reputation to the winds, and dash their heads against Bumbledom. But these exceptions are so rare, and especially so rare in England, that, though very important in themselves, they are hardly worth reckoning as a limitation to the broad rule that he who attacks Bumbledom is he who has not the power and ability to thrive in the world as it is. Thus have I written my own condemnation, immolating myself, as well it behoves me, beneath the irresistible Triumphal Car of our great, our divine Juggernauth—Bumble.

Per Contra: The Poet, High Art, Genius

[*This essay is the "per contra" to "Bumble, Bumbledom, Bumbleism," and should, of course, be read in conjunction with that essay; its publication immediately followed "Bumble" in two installments in the* National Reformer *(November 12, 19, 1865). Thomson's views on the poet as contained herein should be compared with those he had expressed five years earlier in his 1860 essay on Shelley. By 1865, he had concluded, as he put it in the poem titled "Art," that "Statues and pictures and verse may be grand / But they are not the life for which they stand." Thus during this period his poetry, including the famous "Sunday up the River," reflected the attitude expressed in this essay, that one should "live" life rather than writing about it. After "Per Contra," Thomson did not stop writing poetry, but he was never so prolific as he had been before 1865, and that he continued to hold such views is indicated by his decision to reprint "Per Contra" rather than "Shelley" in* Essays and Phantasies.]

I

> *Glendower.* I framed to the harp
> Many an English ditty lovely well,
> And gave the tongue an helpful ornament,
> A virtue that was never seen in you.
>
> *Hotspur.* Marry,
> And I am glad of it with all my heart:
> I had rather be a kitten and cry mew,
> Than one of these same metre ballad-mongers.
>
> —*First Part of Henry IV.*

WHAT ARE the best names to oppose in extreme opposition to the Bumble, Bumbledom, Bumbleism, which are so good and expressive? Even Mr. Matthew Arnold would not, I am sure, recommend us to term the natural enemies of his Philistines, the Jews, the Hebrews, or the Israelites. Children of the light, chosen people, idealists, *idéologues,* are too vaporous and vague: a name is wanted that will stick. The German *high-flyers* is very good.

Bohemians, the favourite denomination just now, is too much associated with loose-living and poverty for my special purpose; nor is it limited to the artist-tribe: Balzac's *Prince de la Bohême* would have quite agreed with Hotspur, although the glorious quaternion of Henry Mürger (*Scènes de la Vie de Bohême*) are a musician, a painter, a poet, and a *philosophe*. Poet and High Art and Genius are terms of serious value, although ludicrous enough now-o'-days from the mouths and pens of so many simpletons drunk with the noble wine of Emerson and Shelley. However, until better denominations are discovered or invented, one must use these, admitting that they are not the very words he should use: Poet standing for the Priest of Beauty in general, whatever material he consecrates to its service (isn't this the correct sort of phrase?); High Art for the loftiest Expression of the Beautiful, in which more or less latent are involved the Good and the True (could our humbug-in-chief, Pinchbeck-Bulwer-Lytton, put it more neatly?); and Genius for the divine (never forget the *divine*) Inspiration of the Poet and Spirit of High Art.

A hundred years ago a good writer was the *ingenious* Mr. Blank, and a hundred years before *that great wit*. In this present year of grace, if we referred to the ingenious Mr. Blank, it would be thought that he had patented a new washing-machine or something of the kind; and if we spoke of a man as that great wit, it would be understood that he punned like Theodore Hook or versified like the author of the *Ingoldsby Legends*.* Nothing will do now as an attribute of praise but Genius. Never before was "the divine right of Genius" so much lectured and written about: "the divine right of Kings" was just such a favourite theme in the reigns of James I., who was despised; of Charles I., who was beheaded; of Charles II., that angel of the Blessèd Restoration; and of James II., who was kicked out of the kingdom. Talent itself has become a word of scorn rather than praise: scarcely a week passes but periodicals of the *London Journal* type have paragraphs of subtle and detailed contrast between Talent and Genius, all odiously to the disadvantage of the former. Were Gubbins, or Gigadibs, or any other of the writers of these profound and sublime paragraphs, to hear your opinion that though

*Theodore Hook (1788–1841), novelist, editor, and writer of "witty" verse. The *Ingoldsby Legends*, written by Richard Harris Barham (1788–1845), were popular in the mid-decades of the century.

certainly a man of very astonishing talents he is not quite a genius, he would detest and despise you ever after. What! he Gubbins, he Gigadibs, merely a man of talent, not a child of genius! Gubbins, who knows perfectly every shade of difference between Genius and Talent! Gigadibs, who can write you out recipes for Shakespeares and Raphaels and Beethovens as readily as Monsieur Soyer could write recipes for puddings and soups! The possession of this or the other special talent you are at liberty to deny to Gubbins or Gigadibs; the possession of indefinite Genius, with a capital G, I warn you to concede.

In the midst of this universal adoration of creative genius, what creative genius have we exerting sublime energies for us? What living artistic genius have we, exercising influence and commanding homage of which a lofty-minded and strong-minded man could justly be proud? We have, I believe, one such poet in verse, whose name is Robert Browning. We have, I believe, not one such poet in music or sculpture. As to architecture I cannot pretend to judge; but the least tepid praises one meets with scarcely point to such a master. In history and philosophy we have Carlyle and Garth Wilkinson.* Of the Fine Arts, proper, only in painting and in the prose fiction which has superseded the old English drama, can three or four of these commanding geniuses be found. Half-a-dozen novels, Carlyle's *French Revolution*, Holman Hunt's *Light of the World*, Ruskin's great works, have probably had more effect on the heart and mind and soul of England than has been wrought by all the music and verse and sculpture and architecture to which this generation has given birth.

Perhaps the briefest and clearest answer to our exuberant dithyrambs on the divine mission and prerogatives of genius, will be drawn out by the simple question: With what expectations do we ordinary people commence the study of a new "work of genius"? Whereto the honest reply is: We look to these grand and glorious and immortal works, which have enraptured the thoughtful critics of journalism, generally for pleasure and amusement, scarcely ever for real delight and education; while

*James John Garth Wilkinson (1812–1899), Swedenborgian, early editor of Blake (see p. 234). Thomson was not alone in esteeming Wilkinson's work; Emerson, for instance, had declared that Wilkinson's preliminary discourses in his translation of Swedenborg had thrown "all contemporary philosophy of England into shade."

as for ecstasy and inspiration, we have not by experience any idea of what these words may mean. Yet History proves beyond a doubt that in old times great works of Art have in the fullest sense of the term inspired their students, and have wrought the hearers or spectators to ecstasy. The same works would not wield the same influence now; and the works that are produced now wield influence of how different a kind. Thus, try to fancy a student sitting down to read a new volume of poems, with the hope of finding therein some breath of a really divine afflatus! Something that will rock the walls and rend the foundations of his old prison-house of habit as with an earthquake, something that will daze and blind his earthly vision as with a great light from Heaven, something that will melt and consume away his old commonplace existence with the fervent heat of enthusiasm! The fancy is too extravagant to be entertained for a moment. Experience has taught us to expect so little; we condescend, and know that we condescend, to be amused. Some pretty and graceful verses, some amiable sentiments, thoughts not too far below the standard of the best current thought; let us find these, and we deign to approve. Can the critics, I wonder, look each other in the face without laughing, when their rapturous eulogies have appeared in print? Set apart some half-dozen works of our generation, and try seriously and thoughtfully to fit the very choicest of the remainder with the choicest epithets; epithets with which the great old works are naturally invested, and with which our periodical critics freely invest scores of works as they appear; epithets such as grand, noble, magnificent, consummate; and you discover that the robes are far too ample and rich, the forms far too petty and mean, for befitting investiture; you must leave the old royal garments sacred to the old regal forms; and for these new forms find garments of another size and fashion, fitting them with pretty, graceful, clever, lively, sparkling, and so forth. In brief, I think it is clear that High Art and Creative Genius exercise now (and, such as they are at present, deservedly exercise) as little influence on the broad world as they ever did. They are resorted to for amusement, not earnestly; and the pleasure derived from them is of scarcely a loftier kind, and is assuredly not greater in degree, than that enjoyed in a game of cards or billiards, or with a pipe and a glass in a Music Hall.

I have not mentioned the Drama among the present Fine Arts, simply because we have no drama now worthy of the name. In the best Novels we have much of the gold that was of yore lavished in Plays; but as a rule the workmanship in the novels is far less vigorous and masterly, and the alloy of a much lower standard. The drama demands more thought and wisdom, more insight and concentrated passion, more power and energy, than the novel. The genuine drama involved in a novel (I mean an English novel) is usually padded out with easy and thoughtless pages of trite reflection, inventory description, and multitudinous insignificant detail. The drama is eminently masculine, the novel eminently feminine. The substitution of the latter for the former has doubtless contributed to the further emasculation of our literature, of which it was primarily a symptom and effect. It is astonishing what a large part of even a good modern book has been written without any exercise of the faculty of thought. Without going back to Shakespeare and Bacon, we may select works from a literary epoch upon which we affect to look down, works such as Pope's *Essay on Man* or Swift's *Tale of a Tub,* wherein nearly every sentence has required a distinct intellectual effort, and which thus, whatever their faults, shame by their powerful virility our effeminate modern books.

But if the divine mission of genius, like many another mission, effects little or nothing upon the commonplace mass of us; surely the divine prerogatives of genius are of inestimable value to the geniuses themselves? This is a question deserving consideration.

Supposing the vitality equal in two men, that which has the more spontaneous and immediate expression—or, to speak grammatically, that which more nearly approaches spontaneity and immediateness in its expression—is undoubtedly to be preferred to the other. Thus the man whose common gestures and words and actions in the ordinary course of life are easy and appropriate and beautiful, are real fugitive poems naturally rhythmic with time and place and circumstance, is much more to be envied than he who can only express himself adequately, that is, with an approximation to adequacy, by painting or sculpture or music or verse, with long and exhausting labour, with frequent heavy disappointments, with unsightly gaps in his career of heartsick languor and dismal stupidity and desolate despair,—all of which he feels most painfully, though the men who come after him are apt to overlook them, seeing only the brilliant crests of his loftiest moments. A poem is praised above all else for this, that it is the expression of eternal truth and beauty, not of transitory accidents. Yet the perfect expression of anything must conspicuously express just those transitory accidents which differentiate it from all similar precedent and subsequent things. What would be the portrait of a man, neither tall nor middle-sized nor short, with eyes and hair of no particular accidental colour, bearing no transitory expression, clothed but clothed in no transitory fashion, and so forth? And the law which applies to the perfect expression of anything, applies equally to the perfect enjoyment. Life is mainly made up of transitory accidents, and he who cannot enjoy these cannot enjoy life. Make a coat to fit every man tolerably well, and it will fit no one man thoroughly well. The rose from which a lasting perfume is distilled has not been allowed to live out its natural and most beautiful life on the tree. Browning gives the whole philosophy of this matter in one pregnant verse: "Sing, 'Riding's a joy!'—for me, I ride." And Mrs. Browning pathetically expresses the same philosophy in her poem of *The Great God Pan* and in *Aurora Leigh*. The Geniuses who nourish our spirits, like the cattle and sheep and pigs which nourish our bodies, must be mulcted of the free existence of their kind, and not spared to die natural deaths.

Let an artist on some great holiday be amongst the multitudes witnessing some procession or pageant. He finds full exercise for his extraordinary faculties of perception and observation; he studies with keen interest countless effects of colour and light and shade, innumerable faces and forms with innumerable expressions and characteristics; but does he thoroughly enjoy the holiday pageant itself? No; for he uses it but as the mean to an end, and not the poorest thing in the world will suffer itself thus used to be perfectly enjoyed. The inmost charm of the pageant, the finest essence of the holiday, are enjoyed by the little ragged boy getting dirtier and more ragged as he writhes eager through the mob; not by the artist who shall give us so magnificent a picture of the scene. Let a poet be of the party in some merry picnic. Do you think he enjoys it as thoroughly as it is enjoyed by the simple youths and thoughtless girls, or even by the stout matrons and old fogies, around him? The probability is, that he proves about the dullest person in the party. He is reflecting and observing while the others are enjoying; he is so used to reflect and observe that he cannot throw off these staid habits and plunge into the glittering stream of the revelry. Yet some days or weeks afterwards, musing upon the elements of delight which existed in the company and the excursion, he distils them into a poem exquisitely delightful, a poem overbrimming with the pure joyousness which he ought to have felt but did not feel, and which the commonplace people about him really did feel; though they could give it only fugitive expression in chatter and laughter and dancing and romping, while he can give it quasi-enduring expression in lovely verse.

A pageant and a picnic are not the most lofty of instances; I might have used as effectively the most solemn or heroic or useful action. The man we call a Poet would be absent-minded, would not enjoy full presence of mind, that is to say, would not fully and intensely live in any one. He sings of that which he cannot enjoy, cannot achieve; if at any time he can enjoy it, can achieve it, be sure that he is not then pondering or singing it. Where and when rich life is present, it lives, and does not content itself with shadowing forth and celebrating life. When and where rich life is not present, the shadowing forth and celebration of life may partially console for its absence, or may even partially illude into the belief in its presence. Yet life remains and ever is as superior to art as a man to the picture of a man. Men abounding and pictures being rare, a picture will often be valued by us far more than would the original; similarly, life being abundant and art rare, we often value a fraction of art more than the fraction of life of which it is the shadow or symbol: but our valuations do not affect the absolute and relative worth of the things in themselves.

II

My opinion is that artistry accuses weakness and lack of vitality in the artist, when not pursued simply as a relaxation or as the least irksome mode of earning the daily bread. If a man, being poor, can earn more and earn it more easily and pleasantly by painting pictures than by ploughing and reaping, let him paint. But in this case he paints to live, he does not live to paint; his art is purely a trade, not a divine mission and holy vocation, as so many of us in these years regard it. If a man, being rich, finds happy filling up of idle hours in making verses, let him make verses: but let us clearly understand that his art is simply a hobby and a pastime. If the poor man and the rich man were endowed with keener intelligence and more puissant vitality, they would prefer a trade and a hobby bringing them into closer and warmer relations with the living world and their fellow-men, demanding more courage and energy and sympathy and fortitude and wisdom. Still, the necessities of the outer life absolve from the extreme accusation of weakness and poverty in the inner life. But when a man devotes himself body and soul to art, becomes willingly the slave of it and glories in the slavery, it is another thing. What should we think of a fellow who, having money to live independently, made himself a flunkey, through admiration of the grand house and the carriage, through pure delight in the plush and powder? What should we think of a wealthy creature who preferred fiddling in the orchestra to dancing and making love with a pretty girl at the ball? What should we think of a noble lord who, rather than feast with the feasters, set himself among the press-gang, enthusiastic to give a glowing report of the feast? or who elected to assist in the cooking rather than the eating of the dinner? The real flunkey and fiddler and reporter and cook may be acquitted on the plea of necessity; they would severally much rather order than serve, dance than fiddle, feast than describe, enjoy than prepare; if in these instances they exercise certain arts of life for the pleasure of others instead of living for the pleasure of themselves, it is because they are obliged to work in order to live. And they do such work as their characters and abilities and opportunities enable them to get and to do. Their work is not their real life, but it earns the means of nourishing such individual life as they have. We admit their plea of necessity, and are only sorry for them that they are not able to do nobler kinds of work. But for the others who, not driven by external need, but led by internal inclination, toiled for the sake of the toil itself, we should have simply compassion and contempt. Yet wise people have not yet ceased to wonder how Shakespeare in the maturity of his faculties, as soon as he had made a comfortable fortune, could renounce the sublime work of producing comedies and tragedies to settle down as a jolly burgess in his native place!

It appears to me that the very greatest geniuses, those whom we really reverence in their complete manhood, have worked at their art with a distinct consciousness that it was but a trade, an apology for better work from which they were shut out by hostile circumstances; or a pleasant relaxation, a hobby to carry them at a canter through dull hours. Dante's work was heart and soul in "the petty and transitory interests" of his native town, until defeat and exile drove him into bitter immortality. Milton threw himself heart and soul into "the petty and transitory interests" of his age and country: his first poems were the refined amusements of youth, his last great poems the consolations of a defeated partisan, old and blind, and cut off from the active life to which the maturity of his powers had been passionately devoted. Shakespeare wrote no more when he could afford to live without writing; and, in his Sonnets cx. and cxi., especially the latter, we may read how he contemned the art which has made him the crowning glory of our literature. Shelley yearned for the direct action of political life, and was disabled and outcast into the mere life of poetry. Novalis expresses himself with the utmost vigour: "Authorship is but a secondary thing; you judge me more justly by the chief thing, by practical life. I only write for self-education." Leopardi devoted himself in despair to scholarship and poetry, because physical infirmity excluded him from active life. Sir Thomas More, Raleigh, Bacon, Selden, Vane, the two Sidneys, Bunyan, Swift, De Foe, Johnson, Scott, and, in fact, nearly all our greatest writers, ever held their authorship as thoroughly subservient to other ends of life. So in a great measure did the truly magnificent masters of Italy with their Art; and I doubt not that they would have done so thoroughly had not Art itself been then one of the most active of careers, bringing its professors into most energetic collision with the most vigorous vitality of the age, as witness the autobiography of Benvenuto Cellini. As it was, consider what Da Vinci, Giotto, Michael Angelo, Raphael, and the rest, did beyond the pale of mere Art. These men drove a flourishing trade in Art, and, at the same time, made the most vigorous career possible of it, and they were universally felt to be greater in themselves than in their works. But the works of the Artist, as he is conceived and worshipped in our days, are greater than himself; he is the slave of a sublime mission, the instrument of a divine inspiration, "the word which expresses what it understands not, the trumpet which sings to battle and feels not what it inspires." As such, I think that he is considerably less than a man; weak, diseased, mutilated, and more or less silly. A man of opulent vitality may be a lyrist, uttering himself now and then in brief snatches of song; but never while healthy and happy, and provided with cash, committing himself to the imprisonment with hard labour of a great work.

If he be imprisoned in the common sense of the term, then his energies in the lack of fitter outlets may overflow into such a work: thus Raleigh wrote his "History of the World," Cervantes his "Don Quixote," Bunyan his "Pilgrim's Progress," in captivity; they dreamed grand dreams in their dungeons because they could not live realities in the free open air. Wine-songs are not written during the wine-intoxication, love-songs are not sung by kissing lips, war-songs are not chanted by the soldier battling breathless and dry-throated: often enough they are written and sung by those who never drink wine, who have no sweetheart, and who never were in battle. Analogies and illustrations crowd in from all quarters, and their abundance is in itself a strong argument for my thesis; for a truth finds brothers and sisters everywhere in the world, but an error can scarcely find anything in Nature to pass off as kith and kin.

Here the questions may be put: But does not everything consummate itself in expression? and is not Art pre-eminently expression? Yes; everything in the world consummates itself (*as the object of our knowledge*) in expression, and Art is pre-eminently expression – but of a peculiar kind. It is slow, mediate, studied, complicate, laborious expression; while the best expression of any being is spontaneous, immediate, instinctive, simple, unlaborious. Ascending into the regions of philosophy, we might discover that, although the world consummates itself to our senses and intellect by expression, the innermost and purest and loftiest soul or essence of all things is supremely inexpressive; and that its expression in the sensible universe, in suns and planets, in trees and animals, is a degeneration; regeneration being only possible (as the wise Hindoos and others have taught) by the gradual extinction of all expression, the restoration to sole and infinite dominion of the primordial spiritual silence, perfect, immutable, eternal, self-involved, self-contemplating. But since it so has been that the Spirit has become the Word, and the Word has been made Flesh, we must admit that the law of our universe is that all things shall "wreak themselves on expression," that "the whole creation groaneth and travaileth in pain until now, and not only it but ourselves also," striving for perfect utterance of the unutterable. Perfect utterance cannot, of course, be attained; but the approach to perfection is in direct ratio to the spontaneous intuitiveness, and inverse ratio to the slow elaborateness. A remarkable instance is afforded by the *Genesis* account of God uttering himself in Creation. His first instinctive expression, "Let there be the light," is the very sublimity of jubilant power; and the morning stars sang together, and all the sons of God shouted for joy. But day after day as the utterance grows more complex and elaborate, the rhetorical imagery more multitudinously profuse, he utters himself worse and worse; until on the sixth day, his figures of speech are cattle, and creeping things, and beasts of the earth, and finally, man and woman. Light in itself, pure, ever-joyous, life-giving, is so magnificent an expression of Deity that the most thoughtful races have worshipped it; but where is divinity in the cow and the viper and polecat? And when one considers Man as the image of God, as the representative of perfect power and holiness and wisdom and love, as the earthly formula of heavenly law, the temporal instrument of eternal Providence, one is constrained to the verdict that if a mere man made a machine for any purpose, so complex and fantastic, so easily disordered and destroyed, and, at the best, wasting so enormous a ratio of power by friction, that machine would not pay, the stupidest men would see that it was a thorough failure; it would be good only to cast into the fire, — and it is not wonderful that Christians in general, believing that man was intended for the image of God, have also believed that mankind on the whole is ultimately good for nothing else.

Artistry, then, as the absolute devotion to Art in and for itself, is, I repeat, a symptom of weakness; amiable weakness, if you like, but none the less privation of power. Coleridge finely said of the great poets, whose character is always superior to their works, that they are feminine not effeminate: of the mass of artists, the swarms of little poets, we may fairly say the reverse, — they are not feminine but effeminate.

To be weak is in itself to be miserable; and for the artist-nature, there is an additional misery in this, that in its spasms of strength, in its highest moments, it is solitary, unsympathising with the world and unsympathised with by the world. Fasting forty days upon the mountain, alone with its God, it descends to find all the people dancing and feasting and worshipping the golden calf; they are all happy and thoroughly understand one another, and have forgotten the poet whose fasting and solitude have been dedicated to their service: so he, the meekest of men, loses his serenity and storms in iconoclastic fury. The poetlings, indeed, may be invulnerable in a brazen armour of vanity and self-conceit, and may glory in their isolation from the vulgar mass as an incontestable proof of superiority; but the really great poet, who is great-hearted, must feel this isolation with terrible pangs and yearnings which he knows are vain, and may starve in this dearth of sympathy like a sailor on a wreck in a shipless sea. And as for the superiority, he knows its true value. He knows into what magnificent thought and imagination an extra ounce of brain will beat out, for what grand creations an inch more breadth in the curve of the skull will make room. He knows that he is great only in comparison, and in a comparison whose standard of measurement is small as small can be; he knows that he is a giant like the king of Lilliput, almost a nail's breadth taller than any of his subjects, striking awe into the beholder.

But is there not an ample compensation for all the disadvantages extrinsic and intrinsic of the poet? Is there not fame? One who is unambitious, and cares not a whit for fame which is renown and notoriety, caring only for some "love disguised" it may contain (an ear of wheat in a bushel of chaff), and for its accidental virtue of making the productions of its minions bring in plenty of cash; such a one is hardly competent to estimate fairly its value. The devotion to it must be deeply set in most species of human nature; for even an actor, who has been for years before the public, who is quite well known as Mr. A. in private life, whose worth as an actor has long been strictly appraised, and whose salary is invariable whatever parts be allotted to him, even he will be wrathful as Achilles if made to appear in a *rôle* which does not suffer him to shine during the two or three hours occupied by the play. An orator will swell with pride and delight when cheered by a lot of people, even if he knows them to be stupid and ignorant. A painter or poet or musician is intensely gratified by the applause of persons who, as he is thoroughly aware, are dunces in painting or poetry or music. Very great men (uncommonly tall pigmies) have been abject suppliants to fame, and have yearned and toiled and suffered for genuine and wide and enduring renown; yet the most genuine is so full of illusion and mockery, the most wide is so narrow and superficial, the most enduring is so infinitesimally brief, that for my own part I am quite unable to understand how any intelligent person can set a high value upon it. Everything, however, as an element of happiness, is relative in its worth; and if a string of glass-beads gives more joy to a savage than would a volume of Shakespeare, the string of beads is undoubtedly of more worth to him; only he judges himself in judging the two objects, and with his preference obtains also our noble contempt for his barbarism. With such measure as ye mete it shall be meted to you again, is a truth of the widest application. Thus the tribe of artists, the poetlings, who in all respects get so much life-happiness from their vanity and conceit, get an immense amount of real happiness *of its kind* from their assurance of posthumous fame. If Sir Richard Blackmore believed that he would go down to remote posterity in a triumph of glory and honour, he was very much mistaken in himself and posterity;* but the delusion was none the less genuine happiness to him alive. Therefore, while considering the absolute devotion to fame as the capital symptom of imbecility and weakness in the poets, I consider it also as the only advantage over common men in actual enjoyment with which they can fairly be credited. Common men live in the present, live while they are alive; these poets live in the future (*i.e.*, they believe they do, and happiness is but a bundle of pleasant beliefs—for the most part illusions), live when they are dead. "Will you have your life living or dead?" Nature asks us all; and these reply, "Dead." Ordinary hearty men live from day to day upon a competence of the current gold of the present; the votaries of fame (that *last* infirmity of noble minds, in another sense than Milton's) exist on the paper money of heavy bills drawn on posterity. Posterity will ruthlessly dishonour nearly all these bills, quite all indeed which are drawn at very long dates; but luckily for the poor devils drawing them, they cannot be protested until after the drawer's death, and can always during his life be converted (negotiated by Vanity, discounted by the millionaire Conceit) into large sums of real enjoyment. In these transactions the poet has the same advantage as a prophet flourishing on predictions to be fulfilled in a century or two; if they should not be fulfilled then, little matters to the prophet: what can have possessed Dr. Cumming when he brought forth prophecies which arrive at maturity in his own generation?† How many

*Sir Richard Blackmore (d. 1729), physician to Queen Anne, prolific writer in verse and prose. His "Creation," a philosophical poem demonstrating the existence and providence of God, was praised by Addison and Dr. Johnson, but is now forgotten.

†John Cumming (1807–1881), preacher and philanthropist, was widely known by his writings on the interpretation of prophecy; he contended that the "last vial" of the Apocalypse was to be poured out from 1848 to 1867.

poets would find a draft on the house of Fame negotiable if it fell due in their own lifetime? We may affirm that the superstition of fame, with the conceit of being superiorly gifted, is a crutch that supports the weakness of which it is an outward and visible sign; the crutch of the lame poets, all the poor beggars of ballad-mongers and painters and sculptors and musicians and philosophers, who, like so many santons, dervishes, fakeers, and mendicant friars, are held in such holy repute at present.

In order to complete the antithesis to Bumble, a few words should be added on the poets as the men of new ideas, the men always in advance of their age. I have only space left to refer to Browning's *Bishop Blougram's Apology*, wherein these men are sketched with a few masterly lines. I refer specially to the passage wherein the saintly bishop compareth these men unto travellers leaving arctic regions for the equator, who never wear the garb suited to the zone they are actually traversing, but always such garb as would suit the zone towards which they journey, and which they may never reach.

Byron writes in the *Prophecy of Dante* —

> Many are poets who have never penned
> Their inspiration — and perchance the best.

And, if poets are they who most intensely live, rejoicing supremely in the harmony and beauty of the world; if the very poets of poets are they who realise in flesh and spirit the loftiest dreams in marble and verse and sound and colour of the men we commonly call poets; then I heartily agree with Byron. But the extremely Byronic reasons why they did not pen their inspiration — that they would not lend their thoughts to meaner beings, and repressed the deity within, and so forth — I humbly opine to be stuff and nonsense. They do not *pen* their inspiration simply because they are able throughout and equably to *live* it; so far from repressing the deity within, they express it every day and hour and moment in their most ordinary words and deeds, an infinitely better kind of expression than that which is found in spasmodic poems of a dozen or two astonishing fyttes.

Indolence: A Moral Essay

(Calculated for a temperature of about 90° in the shade)

[*Thomson, when reprinting this essay in* Essays and Phantasies, *dated it as having been written in 1867. It was first published, however, in three installments in the* Secularist *in 1876 (July 22, 29, August 5). Apparently Thomson had intended it to be a longer essay, including a classification of the "energetic" along with the "indolent," but he seems to have lost interest in the project and probably published it in its present state only when under pressure for* Secularist *material. In any event, the long classification of the "indolent" is rather tedious, and is herein omitted; the essay is primarily of interest for its very un-Victorian comment on Victorian "earnestness," as well as for its observations on some of the eminent Victorians.*]

"This began with me from childhood, being a kind of voice which, when present, always diverts me from what I am about to do, but never urges me on." – Socrates of *his* good Genius, as reported by Plato in the *Apology*.

In this wide inland sea that hight by name
  The Idle Lake, my wandring ship I row,
That knowes her port, and thether sayles by ayme,
  Ne care ne feare I how the wind do blow,
  Or whether swift I wend or whether slow:
Both slow and swift alike do serve my tourne.
Faërie Queene, b. ii. c. vi. st. 10.

A LITTLE boy (that same terrible infant who outflanks all our prudent maxims and moral texts) was so very lazy at his lessons one fine morning, that his mamma was driven to tell him in the solemn words of the poet, that Satan finds some mischief still for idle hands to do. "Ah," he sighed, "but if they felt as idle as me they wouldn't do it for him." With this piece of childish wisdom for a passport, one may venture in the dog-days to steal from out the turmoil of this busy, busy London, and saunter for a few hours in the wild woods which encompass the pleasant

Castle of Indolence; sauntering simply for enjoyment and recreation, revolving no schemes to clear the forest with axe and fire, and utilise the Castle as mill or factory. "If they felt as idle as me they wouldn't do it for him." Our little boy probably knew very little of grammar, and nothing of the momentous controversy which has raged around the personal pronouns *I* and *me*; it is moreover doubtful whether he discriminated between *idle* and *lazy*, but even if he did not, it by no means follows that his retort missed the mark, for idle hands may be idle through a laziness which would no more attempt Satanic than a better class of work. Surely an immense amount of mischief has been done for Satan on this earth of ours; but has the greater part thereof been wrought by indolent or by energetic hands? If we refer to general history and our particular experience for those who have done most harm in their lives, reckoning as harm only what seems sheer preponderance of evil over good, do we find the restless or the placid characters in the majority? A question each must resolve for himself: one could not hope in a brief essay to adduce typical examples in such number as to be of important weight on either side. In my own humble opinion the placid would emerge from this ordeal in rather better case than the energetic.

It may, however, be fairly expected that intelligent and vigorous young England, with Carlyle for its prophet (and take him for all in all few generations have had a nobler), will vehemently condemn the Idlers, the Do-nothings and Eat-alls, and vehemently extol the Earnest, Strong, Able men. For myself, I most respectfully discharge Carlyle from the court when any suit on this matter is pending. His continual cry of Work! Work! Work! is simply the Imperative mood of a doctrine which, couched in the quiet Indicative, reads, "Mankind is a damned rascal."* Cool and languid believers in this hopeful

*It is worth noting that the two deepest and intensest convictions of Carlyle appear to be that "Life is infinitely earnest" and that "All dies, and is for a time only; is a Time-phantasm, yet reckons itself real"; in other words, he regards human life as at once a vanity of vanities and a supremely important reality. These convictions he expresses in many ways, but the one or the other will be found at the root of most he has written; and, a coincidence not to be lightly passed over, the same may be affirmed of the *Thoughts* of Marcus Aurelius. Yet these convictions are absolutely contradictory, and in logic one if not each must destroy the other: but our human nature is not logical; and as George Eliot somewhere remarks, it can accommodate the most hostile principles at the same time without any sense of embarrassment or inconsistency. (Thomson's note.)

doctrine are quite content with the cynical formula; our prophet, being ardent and tempestuous, and overflowing with sympathy as well as grim scorn and rage, tries to forget the formula in thunderous exhortations that yet have no sanction if it is not true. If we humbly inquire, Why work, work, work in this furious fashion? we shall find that the ultimate because is to the following effect: To save yourselves from yourselves; to overwhelm and exhaust the natural (sinful and foolish) man in each of you; to occupy all your hours and make them pass as swiftly as possible, thus distracting yourselves from vain talk and thought and self-consciousness, until you are got into the quiet grave, and securely covered over, impotent for further mischief. And if we continue to question, with a mean and selfish After? we can only learn that After is a black abyssmal Night, inscrutable, utterly void and silent; unless the prophet is in an unusually hopeful mood, when we seem to catch vague glimpses of a sort of Walhalla, whose sky is storm-cloud and whose air sad mist, where the heroes give and get incurable wounds, and where the rations of mead have been long ago stopped. Now these reasons, though very forcible, have not for many years past convinced me that intense and unremitting labour is the supreme good of life; and these prospects, so alluringly cheerful, are the same for all lives, for the indolent no less than for the active. And if the chief end of human life is indeed escape from itself, this end can be attained at any hour by suicide, a much more rapid and easy process than the prolonged galley-slavery or penal servitude enjoined by our austere sage. I am therefore wont to enjoy his terrible Icelandic hurricanes of preaching with perfect tranquillity. In the words of His Most Serene Highness the Lord of the Castle of Indolence (c. 1, 43): —

> At doors and windows threat'ning seemed to call
> The demons of the tempest growling fell,
> Yet the least entrance found they none at all,
> Whence sweeter grew our sleep, secure in massy hall.

Thousands of men, however, middle-aged and practical, who read not and heed not the tough Carlylese, would unhesitatingly decide the question against the indolent, without reference to general history. For personal experience is always ready at the slightest hint to speak through them, in a voice somewhat loud and harsh, affirming that the busy are good and prosperous, and the idle are ne'er-do-weels. (*N.B.*—This applies only to common people; royal and aristocratic personages are the more to be reverenced the less they do.) In England the passion for work, which pervades and to a certain degree ennobles the lust for wealth, has become an irrational idolatry; labour is prized for itself, not as the means to an end. Thus it is now quite a commonplace to extol the blessing veiled under the curse, "In the sweat of thy face shalt thou eat bread." Good people know better than God, and inform him and us that he was quite mistaken, that like Balaam he came to curse but really blessed, that Paradise Lost was in fact a Paradise Gained. Had the curse doomed us all to gulp down some abominable physic every day of our lives, these good people would have proved this also a real benediction, for our constitutions would of course be diseased in horrible harmony with the diurnal dose. The curse is that we are such that we seem to need our punishment no less than our food. Let it not be forgotten that the busiest personage we know of is he who brought upon us this burden of stupendous toil, he whom Charles Lamb so fitly defines "Sabbathless Satan." Whence the shrewder barbarians have offered their prayers and sacrifices not to the Good but to the Evil Spirit; arguing cogently that the former is a quiet, contented, sweet-natured being who can never dream of hurting anybody, while the latter is a restless and malicious imp whom it concerns poor mortals to propitiate if possible. These savages are wiser than our own multitudes who keep up a continual chorus in praise of work, as if all work were necessarily good, quite ignoring the fact which stares us everywhere in the face, that a very large proportion even of what we call honest commercial labour (if the term honest may be applied to any commercial labour) is mischievous as any Satan can find for idle hands to do.

Before discussing the general question I have raised, it will be well to note the different classes of the indolent; for indolence, like genius and love, while perhaps in the deepest deep always and everywhere one and the same, varies greatly with its various votaries in approaching and reaching the surface of expression. Thus there are many species of the indolent, though the world in its coarse and purblind fashion ranks some of them among the nobly assiduous, and huddles together all the rest in one indiscriminate condemnation. I have room here for only the leading divisions.

[*In the section omitted here, Thomson proceeds to describe seven classes of the indolent. First are idlers of the* lazzarone *type, the loftiest and purest since "their inertia is quite free from adulteration or object." The second class are of the Hiberian type, "indolent supremely by independence, a noble abhorrence of the iron bonds of law"; they are "not incapable of strenuous and even prolonged exertion, provided the exertion is thoroughly untainted by any useful or orderly purpose." Idlers of the third class are "idlers by grace"; "we should as soon expect the flowers to toil and spin as these." Next come the "idlers by Fortune," who "appear willing to work, but . . . it always happens that Nature and Circumstance step in between, and do the work for them." The fifth class of idlers are often mistaken for industrious men, for "while possessed by the plenary genius of indolence, they are possessed of vigorous faculties which they employ perforce for the needs of life. Thus they alternately 'toil terribly' and bask in Oriental repose." Idlers of the sixth class are idlers chiefly by profound and continual thought. "They see clearly that the consequences of any act are infinite in number, and quite incalculable in their ultimate results . . . so they preserve a wise indifference, and do as little as possible." The seventh class consists of "idlers chiefly by faith. Providence has the world in hand, and will doubtless make the best of it that can be made; shall one flurry and meddle and muddle to improve this and extinguish that, as if he were wiser and better than Providence?"*]

Inadequate as is the above classification from the philosophical point of view, it may serve to make us pause ere we either condemn or praise any one for indolence. His indolence may be worthy of condemnation (if indeed anything in any man can be worthy of condemnation by any other man or by himself); or it may be the quietude of a spirit cherishing profound thought, supreme faith, ideal beauty. Speaking down to our common tea-table level of morality, since on no other level is the world likely to heed or hear a word one says, and leaving aside the drudgery for daily bread, I would put it that on the one hand no indolence is to be praised which involves conscious shirking and sneaking, with fear more or less definite of the consequences; and on the other hand no industry is to be praised which involves fussing and fuming, and usurps dominion over the general nature of the worker. And we must note that much the greater part of what we term work is mere self-seeking activity, neither noble, nor just, nor wise, nor thorough, and has no moral right to contemn any indolence. Passing over the multitude of wealth-making rogues, how many large fortunes are grubbed together meanly, though honestly and respectably, by years of purblind selfish toil, unwarmed by a spark of generous feeling, unlighted by a gleam of liberal thought! Nor must it be forgotten that in our time and country we have a plague of busy-bodyism, certainly more annoying and perhaps more noxious than the plague of idleness. One comes across many earnest and energetic characters (restless "time-phantasms that reckon themselves real") who are no longer men but simply machines for working out their "missions" (as fads and hobbies are now grandly entitled); who are always in a hurry and bluster, and believe that hurry and bluster are the sole symptoms (if not, rather, essential motive-powers) of active progress; who are quite unable to settle for a time in tranquillity, having a notion that if they pause, the world must come to a full stop; who are sure that every step is a step in advance, though the quiet looker-on can see that nine-tenths of their movement is that of a squirrel in its revolving cage; who are continually vehement about some imminent crisis, as if life like birth or death were but an agony of throes and convulsions; who often whirl away in their rushing tumult modest people far superior to themselves in sense and judicious activity; who claim sympathy for their exhaustion when there has been no need for them to exhaust themselves, and admiration for their indomitable energy when its application has been altogether perverse. Except in those rare cases when sudden supreme emergencies demand supreme raptures of uncalculated toil, I admire the work of no man who is not working within himself, superior to his work. And it seems to me that in our England of to-day there is more peril to be feared from overwork than from underwork, of course leaving out of the case those who can get no work at all; that more are ruined by overwrought faculties than by faculties rusting through disuse. We have adopted in a drudging sense the maxim of Macchiavel, Better repent having done than not having done. The desperate toil demands desperate stimulants and sedatives, and thus tends to extreme dissipation and profligacy. As cool Goethe observes, Unlimited activity, of whatever kind, ends in bankruptcy.

If we appeal to Memory, whose judgments are supposed to be in accordance with the law as laid down by Conscience, we find that her verdicts differ remarkably from what common talk would lead us to expect. Which among our school days and nights do we recall with most satisfaction? Those wherein we learned much, or solved hard problems, or were publicly praised for our diligence, or took some coveted prize from many competitors? Not at all; but those wherein we played truant, or tricked the master, or violated good discipline by a bolstering match, or carried out a foray on an orchard. If you affirm that the chief element of delight in such retrospects is not the indolence but the lawlessness, the insurrection of our wild free nature against the stark pedantry of rules, I reply that the lawlessness cannot be separated from the indolence, and that this very lawlessness, which has been pointed out as the dominant characteristic of the second or Irish type, is an essential element in every species of indolence; it is human nature lying down in a protest of "masterly inactivity" against the bitter old curse, In the sweat of thy face shalt thou eat bread.

Or let us take an instance or two from art. Indolence, like love, of which it is the foster-mother, if not the very mother, inspires the dullest man with genius for a time. The genius of two of our poets has culminated in its celebration. Jamie Thomson, of most peaceful and blessed memory, was indeed constrained in deference to public opinion (besides that he always had a turn for preaching, owing perhaps to his early training) to adduce frightful admonitions and warnings, and make the vulgar moral as clear as a copy-book text in round hand; yet the initiated reader divines and knows well that the end of the first and all the second Canto are but dragon-haunted wood and marsh to affray the crowd, and secure the solitude for those who have the talisman of entry into that serenest Castle of Indolence, "which he has made the House Beautiful, so that all who pass are fain to tarry therein." And the "Lotos-Eaters" is so decidedly the best work of our weak and exquisite Tennyson, that it will preserve his fame as an almost great poet when the hysterics and commonplace philosophy of his *Maud* and *In Memoriam* have passed out of memory, when all his Idylls are idle on the shelf, when nothing else of his save a few tender lyrics and fragments of description shall be cared for by the general public. Now let us take a poem, or at any rate a piece of verse, devoted to energy and perseverance. The sublime *Excelsior* is very popular at present; but I doubt whether any man (soft curates, Sunday-school teachers, and tea-meeting muffs who think beer and tobacco certain perdition, are of course not included) ever read the adventures of its lofty hero without ejaculating, The Ineffable Ass! The Infernal Idiot! And I should like to know what that maiden fair and free, who at first sight tendered such a handsome invitation, really thought of him when he preferred snow and ice to the pillow of her warm bosom, the imbecile *casto Giuseppe*! What possible good could he do himself or anybody else by planting that banner with the very strange device on the top of that mountain? Well, he perished; and I trust that the coroner's jury found a verdict of Serve him right.

We all know, or ought to know, the story of that dauntless philosopher and martyr, Giordano Bruno. His fiery nature would not let him rest, and his restlessness brought him to the prison, the rack, and finally to the stake. If he could only have kept quiet he might have become a prelate, a cardinal, even a pope, and a saint, instead of being "punished as gently as possible, and without effusion of blood," as tender-hearted Mother Church phrased it when she burned her dear children alive. He knew well the inestimable value of that inertia or supreme repose which was denied to him; and in his *Spaccio de la Bestia Trionfante,* or Expulsion of the Triumphant Beast, introduces Indolence nobly vindicating herself before the assembly of the gods (I transcribe from the French of Christian Bartholmèss, not having the Italian original): "It was I, she said, who created the Golden Age, that marvellous time when beneficent Nature offered to the calmest spirits an infinite abundance of apples, chestnuts, acorns, and roots. It was Industry who put an end to this epoch in filling the earth by her fallacious arts with novelties and disorders, and in urging minds and hands to ambitious and corrupting enterprises. Enemy of quietude, she seduces men by false promises, by the phantom of a glory remote and detestable; while I sweetly invite them to enjoy the present. It is I whom Jupiter gave for companion to the first couple, while they were still good; as soon as they became bad they had no other society than that of Labour and Industry. It is I who protected innocence; it is Industry who is the ally of sin. In fine, O gods! hear this invincible sorites: The gods are gods because they are perfectly happy; the happy are happy because they have neither fatigue nor pain; those have neither pain nor fatigue who do not stir or change; now, to live with Indolence is the sure method of avoiding change or stir; therefore the gods are gods because they have Indolence in their midst."

But I remember that it has been noted how the old knights errant, what with fasts and vigils, freezings and scorchings, gashes and mutilations, seemed bent on making themselves as ugly as possible in the service of Beauty; and in like manner I am in danger of growing preposterously industrious in the service of Indolence. Let me then conclude straightway with Lessing in his fragment of an ode: –

PRAISE OF INDOLENCE

Indolence, I will to thee
  Some small song of praise now bring;
Oh – it – sorely – troubles me –
  Thy – great – worth – to fitly sing!
Yet I'll try to do my best;
After labour comes sweet rest.

Highest Good! who has but thee,
  Who untroubled life doth live –
Ah! – I – yawn – tired out – you see –
  So – you – really – must forgive –
For how can I sing your lay
While you kiss my breath away!

On the Worth of Metaphysical Systems

[*This essay, Thomson's most complete statement as to his reasons for rejecting philosophical "systems," appeared in the* Secularist *(May 13, 1876), and was reprinted in* Essays and Phantasies. *His general thesis is illustrated by example in a later essay, "A Few Words on the System of Spinoza," which is not included in this edition but can be found in* Essays and Phantasies.]

A FRIVOLOUS POET observes: "If it is hard to refrain from flippancy when writing mere prose, it is almost impossible when the subject is that broad burlesque, a system of philosophy or theology. Yet we are in general so imposed upon by weight of character and intellect as to regard such a system with serious respect if not adoration. Any despotic absolutism always finds abundant slavishness among men to respond to it, just as the rich always find parasites, mad prophets always daft believers, knaves always natural dupes."

In preaching a short sermon on this flippant text, let me begin by remarking that I throughout adhere to the sense in which the word system seems to be used by the said frivolous poet; meaning a system general and absolute, whether in philosophy or theology; a system which professes to expound the universe in its genesis or its eternity, its development, its final causes or want of the same, its essential relations to the human soul (whose essence is equally expounded), its essential relations to God if the system includes a God (when his essence is indicated if not expounded). Such a system is included in each of the great religions, and in nearly every great philosophy; the latest systems of the latter, those of the great Germans, Kant, Fichte, Schelling, Hegel, Schopenhauer, being among the most elaborate and absolute ever constructed. There are other systems, rightly called philosophical, of a very different kind, being founded on experience not intuition, following Nature instead of trying to transcend her, consciously limited amidst the Illimitable. There is nothing metaphysical in the greater part of what is called the

Idealism of Berkeley; the metaphysic comes when he brings in the Eternal and Infinite Mind to give permanence to the ideal world. There is nothing metaphysical in Kant's demonstration that time and space are but constant forms of our sensibility; the metaphysic comes in when beyond the phenomena of our perceptions he predicates noumena or things in themselves of which we know nothing. There is nothing metaphysical (save by lapse or oversight) in the great modern psychological systems, for these continually appeal to the test of experience, and are in general but working theories more or less comprehensive, always open to modification by new discoveries and to inclusion in wider formulas. And here we have the essential difference between the natural and the extra-natural or supernatural, between the relative and the absolute systems; the former as empirical are ever open to improvement and susceptible of transformations, the latter as imperious and unconditional cannot suffer change without being destroyed. Hence the former are continually advancing and extending, the latter are still where they commenced; the former have established much that is practically certain in their limits, the latter in their deepest depths are each and all as uncertain as ever.

What, then, is the worth of these absolute systems which have fascinated some of the profoundest intellects and noblest spirits among mankind? The fascination itself is not to be wondered at, for no fascination can be stronger to such intellects and such spirits than the hope of securing certitude beneath the transitory and illusive shows of this world and life. So intense, indeed, is this fascination that it has bewitched exceedingly able and good men, who despaired of attaining such certitude by rational inquiry, into abjuring their reason, strangling their doubts, and seeking peace in blind faith and abject submission to authority, mutilating their minds as Origen mutilated his body, as in the deplorable instance of J. H. Newman. But the builders of systems do not, or will not, despair. The subtlest of them recognise quite clearly the practical trustworthiness of what the natural or relative sciences have established within their limits; but they cannot endure the utter blank immeasurable beyond those strait limits, the formless void unfathomable beneath their thin surface. They see plainly what many of the triumphant and triumphing natural philosophers do not see at all, that even the most obvious and commonplace so-called facts are undermined by deepest metaphysical doubts. Admitting the relative truth, they must seek the absolute basis; acknowledging the limited fact, they hunger for the universal law. They will build out of pure thought a faithful counterpart of the world, a microcosm the perfect image of the macrocosm; believing that the laws and processes of the human mind correspond with those of the universe. With gigantic self-sufficiency each labours at his task, in no wise daunted by the manifold and manifest failures of all who have hitherto made the same attempt, in no wise doubting that his mind is a true mirror of the world, though he sees that its reflections are more or less different from those of all other minds. Century after century, sometimes generation after generation, sees the selfsame attempt renewed, the building of a tower whose top shall reach unto heaven. When such a tower has been reared, many of the bystanders believe that its top *does* reach to heaven, for it is generally lost in the clouds, and, as Carlyle observes, what we cannot see over is infinite to us. But as men are removed from it in time, they perceive that its summit gradually sinks beneath the horizon, and they who visit it perceive that the structure announced everlasting is mouldering away and falling to ruin like the vulgarest building man erects for his sojourn. Then a new architect sets to work with the same sublime aspirations, the same indomitable self-sufficiency; a fresh metaphysical tower with a brand-new terminology loses its head in the clouds, to be regarded with awe and reverence by its bystanders, to crumble away and fall to ruin in its turn; for the legend of Babel and the confusion of tongues is the legend of system-building in all ages.

And now that we have seen in history so many such systems arise and disappear, all with the same assurance of plan, all with the same instability of structure, it is natural that we should ask the question I have put, What is their worth? To myself it appears that as systems their worth is, and always has been, little or nothing. The building and study of them has had a great educational worth in developing powers and skill which could scarcely have been called forth in their utmost energy by a hope less immense and sublime; and the study of them may be of great educational worth still. But examining any one of the great systems as a system, we seem to discern that its value consisted altogether in the value of some great thoughts or noble sentiments embodied in it, and that these were not improved but injured by the incorporation. When the structure into which they were built is a ruin, they remain as precious marbles, goodly for use in edifices less vast but less imperfect, more humble but more habitable; only to suit them to his purpose the ancient builder hacked and chipped them into forms inconvenient for anything else, and perchance kept them obscure for ages in sombre crypt or lofty dome. A man discovering some new truth or some new aspect of an old one, will probably only strain and distort it in trying to expand it into a complete system. For to him such truths are not as splendid jewels which he may cut and polish, and set in star or cross or circlet, as his taste may prefer; this is the work of the poet; the philosopher undertakes to cut and set them in the sole best form and order, harmonious with the form and order of sun and moon and stars, and failing in this he damages them for other use. Or, to vary the illustration, if from the depths of a forest we glimpse a fragment of the remote horizon, and mentally complete the circle in accordance with that arc, our ring will not even be the ring of the meeting of earth and sky encompassing our standpoint; ours will be all shipless sea or green valley-bottom, while the true horizon would be sea and shore, vale and river, wood and hill, abounding with various life.

But it is strange that we have to appeal to history to show the worthlessness of absolute systems. How can man, an infinitesimal atom in the infinite universe, embrace that infinity? How can man, whose life is an inappreciable moment in eternal time, comprehend the laws of that eternity? A critic may be very small, and a philosopher or theologian very great (according to our petty human standards), yet the former in relation to the latter must be immeasurably greater than the latter in relation to the universe he has the audacity to expound. Therefore even the most stupid of men is quite justified in rejecting decisively and without examination any universal system whether of theology or philosophy, for beyond doubt it is ludicrously inadequate. During many millenniums some of the best and wisest of our race have devoted themselves to teaching us all about God and our immortal souls, the origin and final causes of the world, and so forth; yet when one comes to reflect on the matter it is overwhelmingly certain that not one of these men has ever really known anything about any of these things, or whether they really exist or not. By studying the signs of the times and commonly recurring sequences, men may learn how (with due adroitness and agility) to pick up a living for their microscopical selves in this shoreless and fathomless ocean of being, of whose main currents they are perforce perfectly ignorant. Let us imagine a small colony of mice in a great cathedral, getting a poor livelihood out of Communion crumbs and taper-droppings. Could any of them by much deep speculation comprehend the origin, the plan, the purpose of the cathedral, the meaning of the altar, the significance of the ritual, the clashing of the bells, the ringing of the chants, the thunderous trepidations of the organ? Yet a mouse explaining the final causes of all these things would be incomparably less absurd than is a divine or sage expounding the mysteries of Nature or God. The discreeter mice would limit themselves to noticing and remembering that certain periods and ceremonies were marked by more numerous tapers burning, whence came more grease on the floor, and by noting the spots where grease did more abound. These would be the practical philosophers among the mice, positivists or utilitarians; and if while grease was to be had, other mice lost their time in demonstrating that the final cause of a great Church festival was to increase the harvest of taper-droppings for their species, these shrewder mice would not stay to dispute the point with them, but would be off to their jolly feast of Candlemas.

I have said that the absolute systems have fascinated some of the profoundest intellects and noblest spirits among mankind. On the other hand, they have equally repelled intellects not less profound and spirits not less noble. And these, it must be added, have been more sane than those, for there is always more or less of insanity in the fascination. As I have elsewhere had occasion to express it,* such a creed or system is a little strait-waistcoat wrought by some little man, and in which he would fain confine Titanic Nature: she laughs with immense good-nature at the puny fellow at first, but if he seriously persists in attempting to force it on her, she inevitably makes him fit for a strait-waistcoat himself.

*In "An Evening with Spenser," published in the *National Reformer* (November 26, 1865), and reprinted in *Essays and Phantasies.*

Stray Whiffs, from an Old Smoker

[*From 1875 to 1881 Thomson's main source of income was the work he did for* Cope's Tobacco Plant. *(Richard D. Altick has written an informative article on this unusual periodical in* Papers of the Bibliographical Society of America, *XL, no. 4 [1951], 333–350.) As the essay indicates, Thomson was an inveterate pipe smoker, and had written in praise of tobacco long before his affiliation with* Cope's. *This essay, however, is the earliest (September, 1875) of his many informal essays on the subject of tobacco written for that periodical, usually printed under the signature "Sigvat." It is reprinted here for the first time, although a few passages from it were included in a pamphlet published in 1889 by the Office of "Cope's Tobacco Plant":* Selections from Original Contributions by James Thomson to Cope's Tobacco Plant.]

IN Lane's admirable and delightful "Account of the Manners and Customs of the Modern Egyptians," which forms so worthy a pendant to Sir Gardner Wilkinson's book on the ancient, we read (chap. xv.): — "The most prevalent means, in most Muslim countries, of exciting what the Arabs call 'keyf,' which I cannot more nearly translate than by the term 'placid enjoyment,' is Tobacco." In chap. v., on the Domestic Life, he tells us that the Tobacco smoked by persons of the higher orders is of a very mild and delicious flavour, mostly from the neighbourhood of El-Ládikeeyeh (in which we may recognise Latakia), in Syria; the best kind being the "mountain Tobacco," grown on the hills about that town. Egyptians and other Orientals draw in their breath freely when smoking, so that much of the smoke descends into the lungs; and the terms they use for "smoking Tobacco" mean "*drinking* smoke," or "*drinking* Tobacco"; for the same word signifies smoke and Tobacco, marking their sense that no other smoke is worth naming in comparison with this. For the Persian pipe, or nárgeeleh, in which the smoke passes through water, and which has a long flexible tube, they use a choice Persian Tobacco called tumbák, which is first washed several times, then put damp into the bowl, and two or three pieces of live charcoal placed on the top. The flavour is very mild and agreeable; but the strong inhalation necessary in this mode of smoking is injurious to persons of delicate lungs. Yet it is often recommended for a cough; and one of Mr. Lane's friends, the most celebrated of the poets of Cairo, who was much troubled by asthma, smoked the nárgeeleh almost incessantly from morning till night. In using this pipe the smoker draws the smoke as freely into his lungs as if he were inhaling pure air. The great prevalence of liver-complaints in Arabia is attributed to the use of the nárgeeleh, and many persons in Egypt suffer severely from the same cause.

I have not, however, referred to Mr. Lane's book in order to dilate on Eastern methods of smoking, which by this time are pretty familiar to most of us, but simply to note the exquisite accuracy of purpose with which these sage and dignified Muslims smoke, aiming steadily at keyf, or placid enjoyment. The dreamer and poet Charles Baudelaire, in "Les Paradis Artificiels," says of this keyf (or, as he spells it, kief): — "It is the absolute happiness. There is no longer any unrest and tumult; it is a beatitude, calm and motionless, a glorious resignation. . . . All the problems of philosophy are solved. All the arduous questions against which the theologians cut and thrust, and which are the despair of reasoning humankind, are limpid and clear. All contradiction is become unison. *L'homme est passé Dieu.*" Here is the real aim of the real smoker, the end which his Tobacco, rightly used, can always approach, if not quite attain; for, be he active and restless at other times as Mercury or mercury, his sole creed with pipe or cigar in his mouth should be that of the lotus-eaters: "There is no joy but calm." The "weed" which is richer than all rich flowers is ever ready to give soothing to the nerves and serenity to the mind of him who will dispose himself, in favourable circumstances and at auspicious periods, to receive in full its benign influence; but it is dissipated and wasted by him who, instead of resting quiet to be brimmed with quietude, suffers himself to be jerked and hurried and agitated. It is hard to fill a jumping cup. Perhaps we Britons are in this respect the greatest of all sinners against "divine Tobacco," as Raleigh's friend Spenser hastened right well to acclaim it; we, fate-driven, strongest of the strong for labour, weakest of the weak for inertia, which is no less essential in its turn for healthy life; we who know how to do almost everything, but not how to do nothing with ease and grace and dignity. This the Orientals can do to perfection, and herein appear to the philosopher as an antique patrician race, while ourselves are ever-bustling plebeian *parvenus*. Strangely enough, this consummate genius for stately repose, which in persons is deemed the distinction of born aristocrats from the ignoble vulgar, is in nations supposed to distinguish the barbarous and semi-barbarous from the civilised; that which in persons is thought the stamp of natural superiority, in nations is thought the stamp of natural inferiority; peoples are dominant by that which marks their individuals subservient. We cannot pretend to compete with the Easterns in doing nothing; but neither can we, I believe, with those Westerns who are usually accounted the most restless and impatient of men. When the citizen of the United States has no immediate business in hand or in head, it may well astonish and abash us to observe with what tranquil contentment he will sit hour after hour on tilted chair, with feet on the hotel-office stove or window-sill, chewing, smoking, reading illimitable newspapers, or very deliberately chatting. With ourselves it is sad and shameful to see what volumes of fragrant incense are gulped in and belched out (call it not inhaling and exhaling), unrelished and ineffectual, by fellows in fierce worry and excitement. Many business men now smoke cigars or cigarettes nearly all day, while frequently fuming more than their ill-used weeds; and if one asks *cui bono*? the only rational reply is, To the Tobacco-grower and the cigar-merchant; to them alone can such tormented consumption of the precious drug prove profitable. It is true that the grave men of the East and the fiery men of the South often make a show of violent excitement while bargaining and smoking; but the hot haggle is with them a mere comedy and pastime, as is perfectly well understood by the disputants on both sides.

Nor is it only in busy and worried smoking that we lose much of the savour and power of Tobacco; even when at leisure and tranquil we are apt to puff the smoke out immediately, instead of retaining it long enough to let it work its full spell. Some, indeed, hold in at intervals, then emit slowly and through the nostrils, which is a good test of the strength and quality of the Tobacco; for the nerves thus affected, being seldom subject to the fumigation, are very sensitive to its influence. I remember in Spain, where the men when not asleep are continually making and smoking cigarettes, chatting with a native gentleman on the subject, and avowing that I usually smoked cigar or pipe because I could not get satisfaction from the little cigarettes, especially in the open air, where they burnt to my lips almost as soon as kindled. My courteous Señor replied that I got no satisfaction from the cigarettes simply because I wasted nearly all their precious incense. He bade me mark how, having slowly inhaled a good mouthful, he kept it on his palate, or somewhere down his throat, for a considerable time, speaking in the meanwhile as comfortably as if his windpipe were not a flue; and how the smoke escaped not from him until it had yielded its utmost sedative aroma. I was fain to admit the vast superiority of his method; but, in trying to practise it, only succeeded in making myself cough and sneeze abominably. Do these Spaniards, like Lane's Egyptians, draw the smoke right into the lungs?

It is generally found that smoking is conducive to meditation; and most of us, when essaying to think out a difficult matter, light pipe or cigar as the preliminary step, taking a bird's-eye view of the whole subject, as a friend terms it, with a pun as mild as his Tobacco. With those of a nervous temperament the thought thus soothed has a decided tendency to vague reverie, to the dreaminess of the mild-eyed lotus-eaters. For such persons, in addition to the charm of the Tobacco, the mere attitude of quiet smoking, the mechanical employment of inhaling and exhaling the gentle vapour, of holding and occasionally tending the pipe, is a sedative to the restless frame, and induces the tranquillity required for intent meditation. For the best way to reach any mood is to put one's-self in the attitude thereof; and nervous people must occupy their fidgety members somehow, and smoking performs this office at least as well as whittling or needlework, while less distracting the attention. Moreover, the deep, slow breath of meditation extracts the inmost subtle aroma of the Tobacco, which is thus the very choice and sacred incense of the Temple of Thought.

I have met with but one instance wherein smoking proved decidedly injurious to philosophy. A young student-friend, perhaps a little beyond his depth in Berkeley, was set upon acquiring a sort of ocular demonstration of the theory that forthright distance, or protension, is not actually seen but only habitually inferred by us, after long practice and education of the senses, sight powerfully aided by touch. For this purpose he used to seat himself, when the speculative mood was strong upon him, in front of a blank wall (he had three such from which to choose in his attic chamber), with nothing between its whitewash and his eyes save viewless air; and, gazing intently in pure abstraction, strove to gaze the wall, as it were, into his retina, and perchance to draw it along the optic nerves even into his central brain; to perceive it as an immediate sensation, not outward, but internal. Again and again he tried this in vain. At length he discovered, with mingled joy and anguish, the flaw that marred the experiment. He always smoked when philosophising; and although his pipe, having a foot-long flexible tube, was not in his level line of vision, he could not but be vaguely conscious of its presence between himself and the wall; while the vapour, which at long intervals sprang blue from the bowl and lingered grey from his lips, was an ever-recurring exponent of the distance of the whitewash beyond. The poor fellow endeavoured the experiment without his pipe; but, no pipe no philosophy; he could not fix his attention at all; and the result was that he had most reluctantly to accept the theory in question on its mere reasonableness, without empirical verification. None the less did he enthusiastically persevere in his noble researches into the unknowable; and when we parted he was so transcendentally befogged in the cloudy metaphysics evolved from the seething brains and profound pipe-bowls of Germany, that I felt justified in assuring him, in an effusion of rapture rapturously reciprocated, that ere long he must attain the beatific vision, with eyes shut introspective clearly discerning the supreme and saving truth that Being and Non-Being are identical. And thus, after all, Tobacco, like wisdom, is justified of her children.

For good thinking, it seems to me that the pipe is preferable to the cigar; for good reading it certainly is. The cigar burning away towards your lips reeks pungently in your eyes and nose, and its ash powders you with perturbation if you do not frequently perturb yourself to knock it off; but the fire of the pipe is as far from you at the close as at the kindling, and its mouthpiece as cool in your lips, and its ash, secure in the censer, disquiets not. Give me a cigar for a placid and pensive stroll, in the sunset, or gloaming, or moonlight, deep in the rich quietude of summer, when the air is so calm that you can strike a vesper unshielded without fear that the tiny taper may be blown out; when the fresh odours of field and wood and garden mingle deliciously with the choice fragrance of the weed; when Venus from her heaven throbs golden replication to its pulsing crimson light, as if she mistook it for earth-wandering Mars.

There are some who can smoke with enjoyment and profit when writing: this I cannot do, either with cigar or pipe, when the writing requires reflection; for either the thought is distracted by the smoke, or the fire goes out in the interest of the thought. But how delightful and inspiring are a few whiffs in the pausing-spaces, when the brain teems with new ideas gradually assuming form, and the palate yearns for the Tobacco savour with a thirst as keen as the water-thirst of the desert—the desert whose cruel mirage, while it cannot be drunk, cannot even be smoked.

The true smoker, born for smoking, to whom Tobacco has been through long years a loyal friend, ever ready to console, never intrusive, can but smile serenely, not without compassion, at the desperate objurgations of the poor creatures afflicted with *nicotophobia* (the peculiar monomania demands some such name, and I know not whether any be yet stamped with authority), permanently inflated and intoxicated with fumes of confusion and delusion, the ever-burning incense of vanity offered by themselves to themselves. But there are other wiseacres of that flaççid sort of mind so well indicated by George Eliot, the type of people who are ready to admit that, speaking generally, the radii of a circle have a tendency to be equal, but who, at the same time, think that the spirit of geometry should not be carried too far; and these are in the habit of saying, with great solemnity, that too much smoking is injurious; as if too much of anything, good or bad, could be otherwise than injurious; as if the whole question were not begged in the very phrase too much. Disregarding these platitudinarians, the smoker knows when he has smoked too much overnight by the languor of the next morning, and the loss of zest in the weed. But the too much of one man is the golden mean of another; for there are smokers and smokers—from him who gets through about a cigar and a box of matches in a week, to the soldier who puts his *brûle-gueule,* or black nose-warmer, to his lips on waking, and drops it under his bed as he drops off to sleep at night. I remember being told of one such in hospital, where Tobacco is strictly forbidden (and where it would be more sanative than all the beastly drugs of the pharmacopœia, as was fairly proved in the Franco-German war), who was enjoying a surreptitious pipe sitting on his bed, which was next to the door, when the doctor and hospital-sergeant unexpectedly visited the ward. He had just time to withdraw the pipe, but the doctor too surely scented the last whiffs still curling in the corner. Our delinquent denied the charge with the coolness of an old soldier also an old smoker, and was vainly searched for the pipe. At length the puzzled doctor, quite sure of the atrocious crime he was quite unable to prove, guaranteed absolution and non-forfeiture of the pipe if the criminal would but confess and tell where he had secreted it. "Then, it's yourself you ought to be searching, doctor, and not me; for it's you is guilty of having a pipe in hospital," said the hardened one, and said sooth; for he had deftly dropped it at the critical right moment into the gaping side-pocket of the doctor's shooting-jacket, as the latter half-passed at first before turning on him. Surely this was not a man to be punished, we cry; even as, having told us of those two condemned ones in the Reign of Terror, who so densely filled their cell with the wholesome vapour, that the janitor entering to summon them to the guillotine, retired in hot dismay, half-blinded, and coughing furiously, our sympathetic Carlyle exclaims, "O my brothers, it is surely not *you* that I would select for execution!" This soldier reminds me of another who was in a light-dragoon regiment at Balaclava, on the right of his squadron. While awaiting orders the light cavalry sat at ease, screened by rising ground from the enemy, and most of them smoking. When the order for the mad charge was communicated, and "Attention!" called, this worthy warrior, while keenly alert, forgot to take his pipe out of his mouth, and kept on smoking in sweet unconsciousness. The officer close by, who must have had some bad blood in him, snarled to the troop-sergeant-major, also close by, "Stop that man's grog for two days," as they rode on up the slope. Scarcely had they crowned it, and were sweeping toward the Russian batteries, when a cannon-ball flew off with that officer's head, "as clean as a couple of billiard-balls." Our philosophic smoker just glanced round and ejaculated, "You beggar! *your* grog's stopped for more than two days, I guess!" The troop-sergeant-major was wounded and taken prisoner; the smoker came safe back and resumed his pipe, and there was no one to stop his grog, which be sure he relished not less than he deserved.

I remember a veteran smoker who loved his old pipes as a sailor loves his old ships, and who, contemplating the remains of a poor dear broken cutty, was so carried away by love and grief, that he placed it in the post of honour in his pipe-rack, with the touching inscription: –

> Neglected now it lies a cold clay form,
> Though late with living inspirations warm:
> Type of all other creatures of frail clay;
> What more than it for epitaph have they?*

And did not another enthusiast apostrophise heathenishly his meerschaum with superbest Olympian flatteries? –

> Cloud-compeller! Foam o' the sea,
> Whence rose Venus fair and free
> On some poet's reverie!

Verily, it is a stupendous subject for solemn meditation and for ardent admiration, that ever since Columbus was certified Great, not so much by the chance discovery of America as by the godlike fortune of thus propagating "divine Tobacco" throughout all lands, its sacred fires, whose fane is our sky-domed earth, whose altars are ubiquitous, and whose vestal virgins are the flower of mankind, have burned without intermission day and night: while the swart Eastern slumbers the white Western keeps them a-glow; while the Western slumbers, the Eastern: as advancing night shrouds these gracious luminaries in one meridian, its withdrawing skirts discover as many in a meridian thousands of leagues remote; the advancing day arouses innumerable votaries to their delightful duty, kindling ever-fresh incense on its path from pipe-bowls as from flower-chalices: with Phosphor of the dawn they glitter splendid, and splendid with Hesper of the gloaming; everywhere they shine forth in the darkness, countless and constant as the stars; nor can thickest clouds veil them, nor at highest noon are they extinguished: and they are the glorious constellations of the glorious Heaven of Keyf, the Paradise of placid enjoyment, the Empyréan of calm beatitude: – O just, subtle, and mighty Tobacco!

*This is Thomson's own epigram, "On a Broken Pipe."

"Jottings" on the Popular Concerts

[*Although Thomson's "Jottings" column in the* National Reformer *frequently contained full-length essays or satires (both "Hints for Freethought Novels" and "A Commission of Inquiry on Royalty" were published as "Jottings"), more often the column was composed of as many as five or six short comments. This one paragraph notice on the Popular Concerts reveals Thomson's lifelong interest in music, and indicates again that not all of his work for the* National Reformer *was concerned with religion or politics. The article appeared in the November 15, 1874, issue, and is reprinted here for the first time.*]

ON MONDAY LAST the Popular Concerts commenced their Seventeenth Season at St. James's Hall. As usual, there will be sixteen Monday evening and sixteen Saturday afternoon performances, extending, with a break for the Yule-tide holidays, well into March. It would be gross ingratitude in me to let slip the chance of acclaiming these lordly and generous musical feasts; for on looking back through several years, I reckon that these Concerts have yielded me more and more pure delight than all the other public entertainments of London put together. It is true that I cannot very ofter hear operas and oratorios; and that it has pleased the austere Archbishop Manning to ruin his choirs by expelling the women—as if boy's voices could be sonant and flexible enough for such *soprani* parts as those of the *Stabat Mater*. Begun as a daring venture to try whether the best chamber music, by the best performers, could be so appreciated by the public that very large audiences would make up for very low prices, these magnanimous concerts have proved a magnificent success, and this without ever lowering their first high intent. Scorning all flashy and ephemeral jinglings, which are to music what a clever leading-article is to literature; scorning the low jugglery of acrobatic execution, whereat the wide-eyed vulgar gape; they are wholly devoted to the Great Masters as interpreted by great artists. There Beethoven is King of Kings and Lord of Lords; "the wind seems in his hair, he seems to hear with his eyes," on his forehead broods the frown of thunder, but his smile is so ravishing and sweet that naught can compare with it save the tenderness in sternness of Dante the Divine: with Handel and Bach, Mozart and Hadyn, Weber and Mendelssohn, throned high but less loftily around him; with Hummel and Dussek, Tartini and Scarlatti, Spohr, Chopin, Hiller, and their peers, as satraps of provinces; and lastly, at his very feet, that notable and but recently discovered pair of Shoes, Schubert and Schumann, whereof the former is indeed lovely but too large and lax, while the latter with its stiff embroidery is of such shape and size that I for one cannot yet wear it with pleasure. And worthy are those who give voice to the silence, charged with thought and passion superhuman, of these greater and lesser gods. First the supreme master of the supreme instrument, "the Lord of the unerring bow," of whom it cannot be too often repeated, "There is one Beethoven, and Joachim is his prophet." Then Mme. Norman-Néruda, of feminine grace and masculine power; Ludwig Straus, the accomplished, who changing the violin for the viola when Joachim comes with the new year, completes the perfect quartet; Ries the severely serious, and Sainton the jolly, who leadeth with the overmuch emphasis of the leader of the hundred-strong Opera band; the grave iron-grey Piatti and his noble Stradivarius violoncello, with its "music yearning like a god in pain": and then the pianists; Arabella Goddard the faultless executant; Mme. Schumann with her soul of "Sturm and Drang," storm and stress; Hallé, the gentle and dreamy, the idyllic and elegiac; Pauer, the intellectual and scholarly; and now the phenomenal Hans von Bülow. Of vocal music there is little, just two or three songs sprinkled like flowers and perfumes in the intervals between the instrumental processions. An impassioned chant of Beethoven; an *aria* from some opera of Mozart, "honey-sweet-throated"; a charming *lied* of Schubert, or pretty French *chanson;* a noble rolling and resonant air from some neglected opera of mighty Handel, like that "Nasce al bosco oscuro" which Mr. Santley trolls with such vigour. And the charges for these banquets of delight are but five shillings in the stalls, three shillings in the balcony, one shilling in the back area and gallery and orchestra. This Jotter goeth always to the orchestra. There you look down over slanting heads to the musicians, and see them clearly, and are near to them; and it is well to be near to them when usually they play not more than four or five together; but how any one, not quite or almost deaf, can be foolish enough to pay heavily for an orchestra stall at the Opera, so as to have the shrieking and blaring and clashing and banging of five-score instruments close to his ears, has always surpassed my comprehension. The stall people looking up at us of the orchestra, behold nothing but a sombre and undistinguished mass, concave, and receding as it ascends to the ignoble organ; to us, gazing forthright down the great hall's long length, the stalled dignitaries are as a brilliant and many-coloured garden, scarlet and azure, white and golden, over which the divine music floats. One hears well-known names attributed to some of those we thus look down upon. One says that George Eliot is always in her place, at least for the Saturday Afternoon Concerts. There have I years ago often seen that one of our poets who appears to thoroughly comprehend all art; music and architecture, painting and sculpture, no less than poetry; who has written "A Toccata of Galuppi's" and "Master Hugues of St. Gotha," "The Bishop Orders his Tomb," "Andrea del Sarto," "Fra Lippo Lippi," and "Cleon"; I have seen Robert Browning, his face beaming with rapture; I have seen him throw up his hands and let them fall helpless, made womanish for the moment with wonder, as Joachim finished Sebastian Bach's *Chaconne*. And there did I see my Lord Chief Justice,* that gay and festive old boy, light and bright and lively as a bird, receiving hearty congratulations from all around him, just two days after he had got rid of that horrible Old Man of the Sea who had weighed upon him for almost a year, two days after he had pitched that huge lump of imposture and blackguardism clean off his shoulders, right into Newgate, to *ricocher* thence into Milbank, where one regrets that it is deprived of the constant companionship of certain of its friends. But I must leave for the present these beloved Popular Concerts, though I would fain dilate much longer on their noble delights. Can any one tell me of such another investment for time and money in London or elsewhere on earth? Two and a half hours of Paradise for a shilling!

*Sir Alexander Cockburn, Lord Chief Justice who presided over the famous Tichborne trial of 1873–74 in which Arthur Orton ("that huge lump of imposture and blackguardism") was convicted of perjury in claiming to be Roger Tichborne, the heir to the Tichborne estate.

The *Saturday Review* on Dr. Newman

[*Although Thomson's most ambitious journalistic endeavors occurred in 1873 when he went to Spain as a war correspondent for the New York* World, *as early as 1864 he attempted to earn a living by writing for a newspaper. This letter to the editor of the* Daily Telegraph *(published on July 1, 1864) led to a very short-lived career with that paper. On July 19, 1864, his article titled "Middle Class Education" appeared, but other articles mentioned in his diary were apparently rejected. Thomson never again published in the* Daily Telegraph, *and in later years he delighted in satirizing the "D.T." (which he liked to pretend stood for* Delirium Tremens*). This letter is also the first of his many attacks upon the* Saturday Review, *a periodical he deplored because of its orthodox position in religion and politics. Finally, the letter splendidly exemplifies Thomson's scorn for careless writing. It is reprinted here for the first time.*]

TO THE EDITOR OF "THE DAILY TELEGRAPH."

SIR—"There is much in what he records of himself which might seem to bring the great Doctor of Oriel down to the deplorable level of an ordinary fanatic; and were it not counteracted by an exhibition of rare keenness of thought, vigour of logic, a wonderful and intimate familiarity with human nature, and the deepest sympathy with other people's minds, *as well as a vigour of vituperation* which shows a proficient in the art of malediction almost equalling St. Jerome himself, *we might almost be tempted to rank the apologist with Swedenborg or Wesley.*"

As soon as this brilliant sentence caught my eye, I was sure that our dear genial friend the S. R. had prepared one of its grand articles for the public this week, and I set about reading, with due humble carefulness. The Doctor so narrowly saved, by his vigour of vituperation and the other things, from being degraded by the S. R. to the deplorable level of Swedenborg or Wesley, is J. H. Newman. The book of his in review is, of course, the "Apologia"; and I can fearlessly assert that the whole article is of even more astonishing magnificence than the first sample led me to expect.

With your kind permission, I would earnestly exhort your readers to beg, borrow, or convey the number containing the article; and, to justify my exhortation, as well as to excite the curiosity and admiration which will doubtless make it effectual, I add a few specimens — a few gorgeous flowers, from a dense and bewildering tropical forest — blossoms that lose half their beauty in being severed from their parent boughs — tendrils with difficulty disentangled from the intricate exuberance.

A great and splendid mind cannot apply itself to any one subject without throwing lustre far around on innumerable things which it has no immediate intention of glorifying. Thus it will be seen that the S. R., while meaning simply to settle once and for ever the *status* of Newman, and the right answers to all the theological problems which the name of Newman suggests, really does also open out views novel and startling in grammar, in mechanics, in history, in meteorology, in logic, in jurisprudence, in medicine, in nearly the whole circle of the arts and sciences. In grammar, above all, I am forced to infer, from the S. R.'s marvellous sentences, that he has elaborated rules of composition which laugh to scorn our Lindley Murray commonplaces.* As the S. R. has not condescended to bestow upon the world these rules in the abstract, contenting himself with the exhibition of them in the concrete of defiant clauses and mysterious sentences — just as Newton, while keeping the secret of fluxions to himself, could overwhelm mathematicians with problems solved, which could only be solved by the aid of fluxions — I will send you, if you like, an annotated copy of *the* article, that you may at once set some eminent hands to work upon the elimination of the doctrines from the practice.

Now for the few and inadequate specimens:

1. Ecclesiastical Mechanics. — "There are very likely deflections from the ideal equilibrium. If the Puritans represent *one depression* of the balance, there must be Romanising on the other hand."

If the Puritans represent *one* depression, there must be another, and the equilibrium is destroyed by each side outweighing the other. How finely is the peculiarly puzzling nature of all Church questions thus symbolised.

*Lindley Murray (1745–1826), grammarian and author of the widely used *English Grammar,* first published in 1795.

2. Mental Hydrodynamics and Meteorology combined.—"There is no real and certain conviction without its preliminary of doubt. Certainty is only given to second-rate minds. Thinkers must *always* be in more or less of a flux." (Let the reader note that the preliminary of doubt thus lasts *always*, and is therefore preliminary only to itself.) "They ebb and flow. At times there is an *apparent* clearness and definiteness in the horizon of mind or conscience, when everything stands out sharp and defined; and this is usually the precursor of a mental tempest." (The sky is clear; furl for the storm!) "*Then* the mind reposes on the haze and softened outline of difficulties."

This is without doubt one of the noblest passages in the essay: but the hasty reader will probably miss some of its grandeur, and for his sake I seek to put it in the simplest style. The mind or conscience is an ocean always ebbing or flowing, or both (for, though plausible reasons might be advanced for so doing, I think it preferable not to connect the "flux" with the process termed "purging of a bias" a few lines before); that is, it is ebbing and flowing as a preliminary to getting settled; but, as it ebbs and flows for ever, the preliminary is a long one, and the settling far off. While this ocean of mind or conscience ebbs and flows, the atmosphere of mind or conscience finds its horizon, because of the ebb or else the flow, apparently clear and definite (and you must remember that things often look clear *un*apparently); and when the horizon is definite, things look defined; and matters being in this state of ebb and flow and definiteness, a storm is imminent; and *then* the mind, this ebbing and flowing ocean, and also this clear atmosphere, finding the storm coming, feels very comfortable, or perhaps very much disgusted, and forthwith sets about reposing on the haze of the clear horizon and on the softened outlines of all the things standing out sharp; the sea reposes upon the sky, the sky reposes upon itself, and when the tempest does appear, it will surely find all snug above and below.

This explanation is rather tedious, but I trust that the dullest and the most careless will find it sufficiently lucid.

3. Psychological Jurisprudence.—"They (doubts) were dismissed only to reappear uninvoked; and when they reappeared, *they silenced their own appeal*."

Can our common law or Chancery procedure produce a feat equal to this?

4. Theological logic.—"At the present moment he (Dr. N.)

holds very distinctly the view that there are only two luminously *self-evident* beings, myself and my Creator."

"A man whose deepest conviction is that he and his Maker are the only *demonstrable* realities."

"If, then, there are men to whom this inner *improved and improvable consciousness* has not been given, they may be atheists," &c., &c.

"Believing in the existence of God, *for no reason whatever*, Dr. N. *goes on*, by strict logical process, to believe in," &c., &c.

The heights and the depths of divinity! Euclid used to make us a present of a few axioms in our school days, on the distinct understanding that we were to accept them as self-evident and undemonstrable; and as self-evident and undemonstrable we took them, and would have been very glad to accept the sequent propositions, one and all, without the slightest insult of investigation, as self-evident and undemonstrable too. But learn, O reader! that in the transcendental theology axiomatic convictions which are self-evident are also demonstrable, and the only propositions that are demonstrable; and they, furthermore, belong to the improved and improvable consciousness, and therefore he who believes in them believes in them for no reason whatever. Of the cogency of this *therefore* a familiar example may be added. You are conscious of pain in your chest; you do not know its cause; you cannot prove to others that you have this pain; you believe, then, in your pain for no reason whatever, imbecile that you are!

5. Ecclesiastical Geometry and Anatomy. — "It was only accidentally, as it were, that the Church of Rome, and its claims to fulfil the idea" (we have been among Platonic ideas, ideals, and types which the ignorant ancient Platonists called archetypes and antetypes), "*crossed the area of his experiments in ecclesiastical vivisection.*"

Would it not make a picture? Dr. N. in a certain area is cutting up live churches; enter the Church of Rome, and crosses said area with claims to fulfil the idea. Or what a problem for the ghosts of Euler and Magendie to work out!*

6. Theological Scandal. — "Dr. Newman's method is the *legitimate parent* of open inquiry."

*Leonhard Euler (1707–1783), Swiss mathematician, considered a founder of modern analysis; François Magendie (1783–1855), physiologist and anatomist.

What an affiliation case! Who or what is the *il*legitimate parent?

7. New Sects Heretical. — "Dr. N.'s religious history forms an apology for Atheism more mischievous than all that the Encyclopædists, or *Darwinists, or believers in the new philosophy of the divinity of the sun,* have ever speculated or suggested."

So Darwin and his followers are Atheists, the rogues! But who are these nineteenth-century English Guebres and Parsees who believe in the divinity of the sun? S. R. ought really to drag them into scathing notoriety.

8. The Poor Common Folk. — "They will go on believing in Christianity upon grounds which they cannot express in *mood and figure.* They only know that they are, and intend to remain, Christians."

Alas! ye poor "chaotic, unintelligent, inarticulate!" not one mood for you? Indicative, Imperative, hopelessly beyond your power, and even Subjunctive too hard? And not one figure? Not a balance, or ocean, or atmosphere, or bias-prophylactic, to assist you in expressing yourselves? You are, and you intend to remain, like ostriches with heads buried in the sand, and only the ignobler parts open to the free air and light. Surely even the S. R. pities you, though inexorable justice makes him proclaim your doom.

9. Relaxation. — (Dr. Newman is) "the one original genius who has risen above the heavy clouds and fogs of the Tractarian *flats.*" Charming pun! d' y' see?

This letter is already so long, that I must refrain from offering any more of these precious samples. One protest only would I offer to the Editor of the *Saturday Review* before concluding, and this protest protests against that editor's conduct in allowing some Jesuitical priest to put a forked sting in the tail of this serpent of wisdom. For with an evil equivoke the last sentence tells us that people won't go over to the Church of Rome because "they would lose more than *they can see* that they would gain." Not more than they would really gain, mark you. I am convinced that this sentence was not written by the learned, subtle, perspicacious, perspicuous, honest, meek, logical, &c. &c. &c., writer of the rest of the article. — I am, Sir, yours, &c.,

June 28. T.J.

France Declares War against Prussia

[*This article, one of Thomson's infrequent efforts as a political commentator, appeared in the* National Reformer *on July 24, 1870, five days after France had declared war against Prussia. It is reprinted here for the first time. At the outbreak of the war, Thomson, ignorant of Bismarck's role in encouraging the conflict, was at one with his countrymen in placing the blame entirely upon France, although Thomson was considerably more optimistic than most as to Germany's chances of success in battle. Six months later, when, as a result of German victories and German insults on English neutrality, the tide of sentiment had turned and most Englishmen were sympathizing with a defeated France, the* National Reformer *also came out against Bismarck. The issue for January 15, 1871, contained a seven-page article by Austin Holyoake explaining the reverse in attitude, but Thomson, who had so vigorously claimed that the German Fatherland was honest and peaceful, had no further comment to make. His next contribution to the* National Reformer *consisted of eight translations from Goethe's poems.*]

A FEW DAYS ago the world was informed by the French Government that the continuance of peace was never more assured. Already the world knows that the French Government must have then been resolved to break the peace as soon as possible. The candidature of Prince Leopold* was as poor a pretext for hostilities as ever a bully made much of; the withdrawal of the Prince took away even that pretext. The French Government proclaimed its intense desire for peace; and proved its veracity by beginning the discussion with threats, carrying it on with insults, and urging it headlong to decision of battle with what looks like fraud, for not even to its own servile Legislature did it dare to produce the documents on which its case rested. However, there is nothing strange in the fact that a Napoleon lies, that the truth which is not in him never comes out of him; the founder

*Prince Leopold of Hohenzollern Sigmaringen, whose candidature for the Spanish throne had been withdrawn on July 12, 1870, one week before France declared war.

of the dynasty stands supreme among great men for lying and selfishness, scarcely approached by Jonathan Wild the Great himself; and the present head of the family is so faithful to the Napoleonic tradition that a perplexed diplomatist said of him, "He is so false that you cannot even believe the opposite of what he affirms."

The true cause of the war is to be found mainly in three facts: the French Government has home difficulties, it knows that the French people dislike and are jealous of the Prussians, it thinks France now strong enough to beat Prussia. It would have declared war the day after Sadowa* had it dared, and has only refrained from doing so during these four years past from a magnanimous feeling that it was more likely to lose than to win. What a pity should it prove even now not stronger than the Government and nation it has forced into fighting!

Many Liberals will separate the French people from the French Government in their verdict upon this last great iniquity of the Empire. But a people which has supported a particular Government for eighteen years is responsible, morally as otherwise, for that Government. A great and noble people, in certain disastrous circumstances, may be surprised and abused by a despicable Government, and remain thus misrepresented for three or four years, but surely never for eighteen. A period so long proves close affinities between sovereign and subjects; his vices or virtues must have counterparts in theirs. The French Government is the outcome and flagrant symbol of the whole corruption of the French nation as it now exists, as surely as an ulcer on the face is outcome and symbol of corruption in the blood. The bruise or gash of an accident from without would have long ago healed; this foul sore has been running for eighteen years. The ignorance of the peasantry, the servile self-seeking of the officials, the cowardice and greed of the middle classes, the dissoluteness of the great towns, the vanity and glory-mania of the people generally, the wild imprudences of some of the Republicans; these and the like peccant humours keep this shameful stigma burning on the fair front of France.

The police, we may fairly suppose, have much to do with the

*The battle of Sadowa on July 3, 1866, concluded the Seven Weeks War; Prussia was victorious over Austria, and subsequently headed the North German Federation.

Parisian and other demonstrations in favour of war. But it seems almost certain that the nation generally approves it. France is jealous of Prussia. Sadowa has dimmed the glory of Solferino.* France, which has really given powerful forward impulses to Europe, France the apostle of the ideas of '89, wishes to reserve her own leadership in the progress of civilisation. Her programme is: Liberty, to do as France inspires; Equality, under France paramount; Fraternity, as of English younger sons and their eldest brother in respect of landed estate. The most recent international societies may have ignored and abolished these French assumptions, but hitherto they have dominated in French literature, and no glorification of Paris and France has been too absurd, too insane, for the best authors to write, and the most sensible readers to swallow with rapture. But little more than a hundred years since, Germany began to develope ideas and a literature of her own; not at all like those of France, yet by no means necessarily antagonistic. And now she is beginning to realise these ideas, being specially and rightly anxious to realise a great German Fatherland for the great German people, of old disintegrated in the most ludicrous and disastrous way. This German unity is really formidable to nothing French save the French supremacy in continental Europe. The Germans can have no motive for injuring France while France leaves them uninjured. France achieved her own unity centuries ago, welding the numerous more or less independent duchies into a strong monarchy. She lately helped Italy in the same process. That idea for which she fought in Italy, she is now fighting against in Germany. She is thus fighting for all that is retrograde in Europe; and would force back the main current of our century which sweeps the strongest down. She is in this war selfish and unjust, untrue to her better self, true only to herself as represented by Chauvinism and Napoleonism. She is acting towards Germany in the latter half of the nineteenth century, as England acted towards herself in the fourteenth and fifteenth centuries, without even the old pleas (or any faith in them, if they existed) of hereditary royal rights. She is prostituting the *Marseillaise*, that supreme heroic cry of a nation in agony, encompassed with enemies, to be the swash-buckler chorus of a war of aggression, a fight for supremacy

*On June 24, 1859, Napoleon III succeeded in seizing and holding Solferino in an important victory against Austria.

over her equals who want no supremacy over her. How much farther can she go on the grand Napoleon road?

I do not pretend that the Prussian or the North German Government is a realised ideal. The best German Liberals have recently refrained, and still refrain, from pressing with their full power for reforms, because they see that the most urgent business just now is to assure German unity. The ship once seaworthy, they will make their vote felt in deciding as to the course it shall sail. The Prussians are at present to Germany much as the Piedmontese to Italy. And a stiff backbone is just what both nations want now, when they are making their first practical endeavours to stand firm and erect in Europe. And when we compare a homely and frugal, though somewhat antiquated kind of hereditary monarchy, like that of Prussia, with the Napoleonism of France, the respectability of the former seems quite venerable and sacred.

One should not omit to express the honour due to those members of the Left, and to M. Thiers* (who has heretofore done much harm in fomenting the Gallic jealousy of its neighbours, and lust of domineering) who opposed though ineffectually the insolent precipitation of the French Chamber in voting war and war subsidies on hearsay.

The war will probably be one of extreme surprises. The period is of such rapid transition in military science and art, that a few months may make a wonderful invention quite obsolete. If the French chassepôt and mitrailleuse† are not much superior to the Prussian needlegun and new artillery, the Prussians seem likely to do more than hold their own. They have better chiefs both in council and field than any French chiefs have yet proved themselves, with the single exception perhaps of MacMahon. And the main bulk of their levies is, I think, rather superior than inferior to that of the French in good soldierly qualities and thorough training. It is said that the very Zouaves of the Zouaves‡ come from Alsace, the German province of France.

But it is idle to speculate on probabilities when the solution is

*Louis Adolphe Thiers (1797–1877), statesman and historian who, after the defeat of MacMahon at Sedan, was responsible for arranging the peace with Prussia; he later served as president of the new republic.

†The chassepot was a new breech-loading rifle, the mitrailleuse, an early machine gun.

‡A crack infantry regiment in the French army.

so near at hand. The certainties are enough for the present. It is certain that many thousands of brave men, who have been drawn from useful labour and family life to live dissolutely in barracks and camps, will be killed, and tens of thousands wounded. It is certain that fields will be trampled, houses plundered and burnt, honest men ruined, throughout large districts among the most wealthy and civilised in Europe. It is certain that nearly every state in Europe will have to squander enormous sums of money in order to secure its house from catching fire while these two neighbours seek to burn each other to the ground. And I think it equally certain that the ultimate union of Germany will be rather accelerated than postponed by the war, whether France conquers or Prussia. I even think it equally certain that the time is not very distant when France will be glad to have in the centre of Europe, between herself and Russia, a solid German Fatherland peopled by forty or fifty millions of Germans, a people on the whole as honest, industrious, frugal, peaceful, kindly, brave, and intelligent, as the nineteenth century can show anywhere in the world.

Whatever the event, this war is disgraceful to France; and disgraceful to Europe is the fact that without warning, without injury received, without discussion, without appeal to friendly arbitration, but in mere spite and blind submission to the will of one wretched man, a nation should dare and be able to wage war upon another, causing immense havoc and injury throughout the whole civilised world.

P.S. — Since writing the above, I have been glad to read in the *Daily News*, with regard to the French press: "We find all the independent journals of considerable circulation, of every shade of the Republican and the Liberal party, both in the capital and in the provinces, opposed to the war; and in its favour are only the journals more or less associated with the Government, the Court, or the Police, and of little or no circulation beyond official circles and the Boulevards." And, further, that not only men like Louis Blanc and Rochefort,* but also the *Internationale,*

*Louis Blanc (1811–1882), political leader and historian who at the time was in exile, not returning to France until after the fall of the Empire; Henri Victor Rochefort (1830–1913), polemical writer, novelist, and dramatist, leader of Republican opposition to Napoleon III, imprisoned at this time but released after the fall of the Empire.

through its French Committee and the French Masonic Lodges, have denounced "this abominable outrage on the rights of nations, and the spurious patriotism that applauds it." If we cannot separate the French people as a whole, we can separate the French Liberals from the Government in this shameful business, and hope that such good leaven will ere long leaven the lump.

On the Way to Don Carlos

[*In 1873 Thomson spent two months in Spain working as a war correspondent for the New York* World*; his assignment was to cover the Carlist revolution, the short-lived rebellion by Carlist royalists against the newly formed Spanish republic. Some years later he published his "Carlist Reminiscences" in the* Secularist *(in four installments, March 11–April 1, 1876), but the following article, herein reprinted for the first time, is taken directly from the* World *(August 12, 1873). This was Thomson's first report, written from Bayonne; it was signed "J. S. T." and appeared on the front page of the* World *under the headline, "On the Way to Don Carlos: Scenes at Bayonne and on the Spanish Frontier." Thomson had many opportunities to observe and to talk with Don Carlos, whom he later described as "an amiable man of somewhat phlegmatic temperament, who would be much happier living as a country gentleman with his wife and three children, than leading the advance-guard or forlorn-hope of the Restoration." This article, which sheds little light on the war itself, is obviously more an informal essay than a newspaper report, and provides a good example of Thomson's interest in and talent for colorful description, an aspect of his work seldom revealed in essays or articles, although his diaries are rich in detailed descriptions of nature.*]

BAYONNE, July 28.—I fear that the good people of Bayonne, however kind-hearted, cannot feel that full amount of decent sorrow for the distresses of their neighbors which humanity and Christianity enjoin, for the troubles of Spain have filled the town to overflowing with excellent guests.

The Spanish guests seem a nice, quiet set of people. Among themselves they doubtless speak warmly on political and religious questions, but they are careful not to risk the stirring up of strife in general company. They lounge in and about the cafes most of the day and up till bedtime, reading many journals, playing cards, and taking quiet refreshments, such as lemonade and cold coffee with sugar and cold water, though warm coffee and cognac and the beer of Angoulême are not totally neglected. The ladies seem to walk about more than the men. Though all appear so tranquil, getting placidly through the day, or letting the day get through them, as Dickens puts it, doing a hundred nothings with perfect dignity and composure, there must be some hot resentments, some sharp sorrows, some fierce hopes throbbing beneath the smooth, white shirt-fronts.

But even without an unusual influx of visitors from Spain, Bayonne would seem almost half Spanish in many respects. Inscriptions and announcements are quite commonly given in Spanish as well as French, and a considerable proportion of the chat you hear in passing such as do not look like temporary visitors is Spanish also.

Altogether it is a pleasant place to loaf in, this Bayonne, with its two rivers and its three divisions—Grand or Old Bayonne, Petit or New Bayonne, and St. Esprit—and the charming green country well wooded all around. Perhaps the streets one likes best are the old narrow ones, with tall houses, all the shutters Venetian-blind fashion, and the shadowy arcades, with massy short pillars in front of the stores. As these arcades not only keep out much of the heat, but also much of the light of the sun, the interior of the stores is rather dark, and thus many stalls are placed under the open arches, and much of the work is done outside. Even where there are no arcades it is the custom to carry on the work in the front shop with the door open. Thus you see young girls with nimble fingers, all natty and clean, working away with a will and chatting gaily, with now and then a glance for the passers-by. This is surely a more rational and benevolent plan than that of withdrawing all the pretty creatures to labor in some dull back room where no eye can see them and they are quite shut in from the cheerful daily life of the world. The frankness with which all kinds of work is carried on in public must sometimes surprise a stranger from countries more reserved. In front of a hair-dresser's, at an archway of an arcade, round a table covered with fluffy hair and I know not what else, you may see two girls and two young fellows, seated like a snug whist party, busily manufacturing those chignons and other postiches, which to the masculine mind seem even more emphatically than ourselves "fearfully and wonderfully made." Yes, even here false braids are worn, though none, so far as I have seen, half so monstrous and tumid as those which abound in London and New

York. The lower classes have the hair neatly wound at the back of the head and covered with a little cap or handkerchief, which to my eye is very attractive. Well-to-do women of the middle classes come out walking or shopping without anything on the head save the rich black braids of hair, and there is something homely in this fashion which makes me admire them much more thus than flaunting the most gorgeous gossamer bonnets or hats. In default of head-dress they carry the fan. Clear aquiline contours abound, with strong black eyes, which look you full in the face with perfect composure.

They have renewed one tower of the old yellow cathedral, and are completing another. I strolled in on Sunday, and found a pretty numerous congregation. Near the western entrance is the fountain, above which the monument, in form of a sarcophagus surmounted by a funeral urn, was erected in 1831 by the people of Bayonne, in memory of the three days of July. It is specially dedicated to a medical student and a journeyman tailor (presumably natives of Bayonne) who died for their country in Paris, on one of those days. There is a high-sounding sentiment engraven on one side: "Les révolutions justes sont le châtiment des mauvais rois." There must have been many bad kings chastised of late years if all the revolutions have been just.

I have made a little expedition by coach to the frontier nearly twenty miles off. The road, which is very well kept, winds up and down towards mountains, through a rolling region of rich verdure, well-cultivated fields, abundant trees. There are sweet banks and hedgerows with honey-suckle, wild roses, heather, manifold wild flowers, and luxuriant ferns. Above are large-leaved platanes, chestnuts, oaks with the crimson flames of red leaves sprinkled among their green in the sunlight, and the omnipresent poplars, standing sentinel-like at gateways or in long stately lines walling the road on either side. "The poplar his pop'lar in France," said a cockney, and grinned with the fatuous assurance of one who thinks he has achieved a pun. The raked hay stripes the yellow meadows; there are numerous fields of maize with the long, drooping flags and the tassels still chiefly erect, and here and there are bits of vineyards with the vines festooned between the stakes. The mountains looked massy as of dull, heavy lead under the cloudy afternoon sky. As we drew nearer they changed into sombre solid green. And again, towards sunset, long, pale light from the west, under the low curtain of cloud, partially transfigured them, contrasting with the long, misty folds which divided the crest from the base.

The frontier at that point is a streamlet over which one might almost or quite jump. It is crossed by a little bridge which forms a sort of neutral ground, the one end being French, the other Spanish. The village is very small, comprehending a decent little hotel, a small military station in France, a custom-house in Spain, and very few cottages. I need scarcely say that the custom-house is in the hands of the Carlists, who levy and are paid with cheerful regularity the usual dues. All these people are Carlists, indeed, or if any peculiar person has another way of thinking he takes care to keep his thoughts to himself. The *Dios, patria, rey* (God, country, king) is the magical charm in this region. The custom-house seems to serve as recruiting depot, and I saw several young fellows, just arrived from Guipuzcoa, I was informed, who were about to join one of the columns. They were not very tall but strongly built, alert and vigorous, and appeared excellent stuff to make good soldiers out of. None of them had the look of having ever suffered want—all had the cheerful bearing of independence and self-respect. I am told and can readily believe that they are wonderful marchers, these mountaineers. But all the peasantry about this region, and even the oldest women, walk erect with a free, graceful carriage and a firm yet light planting of the feet, which makes their movements as pleasant to witness as if they were dancing to music. The *jeu de paume* is very popular here, and I watched several of these young fellows playing it. They played with the bare hands, just as the same game is played in Ireland, and were equally deft in left and right hand, in straightforward and back hitting. Their suppleness, agility, and breathing power could scarcely be surpassed. They put the ball out fairly, and generally as far as possible, while the Irish at fives drop it low and at awkward angles into awkward corners. But then these had not a regular ball-alley, only the side of a house with a piece of smooth ground before it without sidewalls. As the recruits come in they receive a brooch, with the monogram of Carlos Rey, which they affix to the crown of their berretta—if I may speak of the crown of that which is all crown—being a cap just like the lid of a saucepan, of which this brooch takes the place of handle, folded inwardly all round. It is generally of white, blue, or red, and I noticed that this last color did not disagree with the Carlists; some wear tassels of woollen or silver trailing over it. A Carlist aide-de-camp came on horseback from the interior to the frontier while I was there; tall, swarthy, with great black eyes, which suggest forests and sierras, and have nothing in common with cities. He was in uniform, and went and chatted with the French soldiers lounging on the bridge. Soldiers and volunteers are on easy and friendly terms, the only difficulty between them arising from the fact that few of the volunteers know any French and few of the soldiers know any Spanish. Some of the border country people, who know something of both languages, do a good deal of interpreting in a miscellaneous fashion. I must not forget to mention a man who, beating a little drum with the right hand and playing a long whistle having three holes near the bottom with his left, made the quaintest stirring noise. When one who could play the drum took it from him and accompanied with two bits of stick he employed his right hand in beating on the ground with his staff, not merely keeping time, but, as it were, urging and exciting the music.

Returning to Bayonne early in the morning (we started before five) we soon saw plenty of people working in the fields and villages as we passed. More than one old woman walking lightly with handkerchief tied obliquely round the head, recalled forcibly the portraits of Dante; network of minute wrinkles, sharp nose, sharp, strong chin, contracted features, intense regard under sharp brows. All give gracious salutation as we go by, for every one here is intensely and obsequiously polite to every one else. A Dante visage in a poor old peasant crone of the Basses-Pyrenees, who, I daresay, cannot write or read! yet she has had to live out as she could her divina commedia, with very probably a quite excessive share of inferno and purgatorio in it. Panniered donkeys came by, with fresh-faced girls sitting well forward, their feet level with the quadruped's head. Some of the donkeys are hung all round with fern-fronds, and are even plumed with the same like dowagers in turbans and feathers, for the shadow and the coolness and against the flies. So the coupled oxen, drawing the wains, have a thick matting or rather moss on the head, a network veil for the face, and a thin sheet over the back.

Before closing I must call attention to one remarkable announcement, placarded in large letters about Bayonne: "Old England have arrived at Biarritz." Who can this old England be that *have* arrived? I am quite puzzled, and can only guess that it may be the Tichborne claimant,* for the language has a smack of his style. But then, surely, Biarritz is not on the way to any place to which he is likely to be sent?

*See note, p. 167.

In the Valley of Humiliation

[*This article, dated December 16, 1878, and published in the January, 1879, issue of the* Liberal, *is here reprinted for the first time. Thomson's vituperative attack on Disraeli's policies centers upon the "peace with honor" that Disraeli had brought home from the 1878 Congress of Berlin. At that conference, England and Austria had allied themselves in opposing Russian interests, and both nations felt they had obtained their goals in what was inevitably a temporary settlement of the Russo-Turkish War and the impossibly complex "Eastern Question." But Thomson felt that the solution was the establishment by "Concord of the Great Powers," especially England and Russia, of a chain of autonomous states from the Black Sea to the Adriatic, and he feared that the Berlin conference had merely strengthened Russia's position and made her the sole power to whom eastern Europe could turn. The Congress of Berlin had actually climaxed Disraeli's career, and, although Thomson found himself in the "valley of humiliation," the Prime Minister's prestige had never been higher than it was in 1878. Thomson was, however, correct in predicting that Disraeli's policies, both domestic and foreign, would cause his fortunes to wane, and in the general election of 1880 the Conservatives were indeed soundly defeated. In addition to its interest as a criticism of Disraeli, this article is notable as the clearest statement of Thomson's dismay over the "national disease," and his fears about the too-rapid growth of a democratic republic "until we are taught and trained into something like fitness for it."*]

"Dizzy is England while England is dizzy."

NEVER BEFORE, since old enough to take interest in our national policy, have I, for one, as a Briton, felt so vilely and wantonly insulted and humiliated as during these last three years; in which for our manifold sins and stupidities we have been delivered over to the scourging domination of an alien Charlatan, cutting his ignominious capers and posturing with yet more preposterous solemnity to the amazement of the world, on the solid platform of the dense wooden heads of an abjectly servile Parliamentary majority. Truly we are become a byword and a scorn to the nations; our enemies sharpen their eyes on us.

The first fruit of our disasters and disgraces (produce of course of seedlings long since planted) was the bitter fact that Carlyle's "superlative Hebrew Juggler" was borne not merely into office but into power with a sure majority to sustain him there; not, indeed, a majority of popular votes, but of Parliamentary; a majority so sure in its partisan servility, that he was practically installed Dictator for seven years. What made this shameful portent possible? Not only this selfish servility of the Tories, ever ready and willing to sacrifice national to partisan interests: but also the equal selfishness and greater cowardice of the Whigs; the distracted dissensions of the Liberals, each one idolising his own particular god; the contemptible apathy and stupidity of the bulk of the working-classes, steadily refusing to look beyond their own noses; the utterly unscrupulous misrepresentations, calumnies and manœuvres of great greedy "interests"—as the Aristocracy and Landholders, the State Church, the Publicans, the Army and Navy—"interests" whose Tory zeal is in general directly proportioned to their incompatibility with the best interests of the Commonwealth.

Thus it is of little use to lavish our indignation and contempt on the Miracle of Charlatanism now lording it over us; he is but the most prominent symptom of the national disease, or rather complication of diseases, not the complicated disease itself; the ulcer flagrant on England's forehead, which shows how corrupt are the currents of her life-blood. While the blood continues so foul, such ulcers must burn forth on the surface of the body politic, if not in certain places then in others; there can be no real cure by cautery or excision of the ulcers without thorough cleansing of the blood. The man himself, the Dictator of our Degradation, was amusing enough while one never dreamt that he could attain office save temporarily on sufferance; amusing as a very clever antic in a pantomime; agile, adroit, keen-witted, inexhaustible in fantastic tricks, charming in the frank effrontery of his humbug. But what are we to say of the mental and moral condition of England when she elects to have her Government, with all its national and international policy, turned into a Pantomime regardless of expense! to have Clown stealing real millions with a grin, and grabbing a Cyprus or an Afghanistan as if it were a string of dummy sausages, while pelting us, who are the paying audience as well as the shareholders of the theatre, with the most impudent "gag" of solemn mystifications or ludicrous falsehoods; to have Pantaloon playing the most absurd tricks with our interests and our honour; to have Harlequin jesting at horrible massacres and worse than massacres, leaping lightly over all bounds of property, of good faith, of constitutional and international law, and finally flourishing his wand to kindle a real sensational transformation scene—lurid with real fire, real cannon-thunder, real fighting and slaughter, to end with the splendid spectacle of the real burning down of our own National Theatre on our own heads! And this tragic farce is being enacted with the boisterous applause of a large part of the nation!

I need not dwell upon the ignominious events so recently branded into our memories. Blindly selfish refusal to act with the other Great Powers in the Eastern Question, so as to secure its gradual and peaceful solution; blindly selfish jealousy of Russia, which thrust the tributary Provinces into her arms, and precipitated the war which could not but aggrandise her; blindly selfish and unscrupulous collusion with Turkey, encouraging her to a resistance otherwise hopeless in prospect, and which by lack of our material support could not but prove disastrous in result; blindly selfish blustering and brandishing of British interests, changed at a wave of Harlequin's wand into high moral interests of European law; austere declarations against any secret treaties anticipating the Conference, into which we went hampered by secret engagements with Russia, with Turkey, and perchance with Austria. Then the Conference, that Infamy, in which our callous Charlatan of nascent Imperialism and Personal Government at home, made an Unholy Alliance with the effete Imperial Despotisms of the Continent; that Conference which followed as closely as the changed circumstances would permit the infernal impolicy of the Congress of Vienna, without the excuses it had in the terror and amaze of the then recent Great Revolution and stupendous wars. We, by our Supreme Impostor, joined with Austria and Russia, to grab each a portion of that Turkey, whose integrity we had pledged ourselves to maintain; the populations to be handed over like droves of sheep, or shot as insurgents. We, by our mad Harlequin, assumed gratuitously the tremendous and profitless burden (we, staggering already under the burden of India, and the "too vast orb of our fate"!) of a protectorate over that Turkey, whose independence we had equally sworn to maintain; we, by our callous Charlatan, out-Russia'd Russia, deserting the cause of Greece which we specially were bound to vindicate, we having kept her back from enforcing her claims when she could have done so. In brief, we have allied ourselves with all that is blind, deaf, senile, effete, against all that is young, active, vigorous, and promising; we have preferred darkness to light, retrogression to progress, storm to calm, despotism to freedom, falsehood to truth, dishonesty to honesty: we have done all this because by the Parliament we elected we have authorised this prestigious Mountebank to do it for us; and having done it, he comes home to be greeted by applauding crowds, and to announce that he has brought us Peace with Honour! A peace which is no peace, nor even a truce; an Honour of the foulest dishonour. Peace which meant "insurrection" in Bosnia against the Austrians come to take forcible possession, without a shadow of right, but with the connivance of the great predatory Powers, England included; "insurrection" in the old Greek provinces, "insurrection" in the Rhodope districts, an "insurrectionary" league for autonomy in Albania; "insurrectionary" indignation biding its time and opportunity in Montenegria defrauded of what it won, in Greece and Crete defrauded of their rights, in Roumania robbed (by our special collusion) of Besserabia. Honour which meant yielding to Russia, after all our vauntings and menaces, Schouvaloff's* kernel for the shell, essentially all she demanded. The Conference of Berlin was another Harpies' feast, another of those orgies of the great Imperial eagles which are carrion vultures; and in this case the vilest, the most ravenous, the most obscene of the Harpies was England. We have been the best friend of our enemies, the worst enemy of our friends. As if all this Peace were not enough even for our gluttonous Government, we are adding to it a wanton and cowardly war in Afghanistan;† whose "Honour" shines in the burglarious avowal of

*Peter Andreivich Shuvalov (or Schouvaloff) (1827–1889) was the Russian ambassador to London, skillful negotiator with Lord Salisbury during and after the Russo-Turkish War. Contrary to Thomson's impression, after the Congress of Berlin, Russian public opinion considered Shuvalov to have been excessively conciliatory, and reproached him for needlessly giving up advantages won in the war. In 1879 he was replaced as London ambassador.

†This war of 1878–1891 evolved through British fears of Russian designs in Afghanistan, suspicions that were intensified and led to the outbreak of war in

our frontless Premier (we may disregard the pretexts put forward by his underlings), that it is undertaken simply to rectify our frontiers at the expense of our neighbours, the said frontiers being quite secure already! Henceforth let no landholder hesitate to glut his earth-hunger by stealing and enclosing any common land adjacent; he will be simply rectifying his frontiers, substituting scientific for haphazard boundaries; and so carrying out our Imperial principles sanctioned by an overwhelming majority in both Houses of Parliament, consecrated by no fewer than eight of our right Reverend Fathers in God. Was it not in the eternal fitness of things that the man in the Lower House (surely now low enough even for a Grand Vizier) selected to move "that a humble address be presented to Her Majesty thanking Her for Her gracious speech" was *Viscount Castlereagh*? and that his maiden speech in thus moving elicited from his cypher leader the exquisite Tory compliment, "I believe it will be generally felt that the noble lord has broken the ice [would that the Ministry had been drowned in the hole!] in a way which gives us reason to hope that he will sustain the honour of the great name which he bears." (Tory cheers.) No doubt he of the "great name,"*the "carotid-artery-cutting," who before he so righteously cut his own throat had done his worst to cut his country's and liberty's, would have been proud to move such an address in answer to such a speech concocted by such a Cabinet "in Her Majesty's own words" as the lying official formula runs.

This policy of falsehood, dishonesty, and manifold degradation has been and is being carried out at an enormous wanton expenditure during a period of severest commercial depression, affecting more or less gravely every industry of the country — save that of the *chevaliers d'industrie*, whether of the slums, the Press, the clubs, the Stock Exchange, or the purlieus of Parliament; and the prospect of recovery from this depression is still exceedingly dubious and remote, despite the easy optimism,

---

1878 when a Russian mission was accepted at Kabril while a British one was refused.

*Robert Stewart Castlereagh, 2d Marquis of Londonderry (1769–1822), Tory foreign secretary at the time of Waterloo and the Congress of Vienna who committed suicide after his mind became affected from overwork. Thomson undoubtedly knew Shelley's lines from the "Masque of Anarchy" — "I met Murder on the way — / He had a face like Castlereagh."

feigned or unfeigned, but anyhow unsubstantiated, of our Ministers who are our Masters: the only forecast that approaches certainty being that things must get considerably worse before they can begin to get better. And this reckless, unscrupulous, impolitic policy of turbulence and surprises, mysteries and mystifications, keeping the country in continual suspense and alarm, no man knowing what delirious catastrophe the morrow might bring forth, what wild war or onerous engagement, has incalculably aggravated this commercial depression. As Mr. Gladstone said the other day at Woolwich, alluding to the cry of "harassed interests" so perniciously potent at the last General Election: "At the present moment I see but one harassed interest, and that harassed interest is the British nation." Let the hundreds of merchants and thousands of tradesmen now seriously embarrassed or quite ruined, let the myriads of working people and their families now half-starving, reflect with all due gratitude that a very large, and probably the larger, part of their distress and misery and destitution is directly and indirectly owing to the prodigious cost of this interminable Pantomime-Tragedy, wherein the Harlequin they have helped to constitute Dictator revels and shines as the hero, making his Columbine the Queen, whom he first promoted to Empress that she might not be too far beneath the high level of her part. And let these hundreds and thousands and myriads likewise reflect with all due gratitude that although our paternal Government could not spare even a cheap sentence in Her Most Gracious Majesty's speech commiserating their unfantastical sufferings, and although the said sufferings, in Lord Beaconsfield's words, were "not alluded to in the Speech from the Throne because we had no remedial measures to propose"; the same paternal Government, whose unselfish charity neither begins nor ends at home, but which is ever intent on upholding our honour abroad (such Honour as we got with the Peace at Berlin), lost no time in bringing forward a proposal for a vote to relieve the sufferers by the insurrection in the Rhodope Mountains. That is disinterested, noble, at once classical and romantic; not selfish and commonplace and intensely prosaic, as would be the relief of distress in mere Sheffield, Oldham, Burnley, Blackburn, Manchester, and the like grimy towns! Lancashire has grand cause for exultation in the number of Tory members, and even Tory Ministers, it has contributed to our present Legislature!

Yet the financial results of this "Government of Imposition and Impositions," disastrous as they already are, much more disastrous as they threaten to be, are but as the stings of wasps to the stings of scorpions compared with the moral, or rather the immoral. I have not blenched from the fact that such an iniquitous rule is only made possible by the iniquities of the ruled, by the selfishness, corruption and enormous stupidity of those who elect to be thus dominated. But such a Government, once established, becomes in its turn a powerful efficient cause, extending and intensifying all the evils to which it owes its being; every year and month of its continued existence, every fresh unscrupulous triumph it gains over scrupulous opposition, tends to lower yet more the tone of political morality, to discourage the good and encourage the bad, to depress yet further the peaceful and laborious and law abiding citizens—the mainstay of every commonwealth, and to elevate turbulent and thriftless and lawless adventurers—the obscene parasites of every society; in short, to demoralise and degrade the whole community. There is no readier and surer test of the character of a Government than the kinds and classes of the governed that severally rejoice and grieve under it. Of what sort are the men who are blatantly jubilant and arrogant in this our portentous and despicable travesty of an Oriental despotism, with a Grand Vizier slavishly obsequious in outward forms to the Sultana whom he absolutely sways in fact, she, as he told us long since, being morally and physically incapable of herself governing? Our genuine statesmen (we seem to have two or three left)? our great thinkers and writers? our manufacturers and merchants? our shopkeepers, artisans, labourers, peasantry? all those, in brief, who contribute to the wealth and well-being, the stability and genuine grandeur, the wisdom and virtue of our country? Assuredly not these; not the wealth-makers, but the wealth-devourers; not the wise, but the selfishly astute; not the virtuous, but the reckless and vicious; not those who settle, but those who unsettle, a State; not those who make, but those who unmake, a flourishing realm. These are they who exult and triumph: the great lords who have robbed us of our land, at the same time shuffling off its burdens of taxation on to our shoulders; the dignitaries of the adulterous State Church, which has so long embezzled and misused the endowments intended for our national education; all the predatory placemen and wealthy misrepresentatives of the people; all whose families infest, like locusts, the topmost branches of the public service for the public disservice—Army, Navy, Royal Household, Diplomacy, Church, etc., etc., etc.; the swashbucklers of the sword, whose chance of fortune is in bloodshed and rapine; the swashbucklers of the pen, the dregs of journalism, about the very vilest of all vile dregs, shameless sycophants to whom conscience and honour and truth and patriotism are utter mockeries; the dregs of the populace delighting in anarchy; the buffoons of the Music Halls and "comic" Press, and the fools who applaud and echo their blustering buffoonery; the gluttonous gamblers of the Stock Exchange, whose best fishing is in troubled waters; all who are deeply interested in the continuance of obsolete abuses and inveterate wrongs. These have their millennium of beatitude, these are the saintly elect, in this new Avatar of Imperial Charlatanism, which but perished in the man of the 2nd of December and Sedan* to revive in his worthy friend, "the lineal descendent of the impenitent thief on the cross." What plummet can sound the ghastly depths of our ignominy when our patriotic inspiration has come from the laureates and cads of the Music Halls, from the Levites of the *Daily Telegraph*, from the rowdies of Whitechapel and Capel Court, with their so-fit flying emblem, the dead cat?

From of old it has been noted that the professed Conservatives are always the real Revolutionists; therefore we need not wonder that the alien Apostate whom the Tories have been fain to follow in default of leading brains among themselves has strained the constitution almost to snapping-point in order to achieve his ends, and that they have boisterously applauded him in the process. Their late noble and chivalrous leader avowedly took a leap in the dark merely to dish the Whigs, and they would now venture a plunge into the bottomless pit to dish the Radicals—for the Whigs, as we see in their leaders, are dishing themselves most effectually. For myself, I cannot pretend any alarm that this straining of the Constitution to the purposes of Imperialism, this violent wresting of the old political system to Personal Government, will succeed; I feel too sure that the irresistible recoil will follow, and follow soon, clenching the Milo of Toryism in the fatal clench of the British oak. A Queen who for seventeen years has shirked nearly every royal office, save the acceptance

*Napoleon III.

of the Civil List, a Mountebank Mayor of the Palace whose stock of juggleries — sword-swallowing, fire-eating, and all, — is pretty nearly played out, though they may do immense damage in their time, are not very formidable enemies to a Commonwealth not yet effete. What I fear is the unfitness of large and influential masses of the people, if not indeed the main part of the people, for a Democratic Republic when the inevitable recoil from the Charlatan's Imperialism arrives: our lords spiritual and temporal have managed to keep so many of us, and particularly their noble selves, in such dense undisciplined ignorance or worse than ignorance so long! gross ignorance or, worse, gross misunderstanding, of the mutual relations of the various classes in a well-ordered State, of their mutual and common duties, of their common inalienable rights, of the science and art of good citizenship. What ineffable blockheads and bunglers we are in the theory and practice of true statesmanship, true politics, the noble antique discipline of true patriotism, and the yet nobler modern discipline of true internationalism — the comity and solidarity of the Peoples, is proved only too plainly by the single monstrous fact that during these four years past we have been abject and almost impotent under "little Benjamin our ruler," of whom his people's Bible further predicts, "Benjamin shall ravin as a wolf: in the morning he shall devour the prey, and at night he shall divide the spoil." * Wherefore I, though a Republican in principle, am by no means in a hurry for a Democratic Republic in Great Britain, preferring to wait until we are taught and trained into something like fitness for it; and therefore I do not regard the present costly and bloody burlesque of Imperialism with any the less disfavour because it is likely to precipitate the advent of such a Republic. Already, although we hear much lip-loyalty in Parliament and Bumbledom, and read much pen-loyalty in popular newspapers (which always cant to the level of their most idiotic possible respectable readers, the strength of the chain of their circulation being that of its weakest link), I scarcely ever meet with any loyalty in the private political conversation of men. And indeed it would be hard for any man to show how we should suf-

*What a horrible mistake for us the other Israelites committed when they refrained from thoroughly extirpating the whole tribe of Benjamin, as we read in the sweet close of the Holy Book of Judges: — for even to this day Benjamin's mess is five times so much as that of any of his brethren. (Thomson's note.)

fer any loss whatever if the whole Royal Family, with all its attendants and parasites, and with the whole Royal System, evanished to-morrow into eternal Limbo; while nothing is easier than to show that we should gain very much thereby. At any rate, our Queen, suffering herself to be played as a mere Chess-queen in the game of party politics, such a Queen of Sheba to such a Solomon; our Harlequin Renegade aping Napoleon the Little; our Tories with their blustering insolence and arrogant wrong-headedness, who in their brief possession of power show that they have learned nothing and forgotten nothing, who are as imperious in contempt of the people as they are slavish in subservience to their High Priest of the sacrificial mysteries (what would he not sacrifice for a new sensation?); and our effete aristocratic and bureaucratic Whigs, who always grasp at all the spoils of office, and nearly always desert their followers and allies in the day of serious battle; — all these are conspiring to irritate and disgust the People into the extremity of Radicalism. The Queen is not likely to suffer in her time, save in loss of intangible respect; nor the Arch-Impostor in his, for his career is about ended, and he will be highly satisfied to leave the stage in a blaze of fireworks: but the younger Tories and Whigs, who might have had an honourable and influential future? the arrogant Salisbury, who has allowed himself to be dragged in triumph at the chariot wheels of the political adventurer he denounced; Hardy-Cranbrook the bully, and Northcote the weak-kneed and inept; half-hearted Hartington, Forster of the 25th Clause and the false-telegram panic, Goschen, who remembers that his pastoral ancestors had no votes in the land of Goshen; what shall be the future of these?*

*The "arrogant" Salisbury (1830–1903) was Disraeli's foreign secretary at the time of the Congress of Berlin, later prime minister; Hardy-Cranbrook "the bully" was Gathorne-Hardy, 1st Earl of Cranbrook (1814–1906), Disraeli's secretary for war until March, 1878, when he was made secretary for India and supported the Afghanistan war; Northcote "the weak-kneed" was Sir Stafford Henry Northcote (1818–1887), Disraeli's Chancellor of the Exchequer and, in 1876, leader of the House of Commons; "Half-hearted Hartington," Spencer Compton Cavendish, Marquis of Hartington (1833–1908), was leader of the Liberal party in the House of Commons, 1875–1880, and was offered but declined the premiership in 1880; William Edward Forster (1818–1886) is best known for the 1870 Education Act, the 25th clause of which enabled local authorities to pay fees of needy children at denominational schools, thus giving an advantage to church schools, especially in rural districts where there were no board schools; George Joachim Goschen (1831–1907), Liberal statesman and financier who in 1876 was sent to Egypt (Thomson's "Land of Goshen") to investigate its nearly bankrupt financial position.

One immediate or almost immediate practical benefit from this long domination of Benjamin who ravins as a wolf, and thereto cheats like a fox, ought to be Triennial instead of Septennial Parliaments; a subject which will have to be agitated right soon. Seven years' penal servitude is too heavy a punishment for the mistakes of a people in a single General Election; three years' would be quite severe enough in all conscience.

In conclusion, should some of my language dissatisfy any of our readers, I can only confess with the utmost candour that much of it dissatisfies myself because I have not been able to find words that would adequately express the intensity of the indignation, scorn and abhorrence with which I regard the conduct of Him who is our Dictator, of his servile underlings, his slavish supporters, his lying sycophants.

III. Critical Studies and Reviews

Shelley

[*This article was one of Thomson's earliest contributions to the* National Reformer*; it appeared on December 22, 1860, shortly after his twenty-sixth birthday. Thomson was later to reject many of his ideas on the function of poetry and the "inspired" artist, but his interest in Shelley, so exuberantly expressed in this youthful appreciation, never waned. In the 1870's, his lengthy correspondence with William Michael Rossetti was mainly concerned with notations for Rossetti's edition of Shelley; in 1881, just a few months before Thomson's death, his "Notes on the Structure of Shelley's* Prometheus Unbound" *appeared in the* Athenaeum*; and in 1884 Bertram Dobell was able to compile a small volume of Thomson's writings on Shelley,* Shelley, A Poem, With Other Writings Relating to Shelley, by the Late James Thomson (B.V.). *Thomson did not choose to include the essay in* Essays and Phantasies, *but it appears in both* Poems, Essays, and Fragments *and* Biographical and Critical Studies.]

"WHEREFORE I say unto you, all manner of sin and blasphemy shall be forgiven unto men: but the blasphemy against the Holy Ghost shall not be forgiven unto men. And whosoever speaketh a word against the Son of Man, it shall be forgiven him, but whosoever speaketh a word against the Holy Ghost, it shall not be forgiven him; neither in this world, neither in the world to come." Which glorious Scripture we may surely understand to mean, that a man may believe or disbelieve in any book, any historical or legendary personage, any dogmatic formula, and yet be in a state of salvation; that only who rejects and violates the Holy Spirit of love and truth, the Conscience of the World, he cannot (because he will not) be saved. Jesus, though absorbed in his personal mission, could speak this truth of sublime toleration; but eighteen centuries have not taught His disciples the wisdom of believing it and acting upon it. Whom He absolved, they dare condemn.

Probably no man of this century has suffered more and more severely, both in person and reputation, from this rash convictive bigotry than Percy Bysshe Shelley. Florence to the living Dante was not more cruelly unjust than England to the living Shelley. Only now, nearly forty years after his death, do we begin to discern his true glory. It is well that this glory is such as can afford to wait for recognition; that it is one of the permanent stars of heaven, not a rocket to be ruined by a night of storm and rain. I confess that I have long been filled with astonishment and indignation at the manner in which he is treated by the majority of our best living writers. Emerson is serenely throned above hearing him at all; Carlyle only hears him "shriek hysterically"; Mrs. Browning discovers him "blind with his white ideal"; Messrs. Ruskin and Kingsley treat him much as senior schoolboys treat the youngster who easily "walks over their heads" in class—with reluctant tribute of admiration copiously qualified with sneers, pinches, and kicks. Even Bulwer (who, intellectually worthless as he is, now and then serves well as a straw to show how the wind blows among the higher and more educated classes), even Bulwer can venture to look down upon him with pity, to pat him patronisingly on the back, to sneer at him—in "Ernest Maltravers"—with a sneer founded upon a maimed quotation. It was only the other day that a person thought it worth while to send to the *Times* the discovery that Shelley, in his mock-heroic preface to "Peter Bell," had anticipated Macaulay's famous New Zealander!* Now, I do not expect that Shelley—any more than piety and lofty thought and heroic action—will ever be extensively popular; I admit that to himself more than to most poets are his own grand words applicable—"the jury that sits in judgment upon a poet, belonging as he does to all time, must be composed of his peers; it must be impannelled by time from the selectest of the wise of many generations." Yet it was to be expected that men so noble as Kingsley and Ruskin could surrender themselves to generous sympathy with a most noble and generous life, could love and reverence a most loving and reverent spirit; although that life developed itself without the pale of their sanctuary and that spirit dispensed with the theological primer which they conceive necessary to education.

A poet, in our restricted sense of the term, may be defined,

*Macaulay frequently described a ruined London as it would appear to a New Zealander viewing it ages hence; Shelley's dedication to "Peter Bell the Third" similarly describes London in a state of ruin at some distant future date.

an inspired singer; the singing, the spontaneous musical utterance, being essential to the poetical character. Great learning, profound thought, and keen moral insight may all enrich a volume, which shall yet, lacking this instinctive harmony, be no poem. Verse equally with prose may be unpoetic through this fatal want. Through it, George Herbert is almost unread, and the "Heaven and Hell" of Swedenborg is a dull map instead of a transcendent picture; through it—tainting both, but in a less degree—the works of the Brownings are less popular than those of Tennyson, though they in all other noble qualities are so far his superiors.

In musicalness, in free and, as it were, living melody, the poems of Shelley are unsurpassed, and on the whole, I think, unequalled by any others in our literature. Compared with that of most others his language is as a river to a canal—a river ever flowing "at its own sweet will," and whose music is the unpurposed result of its flowing. So subtly sweet and rich are the tones, so wonderfully are developed the perfect cadences, that the meaning of the words of the singing is lost and dissolved in the overwhelming rapture of the impression. I have often fancied, while reading them, that his words were really transparent, or that they throbbed with living lustres. Meaning is therein firm and distinct, but "scarce visible through extreme loveliness"; so that the mind is often dazzled from perception of the surpassing grandeur and power of his creations. I doubt not that Apollo was mightier than Hercules, though his Divine strength was veiled in the splendour of his symmetry and beauty more Divine.

But when we have allowed that a man is pre-eminently a singer, the question naturally follows, What is the matter of his song? Does his royal robe of verse envelop a real king of men, or one who is intrinsically a slave? And here may fitly be adduced Wordsworth's remark, that the style is less the *dress* than the *incarnation* of the thought. Noble features have been informed by ignoble natures, and beautiful language has expressed thoughts impure and passions hateful: great hearts have pulsed in unsightly bodies, and grand ideas have found but crabbed utterance: yet still it is true that generally the countenance is a legible index to the spirit, and the style to the thought.

With this presumption in his favour, we enter upon four inquiries. (1.) What are the favourite subjects of Shelley's song—

great or small? (2.) Is his treatment of these great-minded? (3.) Is it great-hearted? And, rising to the climax, (4.) Is it such as to entitle him to the epithet *inspired*?

(1.) The favourite subjects of Shelley's song, the speculations to which his intellect continually gravitates from the petty interests of the hour, are certainly great and important above all others. (I omit one theme, whose treatment is common to all poets, so that we conceive it as inseparable from the poetic character—the beauty and harmony of the visible universe: in the celebration of which, however, Shelley displays an intense fervour of admiration and love which almost isolates him above his compeers.) The questions concerning the existence of God, the moral law of the universe, the immortality of the soul, the independent being of what is called the material world, the perfectibility of man: these and their kindred perpetually fascinate his mind to their investigation. It may be considered by many—and not without some show of reason—that mere addictedness to discourse on great subjects is no proof of a great mind: crude painters always daub "high art"; adolescent journalists stoop to nothing below epics; nay, Macaulay long since told us that the very speculations of which we speak are distinctive of immaturity both in nations and in men. Nevertheless, believing that the essence of poetry and philosophy is communication with the Infinite and the Eternal, I venture to conclude that to be strongly inclined to such communication is to be gifted with the first requisite for a poet and a philosopher. The valiant heart may prove victorious without the strong arm, but the strong arm without the valiant heart must be beaten ignominiously for ever.

(2.) But have his thoughts and his conceptions a magnanimity befitting these subjects? He upholds strenuously the Manichean doctrine, that the world is the battlefield of a good and an evil spirit, each aboriginal, of whom the evil has been and still is the more powerful, but the good shall ultimately triumph. Let those who scoff so liberally at this account for the existence of evil, and a devil created by an omnipotent, all-holy God. How magnificent is his conception of these hostile powers, symbolised in the eagle and serpent, in the opening of "The Revolt of Islam"; how sublime is it in the "Prometheus Unbound," where they are represented by Jupiter and Prometheus!

He proclaims enthusiastically the Idealism of Plato, of Spinoza, of Berkeley, of Kant. Let those who so stolidly snear at this, expound by what possibility spirit and matter can influence each other without one attribute in common; or let them demonstrate the existence of matter apart from our perception; or let them show, if there be but one existing substance, that it is such as we should call matter rather than spirit. How glorious are his expositions of this philosophy in the "Ode to Heaven" and the speeches of Ahasuerus in "Hellas"!

He devoted himself heart and mind to the doctrine of the perfectibility of human nature, an intrinsic perfectibility to eventuate in a heaven on earth realised by the noble endeavours of man himself; not that which is complacently patronised by many so-called Christians, who are agreed to die and accept a perfect nature as a free gift, when they can no longer live imperfect. As if the severe laws of the universe permitted partial gifts, any more than they permit gainful robberies! Though I must consider Shelley mistaken in this belief, I yet honour and not blame him for it. For his nature must have been most pure and noble, since it could persuade his peculiarly introspective mind of its truth. Right or wrong, it is the very mainspring of his philosophic system. In "Queen Mab," in the "Revolt of Islam," in the "Prometheus Unbound," its expression glows with the solemn inspiration of prophecy. As Scott was the poet of the past, and Goethe of the present, so was Shelley of the future; the thought of whose developed triumphs always kindles him into rapture. However dissident, we cannot but reverence so sublime and unselfish an enthusiasm: perchance, were we more like him in goodness, we should be more like him in faith. Expand the stage from our earth to the universe, the time from one life to an infinite succession of lives; let the *dramatis personæ* be not men only but all living souls; and this catastrophe, if catastrophe there must be, is the most righteous and lofty conclusion ever suggested for the great drama.

Of his opinions concerning the right relations of the sexes, I can only say that they appear to me radically correct. And of his infidelity, that he attacked not so much Christianity as Priestianity—that blind, unspiritual orthodoxy which freezes the soul and fetters the mind, vilifying the holiest essence of all religion. Space being restricted, suffice it to say that in all his thoughts one is struck by a certain loftiness and breadth characteristic of the best minds. It is as if they looked around from the crest of a mountain, with vision unbaffled by the crowd and the chimney-tops. Now, exactly as the height at which a person stands may be calculated from any one object on his horizon as well as from a hundred, so one of these superior thoughts is in itself proof sufficient of an elevated mind. For quantity is the measure of low things, but quality of high. Ten small apples may be worth more than one large; but not any number of small thoughts can equal one great. Ten weak arms may be stronger than one stalwart, but what number of weak minds can equal one that is powerful?

(3.) What moral emotion, pure or impure, noble or mean, generous or selfish, does Shelley effuse through his works? The question has been partly answered already, for, in a poet whose theme is concrete with man and abstract with destiny, the spirit refuses to be analysed into thought and passion, being the identity of the two. Morally, he is indeed sainted. Never yet did man thrill and glow with more love of his fellows, more self-sacrificing sympathy with all life, more hatred of fraud and cruelty—yet hatred interfused with the tenderest pity, more noble independence, candour, and intrepidity, more devoted reverence for goodness and truth. In what is understood by the present age as a truly Christian spirit, he bears comparison with the holiest of Christians. The creeds, the rituals, the ceremonies—those media which common men require to temper the else intolerable splendour of Divine truth—he did not need: his eagle-eye could gaze unblenching upon the cloudless sun; and his life incarnated his poetry. He was his own Prometheus. That fatal *per contra* with which Emerson is obliged to conclude his magnificent summary of Shakespeare cannot be urged against Shelley.* He perceived—who better?—the symbolism of the visible world; he appreciated—who more rapturously?—its Divine beauty; but he did not rest here—he lived higher to the beauty of that which is symbolised, to the beauty which is called "of holiness," to the laws of that realm which is eternal. He was not "master of the revels to mankind," but prophet and preacher. His music was as the harping of David to charm away the evil spirit from Saul.

*Emerson accused Shakespeare of having failed to "explore the virtue" that resides in symbols of nature, of having "converted the elements which waited on his command into entertainments"; Shakespeare "led an obscure and profane life, using his genius for the public amusement."

And thus we have crossed the threshold of our last inquiry—is he entitled, in a high sense, to be called *inspired*? That he was a singer who sang songs beautiful, wise, and pure may be affirmed of many a poet, though of no two with the same emphasis. What is it, then, which differentiates him from the second-class poets, and exalts him to sit with Isaiah and Dante, as one of that small choir of chief singers who are called transcendent? It is that of which I but now spoke; it is that of which he is so often accused under the name of mysticism. I dare affirm that no great writer is less obscure in manner, in expression than he: obscure in matter he is, and ever must be, to those in whom is not developed the faculty correlative to those ideas in whose expression he supremely delights. Were the most of us born deaf, we should reprobate as obscure and mystical those gifted men who dilated upon the ravishment of music. And to the ideal or spiritual harmonies, perfect and eternal, to whose rhythm and melody the universe is attuned, so that it is fitly named Cosmos—to these we *are*, most of us, deaf; and whoever, with reverence and love and rapture, is devoted to their celebration—be it Plato or Swedenborg, Emerson or Shelley—shall for ever to the great mass be as one who is speaking in an unknown tongue, or who is raving of fantasies which have no foundation in reality.

Therefore, the accusations of mysticism but ignorantly affirm that he was most intensely and purely a poet. Plato, in the *Ion* (Shelley's translation) says: "For the authors of those great poems which we admire do not attain to excellence through the rules of any art; but they utter their beautiful melodies of verse in a state of inspiration, and, as it were, *possessed* by a spirit not their own." And again: "For a poet is, indeed, a thing ethereally light, winged, and sacred; nor can he compose anything worth calling poetry until he becomes inspired, and, as it were, mad. . . . For, whilst a man retains any portion of the thing called reason, he is utterly incompetent to produce poetry or to vaticinate." This great truth has been enounced or implied by all true philosophers, though sadly abused by uninspired poetasters, and as obviously obnoxious as the Berkeleyan Idealism to stupid and unavailing sneers. Shelley himself, in that "Defence of Poetry" which is one of the most beautiful prose-pieces in the language, and which, in serene elevation of tone and expanse and subtlety of thought, is worthy of Plato or Emerson, repeatedly and throughout insists upon it as the essential law of poetic creation.

The only true or inspired poetry is always from within, not from without. The experience contained in it has been spiritually transmuted from lead into gold. It is severely logical, the most trivial of its adornments being subservient to and suggested by the dominant idea, any departure from whose dictates would be the "falsifying of a revelation." It is unadulterated with worldly wisdom, deference to prevailing opinions, mere talent or cleverness. Its anguish is untainted by the gall of bitterness, its joy is never selfish, its grossness is never obscene. It perceives always the profound identity underlying all surface differences. It is a living organism, not a dead aggregate, and its music is the expression of the law of its growth; so that it could no more be set to a different melody than could a rose-tree be consummated with lilies or violets. It is most philosophic when most enthusiastic, the clearest light of its wisdom being shed from the keenest fire of its love. It is a synthesis not arithmetical, but algebraical; that is to say, its particular subjects are universal symbols, its predicates universal laws; hence it is infinitely suggestive. It is ever-fresh wonder at the infinite mystery, ever-young faith in the eternal soul. Whatever be its mood, we feel that it is not self-possessed but God-possessed; whether the God came down serene and stately as Jove, when, a swan, he wooed Leda; or with overwhelming might insupportably burning, as when he consumed Semele.

These distinctive marks of the highest poetry I find displayed in the works of Shelley more gloriously than in those of any other poet in our language. As we must study Shakespeare for knowledge of idealised human nature, and Fielding for knowledge of human nature unidealised, and Carlyle's "French Revolution" as the unapproached model of history, and Currer Bell's "Villette" to learn the highest capabilities of the novel, and Ruskin for the true philosophy of art, and Emerson for quintessential philosophy, so must we study, and so will future men more and more study Shelley for quintessential poetry. It was a good nomenclator who first called him the poet of poets.

He was not thirty when he died. Had he but lived for another thirty years? — In the purity of our fervent youth, I think we all consecrate ourselves to an early death; but the gods cannot love us all with a partial love, and most of us must dwindle down through age and decrepitude into the grave. But Shelley, while singing of the millennial future, and chanting beatitudes of our free and pure and love-united posterity, knew with undeceiving prescience that he could not live to see even the first straight steps taken towards the glorious goal. The tomb which he selected and described with almost passionate tenderness in 1821, received his ashes in 1822. And so may we trust that the prophecy of 1821 was fulfilled in 1822: —

> The breath whose might I have invoked in song
> Descends on me; my spirit's bark is driven
> Far from the shore; far from the trembling throng
> Whose sails were never to the tempest given;
> The massy earth and sphered skies are riven!
> I am borne darkly, fearfully afar:
> Whilst burning through the inmost veil of Heaven,
> The soul of Adonais, like a star,
> Beacons from the abodes where the eternal are.

If this meagre essay attracts any worthy student to Shelley, it will fulfil the purpose of its publication, miserably as it fails to fulfil my desire to render honourable tribute of love and gratitude to this poet of poets and purest of men, whose works and life have been to me, from my youth up, a perennial source of delight and inspiration.

Robert Browning's *Men and Women*

[*This essay on Browning was written while Thomson was serving as an army schoolmaster, stationed at St. Helier on the isle of Jersey. It appeared in the* Jersey Independent *(under the signature "T. J.") on February 20, 1862. At that time Thomson's high opinion of Browning was not shared by most reviewers, and in concluding the article he felt it necessary to give a "specimen" of Browning's work. The article actually concludes, then, with a copy of "Evelyn Hope" (here omitted). Apparently not even Bertram Dobell, Thomson's close friend, literary executor, and bibliographer, was aware of the article's existence, and it is here reprinted for the first time. Thomson's admiration for Browning continued throughout his life, and the last two articles he ever published were on Browning (in* Gentleman's Magazine, *December, 1881, and in the* Browning Society's Transactions, *1882). Dobell reprinted both in* Biographical and Critical Studies.]

THE BODY OF Elizabeth Barrett Browning now lies buried, as a soldier's on the field for which he fought,—with those fit emblems of her purity and her fame, the white rose garland at her feet and the crown of laurel at her head—in the land whose cause she pled so nobly, and which has been and still is proving itself worthy of the noblest championship.

Keats and Shelley sleep at Rome,
  She in well-loved Tuscan earth;
Choosing all their death's long home
  Far from their old home of birth:
Italy, you hold in trust
Very sacred English dust!*

Now that the first shock of our bereavement is over, while yet the intensity of interest in everything concerning the Brown-

*This is the third stanza of Thomson's own memorial poem, "E. B. B.," written in 1861.

ings which that bereavement excited among all lovers of genuine poetry is but little abated, it seems to me a fit time to consider carefully the literary worth of Robert Browning. I choose for special consideration the last published of his works, *Men and Women*; two volumes from which a young friend of mine, whose character and ability command profound respect wherever they are known, informed me that he had derived a more powerful moral and intellectual stimulus than even from that history of histories – Carlyle's *French Revolution*.

I am aware that Browning is not a popular poet; but upon whom does this fact cast more reproach, upon him or upon the world of readers? In my poor opinion, undoubtedly upon the latter. The one great fault with which nearly all his readers concur to charge him is obscurity. Few, if any, deny that the richest materials of poetry,—profound and original thought, keen perceptions, knowledge both broad and deep, clear moral insight, wonderful dramatic ability, and passion of the true white heat, abound throughout his works: but on the other hand as few will admit that these materials are thoroughly wrought into the poetic form and brightness which is beauty; it is generally affirmed that his "creations" are not cosmic, but only half-developed from chaos. Although many of the objectors would be fairly answered by the retort that they have no right to a voice in the matter since they have never *studied* him, being wont to lounge over literature as languidly as if they were inhaling perfumes; it must still be admitted that the broad superstructure of this objection is supported by a certain basis of truth. Beauty is not so supreme in his as it should be in all poetry; and it is not, chiefly because of his restlessness of mind, resulting from the strength and activity of his talents as distinguished from, and often rebellious against, his genius. The keen and rapid eye, when it should be fixed upon some sole central figure, remarks every minute object quiescent or stirring about it; the word-rich mouth rattles on with lively cleverness when its speech should be solemn and slow; the vigorous and learned mind, when it should be concentrated on one supreme idea, courses about through the world and the libraries after remote and subsidiary and often merely distracting thoughts. So that it may be fairly asserted that his talents often run away with his genius, or—adopting the magnificent language of Coleridge in reference to Shakespeare—that "the intellectual power and the creative energy wrestle as in a war-embrace."

This restlessness of mind—so inimical to the attainment of that exclusive concentration which, whether serene or impassioned, is the loftiest mood of the poet—is evidenced in many ways, and with peculiar prominence in his rhymed verses. Now it cramps up a good thought into a bad line in its haste to be dealing with another, now it hurries off for the matter of a simile or metaphor into regions so remote that one is puzzled to make out the similarity, anon it perturbs the stream of narrative with sudden exclamations and interrogations like rocks and snags; and soon after we find it throwing off a long succession of rapid, noisy, clattering syllables, about as pronounceable as "Peter Piper picked a peck of pepper," with the mischievous delight of a schoolboy. Nay, the very measures of these rhymed verses nearly all run in a sort of canter, curvetting and prancing on trochaic and anapestic feet.

But some critics (I remember especially a leagued couple in that *Fraser* for which Kingsley used to write poetical critiques!) have found out that his roughness and obscurity are not intellectual, but moral faults, that they are the result of laziness and the lack of conscientious reverence for the Giver of his precious gifts; that he gives out his mind after the fashion in which Carlyle found certain papers given out or edited—"as one might edit a cart-load of stones, by tilting up the cart!" To this charge the best reply is a short passage of his own, in the "Easter Day."

—And if any blame me,
Thinking that merely to touch in brevity
On the topics I dwell on is unlawful;
Or worse, that I trench with undue levity
On the bounds of the holy and the awful;
I praise the heart, and pity the head of him,
And refer myself to Thee instead of him
Who head and heart alike discernest,—
Looking below light speech we utter,
When the frothy spume and the frequent sputter
Prove that the soul's depths boil in earnest.

However, with regard to *Men and Women*, I dare assert that no person of fair intelligence and enough love of poetry to be willing to expend *study* on it, will be baffled in this work by obscurity. It is in fact less obscure than almost any play of Shakespeare or any book of *Paradise Lost*. But a scene may be little worth gazing at, even though unclouded: what positive merits, beyond those implied in this negative one, is the reader to look for? Let me mention one or two of the leading characteristics.

First, the bold, vigorous, healthy spirit; the sterling and complete manhood, interested in the world and able to hold its own in any sphere of it, which is akin to the spirit of Chaucer and the great Elizabethan dramatists. It has been remarked that to read Fielding after Richardson is like emerging from a sick chamber into the free light and air of the open fields; and the remark well applies to the reading of Browning after almost any of our popular poets. They are morbid, melancholy, miserable, neither at home in this world nor likely to be at home in the next; he is genial and joyous in that full and free exercise of his faculties here which is surely the best preparation for whatever world he shall go to hereafter. He has illustrated this difference in a remarkable passage of "Bishop Blougram's Apology." Hence his poems are rich in facts, and his loftiest idealizations are embodied in that Shakespearian flesh and blood reality which is so cordial a contrast to the vague, dim, spectral productions of all but the supreme mystics.

Second, the intensity of the love inspiring many of the poems. Undoubtedly much of this is due to his marriage with the noble woman whose loss we all deplore. No one who has read with feeling her *Sonnets from the Portuguese* can forget the solemn rapture, the devotional fervour, with which she therein utters love; and they have in this work their true antiphonies. The love is so intense and all-absorbing, that when its pure fire has wholly consumed this world and life it flings out its electric flames into the infinite future, thrilling along the endless lifeline of the immortal married souls.

Third, the profound and unsectarian Christianity. Many good people, subject from their childhood to religious influences and quite content with their Bible and a few commonplace pious books, have scarcely any conception of the missionary value of such authors as the Brownings in upholding the sway of Christianity over the minds of young and thoughtful persons who turn with contempt from the abounding trash of tracts, and find most clergymen's books vitiated by the special pleading of hired advocates, and scarcely meet with a minister liberal and wise enough to command their intellectual esteem, and know that modern erudition has beaten down and undermined many of what were once considered main bulwarks and buttresses of the Church, and above all ponder frequently on the fact that not a few of those living writers whom they most revere—men like Carlyle and Emerson, Francis Newman and Froude—have found the Christian formula too strait to cover the whole of now-known truth.

Though these remarks must be very brief, I cannot conclude them without a few words on some of the principal poems in *Men and Women.*

"Saul," in which David relates how he released the first monarch of Israel from the power of the evil spirit, and the "Letter of Karshish, the Arab physician," concerning Lazarus whom Jesus had raised from the dead, may well compare in sublime spirituality and intense imagination with any poems in the language.

"Fra Lippo Lippi," the gloriously genial, and "Andrea del Sarto," the bitterly sad, wonderfully bring to life the two great painters of whom they treat. These, with the letter of Karshish and another of Cleon who is a sort of Greek Goethe, are in blank verse; a metre which Browning always uses with consummate skill and power, without any of that harsh abruptness which deforms some of his rhymed verses. In the same measure are also the half-ironical, trenchant (with both edges) "Apology of Mr. Worldly Wise-man Bishop Blougram," the vigorous dramatic scenes of "In a Balcony," and the quaint description of a poet, entitled "How it Strikes a Contemporary."

"Childe Roland to the Dark Tower Came" is developed from the line in *Lear,* as was Tennyson's "Mariana in the Moated Grange" from a line in *Measure for Measure,* but with far less of precise suggestion in its germ. It is a series of pictures very powerful, weird and Rembrandt-like, elevated above grotesqueness by the stern heroic fortitude of the Childe. It has nothing in common with the yet grander old Scottish ballad of Childe Roland. The "Statue and the Bust," written in a peculiar *terza rima*—with mingled iambics and anapaests giving a sway and sweep to the lines which carry us buoyantly over long years, narrates and moralizes superbly a Florentine historiette. "A Toccata of Galuppi's" makes the music interpret the Venice in and for which the artist composed, the Venice of luxury and debauchery, masks and stilettos, that later Venice against which Ruskin had already hurled the thunders of his fierce wrath and contempt. "Mesmerism" details process and result with such vivid verisimilitude that one can hardly help believing that it narrates an actual experience.

The purely love-poems are very many, and among them must be counted the "In a Balcony" already noticed. Besides this are "Love Among the Ruins," transcendently beautiful; "The Last Ride Together," "One Way of Love," "In Three Days," "In a Year," "Love in a Life," "Life in a Love," "On the Campagna," "The Lovers' Quarrel," "Respectability," "A Woman's Last Word," all vehemently impassioned; "The Serenade at the Villa," stern and almost fierce in rhythm, brief with the conciseness of despair; "At the Fireside," which we may account as directly addressing Mrs. Browning; "Any Wife to Any Husband," the solemn, yearning, hoping-against-hope appeal of a dying wife to her husband to be constant in love for her until their reunion in heaven, which it is inexpressibly mournful to read now; and, fitly concluding the work, an Address to E. B. B.

I find that I have omitted "The Guardian Angel," which is an exposition of a picture by Guercino at Fano, and whose stanza for solemn and pathetic beauty is the finest of all used in the volumes.*

Finishing this very rough and imperfect notice, I confess that the Brownings are for me the two great poets of this generation. In all the loftiest qualities and faculties of our nature I know no other bard—no one devoted to metrical expression—who comes near them. Tennyson is a rare "literary luxury" for us all, and especially for our youths and maidens; but Robert Browning is indeed the poet of Men and Women.

*This stanza is the one Thomson used some eight years later in writing the odd-numbered sections of "The City of Dreadful Night."

The Poems of William Blake

[*This essay was written in 1864, shortly after the publication of Alexander Gilchrist's* Life of William Blake, *and was published in the* National Reformer *in four installments (January 14, 21, 28, February 4, 1866). It thus predates Swinburne's famous 1868 essay in recognizing Blake's position as a major English poet. Although the essay was later reprinted* in Shelley, A Poem, *in* Poems, Essays, and Fragments, *and in* Biographical and Critical Studies, *Thomson himself did not include it in* Essays and Phantasies. *His enthusiasm for Blake faded somewhat in the 1870's when he came to realize that Blake "never grasps or cares for the common world of reality." Section XVIII of "The City of Dreadful Night," in which Thomson denies the possibility of escape into a world of innocence, shuts the door on what he came to think of as the "diseased" Blake. (See George M. Harper, "Blake's* Nebuchadnezzar *in 'The City of Dreadful Night,'"* SP, L [Jan., 1953], *68–80.)*]

> "I assert for myself that I do not behold the outward creation, and that to me it is hindrance, and not action. . . . I question not my corporeal eye any more than I would question a window concerning a sight. I look through it, and not with it."

> The angel who presided at my birth
> Said: Little creature, formed of joy and mirth,
> Go, love without the help of anything on earth.

Before the publication of these volumes* I knew but one of Blake's poems, that on the Human Form, or Divine Image,

*"Life of William Blake, *Pictor Ignotus*, with Selections from his Poems and other Writings." By the late Alexander Gilchrist, author of the "Life of William Etty." Illustrated from Blake's own works, in facsimile, by W. J. Linton, and in photolithography, with a few of Blake's original plates. In 2 vols. London: Macmillan & Co., 1863.

I give the full title, in recommending the work to all good readers. The first volume contains the Life and a noble supplementary chapter by Mr. D. G. Rossetti; the second volume contains the Selections, admirably edited by Mr. D. G. Ros-

quoted by James John Garth Wilkinson in his great work.* The wisdom and the celestial simplicity of this little piece prepared one to love the author and all that he had done; yet the selections from his poems and other writings were a revelation far richer than my hopes. Not only are these selections most beautiful in themselves, they are also of great national interest as filling up a void in the cycle of our poetic literature. I had long felt, and probably many others had felt, that much of the poetry of the present and the last age *must* have had an antecedent less remote in time than the Elizabethan works, and less remote in resemblance than the works of Cowper and Burns; yet, since Macaulay's essay on Byron appeared, Cowper and Burns—and in general these two only—had been continually named as the heralds of that resurrection of her poetry which makes glorious for England the crescent quarter of the nineteenth century. A third herald of that resurrection was undoubtedly William Blake; and although he was scarcely listened to at all, while his colleagues held in attention the whole kingdom, the fact may at length be recognised that by him, even more clearly than by them, was anticipated and announced both the event now already past and the event still in process of evolution.

If it be objected that one who was scarcely listened to at all could not exercise much influence, the reply is that we are concerned not with the influence, but with the accuracy and period of the presage. It is written that mankind did not heed Noah, or heeded only to mock, during the six-score years in which he foretold the Flood and built the Ark ready for it. If the Flood really came as he foretold, it attested the truth of his inspiration; but no one now would think that his prophecies were instrumental in accomplishing their own fulfilment, although this opinion must have been general among those who were being submerged. Or we may answer, applying a metaphor which has been with good reason much used, that the mountain-peaks which in any district first reflect the rays of the dawn exercise little or no influence on the dawn's development, even in rela-

setti, with the assistance of Mr. W. M. Rossetti. There is magnificent prose as well as poetry in the selections, and the engravings in themselves are worth more than most books. (Thomson's note.)

**The Human Body and Its Connexion with Man*. For Garth Wilkinson, see note on p. 131.

tion to the country around them; they cast some glimmer of light into obscure valleys below (whose obscurity, on the other hand, their shadows make trebly deep when the sun is sinking); they prophesy very early of the coming noontide; we may judge as to their positions and altitudes by the periods of their reflection; but the dawn would grow and become noon, and the noon would sink and become night, just the same if they were not there. So the Spirit of the Ages, the *Zeitgeist,* is developed universally and independently by its own mysterious laws throughout mankind; and the eminent men from whom it first radiates the expression of what we call a new aspect (the continuous imperceptible increments of change having accumulated to an amount of change which we can clearly perceive, and which even our gross standards are fine enough to measure), the illustrious prototypes of an age, really cast but a faint reflex upon those beneath them; and while pre-eminently interesting in biography, are of small account in history except as prominent indices of growth and progress and decay, as early effects, not efficient causes. They help us to read clearly the advance of time; but this advance they do not cause any more than the gnomon of a sundial causes the procession of the hours which it indicates, or a tidal-rock the swelling of the seas whose oncoming is signalled in white foam around it and in shadowed waters over it.

The message of Cowper has been heard (it was not a very great announcement, and he uttered it neatly and distinctly and honestly), has been laid to heart by the many for whom it was sufficient, and is now in due season passing out of mind with the fulfilment of its purpose. Very little of his poetry can be expected to survive our century. Burns will live with the language; but it must be remembered that his poetry is not blossom and promise; it is consummate fruition; it points to the past more than to the future; it is the genial life, the heroism, the history, the song of his whole people for ages, gathered up and sublimated in and by one supreme man. This King of Scotland happened to come in the guise of a herald to England, but none the less was he a king, the last and greatest of a glorious line; and no other majesty than his own was behind the messenger. Shakespeare made perfect the English drama, and there has arisen no English drama since; Burns made perfect Scottish song, and there has arisen no Scottish song since. When the genius of a nation has attained (human) perfection in any one form and mode, it leaves to ambitious mediocrity all future rivalry with that monumental perfection, itself seeking to become perfect in some new form or mode.

Blake's first volume of poetry was printed (one cannot add *published*) in 1783, about the same time as the first volume of Cowper and a little before that of Burns; Crabbe's first popular poem, "The Village," was printed in the same year. Seventeen years afterwards, Hayley was in high repute, and Blake went to live near him to engrave illustrations for some of his works. The "Lyrical Ballads" of Coleridge and Wordsworth did not appear until 1798; "The Lay of the Last Minstrel" until 1805. Byron was born in 1788, Shelley in 1792, Keats in 1796. The poems in this first volume had been written by Blake in the interval, 1768–1777, between the ages of eleven and twenty years.

Never, perhaps, was a book of verse printed more strange to the literature of its period; and one scarcely knows whether to account the novelty more or less wonderful because relative and not absolute, because the novelty of the long dead past come back to life rather than of a new future just born. The spirit of the great Elizabethan Age was incarnate once more, speaking through the lips of a pure and modest youth. "My Silks and Fine Array" might have been written by Shakespeare, by Beaumont and Fletcher, or by Sir Walter Raleigh. Its sweet irregular artless cadences are not more different from the sharp measured metallic ring of the rhymes of the scholars of Pope, than is its natural sentiment from the affected sentimentalities then in the mode. Of all the other eighteenth century writers, I think Chatterton alone (as in the Dirge in "Ella") has anything kindred to it; and Chatterton was archaic consciously and with intent. The "Mad Song" immediately reminds us of the character assumed by Edgar in *Lear* (a common character in Shakespeare's time, else Edgar would not have assumed it), and of the old Tom o' Bedlam songs. In the fine specimen of these, preserved by the elder Disraeli in his "Curiosities of Literature," three main elements can easily be distinguished: the grotesque but horrible cry of misery wrung from the heart of the poor, half-witted, cruelly treated vagabond; the intentional fooling of the beggar and mountebank, baiting for the charity that is caught with a laugh in its mouth, maddening for his bread; the genuine lunacy of a wild and over-excited imagination, ungoverned so long that it is now quite ungovernable. The first gives us such lines as these: –

In the lovely lofts of Bedlam,
In stubble soft and dainty;
  Brave bracelets strong,
  Sweet whips ding-dong,
And a wholesome hunger plenty.

The second such as these: –

Of thirty bare years have I
Twice twenty been ragèd;
  And of forty been
  Three times fifteen
In durance soundly cagèd.

The third such as these, which Edgar Allan Poe (a fine artist even in the choice of his mottoes) prefixed to his "Unparalleled Adventure of one Hans Pfaall" –

With a heart of furious fancies
Whereof I am commander;
  With a burning spear,
  And a horse of air,
To the wilderness I wander.

Or these: –

I know more than Apollo;
For oft when he lies sleeping,
  I behold the stars
  At mutual wars,
And the rounded welkin weeping.

As Tom o' Bedlams did not wander the country when Blake wrote, the elements of vagabondage and montebankism are not in his piece; but as an expression of lunacy – the government of reason overthrown, and wild imagination making the anarchy more anarchic by its reign of terror – it is thoroughly of the old Elizabethan strain. Here is a stanza which Edgar might have sung in the storm by the hovel on the heath: –

Like a fiend in a cloud,
  With howling woe

After night I do crowd,
    And with night will go;
I turn my back to the East
Whence comforts have increased;
For light doth seize my brain
With frantic pain.

Mark the appalling power of the verb *crowd*, revealing, as by a lightning-flash, the ruins of sane personality, haunted and multitudinous, literally *beside itself*. Not one poet in twenty would have dared to use the word thus, and yet (although a careless reader might think it brought in merely for the sake of the rhyme) it was the very word to use. The address "To the Muses," sweet, calm, and masterly, as if the matured utterance of a conviction well pondered and of no recent date, yet written by a mere boy, embodies the essence of all that Coleridge, Wordsworth, Keats, and Shelley, many years afterwards, taught and sang in vindication of Pre-Drydenism.

The poems in blank verse "To the Evening Star," "To Spring," and "To Summer," are perhaps even more wonderful than those in rhyme, considering the age of the writer and the epoch of our literature in which they were produced. With the exception of the "Ode to Evening," I do not remember any blank verse of the century at all similar to them in tone. And the Ode of Collins, fine as it is, suffers greatly in the comparison with them; for it does not reach their noble breadth of conception and execution, and it is not quite free from then current affectations. These pieces are not perfect in art, but they are perfect in the spirit of their art; they have certain laxities and redundances of rhythm, and are here and there awkward in diction, but such youthful sweet errors rather grace than spoil "that large utterance of the early gods." They have the grandeur of lofty simplicity, not of laboured pomp, a grandeur like that which invests our imaginations of the patriarchs. By a well beneath a palm tree, stands one who wears but a linen turban and a simple flowing robe, and who but watches browsing sheep and camels drinking; yet no modern monarch, however gorgeously arrayed and brilliantly surrounded, can compare with him in majesty.

The Selections from the first volume printed by Blake include extracts from a dramatic work, "Edward the Third." It was an attempt to revive the great English Historical Drama, an attempt which failed, and of which all repetitions are pretty sure to fail; the English Historical Drama flourished in a period whose history was itself dramatic, and such a period is not likely to revolve again on our England. But one piece from this drama I must quote at length, and it is hardly rash to prophesy that this same piece will be quoted at length for many generations to come in all worthy books of specimens of the choicest British poetry. The time is the eve of Cressy; the scene is the camp of Edward: a minstrel sings: —

> O Sons of Trojan Brutus, clothed in war,
> Whose voices are the thunder of the field,
> . . . .
> Your ancestors came from the fires of Troy
> (Like lions roused by lightning from their dens,
> Whose eyes do glare against the stormy fires),
> Heated with war, filled with the blood of Greeks,
> With helmets hewn, and shields covered with gore;
> In navies black, broken with wind and tide.
>
> They landed in firm array upon the rocks
> Of Albion: they kissed the rocky shore:
> "Be thou our mother and our nurse," they said,
> "Our children's mother; and thou shalt be our grave,
> The sepulchre of ancient Troy, from whence
> Shall rise cities, and thrones, and awful powers."
>
> Our fathers swarm from the ships. Giant voices
> Are heard from out the hills; the enormous sons
> Of Ocean run from rocks and caves; wild men
> Naked, and roaring like lions, hurling rocks,
> And wielding knotty clubs, like oaks entangled,
> Thick as a forest ready for the axe.
>
> Our fathers move in firm array to battle;
> The savage monsters rush like roaring fire,
> Like as a forest roars with crackling flames
> When the red lightning borne by furious storm
> Lights on some woody shore, and the parched heavens
> Rain fire into the molten raging sea.
> . . . .
> Our fathers, sweating, lean on their spears and view
> The mighty dead: giant bodies streaming blood,
> Dread visages frowning in silent death.
>
> Then Brutus speaks, inspired; our fathers sit
> Attentive on the melancholy shore.

Hear ye the voice of Brutus: "The flowing waves
Of Time come rolling o'er my breast," he said,
"And my heart labours with futurity.
Our sons shall rule the empire of the sea.

"Their mighty wings shall stretch from East to West;
Their nest is in the sea, but they shall roam
Like eagles for their prey. . . .
. . . .
"Our sons shall rise from thrones in joy, each one
Buckling his armour on; Morning shall be
Prevented* by the gleaming of their swords,
And Evening hear their songs of victory.
. . . .
"Freedom shall stand upon the cliffs of Albion,
Casting her blue eyes over the green ocean;
Or, towering, stand upon the roaring waves,
Stretching her mighty spear o'er distant lands,
While with her eagle wings she covereth
Fair Albion's shore and all her families."

This is the song of the Minstrel as given in the Selections. I have the highest esteem for the taste and judgment of Mr. Dante G. Rossetti, and the whole reading public owes him no common debt of gratitude for his work in the second volume as well as for the supplementary chapter in the first. It is probable, it is almost certain, that he has published quite as much of Blake's poetry and prose as it was prudent to publish experimentally after the neglect of eighty years. But if the above interlineal points mark omissions, the omitted passages should be reinstated in the next edition; the whole of this song, as it stands in Blake's earliest volume or in manuscript, should be given at any rate in an appendix if not in the body of the work. For this chant belongs to the whole British people; it is one of the most precious among the most precious heirlooms bequeathed to us by our forefathers; it is a national jewel of such magnificence that no one man, however honest and skilful, can be trusted to cut it and set it in accordance with his private opinion.

We English are surely a strange people. Pictures beyond price are bequeathed to us, and our first step towards disposing of them satisfactorily is to bury them away where they cannot be

**Prevented,* I need hardly say, is used here in the old sense of *anticipated.* (Thomson's note.)

seen. A song is chanted for us which should thrill and swell every native heart with patriotic pride, a song great with the grandeur of our national life and history for three millenniums of legends and annals and journals, a song heroic as Cressy, sublime as Trafalgar; and for fourscore years we leave it to that oblivion of oblivions which has never had any remembrance. The poet lives forty years after giving this glorious song to his people, devotedly loyal to his highest inspirations, pure, poor, obscure; and when he dies, it is here and there casually remarked that a clever madman has at length reached the sanity of the grave. Again forty years come and go ere a few admirers worthy of him they admire can venture with much diffidence (surely but too well founded!) to bespeak the favour of his people for this song, in which he has added a great and burning light to their illustrations the most splendid, and for other songs in which he has given them the seed whose harvest is likely to be the wealth and spiritual subsistence of generations yet unborn.

When Blake wrote this, however young in years, he was undoubtedly mature; as Keats when he wrote "Hyperion," as Shelley when he wrote "Adonais," or "The Triumph of Life." We shall all soon know it by heart, and cherish it in our hearts, with the speeches of Henry at Agincourt and the "Scots Wha Hae" of Burns, with Campbell's "Mariners of England," and Robert Browning's "Home Thoughts from the Sea"; and then we shall feel and know that for us it is perfect beyond criticism, except the criticism of reverend interpretation. It is Titanic, and it cleaves to its mother earth like a Titan, like a mountain, like a broad oak-tree; and the grandeur of its strength is the grandeur of a gnarled oak whose vigorous life bursts through all conventional symmetries, the grandeur of a mountain which the central fires have heaved into lines enormous and savagely irregular.

Many years afterwards, in 1789, when Blake was thirty-two, the "Songs of Innocence" appeared; and we learn from them the strange fact that he who was mature in his childhood and youth became in his manhood a little child. A little child, pure in soul as the serenest light of the morning, happy and innocent as a lamb leaping in the meadows, singing all its joy in the sweetest voice with that exquisite infantine lisp which thrills the adult heart with yearning tenderness.* The "Introduction," "The

*"Let the reader try to breathe like a child, and let the auditors of the breath decide whether he succeeds or no. There is indeed in adult breath such a peopling

Lamb," "The Chimney Sweeper," the "Laughing Song," "A Cradle Song," "Holy Thursday," "Infant Joy," "The Divine

---

of multitudinous thoughts, such a tramp of hardness and troubles, as does not cede to the attempt to act the infantine even for a moment." (Dr. J. J. Garth Wilkinson, "The Human Body and Its Connexion with Man," p. 98, note.) What is true of common breathing, is true more conspicuously of breathing idealised and harmonised, of the breathing of song in which psychical have superseded the physical rhythms. The adult cannot sing like a child; but Blake in these Songs does so: he did not *act* the infantine, for he *was* infantine, by a regeneration as real while as mysterious as ever purest saint experienced in the religious life. And this regeneration, so far as we can learn, was effected without the throes of agony and doubt and despair, which the saints all pass through in being born again.

I am merely writing a few remarks on the poet, not sketching the life and character of the man; but I may be allowed to call the attention of readers to this wonderful life and character. Blake was always poor in world's wealth, always rich in spiritual wealth, happy and contented and assured, living with God. As to his soul's salvation, I do not believe that he ever gave it a thought, any more than a child thinks of the question whether its loving parents will continue to feed and clothe and cherish it. He had none of the feverish raptures and hypochondriac remorses which even in the best of those who are commonly called saints excite a certain contemptuous pity in the midst of love and admiration: he was a thoroughly healthy and happy religious soul, whose happiness was thoroughly unselfish and noble. As to the "Christian Evidences," as they are termed, of which the mass of good people are so enamoured, in trying to argue themselves and others into a sort of belief in a sort (and such a sort!) of deity, he would have no more dreamed of appealing to them than he would have tried elaborately to argue himself into belief in the existence of the sun. "I feel the warmth, I see the light and see by the light: what do you want to argue about? You may call it sun, moon, comet, star, or Will-o'-the-Wisp, if so it pleases you; all I know and care for is this, that day by day it warms and lights me." Such would have been the sum of his reply to any questioner; for he was emphatically a seer, and had the disdain of all seers for the pretensions of gropers and guessers who are blind. Like Swedenborg, he always relates things heard and seen; more purely a mystic than Swedenborg, he does not condescend to dialectics and scholastic divinity. Those who fancy that a dozen stony syllogisms seal up the perennial fountain of our deepest questionings, will affirm that Blake's belief was an illusion. But an illusion constant and self-consistent and harmonious with the world throughout the whole of a man's life, wherein does this differ from a reality? Metaphysically we are absolutely unable to prove any existence: we believe that those things really exist which we find pretty constant and consistent in their relations to us — a very sound practical but very unsound philosophical belief. Blake and Swedenborg and other true mystics (Jesus among them) undoubtedly had senses other than ours; it is as futile for us to argue against the reality of their perceptions as it would be false in us to pretend that our perceptions are the same. As, however, Blake was supremely a mystic, it is but fair to add that he (and the same may be affirmed of Jesus) was unlike common Christians as thoroughly as he was unlike common atheists; he lived in a sphere far removed from both. In the clash of the creeds, it is always a comfort to remember that sects with their sectaries, orthodox and heterodox, could not intersect at all, if they were not in the same plane. Blake's esteem for argumentation may be read in one couplet: —

If the sun and moon should doubt
They'd immediately go out. (Thomson's note.)

Image"; what holy and tender and beautiful babe-lullabies, babe joy-songs, are these! The ideal Virgin Mother might have sung them to her infant; lambs and doves and flowers might comprehend them; they are alone in our language, which they glorify by revealing its unsuspected treasures of heavenly innocence and purity. I transcribe one of the shortest of them, "Infant Joy"; a sudden throb of maternal rapture which we should have thought inarticulate—expressible only by kisses and caresses and wordless cradle-crooning—marvellously caught up and rendered into song.

"I have no name,
I am but two days old."
    What shall I call thee?
"I happy am,
Joy is my name."
    Sweet joy befall thee.

Pretty joy!
Sweet joy but two days old,
    Sweet joy I call thee:
Thou dost smile,
I sing the while,
    Sweet joy befall thee.

Five years later come the "Songs of Experience," and the singer is an older child, and even a youth, but not yet a man. The experience is that of a sensitive and thoughtful boy, troubled by the first perceptions of evil where he has believed all good, thinking the whole world cruel and false since some playmate-friend has turned unkind, seeing life all desolate and blank since some coveted object has disappointed in the possession; in short, through very lack of experience, generalising one untoward event into a theory of life that seems more bitterly hopeless than grey-haired cynical pessimism. Even the "Garden of Love," "The Human Abstract," "The Two Songs," "To Tirzah," and "Christian Forbearance" (one of the keenest arrows of Beelzebub shot straight back with wounding scorn at the evil-archer), are not in thought and experience beyond the capacity of meditative boyhood. "The Tiger" is a magnificent expression of boyish wonder and admiring terror; "The Crystal Cabinet" is a fairy dream of early youth; "The Golden Net" is a fine dream of adolescence. Perhaps in only three more of his briefer poems do we find Blake mature (it must be borne in mind that his second maturity unfolded itself in pictures rather than songs); "Broken Love," "Auguries of Innocence," and the Letter in verse, dated from Felpham, to his friend, Mr. Butts. These are mature as to their conception, as to the amount and quality of experience and thought involved in them, but occasionally very immature in execution. There is, indeed, one piece of twenty lines mature in every respect, although written so late as 1807: I mean the verses to Queen Charlotte with his illustrations of Blair's "Grave": –

The door of death is made of gold,
That mortal eyes cannot behold;
But when the mortal eyes are closed,
And cold and pale the limbs reposed,
The soul awakes and wondering sees
In her mild hand the golden keys.
The grave is Heaven's golden gate,
And rich and poor around it wait:
O Shepherdess of England's Fold,
Behold this gate of pearl and gold!

To dedicate to England's Queen
The visions that my soul hath seen,
And by her kind permission bring
What I have borne on solemn wing
From the vast regions of the grave,
Before her throne my wings I wave,
Bowing before my sovereign's feet:
The Grave produced these blossoms sweet
In mild repose from earthly strife,
The blossoms of eternal life!

And here are a few more lines almost as majestically mature as one of his inventions for the "Books of Job": –

Jesus sat in Moses' chair;
They brought the trembling woman there:
Moses commands she be stoned to death;
What was the sound of Jesus' breath?
He laid his hands on Moses' law:
The ancient heavens in silent awe,
Writ with curses from pole to pole,
All away began to roll:
"To be good only, is to be
A God, or else a Pharisee."

The man who wrote this might well proclaim: "I touch the heavens as an instrument to glorify the Lord."

"Broken Love" needs no comment here: Mr. W. M. Rossetti has done the best that could be done by the most subtle and patient sympathy to interpret it. I subjoin half-a-dozen lines from the "Auguries of Innocence": —

> A Robin red-breast in a cage
> Puts all Heaven in a rage;
> A dove-house full of doves and pigeons
> Shudders Hell through all its regions;
> A skylark wounded on the wing
> Doth make a cherub cease to sing.

It has been objected (strangely enough, in *Macmillan's Magazine*) to such couplets as these, that they express a truth with such exaggerated emphasis as wholly to distort it, as to make it virtually an untruth. No objection could be more unwise, for it is the result of reading the author's intention precisely *backwards*. His object was not to expand a small fact into a universal truth, but to concentrate the full essence of a universal truth into a small fact. He was intent on making great laws portable, not little events insupportable. "Are not two sparrows sold for a farthing? and one of them shall not fall to the ground without your Father. But the very hairs of your head are all numbered." — "But I say unto you, That every idle word that men shall speak, they shall give account thereof in the Day of Judgment." "For verily I say unto you, If ye have faith as a grain of mustard-seed, ye shall say unto this mountain, Remove hence to yonder place; and it shall remove; and nothing shall be impossible unto you." "But whoso shall offend one of these little ones which believe in Me, it were better for him that a millstone were hanged about his neck, and that he were drowned in the depth of the sea." These texts from the mouth of one of the sublimest of mystics realise the very same object in the very same manner. The sharply cut symbol leaves a distinct and enduring impression, where the abstract dogma would have perhaps made no impression at all. Briefly, in almost every couplet of his poem, Blake has attempted what all profound poets and thinkers have ever most earnestly attempted — to seize a rude but striking image of some sovereign truth, and to stamp it with roughest vigour on the commonest metal for universal circulation. To such attempts we owe all the best proverbs in the world; the abounding small currency of our intellectual commerce, more invaluably essential to our ordinary daily business than nuggets of gold, than rubies, and pearls, and diamonds.

As to the longer poems produced after the "Songs of Experience" — "Visions of the daughters of Albion, Europe, Jerusalem, Ahania, Urizen, &c.," — the Selections given by Mr. Gilchrist are not sufficient to enable one to form a settled opinion. This may be said, that a careful study of the whole of them, in the order of the years in which they were written, would probably reveal that they are much less wild and incoherent than even Mr. Gilchrist supposed. Every man living in seclusion and developing an intense interior life, gradually comes to give a quite peculiar significance to certain words and phrases and emblems. Metaphors which to the common bookwrights and journalists are mere handy counters, symbols almost as abstract and unrelated in thought to the things they represent as are the *x* and *y* and *z* used in solving an algebraic problem, are for *him* burdened with rich and various freights of spiritual experience; they are ships in which he has sailed over uncharted seas to unmapped shores, with which he has struggled through wild tempests and been tranced in Divine calms, in which he has returned with treasures from all the zones; and he loves them as the sailor loves his ship. His writings must thus appear, to any one reading them for the first time, very obscure, and often very ludicrous; the strange reader sees a battered old hull, where the writer sees a marvellous circumnavigation. But we ought not to be kept from studying these writings by any apparent obscurity and ludicrousness, if we have found in the easily comprehended vernacular writings of the same man (as in Blake's we certainly *have* found) sincerity and wisdom and beauty. Nor is it probable that even the most mysterious works of Blake would prove more difficult to genuine lovers of poetry than many works of the highest renown prove to nine-tenths of the reading public.

> Sie haben dich, heiliger Hafis,
>   Die mystische Zunge genannt;
> Und haben, die Wortgelehrten,
>   Den Werth des Worts nicht erkannt.*

*First stanza of Goethe's "Offenbar Geheimnis" in "Buch Hafis" of the *West-Östlicher Divan.*

For many intelligent persons Carlyle at his best is almost or quite as unintelligible as if he were using an unknown language; and the same may be asserted of Shelley and Robert Browning. (I do not select lofty *old* names, because in their cases the decisions of authoritative judges accumulating throughout centuries overawe our common jurymen into verdicts wise without understanding; so that a dullard can speak securely of the sublimity of Milton, for example, although we are pretty certain that he never got through the first book of the "Paradise Lost," and that he would find himself in a Slough of Despond when twenty lines deep in the opening passages of "Samson Agonistes.") Indeed, I doubt whether it would be an exaggeration to assert that, for a very large majority of those who are accounted educated and intelligent people, poetry in itself is essentially an unknown tongue. They admire and remember a verse or a passage for its wit, its cleverness, its wisdom, its clear and brief statement of some fact, its sentiment, its applicability to some circumstance of their own life, its mention of some classic name, its allusion to some historical event; in short, for its associations and not for its poetry *per se*. Yet assuredly there are still men in England with an infallible sense for poetry, however disguised and however far removed from ordinary associations; men who know Shakespeare in despite of the commentators, and understand Browning in contempt of the critics, and laugh quietly at the current censures and raptures of the Reviews: and these men would scarcely consider it a waste of time to search into the meaning of the darkest oracles of William Blake.

I wish to add a few words on the relations subsisting between our author and succeeding English poets. In his early maturity, as a reincarnation of the mighty Elizabethan spirit, the first fruit of a constructive after a destructive period, his affinity to the great poets who flourished a few years before his death (he died in 1827) will be readily understood. Thus in the Minstrel's Song, before quoted, we at once discern that the rhythm is of the same strain as the largest utterance of Marlowe and Webster and Shakespeare precedent, and as the noblest modern exemplar, the blank verse of "Hyperion" subsequent.* It is not, however, in

*Keats avowed imitation of Milton in the structure of his rhythm. Similarity to the Council in Pandemonium there of course could not but be in the Council of the overthrown Titans; but the verse of Keats (if I have any ear and intelligence for

this early maturity, but in his second childhood and boyhood and youth, when he was withdrawn from common life into mysticism, when moonlight was his sunlight, and water was his wine, and the roses red as blood were become all white as snow, in the "Songs of Innocence," the "Songs of Experience," and the "Auguries of Innocence" (always *Innocence*, mark, not *Virtue*) that the seeds may be traced of much which is now half-consciously struggling towards organic perfection, and which in two or three generations may be crowned with foliage and blossoms and fruit as the Tree of Life for one epoch.

The essence of this poetry is mysticism, and the essence of this mysticism is simplicity. The two meanings in which this last word is commonly used—the one reverential, the other kindly contemptuous—are severally appropriate to the most wise and the least wise manifestations of this spirit of mysticism. It sees, and is continually rapturous with seeing, everywhere correspondence, kindred, identity, not only in the things and creatures of earth, but in all things and creatures and beings of hell and earth and heaven, up to the one father (or interiorly to the one soul) of all. It thus ignores or pays little heed to the countless complexities and distinctions of our modern civilisation and science, a knowledge of which is generally esteemed the most useful information and most valuable learning. For it "there is no great and no small"; in the large type of planets and nations, in the minute letters of dewdrops and worms, the same eternal laws are written; and merely as a matter of convenience to the reader is this or that print preferable to the other. And the whole universe being the volume of the Scriptures of the living word of God, this above all is to be heeded, that man should not dwell contented on the lovely language and illustrations, but should live beyond these in the sphere of the realities which they signify. It is passionately and profoundly religious, contemplating and treating every subject religiously, in all its excursions and discursions issuing from the soul to return to the soul, alone, from the alone, to the alone; and thus it is by no means strict in its theology, being Swedenborgian in one man and Pantheistic in another, while in the East it has readily assimilated Buddhism and Brahminism and

verse) is as different from the verse of Milton as with the same language and the same metrical standard it possibly could be. It is in my judgment even more beautiful and more essentially powerful and sublime than Milton's. (Thomson's note.)

Mohammedanism. Its supreme tendency is to remain or to become again childlike, its supreme aspiration is not virtue, but innocence or guilelessness: so that we may say with truth of those whom it possesses, that the longer they live the younger they grow, as if "passing out to God by the gate of birth, not death."

These few hints may serve as points of departure for some slender lines of relation between William Blake the Second and the principal subsequent poets. It must be borne in mind that the object here is not a survey of the full circle of the powers of any of these poets; they may be very great or very small in various other respects, while very small or very great in respect of this mystical simplicity. The heads of Da Vinci and Titian and Rembrandt, the bodies of Correggio and Rubens, would all count for nothing were we instituting a comparison between the old masters simply as painters of the *sky*.

Wordsworth ever aspired towards this simplicity, but the ponderous pedantry of his nature soon dragged him down again when he had managed to reach it. He was a good, conscientious, awkward pedagogue, who, charmed by the charms of childhood, endeavoured himself to play the child. Were it not rather too wicked, I could draw from Æsop another excellent illustration. He was not wrong when he proclaimed himself eminently a teacher; 'tis a pity that six days of the seven his teaching was of the Sunday-school sort.

Coleridge had much of this simplicity. In the "Ancient Mariner" it is supreme; in "Christabel" it does not lack, but already shows signs of getting maudlin; afterwards, "Lay Sermons" with Schelling and the Noetic Pentad, almost or quite extinguished it. He was conscious of the loss, as witness the lines in his great Ode: –

> And haply by abstruse research to steal
> From my own nature all the natural man.

Scott, a thoroughly objective genius, lived and wrote altogether out of the sphere of this simplicity. He had a simplicity of his own, the simplicity of truthfulness and power in his "magnificent and masculine grasp of men and things." Expansive not intensive, he developed no interior life, but diffused himself over the exterior life. His poetry is of action, not of thought; he is as a mighty and valiant soldier, whom we seek on the field of battle, not in the school of the prophets.

Byron had it not at all. He is great, exceedingly great; but great as the expression of intense life, and of such thought only as is the mere tool and weapon of life, never great as the expression of thought above and beneath life commanding and sustaining it. He had just ideality enough to shed a poetic glow upon powers and passions all essentially commonplace, but very uncommonly vigorous, overflowing with the energy of dæmonic possession—an energy most mysterious, but in itself most impatient of mysticism.

Keats, who shall dare to judge? I doubt not that everything pure and beautiful would have had its season in him who, dying at twenty-four, wrote "Hyperion" a few years after "Endymion." But this plastic genius would have proceeded in triumphant transmigrations through all fairest forms ere it could have found eternal tranquillity in the soul of all form. Had he been spared, all analogies, I think, point to this end.

Shelley possessed, or rather was possessed by, this simplicity to the uttermost. Although he and Keats were twin brothers, Greeks of the race of the gods, their works do not resemble but complement each other. The very childlike lisp which we remarked in Blake is often observable in the voice of Shelley, consummate singer as he was. The lisp is, however, not always that of a child; it is on several occasions that of a missionary seeking to translate old thoughts from his rich and exact native tongue into the dialect, poor and barbarous, of his hearers. He (while doing also very different work of his own) carries on the work begun by Blake, sinking its foundations into a deeper past, and uplifting its towers into a loftier future. Both Shelley and Keats are still so far beyond the range of our English criticism that they would not have been mentioned thus cursorily here had it been possible to omit them.*

*Perhaps the astonishing difference in kind between these glorious poets and their contemporaries can best be put in clear light by thus considering them young Greeks of the race of the gods, born three thousand years after their time, in Christian England. Shelley has been called "The Eternal Child," and Keats "The Real Adonis"; and Novalis says well, "Children are ancients, and youth is antique" (*Die Kinder sind Antiken. Auch die Jugend ist antik*, vol. iii. p. 190). The ideas and sentiments of the race among whom they were reared were naturally strange, and in many respects repugnant to them both. Keats, simply ignoring the Bumbleism and Christianity, except in so far as the Bumbleism obstructed his poetic career, unperturbed save by the first throes of creative art, developed himself in the regions from which he sprang—Pagan and Hellenic in his themes, his ideas, his perceptions, his objects. Shelley, on the other hand, started from the time and

Tennyson has no more of this simplicity than had Byron: his chief youthful fault was such a young ladyish affectation as could not exist together with it. But he is fully aware of its value, and woos it like a lover, in vain, as Byron wooed it in the latter parts of "Childe Harold" and in "Manfred." Perhaps each of them should be credited with one great exception, in addition to a few short lyrics: Tennyson with the "Lotos-Eaters," Byron with the "Dream." Scarcely any other artist in verse of the same rank has ever lived on such scanty revenues of thought (both pure, and applied or mixed) as Tennyson. While it cannot be pretended that he is a great sculptor, he is certainly an exquisite carver of luxuries in ivory; but we must be content to admire the caskets, for there are no jewels inside. His meditation at the best is that of a good leading-article; he is a pensioner on the thought of his age. He is continually petty with that littleness of the second degree which makes a man brag aloud in avoiding some well-known littleness of the first degree. His nerves are so weak that any largish event—a Crimean War or a Volunteer movement—sets him off in hysterics. Nothing gives one a keener insight into the want of robustness in the educated English intellect of the age than the fact that nine-tenths of our best-known literary men look upon him as a profound philosopher. When wax-flowers are oracular oaks, Dodona may be discovered in the Isle of Wight, but hardly until then. Mr. Matthew Arnold's definition of "distilled thought in distilled words" was surely suggested by the processes and productions of a fashionable perfumer. A great school of the poets is dying out: it will die decently, elegantly, in the full odour of respectability, with our Laureate.

Robert Browning, a really great thinker, a true and splendid

---

place of his birth to reach the old dominions of his ancestry. In this enterprise he had to conquer and destroy the terrible armies of fanaticism, asceticism, cant, hypocrisy, narrow-mindedness, lording it over England; and at the same time the spirituality of the new religion, the liberty and equality and fraternity of the new political systems, all things lovely and true and holy of the modern life, he would bear with him for the re-inspiration of the antique. He aspired not to a New Jerusalem in the heavens, but to a new Hellenic metropolis on earth: he looked for redemption and victory, not to Christ on Calvary, but to Prometheus on Caucasus.

These young Greeks could not live to old age. The gloom and chill of our English clime, physical and moral and intellectual, could not but be fatal to these children of the sun. England and France are so proudly in the van of civilisation that it is impossible for a great poet to live greatly to old age in either of them. (Thomson's note.)

genius, though his vigorous and restless talents often overpower and run away with his genius so that some of his creations are left but half redeemed from chaos, has this simplicity in abundant measure. In the best poems of his last two works, "Men and Women" and "Dramatis Personæ," its light burns so clear and steadfast through the hurrying clouds of his language (Tennyson's style is the polished reflector of a lamp) that one can only wonder that people in general have not yet recognised it. I cannot recommend a finer study of a man possessed by the spirit of which I am writing than the sketch of Lazarus in Browning's "Epistle of Karshish, an Arab Physician."

Elizabeth Barrett Browning, also, had much of it, yet never succeeded in giving it fair expression. The long study of her sick-bed (and her constant chafing against the common estimate of the talents and genius of her sex) overcharged her works with allusions and thoughts relating to books, and made her style rugged with pedantry. She was often intoxicated, too, with her own vehemence. "Aurora Leigh" sets out determined to walk the world with the great Shakespearian stride, whence desperate entanglement of feminine draperies and blinding swirls of dust. The sonnets entitled "From the Portuguese" reveal better her inmost simple nature.

Emerson stands closest of all in relation to Blake, his verse as well as his essays and lectures being little else than the expression of this mystical simplicity. Were he gifted with the singing voice we should not have to look to the future for its supreme bard. But whenever he has sung a few clear sweet notes, his voice breaks, and he has to recite and speak what he would fain chant. His studies, also, have somewhat injured his style with technicology, making him in his own despite look at Nature through the old church and school windows, often when he should be with her in the rustic air. In some of his shorter poems, however, and in the snatches of Orphic song prefixed to some of his essays (as "Compensation," "Art," "History," "Heroism"), any one with ears to hear may catch pregnant hints of what poetry possessed by this inspiration can accomplish, and therefore *will* accomplish; for no pure inspiration having once come down among men ever withdraws its influence until it has attained (humanly) perfect embodiment.

In eighty years the influence of this spirit has swelled from the "Songs of Innocence" to the poems of Emerson — a rapid increase of the tide in literature. Other signs of its increase meet us everywhere in the best books of verse published during the last few years. And perchance the increase has been even more rapid than the most of us have opportunity to learn, for we are informed by Mr. Rossetti that James John Garth Wilkinson has not only edited a collection of Blake's Poems, but has himself produced a volume of poems entitled "Improvisations of the Spirit," * bearing a strong family likeness to those of Blake; and it may be that Wilkinson has the singing voice which Emerson has not. It would be a boon to the public, at any rate, to make these two volumes easily accessible.

Emerson and Garth Wilkinson, the former undoubtedly the supreme thinker of America, the latter as undoubtedly second to none in England, are surely in themselves sufficient attestation to the truth and depth of the genius of their forerunner, William Blake.

He came to the desert of London town,
Grey miles long;
He wandered up and he wandered down,
Singing a quiet song.

He came to the desert of London town,
Mirk miles broad;
He wandered up and he wandered down,
Ever alone with God.

There were thousands and thousands of human kind
In this desert of brick and stone:
But some were deaf and some were blind,
And he was there alone.

At length the good hour came; he died,
As he had lived, alone:
He was not missed from the desert wide,
Perhaps he was found at the Throne.†

*Thomson later reviewed this book in the *Liberal* (September–December, 1879); the review, titled "A Strange Book," is reprinted in *Biographical and Critical Studies*.

†This is Thomson's own poem on Blake, written March 11, 1865, and first published in this essay.

Review: Frederic Harrison, *The Meaning of History*

[*This brief review, more of biographical and historical than of literary interest, appeared in the* National Reformer *on January 3, 1863, under the signature "B.V."; a few weeks later, an incensed reader wrote a letter to Bradlaugh complaining that the review was a flippant and unjust criticism: "It was not written by a Secularist, but apparently by a Theist or Christian as the writer adopted the fable of a 'golden age.'" Thomson did not defend his review, and two years were to pass before he again wrote for the* National Reformer, *at which time his iconoclastic essays would hardly have qualified him for the title of Theist or Christian. The article is here reprinted for the first time.*]

IN A BRIEF PREFACE the author states that the view of history put forward by him, is drawn with some care from the various writings of Auguste Comte; and that opposite opinions, though not noticed, have been carefully weighed. As I have not read the works of Comte, I cannot pretend to judge whether or not his historical ideas have been fairly applied by Mr. Harrison; but if they have, they are by no means original.

The first lecture is on the use of history, and some pages of it are devoted to the refutation of those who assert that history is of no use at all. Surely these contemners of history are neither numerous nor important, but it is tempting to deal with them, as their refutation gives scope for any amount of easy and fluent commonplace. The lecture goes on to assert that history should be mainly a history of the good, that the "riotings and intrigues and affectations of worthless men and worthless ages" should be all passed by in contempt and pity. To which the reply is: in the first place, you cannot picture a good and noble life without picturing also a vast amount of evil, for a life is good and noble simply in virtue of its persistent battling with evil; and secondly, it is just as weak-headed to dwell altogether on the fair side of human nature, as it is bad-hearted to dwell altogether on the foul;

the genuine historian is he who is naturalistic, discerning and describing both the beauty and the deformity.

The second lecture is on the connection of history, and in about fifty pages gives a sketch of human progress from the author's (or Comte's) point of view. It commences with primitive man, "not yet the lord of the creation, inferior to the brutes in strength, only just superior to them in mind—nothing but the first of the animals"; when "language, family, marriage, property, tribe, were not, or only were in germ"; when "a few cries assisted by gesture, a casual association of the sexes, a dim trace of parentage or brotherhood, were all that was," and so forth. What authority has Mr. Harrison or M. Comte for this charming picture? Do not the traditions of nearly all races lead us back to see our first fathers, not groping their way up from the pit, but descending from the empyreum? What antique records place the iron age first before the golden? What savage tribes have been known to civilise themselves? One of our three or four supreme living writers, J. J. G. Wilkinson, in "The Human Body and Its Connexion with Man," says well in reference to this hypothesis of our primal degradation (with no preceding higher rank to be *degraded* from) that if God had planted the world on such a plan, he would have been worse than a Colonial Secretary peopling a new Continent with scum; and that the human boat, launched with such a hole in its bottom, must have foundered on the brink of the year one.

It is not worth while to follow the lecturer in tracing man's progress by imaginary steps from this imaginary situation. Almost any reader could do the tracing about as well for himself; a very little superficial knowledge, and a slight tincture of trashy French ingenuity being all that is requisite for the operation. Nor need we dwell upon the sketch of the growth and decay of the various great empires and systems up to the present time: what is new in it, appears to me not true, what is true not at all new.

The style is easy, but frequently loose and inaccurate. There are also two or three strange slips in matters of fact. For instance, what does the reader think of this—"For *three* days Leonidas and his 300 held the pass against the Asean host, and *lay down each warrior at his post* calmly smiling in death!" On the whole the unfortunate reviewer is constrained to confess that he cannot commend this pamphlet as at all instructive, but he can also state that here and there an indolent reader might find it amusing.

Mill on Religion

[*This is the first section of a long review of Mill's* Three Essays on Religion*; it was published in eight installments in the* National Reformer *(November 8–December 27, 1874), and was one of the last articles Thomson ever wrote for Bradlaugh. Most of the "review" consists of long quotations from Mill's book; only this first section, herein reprinted for the first time, is of interest as critical comment upon Mill's life and work.*]

ALBEIT I have never from the time I first studied the "System of Logic, Ratiocinative and Inductive," now more than twenty years ago, worshipped its author with such ardour of devotion as might have made me one of the elect, in an age which has been wittily and not unaptly termed the John-Millennium, I have always regarded him with great respect as a sincere and very brave man of most generous sympathies, and also with considerable admiration as a patient, acute, and unprejudiced thinker. I was therefore, in common with many others, not a little grieved when his posthumous Autobiography, published about a year since, made the clear and blunt announcement (written so early as 1861) of what he had never, I believe, unequivocally declared in his lifetime: "I am thus one of the very few examples, in this country, of one who has not thrown off religious belief, but never had it: I grew up in a negative state with regard to it. I looked upon the modern exactly as I did upon the ancient religion, as something which in no way concerned me." He had long been in good pecuniary circumstances, he had long wielded a vast intellectual influence, he was the honoured leader and teacher of the most numerous, able, and energetic School of the younger Liberals; he had proved quite fearless, and regardless of consequences to himself, in the advocacy of extreme and extremely unpopular political and social changes: if such a man, on whatever grounds, thought it expedient and permissible to hide the full extent of his religious heresy until after his death, how could we hope that the thousands and thousands of educated men, less distinguished, less daring, less influential, less favourably circumstanced, who are unavowed Sceptics and disbelievers, would soon gather courage to declare themselves?

The friends and disciples of Mr. Mill have much to adduce in his favour on this point; they have not found it hard to vindicate him relatively to the bulk of his assailants; but I fear that they cannot vindicate him absolutely. One says that he could not well publish his Autobiography in his lifetime; but even if not, he had plenty of opportunities in his other works of fully explaining his opinions. Another urges that by doing so he would have lessened his influence in other and very important spheres; but surely the influence would have suffered less from the living than from the posthumous avowal, and his reputation for courageous candour would have stood even higher than it now does. Another affirms that intelligent readers could divine the full measure of his religious heresy from various passages in his previous books: the question, however, is not as to what might be divined, but as to what ought to have been clearly proclaimed; and, moreover, no one has the right to infer, nor can he do so with any assurance of being correct, that because a man holds certain opinions, he therefore holds certain others which seem logically deducible from them. It is true that in previously published works, as in the "Liberty" and the "Examination of Sir William Hamilton's Discussions on Philosophy," there are passages depreciative of Christianity; it is probably true that the leading tendencies of all his works are against Supernaturalism; but I am not aware that while alive he ever publicly avowed that he rejected and never had accepted Revelation. Even the celebrated retort to Dean Mansel only says in effect: If the goodness of your God is not of the same kind as that of the best men, I refuse him my worship; and if he will send me to hell for this, to hell I will go: and is thus quite ambiguous, leaving open the questions, whether he believed in a God, not the God of Mansel; and whether he believed in Revelation, not as interpreted by Mansel. (Compare "Utilitarianism," pp. 30, 31.)

Lastly, his step-daughter, Miss Helen Taylor, writes in her brief Introductory Notice to these Essays on Religion: — "The fact that the author intended to publish the Essay on Nature in 1873 is sufficient evidence, if any is needed, that the volume now given to the public was not withheld by him on account of reluctance to encounter whatever odium might result from the free expression of his opinions on religion. . . . He declined altogether to be hurried into premature decision on any point to which he did not think he had given sufficient time and labour to have exhausted it to the utmost limit of his own thinking powers. And, in the same way, even after he had arrived at definite conclusions, he refused to allow the curiosity of others to force him to the expression of them before he had bestowed all the elaboration in his power upon their adequate expression, and before, therefore, he had subjected to the test of time, not only the conclusions themselves, but also the form into which he had thrown them." I regret that I cannot accept this explanation as quite satisfactory. The Essays on Nature and the Utility of Religion were composed before 1858; the Essay on Theism, written after 1870, endorses the first, showing that no substantial change in his opinions had taken place in the interval; nor, indeed, was any to be expected on such a subject, seeing that in 1858 he was fifty-two years old. In the part of the Autobiography written and revised not later than 1861, he enounces briefly the main conclusions of all the three essays. And so early as 1822 the manuscript of a book on the Utility of Religion, founded on some of Bentham's papers, and written by George Grote, but published under the pseudonyme of Philip Beauchamp, was put into Mill's hands by his father, and he made a marginal analysis of it, and records it as one of the books which produced the greatest effect on him. Which of his works other than these on Religion did he keep back from the public for over fifteen years? What need could there be of so long a period for maturing his thoughts and revising their expression, when the subject had occupied him from early youth, and the composition was the deliberate work of so ripe an age? The fact that in the year of his death he was about to publish the first of these essays, seems to show that the "purification of the conscience," which was always advancing in him, had at length brought him to realise thoroughly the responsibilities of his eminent position, to recognise clearly the duty that lay on him of speaking out his whole heart and mind.

Let us consider a few of Mill's own words on this matter, in the Autobiography. "In giving me an opinion contrary to that of the world, my father thought it necessary to give it as one which could not prudently be avowed to the world. . . . I think that few men of my father's intellect and public spirit, holding with such intensity of moral conviction as he did, unpopular opinions on religion, or on any other of the great subjects of thought, would now either practise or inculcate the withholding of them from the world, unless in the cases, becoming fewer every day, in which frankness on these subjects would either risk the loss of means of subsistence, or would amount to exclusion from some sphere of usefulness peculiarly suitable to the capacities of the individual" (pp. 43–5). (Compare "On Liberty," p. 18, col. 2, People's Edition.) I submit that men who aspire and claim to be the apostles of Liberal thought, the leaders in Liberal reforms; men of intellect, public spirit, and intense moral convictions; cannot have a sphere of usefulness more suitable to them just now than that of open warfare, and warfare *à outrance*, against the degrading absurdities and anti-progressive dogmatism of the supernatural religion called Christianity, under which our country still crouches; and if such men dare not for the sake of their moral convictions risk the loss of their means of subsistence, the said moral convictions cannot be very intense. I can understand a heretic keeping quiet because he fears that the overthrow of religion may do more harm than good, by removing certain restraints from the vulgar; but I do not believe that any considerable number of intelligent and unprejudiced persons have now any such fear that truth and frankness are likely to be more noxious than falsehood and humbug. I can understand a heretic keeping quiet, who does not set himself up as a teacher or leader, or who has a scornful indifference for all creeds and systems; or because he is hopeless of any improvement in mankind, and believes that if dragged out of one pitfall, they immediately stumble into another as deep and dangerous. But I do not understand how one who believes in the improvability of mankind, and the manifold harmfulness of religion, a Liberal leader and teacher, a man of intellect, public spirit, and intense moral convictions, can conceal his heresy rather than "risk the loss of his means of subsistence." These unfortunate words imply about the meanest doctrine of the heroic apostolic life of a champion of Truth I have ever heard or read; and they are the more lamentable and astounding as coming from a really brave, high-minded, and disinterested reformer. Farther on he says: "The world would be astonished if it knew how great a proportion of its brightest ornaments—of those most distinguished even in popular estimation for wisdom and virtue—are complete sceptics in religion." (Compare "On Liberty," p. 30, col. 1; and indeed the whole of the chapter, On the Liberty of Thought and Discussion.) Thus it is clear, that if all spoke out, the heretics would prove so imposing a minority, powerful by their numbers, far more powerful by their character and intelligence; and I here mean only the conscious, logical heretics, for the practical infidels compose at least 9,999 out of every 10,000 of our "Christian" population; that the "social stigma" and the loss of the means of subsistence would cease to be the consequences of unbelief. It is through the cowardice and hypocrisy of so many secret sceptics that the "Christians" seem so strong, and are enabled to be so overbearing.

Writing, about 1861, of the years soon after 1840 (Autobiography, p. 230) he says: "I was much more inclined, than I can now approve, to put in abeyance the more decidedly heretical part of my opinions, which I now look upon as almost the only ones, the assertion of which tends in any way to regenerate society." When he wrote this wise sentence, the Essays on Nature and the Utility of Religion had already remained in manuscript for periods between three and eleven years; he lived twelve years more; yet it was only in the year of his death that he had made up his mind to give some practical effect to this long-cherished conviction, by publishing the Essay on Nature. Would that he had spoken out earlier, in the prime and vigour of his intellectual life! would that he had avowed publicly and frankly the extreme main conclusions of his heresy, taking as many years as he pleased for their dialectical exposition and defence!

If I preface my review of these posthumous Essays on Religion with this painful discussion, it is because I deem it necessary and particularly called for at the present time; not because I would willingly depreciate the character of their author, who was far more Liberal, more courageous, and more candid, than all save a very few of our speakers and writers. "Not that I loved Cæsar less, but that I loved Rome more." Not that I esteem Mill less, but that I esteem Truth more; and can see no hope for truth save in the free expression of free thought. As things are, in Britain, the tremendous task of openly attacking, hewing down, and extirpating the mental and moral tyranny of a supernatural religion, whose roots cling deep in the past, whose branches and scions extend over all regions of the earth, whose evil shadow chills and darkens our richest fields of culture and civilisation, is left almost wholly to us of the *National Reformer* and the Secular Societies, to us who for the most part are poor, uneducated, and uninfluential; while thousands and thousands of men with wealth, leisure, scholarship, and influence, who in their hearts and minds are just as antagonistic to Christianity as we ourselves, submit to be negative if not positive dissemblers and hypocrites, rejecting on us the heavy burden of odium and disabilities, which they by a manly avowal would at once remove from us without bringing it on themselves.

Had the early Reformers and Freethinkers availed themselves of the excuse sanctioned by John Stuart Mill, we should now be under the absolute despotism of the Holy Roman Catholic Church, with all its incredible dogmas and degrading superstitions; for they would have kept their free thoughts to themselves. What would Wycliffe, Luther, Huss, Savonarola, Sarpi, Knox; what would Berquin, Dolet, Des Periers; what would Bruno, Campanella, Vanini; what would Socrates and the two Zenos, Epictetus and Marcus Antoninus; what would Puritans, Huguenots, and Covenanters; have thought of a theory of apostleship based on "intense moral conviction," allowing silence and inertia, which mean dissimulation, in cases where there is "risk of the loss of means of subsistence"; they, most of whom risked their lives, and lost them abundantly? And many of these men, and others like them, had not merely the courage to die dreadful deaths rather than falsify their moral and intellectual convictions; they had the yet grander courage, the courage which is the most imperial crown of true manhood, to be loyal to their conscience and their reason, loyal to the extremity of martyrdom, when these were reprobated by the consensus of nearly every one else in their world, the great, the good, the learned, the wise, the famous, as well as the ignorant multitude. Try to imagine what it must have been to confront death alone for disbelief in a nation of undoubting believers; all firmly convinced that the rack and the stake but hurried the martyr into the infinitely more cruel torments, the infinitely fiercer fires, lasting for ever and ever, of Hell. As for a large number of our high-spirited gentlemen, who are cowed into servile conformity with what their reason disdains and their conscience rejects, let Mill himself pass sentence on them (On Liberty, p. 18, col. 2): "Those whose bread is already secured, and who desire no favours from men in power, or from bodies of men, or from the public [how tenderly anxious he is to give them every possible chance of evasion!], have nothing to fear from the open avowal of any opinions, but to be ill-thought of and ill-spoken of, and this it ought not to require a very heroic mould to bear. There is no room for any appeal *ad misericordiam* in behalf of such persons." I rather think not! And, as already observed, if all heretics declared themselves, they would be found so numerous and powerful, that even the "ill-thought of and ill-spoken of" would no longer apply; the "social stigma" for heresy would vanish away to that Limbo, whither have preceded it the boot, the thumbscrew, the wheel, the gibbet, the block, and the stake.

Heinrich Heine

[Thomson's admiration for Heine was lifelong; as early as 1862 he had published translations of Heine's poems, and he continued to translate from both the prose and the poetry during the 1860's and 1870's. This essay, which appeared in the Secularist *in six installments (January 8–February 12, 1876), is probably the best of Thomson's many "biographical essays," works intended to introduce his readers to what were then little-known authors such as Whitman, Leopardi, and Stendhal. It was occasioned by the publication of William Stigand's* The Life, Work, and Opinions of Heinrich Heine *(London, 1875), a volume that Thomson attacks with painstaking and devastating documentation, showing that the book abounds with "gross, obvious, and vulgar mistakes," that Stigand's style, when not absolutely incorrect, "is nearly always clumsy, and not seldom barbarously uncouth," that translations from Heine are often "criminally unfaithful," and that there are "conspicuous inconsistencies in plain statement of fact." Since several other examples of Thomson's rather picayune dissections have been included in this edition, the two sections treating Stigand's volume have been omitted; the essay proper is reprinted here for the first time.]*

HEINE WAS BORN at Düsseldorf in what is now Rhine Prussia, probably on the 12th or 13th Dec. 1799, and died at Paris the 17th Feb. 1856, after lying helpless and wasted and tortured in body, supremely clear and vigorous in mind, for upwards of seven years on his "mattress-grave." I can here only indicate the leading features of his life. He owed his earliest education to his mother, a woman of character and intelligence, who had a taste for art, especially music, and loved literature, especially Goethe and Rousseau. She lived till more than eighty, surviving her famous eldest son. Düsseldorf had been occupied by the French from 1795 to 1801, and was again in their possession from 1806 to 1813, so that Heine's boyhood was trained under their influence. And it must be remembered that to the lower classes of Germany, who had been hitherto held in vassalage, the French occupation was on the whole beneficial, until the inordinate exactions and conscriptions of Napoleon overbalanced the boons of legal enfranchisement and civic equality, and produced that spirit of patriotism, that passionate yearning for unity, which was at length crowned with triumph at Versailles. To Heine's own people, the Jews, above all others, was the French occupation a blessed deliverance. These were treated as outcasts and Pariahs. In most German cities they were confined to one quarter, like the infamous Ghetto of Papal Rome, whose gates were shut nightly at a certain hour. On Sundays they were forced to wear a peculiar dress. A Jew appearing on a public promenade ran great peril of being stoned. In Frankfort on the Maine, the great imperial and financial capital, only five-and-twenty Jewish marriages were allowed each year, that the numbers of the accursed race might be restricted. Against insult, violence, robbery, and even murder, they were almost wholly unprotected. Late in the 18th century massacres of them took place in several German towns. At Easter-tide and other festivals the Christian populace were accustomed to the sport of hunting Jews through the streets and breaking their windows; and sometimes the sport included the sacking of their houses. For an educated Jew the only profession open was that of medicine, and this solely for practice among his own people, unless he submitted to be baptised and make profession of the Christian faith. Frederick the Great, indeed, being an impious and enlightened Infidel, conferred upon them certain fixed rights and privileges, but even he could not venture to place them on an equality with the rest of his subjects. From all these oppressions the French occupation delivered them. Under the Republic they were of course free citizens, under the *Code Napoléon* they were at least equal subjects with their fellow-countrymen. Yet with these, the Jews took part nobly in the War of Liberation, volunteering by thousands; for love of the mother-country strikes deep roots even in those to whom she is but a heartless step-mother; and, moreover, the German princes, in their sore need, made fine promises to the Jews as well as to the rest of their peoples. And the poor peoples trusted them with a sublime credulity. One of Shakespeare's kings has declared

> Uneasy lies the head that wears a crown.

Yet if it lies uneasy, how easily it lies! — none more easily, unless it be the head that wears a mitre, or that which wears crown and mitre in one, the triple tiara. The proverbial "As easy as lying," doubtless sprang from one conversant with kings and priests. When He was overthrown and captive,

> Whose grasp had left the giant world so weak
> That every pigmy kicked it as it lay;*

when "Kings crept out again to feel the sun"; these kicking pigmies, these creeping kings, had small thought of redeeming in their triumph the pledges they had given in their necessity; the people were taught practically for the thousandth time that great lesson, Put not your trust in princes; and among the rest, and most pitiable of all, the poor Jews were degraded into their old condition; this was their special reward for fighting so well for God and King and Fatherland. Even Jews who for distinguished conduct in the field had been made officers, were ordered out of the service if they would not return to the ranks. Encouraged by such princely example, the populace of Frankfort in 1818, hunted the Jews like mad dogs from street to street, and assailed their houses with volleys of stones. They were again pent in their ghettos until the Revolution of 1848 released them. Heine's own uncle Solomon, the wealthy banker and benefactor of Hamburg, who sustained and saved its credit after the great fire of 1842, and endowed it with munificent charities for Christians as well as Jews, was excluded from the Chamber of Commerce there, on account of his creed, and never had the rights of a citizen. I have dwelt at some length on these facts, because, without keeping them in view, Heine's character and career cannot be fairly judged.

At the age of ten he went to the *Lycée*, or French Government School, where the teaching was in French, and one third of the time was given to French grammar and literature, where the pupils wore a uniform and were subjected to a strict discipline; where, in short, everything possible was done to enregiment the new generation under the Empire. Heine as a boy saw the great Napoleon twice; first in 1810, and then in 1812, when he reviewed some troops previous to the Russian campaign; and for many years afterwards Heine adored him and

*Shelley, "The Triumph of Life," ll. 226–227; "He" refers, of course, to Napoleon.

dared to worship him openly even in the Germany of the Holy Alliance. Nevertheless he volunteered, boy-like, for the War of Liberation in 1813. Delightful sketches of his early days are to be found in his *Reisebilder* or *Pictures of Travel*, a book which has been translated, and I suppose well translated, by Mr. Leland, author of the *Breitmann Ballads*. After school he was sent to Frankfort, where a fortnight in a banker's office proved enough for him. He was then sent to Hamburg, where his uncle Solomon tried in vain to make a commercial man of him. There he published his first poems, while still under twenty, and fell in love with his cousin Amalie, one year younger than himself. His suit did not prosper; in 1821 she married another; and many of the pieces in his *Book of Songs*, which also has been translated by Leland, are devoted to this frustrate affection. His gruff but generous uncle, illiterate and prosaic, could never understand him, and knew not what to do with him; growling long afterwards when Heine was the greatest of German poets, If the stupid youngster had learned what he ought, he would not have needed to write books. At length Solomon agreed to pay for his university training, on condition that he studied for the law, although to practise this he would have to profess himself a Christian. He accordingly went to Bonn, and then to Göttingen, where he was soon rusticated for six months for challenging another student to a duel. He then repaired to Berlin, in Feby. 1821, and remained there for upwards of two years. There he was brought under the influence of Hegel, and became intimate with Varnhagen von Ense and his wife the Jewess Rachel Levin, "the dear good little lady with the great soul," whose house was frequented by some of the most notable persons of the capital, including De La Motte Fouqué, the author of *Undine*, and Chamisso, the author of *Peter Schlemil the Shadowless Man*. There also with the leaders of the young Jewish party of reform, Gans, the pupil of Hegel, Leopold Zunz, Moses Moser, Ludwig Markus, he tried to establish that Society of Jewish Culture and Science, which so soon failed; and already in 1823 he was looking to Paris as the only place where he could work in freedom. In Jany. 1824 he returned to Göttingen, stuck as hard as he could to the law which he detested, passed his examination in May, and received his Doctor's degree in July, having on June 28 submitted to baptism and professed himself a Protestant. He took this step with profound repugnance, and always looked back on it with bitter regret. But without it he could not enter upon any career, and he looked not simply to the practice of the law, but had hopes of a government appointment. Really he surrendered no religion as really he adopted none, believing neither with the Jews nor with the Christians. The ceremony was strictly private, his godfather as well as his baptiser being a clergyman, as if he would cast on the church all the disgrace of the sham apostacy. Many other eminent Jews went through the same form, for instance, Mendelssohn and Gans himself. In 1799, Friedländer, then the leader of Jewish reform, wrote to Teller, the Provost of the University of Berlin, asking whether it was not possible for enlightened Jews to be received into the community of those "who called themselves Christians, without going through the hypocritical form of conversion?" and got an unfavourable answer. On whom did the shame of these sham conversions rest; on the bigots who imposed them, or the victims who adopted them, as the only means of escape from political degradation and civic outlawry? Years afterwards Heine wrote: "The certificate of baptism is a card of admission to European culture." And again: "If Montalembert became Minister, and could drive me away from Paris, I would turn Catholic. *Paris vaut bien une messe*" ("Paris is well worth a mass"; the famous excuse of Henry of Navarre for *his* apostacy). In his first letter after his baptism to his friend Moses Moser, he says: "I recommend to you Golowin's *Journey to Japan*. . . . I will be a Japanese. They hate nothing else so much as the Cross. I will be a Japanese." Reminding us of Goethe's bitter epigram: —

> Very much can I endure. Most things that are hard to put up with
> I in tranquillity bear, as if imposed by a god.
> Some few however I find as hateful as poison and serpents;
> Four: the smoke of tobacco, garlic and bugs and the Cross.*

In Sept. 1824 he had made the walking tour in the Harz Mountains recounted in his *Pictures of Travel,* and paid his respects to Goethe at Weimar. He tells us that he had often lain awake at night meditating what striking remarks he could address to the grand veteran, face to face with whom he could only

*Thomson's own translation, which he had published earlier as "Cross Lines from Goethe" in the *National Reformer* (April 23, 1871).

say that the plums on the road from Jena to Weimar were very good. Soon after taking his doctor's degree he spent some time at the isle of Nordeney off Holland, having previously spent six weeks at Cuxhaven for the cure of the nervous headaches from which he suffered acutely; and these visits, with a second to Nordeney in July, 1826, gave birth to the North Sea poems which are so original a feature in the *Book of Songs.* In Novr. 1825 he went to Hamburg, ostensibly to practise law: This it need hardly be said, he did not practise; and Solomon in utter perplexity about him appealed to Professor Zimmermann, Tell me, Professor, is there really anything in my nephew? Here on this occasion Heine made the acquaintance of Julius Campe, the publisher, whose books from 1830 to 1848 were absolutely prohibited in most German states. Yet, with immense energy and ingenuity he managed to smuggle them in everywhere, often sending the most wicked sheets under cover of a most innocent title-page. Consequently all the German writers under ban at that period had to publish through him. Börne, Vehse, Immermann, Gützkow, Weinbarg, Dinglestedt, Hoffmann, etc., and chief of all Heine himself, of whose complete works in German he ultimately became proprietor. As usual, author and publisher had many a quarrel, Heine complaining again and again that Campe unnecessarily submitted his works to the ruthless castration of the censorship, and also complaining, it appears with reason, that they were miserably paid for. It is said that he never gave Heine more than about £80 for a volume, and that for the first volume of the *Pictures of Travel* he gave but £40; and Heine was wont to say that he had at least one great monument in his native country, the fine house which Campe erected in Hamburg. This flourishing commercial city Heine hated intensely; he dates from it as *Verdammtes* Hamburg, a vigorous epithet which needs not translation. In 1827 he visited England; staying in London, where he lodged at 32, Craven Street, Strand, with the exception of a fortnight at Ramsgate, during the period of Canning's premiership. He read the journals, and attended the sittings of Parliament, and studied London life; and took away with him an immense disgust for England and the English, which often finds the most whimsically extravagant expression in his works. In Novr. 1827, he went to Munich, invited by the well-known publisher Cotta, with the prospect of permanent literary employment, but was disappointed, and in July 1838 went to Italy. Here everything fascinated him, and he has left a vivid record of his impressions in the *Pictures of Travel*. He had two years more to pass in Hamburg, suffering much from the headaches, suffering always from a general *malaise*; without assured future or definite prospects, with surroundings he abominated. His nerves were so sensitive, that a friend at whose house he slept, says that not only the clock in his own room, but that in the adjoining had to be stopped at night, as the ticking murdered his rest. He was in Heligoland when the news of the Three Days arrived; and in some remarkable letters, included in the *De l'Allemagne* (*On Germany*), has described the general enthusiasm excited; himself being the most enthusiastic of all. One of these letters is specially noteworthy as recording an anticipation of the news; something strange and electric was in the air, the sea had an odour of cates, people felt joyous and expectant, they knew not why. The recoil of this Revolution, as it smote his own people in Hamburg, was the infamous Jew-hunt of Septr. 1830, which the sagacious burghers have recorded as the *Jew-riot*, thus making the victims the aggressors. At length after much hesitation and anguish, despairing of any free and honourable career in his own country, fearing even for his personal liberty, he resolved to expatriate himself; and crossing his Rubicon the Rhine, never but twice to cross it again, and then only for flying visits to his mother and publisher, entered Paris on the 3rd May, 1831. Henceforth he was to be not only the first, without a second, of living German poets, but also one of the greatest of European writers; one of the foremost champions in the western world, and perhaps among all the most radiant and redoubtable, of Liberalism and Freethought; publishing in French as well as in German, publishing often completely and faithfully in French what could only be got published mutilated and distorted in German.

The Paris which he loved treated him well. He was soon on intimate terms with the leading celebrities of literature and art. In the *Confessions* (1854) he has described with his most exquisite light humour his first impressions and experiences of the splendid capital. In 1831-2 he wrote to Cotta's *Allgemeine Zeitung* (*Universal Times*) of Augsburg, a series of letters on the political condition of France. When these were perforce suspended, he turned from interpreting France to Germany to interpreting Germany to France; and in the *Revue des Deux*

Mondes and elsewhere, he published the magnificent essays which are now résumćd in the *De l'Allemagne,* on the philosophy, the poetry, and the popular beliefs of his own country. In the meantime he was writing to Germany on the art and literature and social aspects of Paris. From 1840 to 1843, he was able again to write on the political situation to the *Allgemeine Zeitung.* A collection from these series of letters will be found in *Lutèce* and the *Salon.* In 1841 he visited Cauterets in the Pyrenees (celebrated already in the *Heptaméron* of Marguerite of Navarre), and then produced the poem of *Atta Troll, a Summer Night's Dream.* In 1843 he visited his mother, then seventy-two years old, and this visit produced the poem of *Germany, a Winter's Tale.* Other poems and essays followed up to the year of his death, including the *Romancero,* the *Lazarus,* and the *Last Poems.*

In Octr. 1834 he first met Mathilde Crescence Mirat, his dear Nonotte, whom he married, before a duel, August 31, 1841, after living with her for some time. She was of the *grisette* class, quite ignorant, but handsome and cheerful and true. She said frankly, People tell me that Henri writes very clever books, but I know nothing at all about them. Some time after their marriage, he writes: "We both live happily; that is, I have not a quarter of an hour's peace day or night." And again in 1843: "For eight years I have had a frightful quantity of happiness." Throughout his long, horrible malady she was ever tender and devoted and cheerful, never till the end despairing, of his ultimate recovery. As for him, well and ill he adored her. They lived very simply together, for he was never rich. Mr. Stigand reckons his yearly income at £160 from Solomon Heine (subsequently increased to £192, of which half was to be continued to the wife, if she outlived him), and only on the average £120 from his literary work, which was making the fortune of Campe; and Heine avows that he was a bad manager. After the death of Solomon Heine, in Decr. 1844, the sons seemed resolved to cut off Heine's pension, though it had been promised by the old man, as above stated, for the joint lives of Heine and his wife; but after a quarrel, which is said to have brought on the decisive attack of his malady, the pension was continued though burdened with some mean conditions. The estate of Solomon was valued at forty-one million francs, of which, fifteen millions or £600,000 went to the next head of the house. Surely Heine's allowance was not a very serious deduction from this. In 1843 he ceded to Campe the copyright of his works for £90 a year, commencing in 1848, during the lives of himself and his wife. He also for some years, down to 1848, received a pension of nearly £200 a year from the French government. Very flattering offers were also made to him of employment under this government, but he could not make up his mind to renounce his German nationality, though as early as 1835 the German governments by an edict of the Diet of Frankfort (how ancient seem the names Diet and Bund already!) had done its worst to bring him to starvation by absolutely prohibiting all his writings. I have said that the first attack of paralysis has been attributed to the agitation and anxieties of the dispute with his Hamburg relatives, on the result of which depended in large measure his own future subsistence, and, what he cared for infinitely more, the subsistence of his wife if left a widow; and in 1846, he wrote to Ferdinand Lassalle, also a Jew, and afterwards a leader of the German Socialists, who was shot in a duel near Geneva in 1866: "I am more unfortunate and wretched now than I have ever been, and had I not a helpless wife to leave behind me, I would quietly take my hat and say good-bye to the world." He had still the use of his limbs; but his left eye was wholly closed, and of the right the vision was darkened, and the lid he had to lift with his hand. His heart felt bound as by an iron frost; his lips he could not move freely, and they were so insensible that, in his own words, even kissing had no effect on them. "I sit whole evenings silent by the fireside with my wife. *Quelle conversation allemande,* What a German chat! she says sometimes with a sigh. The palate, too, and a part of the tongue are affected, and all that I eat tastes like earth." In this state he wished to consult his old fellow-student Dieffenbach, the famous surgeon, and wrote to his friend Alexander von Humboldt, then much with the king, to procure him if possible a permit to visit Berlin for medical advice. So extreme was the rancour of the Prussian government against him, and so heartless and cowardly in its extremity, that Humboldt after using his best efforts, counselled Heine in the interest of his personal safety not to touch Prussian soil.

In the preface to the *Romancero,* dated Paris, September, 1851, in which poetry and pathos, humour and irony, are so wonderfully intermingled, Heine says: "I had then still some flesh and heathenism in me, and I was not yet emaciated to the spiritualistic skeleton which now attends its complete dissolution. But do I really still exist? My body is so dwindled away that scarcely anything but the voice is left, and my bed reminds me of the sounding grave of the wizard Merlin, which lies in the forest of Broceliand in Brittany, beneath high oak-trees, whose crests burn like green flames to heaven. Ah, those trees and their fresh waving I envy you, colleague Merlin; for no green leaf rustles in to my mattress-grave at Paris, where early and late I hear only the rattle of vehicles, perpetual hammering, and scolding, and piano-strumming. A grave without rest, death without the privileges of the dead, who have to pay no bills and write no letters nor even books,—this is a sad condition. They have long since taken the measure for my coffin, and also for my obituary, but I am so long a-dying that at last it becomes as tedious to myself as to my friends. But patience; everything has an end. Some morning you will find the booth closed where the puppet-play of my humour so often delighted you."

And again: "When one lies on his death-bed he grows very sentimental and soft-hearted, and would fain make his peace with God and the world. I confess it, I have scratched many, bitten many, and been no lamb. But, believe me, those belauded lambs of gentleness would have shown themselves less tame had they possessed the teeth and the claws of the tiger. I can boast that I have but rarely made use of these natural weapons. Since I have myself needed the mercy of God, I have granted an amnesty to all my foes; many fine pieces, aimed at very high and very low persons, are therefore not admitted into the following collection. Poems which were only half satirical against dear God himself, I have, with the most anxious zeal, given to the flames. It is better that the verses burn than the versifier. . . . Yes, I have turned back to God, like the prodigal son, after long keeping swine with the Hegelians. Was it misery that drove me back? Perhaps a less miserable cause. The heavenly home-sickness fell upon me, and drove me forth through woods and ravines, over the dizziest mountain-paths of dialectics. On my way I found the God of the Pantheists, but of him I could make no use. This poor visionary being is interwoven and blended with the world, as it were imprisoned therein, and gapes at you without will or power. To have a will one must be a person, and to manifest it one must have the elbows free. If we want a god who can help us—and this is the main point—we must accept also his personality, his independence of the world, and his holy attributes, the all-goodness, the all-wisdom, the all-righteousness, and so forth. The immortality of the soul, our continuance after death, will be then as it were given us into the bargain, like the fine marrow-bone which the butcher, when he is satisfied with his customers, thrusts gratis into their basket. Such a fine marrow-bone is called in French kitchen-slang, *la réjouissance*, and most excellent strengthening broth is made with it, very strengthening and refreshing for a poor, pining sick man. That I did not reject such a *réjouissance*, but on the contrary took it to my heart with delight, every feeling man will approve."

And yet again: "As for myself, I cannot boast of any special advance in politics; I continue loyal to the same democratic principles which my earliest youth embraced, and for which thenceforward I ever more ardently glowed. In theology, on the other hand, I am guilty of retrogression, having, as already avowed, turned back to the old superstition, to a personal God. This can no longer be kept secret, as many enlightened and well-meaning friends have wished. But I must expressly contradict the rumour that my relapse has led me to the threshold, or indeed into the bosom, of any Church. No, my religious convictions and views have remained free from every ecclesiasticism; no church bells have allured, no altar-tapers have dazzled me. I have juggled with no symbolism, nor wholly renounced my reason. I have abjured nothing, not even my old heathen gods, from whom I have indeed turned away, but parting in love and friendship. It was in May, 1848, on the day that I went out for the last time, that I took leave of the gracious idols whom I adored in the period of my happiness. Only with pain could I drag myself to the Louvre, and I was nearly exhausted when I entered the lofty hall where the Most Blessed Goddess of Beauty, Our Dear Lady of Milo, stands on her pedestal. I lay long at her feet, and I wept so violently that even a stone could not but have compassion. And the Goddess did look down on me with pity, but at the same time without consolation, as if she would say: 'See you not that I have no arms, and so cannot help you?' "

In October, 1846, he had written: "I remain here the winter in any case, and dwell for the present pretty commodiously at Faubourg Poissonière, No. 41: if you find me not here, look for me, please, in the *Cimetière Montmartre*, not at *Père-la-Chaise*, which is too noisy for me." L. Schücking, who visited him in 1847, writes: "The former glow of health had faded from his face, which was of a delicate waxen pallor; all his features were refined, they were transfigured, spiritualised; it was a head of infinite beauty, a true Christ-head. I said to myself that he could not live six weeks more. Yet he lived full eight years."

In the same year, with regard to the question, What becomes of man after death? Heine said: "What becomes of the wood there on the hearth? The flame destroys it. Let us warm ourselves at it until the ashes are scattered to the winds." A young man present remarked: "All humanity is but one man, therefore no one is lost by death; every individual lives onward as a point in humanity, which is as a nerve from Adam unto us, and from us to our descendants; nothing dies which has once been alive." "Well said, young mole," added Heine with a laugh; "the history of the world is a life-assurance for those who live upon an income."

In 1848, speaking of his immense and indestructible love of life, he said: "In my present state of suffering this seems to me something ghastly. My love of life is like the spectre of a gentle nun in the ruins of an old cloister: it haunts the ruins of my *ego*." In June, 1848, he wrote: "My legs are like cotton, and I have to be carried like a child. The most horrible convulsions. My right hand begins to die. God knows whether I can write to you. Dictation is painful to me on account of the crippled state of my jaws." And in September: "So much is certain, that I have endured more torments in the last three months than the Spanish Inquisition ever invented. This living death, this no-life, is intolerable, and if other pains were to be added—. Even if I do not die soon, life is lost to me for ever, and I love life still with such vehement passion!" In 1849 he said to Alfred Meissner: "A religious reaction has set in upon me for some time. God knows whether the morphine or the poultices have anything to do with it. It is so. I believe again in a personal God. To this we come when we are sick, sick to death and quite broken down. If the German people accept the King of Prussia in their need, why should not I accept a personal God? My friend, hear a great truth. When health is used up, money used up, and sound human sense used up, Christianity begins." And in 1850, to Adolph Stahr: "It is strange that we have such universal religions, while religions must necessarily be of the most personal character. For my part, I am convinced that people in good health and people in bad health need quite different religions. For the man in good health Christianity is an unserviceable religion, with its resignation and one-sided precepts. For the sick man, however, I assure you it is a very good religion." And again to Meissner, after speaking of the terrible tortures which afflicted him even in his dreams: "But I too have my faith. Do not think that I am without a religion. Opium, that also is a religion. If when a pinch of grey powder is shed upon the fearfully painful wounds of my burns [from the blisters] the pain immediately ceases; shall it not be said that there is in this the same soothing power as shows itself active in religion? There is nearer relationship between opium and religion than most men dream of. I can endure my sorrows no longer; I take morphine. I cannot destroy my foes; I leave them to Providence. I can no longer manage my affairs; I resign them to God. Only," he added after a pause, with a smile, "I prefer to keep charge of my money affairs myself." In November, 1851, he writes to Herr Weerth: "I am delighted that my preface to the *Romancero* has pleased you: I had neither the time nor was I in the mood then to explain as I wished, that I die as a poet who has no need of either religion or philosophy, and will have nothing of either. The poet understands the symbolic idiom of religion, and the abstract logical jargon of philosophy, but neither the professors of religion nor of philosophy will ever understand the poet. Through this incapacity both these sets of gentlemen think that I am become a devotee." Speaking to Meissner: "I could not sacrifice myself exclusively, as others have done; I enter the ranks of no party, either as republican or patriot, Christian or Jew. In this I am like all artists, who do not write for enthusiastic moments but for centuries, not for one country alone, but for all the world, nor for one race alone but for all mankind." And to Adolph Stahr, on the immortality of the soul: "A strange conflict goes on in me as to this. All my reason and all my knowledge tell me that the belief in a personal continuance after death is an illusion. There is no trace of this belief in the Old Testament. Moses was much too healthy a man for it. That sickly sect which proceeded from Christ to Christianity, and subsequently to asceticism, invented immortality. In my understanding I am thoroughly convinced of the cessation of our existence. I cannot conceive or comprehend it, because I exist. I only understand that with egotists the thought of the cessation of existence must be consoling. To a loving heart it is, in spite of all science, inconceivable. I cannot imagine, for instance, that I shall leave my wife alone, and I always tell her that I shall come to her in an invisible form to keep her affairs in order,—but she is afraid of ghosts and begs me not to come." To Gérard de Nerval (who translated his *Book of Songs* into most exquisite French prose, and also wrote exquisitely appreciative criticisms on the poems and the poet): "Do me the favour to inquire in Germany in what faith one dies most easily. I am occupying myself very seriously with this question, and the German philosophers seem to know something about it, since one hears nothing of them lately." To Meissner, with a sigh: "If I could even get out on crutches, do you know whither I would go? Straight to church." And when Meissner looked incredulous: "Most decidedly to church. Where else should one go with crutches? Faith, if I could walk out without crutches, I should prefer to stroll along the lively boulevards, or to the Jardin Mabille." Long before, about 1835, he had written in relation to Schelling: "The thinker who of old developed the most daringly in Germany the religion of Pantheism, who proclaimed the most loudly the sanctification of Nature, and the re-integration of man in his divine rights, this thinker is become apostate to his own thought; he has deserted the altar which he himself consecrated; and he now preaches a God extra-mundane, a personal God *who has had the folly to create the world*. The old believers may, if they like, ring their bells and chant their *Kyrie Eleison* in honour of such a conversion. This proves nothing for their doctrine; it proves only that man turns to religion when he is old and weary, when his forces, physical and spiritual, abandon him, when he can no longer enjoy or think. So many free-thinkers have been converted on their death-beds! But, at any rate, do not boast of them. These legends of conversions, at the best, pertain to pathology, and furnish but a sorry testimony in favour of your cause. In fine, they only prove after all, that it was impossible for you to convert these thinkers while they were sound in body and mind."

In his last will, drawn up in French in 1851, he left all his little property to his wife, "who, as true as she is beautiful, has cheered my existence"; begging Campe to pay her regularly the stipulated annuity, and appealing to Karl Heine to pay her the pension guaranteed by Solomon in case of her widowhood. The will goes on: "To my noble, high-hearted mother, who has done so much for me, as well as to my dear brothers and sister, with whom I have always lived in unbroken harmony, I bid a last farewell. Farewell, thou German home, land of enigmas and sorrows; be thou serene and happy. Farewell, you kindly bright-witted French, whom I have loved so much. I thank you for your cheerful hospitality." The seventh clause gives instructions for his burial in the cemetery of Montmartre, as he had passed in that quarter the happiest years of his life; and contines: "I desire that my funeral be as simple as possible, and that the costs do not exceed the ordinary expense of that of the simplest citizen. Although by my baptismal act I belong to the Lutheran confession, I do not wish that the clergy of this church should be invited to my funeral; also I decline the official assistance of any other priesthood in the celebration of my funeral rights. This desire springs from no whim of a free-thinker. For four years now I have renounced all philosophic pride, and have returned to religious ideas and feelings. I die in the belief of one only God, the eternal Creator of the world, whose pity I implore for my immortal soul. I lament that I have at certain times spoken of sacred things without due reverence, but I was carried away more by the spirit of my time than by my own inclinations. If I unwittingly have violated good manners and morality, which is the true essence of all true monotheism, I pray both God and man for pardon. I forbid that any speech be spoken at my grave either in German or in French." This is solemn, and perhaps genuinely serious; I say perhaps, because one can never, however subtle-witted and sympathetic, be quite sure with Heine, and I believe that he could not be quite sure himself, where the seriousness ends and the humouristic irony begins. He tells us that the first book which fascinated his childhood when he was just able to read for himself, was *Don Quixote*, and says, "I was an infant; and knew not the irony which God has created in his world, and which the grand poet has copied in his." This irony, which the simple child knew not, became the master-spirit of the man in all thought and speculation, in all that did not intimately concern his profound and constant home-affections, or his burning love of the beautiful in nature and in art. But whether this passage of the will be thoroughly serious or not, it was not his last word; and I shall have to quote later utterances on God and the soul. Perhaps I cannot more fitly conclude this section than with a piece from the *Last Poems,* which are dated 1853-5, entitled *Body and Soul*: it is worth pondering. My translation, such as it is, was published eleven years since: –

The poor Soul speaketh to its Clay:
I cannot leave thee thus; I'll stay
With thee, with thee in death will sink
And black Annihilation drink!
Thou still hast been my second *I*,
Embracing me so lovingly;
A satin feast-robe round my form,
All lined with ermine soft and warm.
Woe's me! I dare not face the fact, –
Quite disembodied, quite abstract,
To loiter as a blessed Nought
Above there in the realm of Thought,
Through Heavenly halls immense and frigid,
Where the immortals dumb and rigid
Yawn to me as they clatter by
With leaden clogs so wearily.
Oh, it is horrible! Oh, stay,
Stay with me, thou beloved Clay!

The Body to the poor Soul said:
Oh, murmur not, be comforted!
We all should quietly endure
The wounds of Fate, which none can cure.
I was the lamp's wick, and to dust
Consume; but thou, the Spirit, must
Be saved with care, and lifted far
To shine in heaven a little star
Of purest light. – I am but cinder,
Mere matter, rubbish, rotten tinder,
Losing the shape we took at birth,
Mouldering again to earth in earth.
Now fare thee well, and grieve no more!
Perchance life is not such a bore
In Heaven as you expect up there.

If you should meet the old Great Bear
(Not Meyer-beer)* i' the starry climes,
Greet him from me a thousand times!

From Oct. 1848 to Nov. 1854, the mattress-grave of Heine was at No. 50, rue d'Amsterdam, in an apartment at the back of the house, up two steep flights of stairs, with windows looking on the court, and into which the sun only shone at noon. Mr. Stigand says: "In the winter of 1848-9, the suffering from his malady—which was finally found to be a softening of the spinal marrow—reached an almost unendurable pitch, and he was forced to have constant recourse to opium; his blindness increased, his back became bent and twisted, his body wasted away, as did also his legs, which last became soft and without feeling, 'like cotton,' as he expressed it. He lost, too, the use of his hands and arms to such a degree that he ceased to write his letters with his own hands [*sic*] after July, 1848, and he had *moxas* frequently applied to his back, whose burning wounds alleviated the yet more horrible cramps of his back-bone." Meissner, who visited him in Jany. 1849, reports: "He told me of his almost uninterrupted torments, of his helplessness, and his Job-martyrdom, which had now lasted so long. He depicted to me how he himself had become, as it were, a ghost; how he looked down on his poor, broken, racked body, like a spirit already departed and existing in a sort of intermediate state. He described how he lived in images and intuitions of the past, and how gladly he would yet compose, write, and create, and how his blind eye, his unsteady hand, and his ever-recurring pain, effaced everything from his spirit. He described his nights and their tortures, when the thought of suicide crept nearer and nearer to him, until he found strength to hurl it away by thinking of his beloved wife, and the many works he might yet bring to completion; and truly horrible was it when he at last said, 'Think of Günther, Bürger, Kleist, Hölderlin, Grabbe, and the wretched Lenau;—some curse weighs heavy on the poets of Germany.'"

In April, 1849, he wrote to the *Allgemeine Zeitung* correcting various rumours regarding him then current in Germany.

*Meyerbeer, the great musician. Heine in his later years lost no opportunity for a skit at him. The poet is also alluding to his own "Atta-Troll," whose title-hero is a bear. (Thomson's note.)

In the course of this letter he says: "In many moments, especially when the cramps are too painfully lively in the spinal column, a doubt quivers through me whether man is really a two-legged god, as the late Professor Hegel assured me in Berlin five and twenty years ago. . . . I am no more a divine biped. I am no more 'the freest of the Germans after Goethe.' I am no more the great heathen number two, who was compared to Dionysos crowned with vine-leaves, while to my colleague number one was given the title of a Grand-ducal Weimarian Jupiter. I am no longer a Hellene of jovial life and somewhat portly person, who laughed cheerfully down upon dismal Nazarenes. I am now only a poor death-sick Jew, an emaciated image of suffering, an unhappy man."

To Stahr and his wife, Fanny Lewald, who visited him in October, he said: "I suffer unceasing severe pain. Even my dreams are not free from it. Yesterday I hung, as John of Leyden, in a cage in the air, and my pains surrounded me as wild visions. The cramps are gradually extending higher, and now I lie waiting for them to reach my heart." And again: "That which ever sustains me is the thought that I endure all these agonies of my own free will, and can put an end to them as soon as I like. See here, with my hand I can reach out to take a dose of opium after which I should not wake again; and close by there lies a dagger which I have still strength to use if my tortures grow intolerable. That I possess this freedom gives me courage, and makes me, in a certain sense, cheerful."

Dr. Gruby, a Hungarian, who first divined his real malady, did him some good, so that he "was able to place himself in a sitting posture, the use of his hands was in a measure restored, his sight was improved, though still in order to see at all he was obliged to lift up his eyelid with his hand, and the powers of eating and digesting were also partially restored, together with his faculty of taste." He had read to him medical treatises on his malady, saying that these studies would be of use to him by-and-by, as he would be able to give lectures in heaven, and convince his hearers how badly physicians on earth understood the treatment of softening of the spinal marrow.

During the Exhibition at Paris, in 1855, he remarked that if his nerves could be exhibited he was sure they would gain a gold medal for superior wretchedness. He suffered much through being scarcely able to write, as he could not dictate to satisfy himself, needing pen in hand to attain perfection of form. His later poems he pencilled painfully. In May 1850, Meissner found him one day dictating a letter to his mother: "And does she live yet," I asked, "the old lady who dwells by the *Dammthor*?" "Ah, yes! very old though, sick and feeble, but still the warm mother-heart." "And do you write often to her?" "Regularly every month." "How unhappy she must be at your condition!" "At my condition! Oh, as for that we hold peculiar relations. My mother believes me to be as well and sound as I was when I last saw her. She is old, and reads no newspaper. The few old friends she sees are in the like case. I send word to her as well as I can in a cheerful humour, and tell her of my wife, and how happy I am. If she remarks that only the signature is mine, and that all the rest is in the handwriting of my secretary, the explanation is that I have pains in the eyes which will soon pass off, but which hinder me from writing everything myself. And thus she is happy. For the rest, that a son could be as sick and wretched as I am no mother would believe." As for his conduct to his wife, Meissner says: "I fully believe that the poet loved his Mathilde more than he had loved any other being on earth. On his sick bed, in the midst of his most terrible pains, his thoughts were always directed to preserving her honour before the world, and making her subsistence sure for the remainder of her days. . . . It was only for her that he strained his powers to work to the last, and every clause of his will gives proof of a care for her which was prolonged beyond the grave. She was his doll, whom he loved to dress elegantly in silk and lace, whom he would gladly have adorned with the finest of all to be found in Paris. He sent her out to walk, sent her to theatres and concerts, smiled whenever she approached him, and had for her only jests and words of endearment. She never participated in the evolutions of his spirit, and never knew anything of his struggles, but she lived only in him, and she stood faithfully by his side for twenty years." Whence one seems to learn that irony may have its covert tenderness, not less real than is effused by the most gushing candour; and that there may even be dreadful cynics more beloved at home than are some philanthropic saints. Mathilde thus deluded by him would never give up hope of his recovery; and her cheerful confidence in its turn cheered him, for he thought that she could never at the worst be very unhappy. "Such are the angels," he said; "they do not discount their future, they have always ready money." Yet, as stated, he was continually concerned about her future, and on one occasion he said: "My wife laughed yesterday when I gave her some money, for I counted it out to her not as one *louis,* two *louis,* three *louis,* but as one friend, two friends, three friends, etc."

With regard to the state of his brain, he said: "It is a great consolation to me that I have never lost the track of my thoughts, that my understanding is always clear. I hold this to be so essential for me that I have constantly occupied myself in the spirit during my whole illness, although my doctors dissuaded me from it as prejudicial. I think, on the contrary, that it has kept my state from being worse." And he writes: "My body suffers great pain, but my soul is as serene as a lake-mirror, and has sometimes its beautiful sunrises and sunsets." And again: "Only two consolations are left me, and sit caressingly by my pillow,—my French wife and my German muse. I string together a good many rhymes, and some of them magically soothe away my pain when I hum them to myself. A poet remains an idiot to the last." And at the commencement of his illness he once went so far as to say, "Like a nightingale that has been made blind, I shall now but sing the more beautifully." One day when Meissner was visiting the poet, he pointed to a box which stood on a chest of drawers opposite his couch, and said: "Look you! there are my *Memoirs;* therein have I been collecting for many years past a series of portraits and frightful *silhouettes.* Many people know of this box and tremble. In it is shut up one of the greatest, but by no means the last of my triumphs." These are the *Memoirs* which it is said his family sold to the Austrian government after his death, and which are supposed to be reserved in the secret archives of the Imperial court. Until these *Memoirs* are published unmutilated and undistorted, no conclusive judgment upon Heine's life can be delivered.

In Nov. 1854 he removed to No. 3, Avenue Matignon, where he remained till his death. His apartment was on the fifth storey, with a balcony commanding the Champs Elysées; there, in fine weather, he could be laid on a couch under a small tent, with screens of drapery, and with eyelid held up, and through an opera-glass, look at the green trees and the gay crowds promenading the Grande Avenue.

Adolph Stahr, who with his wife visited him in Oct. 1855,

writes: "I found him in a small room one hundred and five steps high, and in the same condition in which I had seen him five years before. He was lying on a low couch with a pencil and portfolio before him, having been attempting to write a little in the absence of his secretary. He expressed hearty joy at seeing us again. 'It must appear fabulous to you,' he said, 'to find me still among the living; it seems to me at times that I must be perpetrating a lie upon myself when I wake up out of my opium-sleep and find myself in my room!' . . . He bade us step out on the balcony, and enjoy the prospects of the trees, and the distant gay life of the Champs Elysées. I admired both as they deserved, and he remarked: 'You cannot conceive what I felt when after so many years I first beheld the world again with half an eye for ever so short a glimpse. I had my wife's opera-glass on my couch, and I saw with inexpressible emotion a young vagrant vendor of pastry offering his goods to two ladies in crinoline with a small dog. I closed the glass, I could look no more, for I envied the dog.' His nurse came to give him a draught of medicine, and bore him off from his couch as one carries a child, and put him on his bed. '*Sic transit gloria mundi*—So passes the glory of the world,' he exclaimed to a visitor on a similar occasion. On the whole I found him suffering still more than five years ago, and his productive power and conversation no longer so incessantly brilliant. A fearful cough, which had set in some time back, often interrupted his conversation with such spasms that at whiles I thought he must be suffocated. His humour, however, did not desert him even in the extremity of his anguish. Once the doctor, who was examining his chest, asked him, '*Pouvez vous siffler?*' He replied, '*Hélas non! pas meme une comedie de M. Scribe.*' He expressed himself very positively as to the condition of France and the French. 'All is of no use; the future belongs to our friends the Communists, and Louis Napoleon is their John the Baptist.'"

In Lord Houghton's "Monographs" is a letter from a lady with whom, when she was a child, Heine had been very friendly at Boulogne, recording two visits she paid to him during his illness; the first after twenty years, in the rue d'Amsterdam, the other five years later in the Avenue Matignon. Of the former she says: "He lay on a pile of mattresses, his body wasted so that it seemed no bigger than a child's under the sheet which covered him, the eyes closed, and the face altogether like the most painful and wasted *Ecce Homo* ever painted by some old German painter. His voice was very weak, and I was astonished at the animation with which he talked; evidently his mind had wholly survived his body." And of the second: "I climbed up four storeys to a small room, where I found him still on the same pile of mattresses on which I had left him five years before—more ill he could not look, for he looked like death wasted to a shadow. When I kissed him his beard felt like swan's-down or a baby's hair, so weak had it grown, and his face seemed to have gained a certain beauty from pain and suffering. He was very affectionate to me, and said [in German], 'I have made my peace with the whole world, and at last with dear God also. He now sends me you as a beautiful Angel of Death: I shall certainly die soon.' On the whole, I never saw a man bear such horrible pain and misery in so perfectly unaffected a manner. He complained of his sufferings, and was pleased to see tears in my eyes, and then at once set to work to make me laugh heartily, which pleased him just as much. He neither paraded his anguish, nor tried to conceal it, nor put on any stoical airs. I also thought him far less sarcastic, more hearty, more indulgent, and altogether pleasanter than ever."

Mr. Stigand says: "The winter of 1854-5 was for Heine a most severe one, and there was yet another to go through before all was over. A severe cold, caught soon after his arrival in his new quarters, aggravated his sufferings immensely; cramps in the chest and throat sometimes lasted the night through, and bade fair to suffocate him, and he was threatened with total blindness of the right eye." The closing months of his long agony caught a glamour of strange beauty from a pathetic romance which calls to memory that of the dying Burns and Miss Jessie Lewars, the heroine of his lovely last song—

Here's a health to ane I lo'e dear,
Here's a health to ane I lo'e dear;
Thou art sweet as the smile when fond lovers meet,
And soft as the parting tear—Jessie!

Although thou maun never be mine,
Although even hope is denied!
'Tis sweeter for thee despairing
Than aught in the world beside—Jessie!

A young lady, beautiful and brilliant, who from childhood had been fascinated by his songs, was brought by chance to his room in Oct. 1855. Her name is not revealed, she is shrouded in sweet mystery; we know only that she was of German birth, for he writes of her "dear lovely Suabian face." He found such pleasure in her society that he begged her to come again, and she came; and soon he could scarcely endure her absence for a day. He called her his dear *mouche,* or fly, and he wanted to have her always hovering and buzzing about him. Probably one of her sweetest charms to him was the fact that she buzzed in his dying ears the dear old mother-speech, for the death-bed ever yearns backward to the cradle. Meissner says: "A hundred sheets of paper at least lie before me written over in pencil by Heine's own hand, which he sent from the solitude of his sick room to the maiden to call her to his side. Just as the prisoner loves the little bird that comes to perch on the sill of his window, and tenderly supplies it with food in order to lure it back again, and make the spot so pleasant that it may at whiles forget the green and spacious wood, so Heine overwhelmed this friend and companion with little presents expressive of his good wishes in a hundred forms, and strained daily a hand, now scarcely capable of writing at all, to write little letters which incessantly, with ever-fresh words of flattery, invited to fresh visits. When one sees these great, delicate, noble characters, one can hardly credit that they came from the withered hand of a shattered organism; and when one reads the sense of which they are the interpreters, one cannot sufficiently marvel at the deep, ineradicable energy of life to which they bear witness. . . . These letters will never be divulged: the name of the maiden herself is a secret. A strange chance brought me, after Heine's death, into contact with their possessor. I was allowed to cast a look into this treasure, which contains many poems, and I give a few of the letters which I have been permitted to publish." Of these I can give but two: "Wednesday, 3 o'clock—Dearest soul! I am very wretched—have coughed horribly for twenty-four hours together: hence to-day pain in the head, probably tomorrow also; therefore I pray the sweetest one to come on Friday instead of tomorrow. I must pine till then. My Scrinsky [his secretary] has excused himself on the ground of sickness for a week past. What an unpleasant state of things! I am almost mad with vexation, sorrow, and impatience. I shall lodge a complaint against dear God (*den lieben Gott*) before the Society for the Prevention of Cruelty to Animals. I reckon on Friday; meanwhile I kiss in thought the little *pattes de mouche*. Your crazy H. H." And here is the last: "Dearest friend, — I am still steeped in headache, which will perhaps be gone to-morrow, so that the darling will be able to see me next day. What anguish! I am so sick! *My brain is full of madness and my heart of sorrow* [in English in the original]. Never was a poet so unhappy in the fulness of fortune, which seems to make a mock of him. Farewell! — H." Another note to her is signed, "Nebuchadnezzar II., once a Prussian Atheist, now a devotee of the Lotusflower." Some of his published *Last Poems* were also inspired by this lady, notably that *Fur die Mouche — For the Fly*. Others of the most tender and pathetic of these *Last Poems* are devoted to his wife.

His end is thus related by Meissner: "A fit of vomiting came on, and continued for three days, and could not be stopped, and it became clear to all who attended him that this time he must succumb. The monstrous doses of morphia to which he had gradually accustomed himself had often brought on similar symptoms, but not so violent or persistent. Yet he was still defiant, and hoped to survive even this struggle. He began to make a new will, without however, being able to get beyond the first paragraph, yet retaining always his consciousness. Even his wit never left him. Some hours before he died a friend came into his room to see him once more. Soon after his entry he asked Heine whether he was on good terms with God. 'Set your mind at rest,' said Heine, 'God will pardon me, it is his trade (*Dieu me pardonnera, c'est son metier*).' Thus the last night arrived, the night of Feb. 16, 1856. The physician came, and Heine asked him whether he must now die. Dr. Gruby thought that he should be told the truth. The sick man received the verdict in perfect peace. About four o'clock the next morning he died. His wife had gone to bed about one, and did not see him again until his eyes were closed for ever. He was more beautiful as a corpse than he had ever appeared in life; the physician declared that he had never seen even youthful features so wonderfully transfigured by death. The plaster cast which was taken preserved faithfully the expression." He was buried on the 20th in the Cemetery of Montmartre. Some of his best friends and warmest admirers followed the funeral; Alexandre Dumas, Théophile

Gautier, Mignet the historian (one of his executors), Paul de Saint-Victor, Alexander Weill, and a small band of German authors and journalists. It was remarked that the coffin was very large, long and heavy for the wasted form, bringing to mind that early poem which concludes: —

> Why so great the coffin
> And heavy, ye would know?
> I likewise bury in it
> All my love and woe.

Théophile Gautier in his brief prefatory notice to the French edition of the *Reisebilder*, says: "His friends should have rejoiced that such atrocious tortures were at length terminated, and that the invisible executioner had given the *coup de grace* to the poor victim; yet to think that of this luminous brain, all sunbeams and ideas, whence images swarmed humming like golden bees, nothing now is left but a little greyish pulp, gives a pang one cannot accept without revolt. It is true that he was nailed alive in his bier, but bending down one heard the poetry singing beneath the black pall. What grief to see one of those microcosms more vast than the world, though contained in the narrow vault of a skull, ruined, lost, annihilated! What slow combinations it will cost Nature to produce another such head!"

I have dealt at such length on the long agony of Heine, because this differentiates him from most men, and even from most men of letters. Nearly all of us, in rare moments of health, and in rare attacks of serious illness, are brought face to face with the sombre mysteries of death; but he who had revelled in surpassing opulence of life, physical and intellectual, was stricken down while yet in his prime, and for seven years, palsied in body and lucid in mind, lay on the very verge of that unfathomed abyss into whose cold shadow-haunted gloom we common men in our common lives cast but a few swift yearning and shuddering glances. In all moods — tender, imaginative, fantastic, humourous, ironical, cynical; in anguish and horror; in weariness and revulsion, longing backward to enjoyment, and longing forward to painless rest; through the doleful days and the dreadful immeasurable sleepless nights; this intense and luminous spirit was enchained and constrained to look down into the vast black void which undermines our seemingly solid existence, and in which he all that time was as near immersion as a sailor alone on a leaking boat in a solitary sea; and his intense and luminous genius of expression has bequeathed to us records of all those moods of sunless day and starless night, though doubtless much of thought and feeling and phantasy remained even for him ineffable. Of his contemporaries with whom I am acquainted, there are three poets, all born in the decade of his birth, who have some affinity to him in this respect: Keats, with a marvellous sensuous prescience; Shelley, with a prescience more marvellously spiritual, of early death, radiated strange flashes of insight, and thrilling pulses of passion, into the depths of the obscure gulf; Leopardi, throughout a longer, though never quite helpless and motionless, agony, confronted it with a most desperate, undaunted, steadfast, and profound regard: but Heine alone lay for years outstretched on a mattress-grave, paralyzed in the weird border-land of Death-in-Life or Life-in-Death, a restless and fiery mind in a passive and frost-bound body. And as he himself was fascinated with an appalling fascination by the fulness of life behind, and the emptiness of death before, so we are fascinated and appalled by what he has revealed to us of his visions from that alien and terrible point of view. And the power of the spell on him, as the power of his spell on us, is increased by the fact that he thus in Death-in-Life brooding on Death and Life, was no ascetic spiritualist, no self-torturing eremite or hypochondriac monk, but by nature a joyous heathen of richest blood, a Greek, a Persian, as he often proudly proclaimed, a lusty lover of this world and life, an enthusiastic apostle of the rehabilitation of the flesh.

Any one who wishes to realise not quite inadequately this sad and strange last stage of the poet, must of course study for himself the poet's last works, as well his recorded speech. In addition to what I have already quoted I have space here for but a few scanty selections from those works. In the *Last Poems* we see, as by lightning flashes in the gloom, the struggle raging between his love of life and his revulsion from its horrible tortures; nor is it easy to discern with which side the alternating victory rests at last. In one piece he says: —

> Slumber is good, and death is better, — truly
> It were the best to never have been born;

and in another cries to Atropos: "Oh, hasten and cut asunder the thread, the evil, and let me recover from this horrible malady of life!" and in another: "Have mercy on me, and give me rest, O God, and finish the terrible tragedy." But elsewhere he recoils:

> The heavenly meads allure me not
> In Paradise, the blessed land;
> I find no lovelier women there
> Than I already found on earth.
>
> O Lord! I think it were the best
> You left me still in this old world;
> Cure only first my body's ills,
> And likewise furnish some more cash.
>
> Only good health and wealth enough
> Desire I, Lord! Oh, let me glad
> Live on yet many pleasant days
> Beside my wife, *in statu quo*!

And elsewhere again:

> O God! how loathly bitter is this dying!
> O God! how sweet and cosy can we live
> In this most sweet and cosy earthly nest!

Just as he had written nearly thirty years before, in 1826, in the book of *The Drummer Legrand,* included in the *Pictures of Travel*: "Let others enjoy the fancy that their beloved will adorn their grave with flowers, and water it with tears.—Oh, women! hate me, mock me, scout me, but let me live! Life is so wildly sweet, and the world is so pleasantly topsy-turvy! It is the dream of a God overcome with wine, who steals off without leave-taking from the celestial banquet, and goes away to sleep in a solitary star, ignoring that he creates all that he dreams. . . . And the images of his dream arise, now in a motley extravagance, now harmoniously reasonable. . . . But this will not last long: the god will awake; he will rub his drowsy eyelids; he will smile! and our world will vanish into nothingness. It will never have existed. No matter; I live. Though I be but a shadow, or an image of a dream, still this is better than the chill gloom and the emptiness of death. Life is the greatest of all blessings; and the worst of all evils is death."

In the first of the additional pieces to the *Lazarus,* — which Lord Houghton has attempted in verse with small success, and which I must reproduce in baldest prose, — Heine exclaims with a savage energy of concision: —

Leave your holy parables,
Leave your pious suppositions;
Try to give straightforward answers
To the damnable old questions —

Why must Right, a bleeding outcast,
Trail the burden of the Cross,
While exultant as a victor
Riding the high horse goes Wrong?

Where, then, lies the fault? Perchance
Our Lord is not quite Almighty?
Or himself he works the mischief?
Ah, but this were too degrading.

Thus we ask, and ask for ever,
Till at length our mouths are stopped
With a handful of mere earth; —
But can this be called an answer?

Perhaps the strongest expression of his *Lebenslust,* or lust of life, is to be found in a piece of which I have elsewhere written: —

Grossness here indeed is regnant,
But it is the grossness pregnant;

and which is of supreme significance as having been entitled by himself the *Epilogue* to the *Last Poems,* and therefore placed at the end of his complete works, as his ultimate utterance, the deliberate sum and conclusion of his philosophy. The following version was published several years since: —

Glory warms us in the grave.
Stupid words that sound so brave!
Better warmth would give to us
Molly Seagrim* amorous,

*The original is *Eine Kuhmagd,* which might read, "Any farm-wench"; but for the English reader it is, or ought to be, emphasized by remembrance of the famous scene in *Tom Jones,* which probably enough Heine himself had in mind, as he was familiar with Fielding (see *De l'Allemagne,* I. 359). (Thomson's note.)

Slobbering kisses, lips and tongue,
And yet reeking from the dung.
Better warmth would also dart
Through the cockles of one's heart
Drinking mulled wine, punch or grog
Until helpless as a log,
In the lowest den whose crowd is
Thieves and drabs, and ragged rowdies,
Mortgaged to the gallows-rope,
But who meanwhile breathe and hope,
And more enviable far
Than the son of Thetis are.—
Yes, Pelides was a judge:
Better live the meanest drudge
In the upper world, than loom
On the Stygian shore of gloom,
Phantom leader, bodiless roamer,
Though besung by mighty Homer.*

We now come to his last prose-work, the *Confessions,* of 1854, which let no dullard think to read aright. It is a Capitolian triumph of audacious genius and truth, but these are charioted by a whirling complexity of irony within irony, as dazzling and bewildering as the wheels within wheels of Ezekiel's vision, whose work was like unto the colour of a beryl, and which went upon their four sides yet turned not as they went; and, "As for their rings they were so high that they were dreadful; and their rings were full of eyes round about them. . . . Whithersoever the spirit was to go they went, thither was their spirit to go: for the spirit of the living creature was in the wheels." And be assured that this triumph of Heine is not without its captive victims, from Zenobia De Staël (whose Longinus Schlegel had been previously vivisected till there was no life in him), to Heraclitus Hegel, the illustrious obscure. I regret that there is room here for but two or three extracts from these hundred peerless pages.

The first relates to what he had done twenty years before in the way of expounding German philosophy to the French people and those who read French:—

"Yes, with regard to German philosophy, I had divulged without reserve the secret of the school; enveloped in scholas-

*Thomson's translation appeared as the "Epilogue" to his 1864 poem, "Vane's Story."

tic formulas, it was known only by the initiated of the highest class. My revelations excited the utmost astonishment in France, and I recollect that eminent thinkers of this country have avowed to me naively that they had always fancied that German philosophy was a sort of mystical haze in which the deity was hidden as in a sanctuary of clouds, and that the German philosophers had always seemed to them ecstatic visionaries, who breathed only piety and the fear of God. It is not my fault that this has never been the case, and that the German philosophy is exactly the opposite of what we have hitherto been accustomed to call piety and the fear of God. The most consistent of these *enfants terribles* of philosophy, our modern Porphyrius, who actually bears the name of *Fire-flood* (Feuerbach), proclaimed, in concert with his friends, the most radical Atheism as the ultimate conclusion of our metaphysics. With a frenzy of bacchantes these impious zealots rent the azure veil of the German heaven, shouting: 'See, all the divinities have fled, and on high there dwells but an old woman with hands of iron and disconsolate heart — Necessity.'"

The next, concerning the people and its flatterers the demagogues, tells some stern truths which we who are of the people may well lay to heart: —

"I love the people, but I love it at a distance; I have always combated for the emancipation of the people; this has been the great business of my life; yet in the hottest moments of my struggles I avoided the slightest contact with the multitude. I have never lavished hand-shakings on it. A rabid democrat of my country said to me once that he would put his hand in the fire to purify it if he had the misfortune to touch that of a king; as for me, I answered that if his majesty the people, the sovereign in whom dwells all legitimate power, grasped my hand, I would wash it. The people, this poor king in rags, has found sycophants and courtiers more brazen than were ever those of Byzantium or Versailles. These flatter the people continually, going into ecstacies over its perfections and virtues. They bawl: 'Ah, how beautiful is the people! how good is the people! and how intelligent is this beautiful and good people!' — No, the people is not beautiful; on the contrary it is ugly; but its ugliness is owing to its dirt, and will disappear as soon as public baths have been erected where his majesty, the people, can bathe for nothing. Nor is the people good, it is rather very mischievous, but it bites because it is hungry; food must be given it, and then the naughty big baby will become quite gentle and gracious, and will smile as all kings do when they have dined well. Nor is the people intelligent, it is as stupid as is allowable in a monarch; it is sometimes as brutish as those Brutuses whom it elects to represent it when it obtains for a moment absolute power: — it confides only in the ambitious who speak the jargon of its passions, and it abhors the honest man who attempts to enlighten it as to its real interests. Allow the people to choose between the justest of the just and the most arrant robber, and it will always cry: 'We want Barrabas! Long live Barrabas!' At Paris, as at Jerusalem, always the same cry! To put an end to this popular ignorance, it is necessary after feeding the people (for food is the chief thing), it is necessary, I say, to establish free schools where the people shall be taught, where it shall receive also the nourishment of the mind, and then you will see how these ferocious animals will become humanised, how they will become intelligent, perhaps even as bright-witted as ourselves."

The next describes, as only he could describe, his conversion from Hegelianism to Theism; the theology being as Heinesque, that is to say as unique, as the philosophy: —

"I was never a great metaphysician, and I had accepted without examination the synthesis of the Hegelian philosophy, whose conclusions tickled my vanity. I was young and proud, and my pride was not a little flattered by the idea that I was a god. I had never consented to believe that God had become man: I taxed this sublime dogma with superstition, yet afterwards I believed Hegel on his bare word when I heard him declare that man was God. Such an idea charmed me; I took it quite seriously, and I sustained my divine character as honourably as possible. . . . The costs of representation of a god who cannot be stingy, and who economises neither his purse nor his body, are enormous; to play this magnificent part one must above all be endowed with plenty of money and plenty of health. Now, one fine morning — it was at the end of Feby. 1848 — these two things failed me, and my divinity was in consequence so shaken that it collapsed miserably. . . . Like many other gods overthrown by the revolution of Feby., I had to abdicate my divinity, and I redescended to the condition of a mere mortal. I re-entered the sheepfold of faith, and I willingly recognised the omnipotence of the Supreme Being who regulates the destines of the world, and to whom since then I have confided also the administration of my own affairs, very involved when I managed them myself. I have now fewer cares in relying on the providence of my celestial steward; and the existence of a God is a great happiness for me; I draw from this belief the greatest comfort, and it is no less convenient than economical. I no longer trouble myself with irksome responsibilities; as a true devotee I no longer encroach on the prerogatives of the good God, and I no longer give anything to the poor, to whom, of old, I distributed succours. I have piously announced to these unfortunates that I no longer have any part in the government of the world, and that they must henceforward seek the aid of the Lord who dwells in the heavens, whose budget is as infinite as his compassion, while I, in order to satisfy my divine propensities, was sometimes forced to pull hard to make both ends meet (*tirer le diable par la queue*—pull the devil by the tail), which was very unbecoming for a god. It is not I who will henceforth carry on the propaganda of Atheism; in addition to my financial collapse, I no longer enjoy brilliant health, I am even affected with an indisposition, truly very slight according to my doctors, but which has already kept me more than six years in bed. In such a condition it is for me a great solace to have some one in heaven to whom I can address my groans and lamentations during the night, after my wife has gone to bed. What a terrible thing to be ill and alone, without any body to importune with the litany of one's complaints!"

In the book of *The Drummer Legrand,* already referred to, he had written in the full riot of his youth: —

"Life is so fatally serious that it would not be endurable without the alliance of the pathetic and the comic. Our poets all know this. . . . Aristophanes, Goethe, and Shakespeare have all copied the great primitive poet, who in his universal tragedy in a thousand acts, has pushed to the extreme this Humour, as we see every day. . . . Even in the most sublime scenes of the tragedy of the world, some comic traits slip in; and the desperate republican who, like Brutus, plunges a knife into his heart, has perhaps first made sure that the blade did not smell of herrings. On this vast stage of the world all proceeds as on the miserable boards of our theatre: there, also, are drunken heroes, kings who do not know their parts, prompters who prompt too loudly, costumes which are the principal matter.—And in heaven, above there, in the dress circle, is seated all the while the good company of the angels, who quiz us performers, and the good God sits grave in his royal box, perhaps much bored, or calculating that this theatre cannot be kept open long, because some of the actors have salaries too large, and others have salaries too small, and likewise because they all play too badly."

Now, nearly thirty years later, lying at the door of death which will soon open to him who has lain before it so long, he writes thus on the same theme in concluding these *Confessions*:—

"The great pot is before me, but I have no spoon. What does it profit me that my health is drunk at banquets from cups of gold, and in the most exquisite wines, if during these ovations, remote and cut off from all the pleasures of the world, I can but moisten my lips with vapid barley-water? What does it profit me that all the roses of Shiraz open and burn for me, fulgent with passion? Alas! Shiraz is two thousand leagues from this sad sick chamber I have occupied so long, and where I smell no perfumes save perchance those of hot towels. Alas! the mockery of God weighs heavy on me. The great author of the universe, the Aristophanes of Heaven, has resolved to make the petty earthly author, the so-called Aristophanes of Germany, feel keenly that his wittiest sarcasms are in fact but pitiful pinpricks compared with the thunder-bolts of satire which the Divine humour can launch against frail mortals.

"Yes, the bitter flood of railleries which the great Master outpours on me is terrible, and the cruelty of his epigrams makes me shudder. I humbly recognise his superiority, and I prostrate myself before him in the dust. Yet feeble as is my creative energy in comparison with that of the great Creator, the eternal reason shines none the less in my head, and I have the right to summon before the tribunal of this reason, and to submit to its respectful criticism the pleasantry of God, my Lord and Master. Wherefore in all humility I venture to remark first that the atrocious pleasantry he inflicts on me, appears to be protracted a little too long; it has already lasted more than six years, and at length becomes tedious. Then I would also remark, in all humility, that this pleasantry is not new, that the great Aristophanes of Heaven has already practised it on several others, and that he is thus guilty of plagiarism from his own works.

In support of this charge I will cite a passage from the *Limburg Chronicle*. . . . It tells us that in the year 1480 they were strumming and humming throughout all Germany songs more sweet and delightful than they had ever known there before: and that young and old, and especially the women, doated on them to distraction, so that they resounded from morning to night. But these songs, adds the *Chronicle,* had been composed by a young clerk who was a leper, and lived apart from the world in some desert place. You are not ignorant, dear reader, what a frightful disease leprosy was in the Middle Ages, and how the poor creatures afflicted with this incurable evil were thrust out from all society, and had to keep themselves at a distance from other human beings. Like living corpses, enveloped to the feet in a grey frock, with the hood drawn over the face, they went about carrying an enormous rattle, termed the rattle of St. Lazarus, with which they announced their approach, in order that everybody should have time to avoid them. The poor clerk, of whom the said *Limburg Chronicle* recounts the glory he had acquired as a poet, was such a leper, and he pined away in the sad solitudes of his wretchedness, while, joyous and tuneful, all Germany praised his songs. Oh! this glory also was the mockery of God, the cruel mockery, which at bottom is always the same, though it appeared then under the more romantic costume of the Middle Ages. The *blasé* King of Israel and Judah said with reason: 'There is nothing new under the sun.' Perhaps the sun itself is simply an old pleasantry warmed up again, a showy, second-hand lustre, which, dressed out with fresh rays, sparkles now aloft in such dazzling style!

"Sometimes in my sombre visions of the night, I seem to see before me the poor leprous clerk of the *Limburg Chronicle,* my brother in Apollo, and through the grey hood his doleful eyes regard me with a fixed and strange regard; but in a moment he disappears, and I hear, losing itself in the distance, like the echo of a dream, the hollow creaking of the rattle of St. Lazarus."

A Note on Forster's *Life of Swift*

[*This review of John Forster's* The Life of Jonathan Swift, *Volume I (London, 1875), appeared in the* Secularist *(May 20, 1876). Thomson had also reviewed Forster's book in* Cope's Tobacco Plant *(April, 1876), and when reprinting the* Secularist *review in* Essays and Phantasies *(as "A Note on Forster's Life of Swift") he included an excerpt from the* Cope's *review in his footnote. The text here is taken from* Essays and Phantasies.]

IT IS MUCH to be regretted that Mr. Forster did not live to complete this work, which he meant to occupy three volumes; it is much to be desired that the materials he gathered during many years of preparation should be entrusted to some competent literary man, so that we may have a full and accurate biography not quite unworthy of the subject. As to this first volume, which is all that Mr. Forster accomplished, it merits the highest praise for its elaborate carefulness. We miss, indeed, the energy of the *Lives of the Statesmen of the Commonwealth*, and intense energy is demanded for the *Life of Swift*; we miss, also, some of the finer qualities that make the *Life of Oliver Goldsmith* such charming reading: the central figure and the central interest are here and there obscured by the multitude of subsidiary details; the contours are not always firm, nor the colours always clear; and we lament that the artist was not in a position to attempt this great picture in his prime, ere his hand grew somewhat tremulous, and his sight somewhat dim, and his natural strength was abated. But it is evident that what honest and earnest labour could effect he has effected, sparing no trouble to master and state the truth, the whole truth, and nothing but the truth; and this thoroughness of patient workmanship is so rare and precious in our current literature, that we might well for its sake condone far more serious deficiencies than we find here. With the work finished in the style of this volume, we should have, if not the classic Life of Swift, at any rate abundant and well-tested materials for such a Life, stored up and arranged with workmanlike skill and care. I must not omit to mention two things for which students will be grateful; a full index, and marginal notes of all the leading matters in the text.

In his Preface Mr. Forster states: —

"The rule of measuring what is knowable of a famous man by the inverse ratio of what has been said about him, is applicable to Swift in a marked degree. Few men who have been talked about so much are known so little. . . . Swift's later time, when he was governing Ireland as well as his deanery, and the world was filled with the fame of *Gulliver*, is broadly and intelligibly written. But as to all the rest, his life is a work unfinished, to which no one has brought the minute examination indispensably required, where the whole of a career has to be considered to get at the proper comprehension of single parts of it. The writers accepted as authorities for the obscurer portion are found to be practically worthless, and the defect is not supplied by the later and greater biographers. Johnson did him no kind of justice because of his too little liking for him; and Scott, with much hearty liking as well as a generous admiration, had too much other work to do. Thus, notwithstanding noble passages in both memoirs, and Scott's pervading tone of healthy, manly wisdom, it is left to an inferior hand to attempt to complete the tribute begun by those distinguished men."

Mr. Forster tells us that more than a hundred and fifty new letters had been placed at his disposal. He obtained additions to the fragment of autobiography first printed by Mr. Deane Swift; and questions raised by that autobiography in connexion with Swift's university career are settled by one of the Rolls of Trinity College which fell into his hands. "Two original letters written from Moor Park clear up that story of the Kilroot living which has been the theme of extravagant misstatement. Unpublished letters in the palace at Armagh . . . show clearly Swift's course as to questions which led to his separation from the Whigs." Mr. Forster also secured Swift's note books and books of account; a large number of unpublished pieces in prose and verse interchanged between himself and Sheridan; the copy of the Life by Hawkesworth enriched with MS. notes by Dr. Lyon, who had charge of Swift's person in his last illness; letters relating to *Gulliver*, some to Stopford, and some to Arbuthnot of peculiar value; an unpublished journal in Swift's handwriting, singular in its character, and of extraordinary interest, written on his way back to Dublin, amid grave anxiety for Esther Johnson (Stella), then dangerously ill; a copy of the first edition of *Gulliver*, interleaved for alterations and additions by the author, and containing several interesting passages, mostly in the Voyage to Laputa, which have never yet been given to the world; a copy of Swift's correspondence with his friend Knightley Chetwode during the seventeen years (1714–1731) which followed his appointment to the Deanery of St. Patrick's, "the richest addition to the correspondence of this most masterly of English letter-writers since it was first collected." To my mind the most interesting novelty in this first volume is contained in the Sixth Book (Appendix), under the heading of "Unprinted and Misprinted Journals"; being the restoration, by collation with the originals in the British Museum, of the genuine and complete text of the first one and the last twenty-four of the letters which make up what is called the Journal to Stella. Here for the first time we read, just as they were written, the "little language" and the caressing diminutives and abbreviations Swift used with his darling; the delightful, fantastic, secret, childish, infinitely tender babblement, never weary of repeating itself, welling up amidst and around the records of the ruggedest affairs of State, like perennial springs of pure sweet water in a region of savage rocks. He was fighting Titanically a Titanic battle; and night and morning, in bed before he rose, in bed before he slept, he found refreshment and peace in these infantine outpourings of innocent love. The sternest cynics have such soft places in their heart of hearts! incomparably softer than the softness of unctuous sentimentalists; liquid with living fountains where these are boggy with ooze.

I have quoted Mr. Forster's very fair judgment on the biographies by Dr. Johnson and Sir Walter Scott. It must be added that of the two writers of most authority who have since dealt with the life and character of Swift, Macaulay does him even less justice than did Johnson, and Thackeray not much more. Both, and Thackeray in particular, were impressed by the supremacy of his genius; but both were essentially out of sympathy with the man. Thackeray, although vulgarly charged with cynicism, was less a cynic than a worldling of genius who had cynical moods. He had a great deal of genuine respect for the established, the customary, the common-place, and was altogether more ironical in tone than in fact when he classed himself among the Snobs he satirised so keenly, though he was certainly a very superior specimen of the class. One of the common threads interwoven with the finer and richer threads of his fabric, was a very soft sentimental "religious" nerve connecting his heart and brain, and this was terribly shocked by Swift's daring and strenuous handling of the most formidable problems presented by our religions, our life, and our world. Moreover, Thackeray's thoroughly English domestic sentiments, his English worship of home and the ordinary public strict relations of husband and wife and family, were revolted by the mysterious duplex relations of Swift with Stella and Vanessa; relations, I may observe, whose full tragic development does not come within the scope of this volume, and which in their worst entanglement it does not appear that Mr. Forster could have done much to unravel.

Macaulay, historiographer in chief to the Whigs, and the great prophet of Whiggery which never had or will have a prophet, vehemently judged that a man who could pass over from the celestial Whigs to the infernal Tories must be a traitor false as Judas, an apostate black as the Devil. In truth, Swift was never an extreme partizan of either faction, and tried to moderate both; being Whiggish in his acceptance of the Revolution, and Toryish in his Church views. However, Macaulay, who has always exquisite pleasure and conscientious satisfaction in showing that our great writers who were not steadfast Whigs were just as ignoble morally as they were noble intellectually, paints him in the most lurid colours, and gives us a very terrific portrait indeed, which has merely the disadvantage of being altogether unlike the original, or any other man known to sober history. This, by the way, is a disadvantage pretty common to Macaulay's portraits, which are not developed organically like Carlyle's, but put together in mosaic work, and on glass for the love of brilliancy; he having a fine eye for the dazzle and contrast of colours, if none for their temperance and harmony. He diligently gathers all the pieces required for his purpose, shows them to us one by one, and announces triumphantly: All the materials are here, as you see for yourselves, gentlemen, each duly numbered and authenticated; and we expect to behold a likeness, though a glaring and composite one. But at the last moment he puts them in the kaleidoscope (or kakeidoscope) of his idosyncrasy, gives some rapid twirls and flourishes, and no mortal can guess what strange shape they shall have taken when finally settled for exhibition. In contemplating, not without bewilderment, his portrait of Swift, one cannot help muttering: This is really very fine in the way of the dreadful, my rhetorical lord; but if we could only have, to hang beside it, Swift's portrait of *you*!

Though, his parents being thoroughly English, Swift was in no sense Irish save by accident of birth-place and the mockery of fortune which banished him to Ireland for the last thirty years of his life, the warm-hearted Irish have never ceased to love and revere the memory of the Dean, who was not only a model of sagacious private charity, but who championed the cause of their then oppressed and outraged country with a courage and constancy equalled by few, with a power and effect equalled by none, for no one else has approached him in massiveness and energy of genius. The English generally, like Dr. Johnson, have done him no kind of justice because of too little liking for him. It is doubtful whether they even read him. The children, of course, delight in the fabulous marvels of *Gulliver*, but the grown-up people care not to study its lessons. At first I was tempted to blame Mr. Forster for occupying space in a book like this, not intended for the uneducated vulgar, with accounts of such classics as the *Battle of the Books* and the *Tale of a Tub*. But on reflection it seemed highly probable that Mr. Forster was much better acquainted than myself with the public of Mudie and Smith,* and that the information he furnished was accurately gauged to their ignorance. It is queer to think of our so-called educated classes needing formal introductions to these works, and then read how a gardener's lad of eleven, trudging in blue smock frock, with red garters tied under his knees, from Farnham to Kew, spent his last threepence at Richmond on the *Tale of a Tub*, and records: "It delighted me beyond description, and produced what I have always considered a sort of birth of intellect. I read on until it was dark without any thought of supper or bed." He slept where he had been reading, in a field by a haystack, and goes on to say of his wonderful threepenny book: "I carried it about with me wherever I went, and when I — at about twenty years old — lost it in a box that fell overboard in the Bay of Fundy in North America, the loss gave me greater pain than I have since felt at losing thousands of pounds." But this rustic was William Cobbett, the only man since Swift who has

*Mudie's and Smith's were the major circulating libraries in England in the last half of the century, and Charles Mudie in particular was influential in controlling the taste of the reading public, refusing to purchase and circulate books he considered in any way immoral.

known how to write in prose for the masses with something of the same irresistible directness and vigour.

Too strong and terrible for Thackeray and Macaulay, Swift is much more so for the average middle-class John Bull, who, while among the bravest of the brave in many respects, is one of the most timorous of mortals face to face with disagreeable truths, truths that perturb his eupeptic comfort, truths hostile to his easy old-fashioned way of thinking without thought, especially if these truths affront his fat inertia in religious, moral, or social questions.* This middle-class John Bull, well-fed, well-clothed, well-housed, with a snug balance at his banker's, is the most self-satisfied of optimists, and is simply disgusted and alarmed by a fellow, who as a Dean ought surely to have been contented and sleekly jolly, who never omitted when his birthday came round to read the words of Job: "Let the day perish wherein I was born, and the night in which it was said, There is a man child conceived"; who asked a friend, "Do not the corruptions and villanies of men eat your flesh and exhaust your spirits?" and who wrote of himself in his epitaph: *"Ubi sæva indignatio ulterius cor lacerare nequit."*

*Elsewhere I had written on the same occasion: "To our mind, for sheer strength and veracity of intellect, Swift is unsurpassed, and scarcely equalled, in the whole range of English writers, rich as the greatest of these are in energy and sincerity. He was much too strong and veracious even for such men as Johnson, Macaulay, and Thackeray; Scott alone of his biographers was genial and large-minded enough to appreciate him, and Scott had not the time to hunt out and sift the necessary documents. As for the general English public, with its soft-hearted and soft-headed sentimental optimism, a genius of such stern and unblenching insight is damned at once and for ever by being denounced as a cynic. It loves to blubber till tear-dry over its Dickens and Farjeon." — *Cope's Tobacco Plant,* April 1876. (Thomson's note.)

A Note on George Meredith

[*This article originally appeared in the* Secularist *(June 3, 1876) as a much longer review of Meredith's* Beauchamp's Career. *When reprinting it in* Essays and Phantasies *(as "A Note on George Meredith"), Thomson revised slightly and omitted the last half of the review, which was little more than a plot summary of Meredith's novel. The revised text is followed here, including Thomson's footnote with an excerpt from his later review of* Richard Feverel *(in* Cope's Tobacco Plant, *May, 1879). He also reviewed* The Egoist *in* Cope's *(January, 1880), and all three reviews were collected in the privately printed edition,* James Thomson ("B.V.") on George Meredith *(London, 1909). Meredith greatly admired Thomson's poetry, and, after reading* The City of Dreadful Night and Other Poems, *told Thomson that he had "not found the line I would propose to recast" and that there were "many pages that no other English poet could have written." The two men corresponded in the late 1870's, and in June, 1880, Thomson spent a day with Meredith at Box Hill, a day that was for Thomson, as he put it, "a real red-letter day in all respects."*]

George Meredith stands among our living novelists much as Robert Browning until of late years stood among our living poets, quite unappreciated by the general public, ranked with the very highest by a select few. One exception must be made to this comparison, an exception decidedly in favour of the novelists and novel-readers; for whereas Tennyson, the public's greatest poet, is immeasurably inferior to Browning in depth and scope and power and subtlety of intellect, George Eliot, the public's greatest novelist, is equal in all these qualities, save, I think, the last, to her unplaced rival, while having the advantage in some deservedly popular qualities, and the clear disadvantage in but one, the faculty of conceiving and describing vigorous or agonistic action,—in the fateful crises her leading characters are apt to merely drift. The thoughtful few have succeeded in so far imposing their judgment of Browning upon the thoughtless many, that these and their periodical organs now treat him with great respect, and try hard to assume the appearance of understanding and enjoying him, though doubtless their awkward admiration is more genuine in the old sense of wonder or astonishment than in the modern of esteem or love. But the thoughtful few are still far from succeeding to this extent in the case of George Meredith. Even literary men are unfamiliar with him. For having in some freak of fun or irony specified only two of his other books, and these among the earliest, on his title-page; leaving etcs. to represent *Farina, Evan Harrington, Rhoda Fleming, The Adventures of Harry Richmond, Modern Love and other Poems,* with his great masterpieces, *Emilia in England,* and its sequel *Vittoria*; he has reaped the satisfaction of learning that many of his well-informed reviewers manifestly know nothing of these obscure writings. For the rest, the causes of his unpopularity are obvious enough, and he himself, as he more than once lets us know, is thoroughly aware of them. Thus he interjects in the present work (III. 218–9): —

"We will make no mystery about it. I would I could. Those happy tales of mystery are as much my envy as the popular narratives of the deeds of bread and cheese people, for they both create a tide way in the attentive mind; the mysterious pricking our credulous flesh to creep, the familiar urging our obese imagination to continual exercise. And oh, the refreshment there is in dealing with characters either contemptibly beneath us or supernaturally above! My way is like a Rhone island in the summer drought, stony, unattractive and difficult between the two forceful streams of the unreal and the over-real, which delight mankind — honour to the conjurors! My people conquer nothing, win none; *they are actual, yet uncommon. It is the clockwork of the brain that they are directed to set in motion, and — poor troop of actors to vacant benches! — the conscience residing in thoughtfulness which they would appeal to;* and if you are there impervious to them, we are lost: back I go to my wilderness, where, as you perceive, I have contracted the habit of listening to my own voice more than is good."

Not only does he appeal to the conscience residing in thoughtfulness; he makes heavy and frequent demands on the active imagination, — monstrous attempts at extortion which both the languid and the sentimental novel-reader bitterly resent, and which indeed if they grew common with authors (luckily there is not the slightest fear of that!) would soon plunge the circulating libraries into bankruptcy. The late Charles Dickens, who coincided at all points with the vulgar taste as exactly as the two triangles of the fourth proposition of the first book of *Euclid* with one another, carried to perfection the Low-Dutch or exhaustive style of description, which may be termed artistic painting reduced to artful padding; minutely cataloguing all the details, with some exaggeration or distortion, humorous or pathetic, of each to make them more memorable; so that every item can be checked and verified as in an auctioneer's inventory, which is satisfactory to a business-like people. George Eliot with incomparably higher art paints rich and solid pictures that fill the eye and dwell in the mind. But George Meredith seldom does this, either in the realm of Nature or in that of Humanity, though the achievement is well within his power, as none of our readers can doubt who studied, being fit to study, those magnificent selections from his "Vittoria" in the *Secularist* (No. 10, March 4), entitled *Portrait of Mazzini* and *Mazzini and Italy*. He loves to suggest by flying touches rather than slowly elaborate. To those who are quick to follow his suggestions he gives in a few winged words the very spirit of a scene, the inmost secret of a mood or passion, as no other living writer I am acquainted with can. His name and various passages in his works reveal Welsh blood, more swift and fiery and imaginative than the English. And he says in the *Emilia,* with fair pride of race: "All subtle feelings are discerned by Welsh eyes when untroubled by any mental agitation. Brother and sister were Welsh, and I may observe that there is human nature and Welsh nature." If his personages are not portrayed at full length, they are clear and living in his mind's eye, as we discern by the exquisitely appropriate gesture or attitude or look in vivid moments: and they are characterised by an image or a phrase, as when we are told that the profile of Beauchamp "suggested an arrow-head in the upflight;" and of Renée: "her features had the soft irregularities which run to rarities of beauty, as the ripple rocks the light; mouth, eyes, brows, nostrils, and bloomy cheeks played into one another liquidly; thought flew, tongue followed, and the flash of meaning quivered over them like night-lightning. Or oftener, to speak truth, tongue flew, thought followed: her age was but newly seventeen, and she was French." And as with the outward so with the interior nature of his personages. Marvellous flashes of insight reveal some of their profoundest secrets, detect the mainsprings and trace the movements of their most complex workings, and from such data you must complete the characters, as from certain leading points a mathematician defines a curve. So with his conversations. The speeches do not follow one another mechanically adjusted like a smooth pavement for easy walking: they leap and break, resilient and resurgent, like running foam-crested sea-waves, impelled and repelled and crossed by under-currents and great tides and broad breezes; in their restless agitations you must divine the immense life abounding beneath and around and above them; and the Mudie novice accustomed to saunter the level pavements, finds that the heaving and falling are sea-sickness to a queasy stomach. Moreover he delights in the elaborate analysis of abstruse problems, whose solutions when reached are scarcely less difficult to ordinary apprehension than are the problems themselves; discriminating countless shades where the common eye sees but one gloom or glare, pursuing countless distinct movements where the common eye sees only a whirling perplexity. As if all these heavy disqualifications were not enough, as if he were not sufficiently offensive in being original, he dares also to be wayward and wilful, not theatrically or overweeningly like Charles Reade, but freakishly and humoristically, to the open-eyed disgust of our prim public. Lastly, his plots are too carelessly spun to catch our summer flies, showing here great gaps and there a pendent entanglement; while his catastrophes are wont to outrage that most facile justice of romance which condemns all rogues to poverty and wretchedness, and rewards the virtuous with wealth and long life and flourishing large families.

In exposing his defects for the many, I have discovered some of his finest qualities for the thoughtful and imaginative few, and need now only summarise. He has a wonderful eye for form and colour, especially the latter; a wonderful ear for music and all sounds; a masterly perception of character, a most subtle sense for spiritual mysteries. His dialogue is full of life and reality, flexile and rich in the genuine unexpected, marked with the keenest distinctions, more like the bright-witted French than the slow and clumsy English. He can use brogue and *baragouinage* with rare accuracy and humorous effect; witness the Irish Mrs. Chump and the Greek Pericles in *Emilia*. Though he seldom gives way to it, he is great in the fiery record of fiery action; thus the duel in the Stelvio Pass, in *Vittoria*, has been scarcely equalled by any living novelist save by Charles Reade in that heroic fight with the pirates in *Hard Cash*. He has this sure mark of lofty genius, that he always rises with his theme, growing more strenuous, more self-contained, more magistral, as the demands on his thought and imagination increase. His style is very various and flexible, flowing freely in whatever measures the subject and the mood may dictate. At its best it is so beautiful in simplest Saxon, so majestic in rhythm, so noble with noble imagery, so pregnant with meaning, so vital and intense, that it must be ranked among the supreme achievements of our literature. A dear friend said well when reading *Vittoria*: Here truly are words that if you pricked them would bleed. For integral grandeur and originality of conception, and for perfectness of execution, the heroine of his *Emilia* appears to me the sovereign character of our modern fiction: in her he has discovered a new great nature, whom he has endowed with a new great language. In fine, I am aware of no other living English writer so gloriously gifted and so little known and appreciated except Garth Wilkinson: and Garth Wilkinson has squandered his superb genius in most futile efforts to cultivate the spectral Sahara of Swedenborgianism, and, infinitely worse, the Will-o'-the-wisp Slough of Despond of Spiritism; while George Meredith has constantly devoted himself to the ever-fruitful fields of real living Nature and Human Nature.*

*Elsewhere I have written, on the occasion of the one volume edition of "Richard Feverel": — "He may be termed, accurately enough for a brief indication, the Robert Browning of our novelists; and his day is bound to come, as Browning's at length has come. The flaccid and feeble folk, who want literature and art that can be inhaled as idly as the perfume of a flower, must naturally shrink from two such earnestly strenuous spirits, swifter than eagles, stronger than lions, in whom, to use the magnificent and true language of Coleridge concerning Shakespeare, 'The intellectual power and the creative energy wrestle as in a war-embrace.' But men who have lived and observed and pondered, who love intellect and genius and genuine passion, who have eyes and ears ever open to the mysterious miracles of nature and art, who flinch not from keenest insight into the world and life, who are wont to probe and analyse with patient subtlety the intricate social and personal problems of our complex quasi-civilisation, who look not to mere plot as the be-all and end-all of a novel reflecting human character and life, who willingly dispense with the childish sugar-plums of so-called poetical justice which they never find dispensed in the grown-up work-o'-day world, who can respond with thought to thought, and passion to passion, and imagination to imagination; and, lastly, who can appreciate a style vital and plastic as the ever-evolving living world it depicts, equal to all emergencies, which can revel with clowns and fence with fine ladies and gentlemen, yet rise to all grandeurs of Nature and Destiny and the human soul in fieriest passion and action: such men, who cannot abound anywhere, but who should be less rare among meditative smokers than in the rest of the community, will find a royal treasure-house of delight and instruction and suggestion in the works of George Meredith." — *Cope's Tobacco Plant*, May 1879. (Thomson's note.)

Review: Principal Shairp, *Robert Burns*

[*In 1879–80, in a* Cope's *column titled "Our Smoke Room Table," Thomson reviewed each volume of the "English Men of Letters" series as it appeared—twelve reviews in all. This spirited attack on Shairp's book was published in the September, 1879, issue, and is here reprinted for the first time. Thomson was, of course, very familiar with Burns's work, and felt that "Burns will live with the language"; an earlier essay on Burns, one of Thomson's first works to appear in print, was published more than twenty years before he wrote this review.*]

THE AUTHOR of this little book has published many other works, as we learn from a catalogue, not having had the fortune to read any of them. Beginning with an Oxford Prize "Poem," so far back as 1842, we find, among the rest, an "Essay on the Author of the Christian Year," "Culture and Religion in some of their Relations," "Kilmahoe, a Highland Pastoral, and other Poems," "Studies in Poetry and Philosophy," "On the Poetic Interpretation of Nature." His studies and works have brought him high honours; he has been Principal of a Scotch University, he is Professor of Poetry at Oxford—a dignity Ruskin sought in vain. He has now crowned all his splendid achievements by one of the worst essays on Burns that we have ever come across. A Scot, he has no national fervour; an old student of poetry and at least a would-be poet, he has no poetic sympathy; a successor of Matthew Arnold, he has no sweetness and very little light. Of course we speak of him as he shows himself in this, the one book of his we have read; and having read, are little likely to read another. This Oxford graduate and professor has none of the liberal grace and urbanity of culture, but writes with the stark dogmatic narrowness of some remote provincial Calvinist. He might be one of those Auld Light ministers whom Burns scarified; he seems to resent the Address to the Unco Guid or Rigidly Righteous as aimed by anticipation at himself; he is continually sermonising on the great-hearted poet as a Sunday-school teacher might lecture his class on a life which was an awful warning. He is Cauld

Kail in Aberdeen (or should we say St. Andrews?) preaching against hot haggis; the coldest of cold water prelecting on the ardours of whisky. His voice is pitched to the pious twang of that Pharisee who thanked God that he was not as this Publican. He is a raven croaking immensely self-satisfied over a dead thrush. His blood is of the fishy temperature, and he swims serene in a sea of moral platitudes. His body may be in a great University, but his mind is in a little conventicle. He is frigid as the book of Euclid, writing on the most passionate of poets; he is bitter as the dogma of eternal damnation, discoursing on the sweet-souled singer; he is dull as ditch-water for quenching this fiery genius. Burns could cordially sympathise with a wee field-mouse and a mountain daisy: this man has no sympathy even with a Burns.

The style and construction of the booklet are worthy of the spirit, that is to say, the want of spirit, in which it is conceived. The style is dull and common-place, not always even grammatical; not one sentence, of his own, makes itself remembered—save against himself. The construction is out of all proportion: scarcely any space is given to the pregnant period of development, of education and self-education, though the long letter of Burns to Dr. Moore, with his brother Gilbert's supplement, gives us such precious information thereon. There is actually no allusion to the significant passage: "In my infant and boyish days, too, I owed much to an old woman who resided in the family, remarkable for her ignorance, credulity, and superstition. She had, I suppose, the largest collection in the country of tales and songs concerning devils, ghosts, fairies, brownies, witches, warlocks, spunkies, kelpies, elf-candles, dead-lights, wraiths, apparitions, cantraips, giants, enchanted towers, dragons, and other trumpery. This cultivated the latent seeds of poetry"—Principal Shairp writes, "not only the traditional life of Wallace and other popular books of that sort, but the *Spectator*, odd plays of Shakespeare, Pope (his Homer included), Locke on the Human Understanding, Boyle's Lectures," &c., were among the early reading of Burns. Mark the contempt with which the man of no insight mentions casually the life of Wallace "and other popular books of that sort"; as if the inspiration of the poet was derived from the *Spectator* and the rest, which, in truth, were mainly responsible for the ambitious and often inflated English of his letters, he being fully himself in all his pith and raciness only in his native Doric. But see what Burns himself says, writing in his 29th year: — "The story of Wallace poured a Scottish prejudice into my veins, which will boil along there till the flood-gates of life shut in eternal rest." We have here one of the sources of "Scots Wha Hae," "The Vision," "On My Early Days." Again, there is no allusion to the striking sentence: "I had felt early some stirrings of ambition, but they were the blind gropings of Homer's Cyclops round the walls of his cave." Nor are the mutual improvement clubs at Tarbolton and Mauchline, in which he took the leading part, mentioned in the account of his youth; but there is a most absurd mention of them in the account of the Edinburgh jovialities, p. 58: "The scenes which Burns there took part in far exceeded any revelries he had seen in the clubs of Tarbolton and Mauchline." Would the unacquainted reader believe that these "revelries" cost each of the members, who were mere country lads, the enormous sum of threepence at each monthly meeting? In the words of Dr. Currie, who gives the rules of the Tarbolton Club: "The sum expended by each was not to exceed threepence; and with the humble potation [Shairp's revelry!] that this could procure they were to toast their mistresses, and to cultivate friendship with each other. . . . The regulations of the club at Mauchline were nearly the same as those of the club at Tarbolton; but one laudable alteration was made. The fines for non-attendance had at Tarbolton been spent in enlarging their scanty potations: at Mauchline it was fixed that the money so arising should be set apart for the purchase of books." Oh, the devilry of such revelry!

As for the style, it is, as we have said, dull and lifeless throughout. We can spare space for but two or three examples of its absolute incorrectness. Of *two* young ladies we are told, p. 80, that Burns addressed songs of affection "now to one, now to *an*other." On p. 196, "*none* of his poems that does such justice" to his better nature as "The Cotter's Saturday Night"; meaning *no other,* for *it* clearly does precisely such justice. On p. 114 we read "He was suffering from nervous derangement, and this, as usual with him, made him despondent." The abnormal being, whom nervous derangement usually made despondent! But this is not ungrammatical, it is only thoroughly stupid. On pp. 44–5, we are told that "the greatest *name,* that of David Hume, had disappeared about ten years before Burns arrived in the capital." For meanness of expression take p. 69, "the *knowing* Lockhart," *i.e.,* the

Lockhart who knew, or was well acquainted with, not *knowing* in the slang sense; p. 143, "The French Revolution was *in full swing*." Thou successor of Matthew Arnold!

As for the criticism, p. 20 says of "The Twa Herds," "Holy Willie's Prayer," "The Ordination," "The Holy Fair," "I cannot but think that those who have loved most what is best in Burns' poetry must have regretted that these poems were ever written." Of "The Jolly Beggars," p. 126 says, "unpleasant as from its grossness it is"; and p. 201, more emphatically, "the materials are so coarse, and the sentiment so gross, as to make it, for all its dramatic power, decidely offensive." This is the piece of which the lascivious Carlyle writes in his Essay on Burns: "the most strictly poetical of all his 'poems' is . . . 'The Jolly Beggars.' The subject truly is among the lowest in nature; but it only the more shows our poet's gift in raising it into the domain of Art. To our minds, this piece seems thoroughly compacted; melted together, refined; and poured forth in one flood of true *liquid* harmony." Coarse Carlyle! Saintly Shairp! Concerning "Scots Wha Hae," Carlyle is indeed quoted to the effect that it should be sung with the throat of the whirlwind, that it is the best war-ode ever written; but the scrupulous Professor is careful to add that Wordsworth and Mrs. Hemans (!) agreed that it *"was* not much more than a common-place piece of school-boy rhodomontade about liberty." Peace to the good Mrs. Hemans,* whose "warrior *tamed* his heart of fire," presumably by pouring Shairp-cold water into it. Peace, likewise, to the prosaic-poetic Sunday School pedagogue, Wordsworth; the placidly ferocious, for whom "Carnage is God's daughter"; whose Solitary in the "Excursion" (Second Book) became

> Chaplain to a military troop
> Cheered by the Highland bagpipe, as they marched
> In plaided vest,—his fellow-countrymen.

There's martial fire for you! the rapture of battle! the rushing pomp and glory of war! no "school-boy rhodomontade"! Burns and Carlyle, with their mere Bannockburn and Taking of the Bastile, could never have written that! Why, Burns actually sees, and Carlyle actually admires his vision, Scottish warriors

*Felicia Dorothea Hemans (1793–1835), poetess, acquainted with Scott and Wordsworth.

plunging through the battle "*red-wat shod.*" How revolting, in contrast with that picturesque "plaided vest"! Scott writes to his friend Geo. Ellis, toward the close of 1805, "I will not castrate John Dryden. I would as soon castrate my own father, as I believe Jupiter did of yore." Scott would not, but Shairp would with the greatest pleasure. He would favour us with a Burns *minus* "The Holy Fair," "Holy Willie's Prayer," "The Jolly Beggars," and a few other pieces; and so with all our poets and dramatists and novelists; and we should rejoice in a literature moral as Dr. Watts, fascinating as Mr. Tupper's "Proverbial Philosophy," sexless as Origen or Abelard.

As for the Principal's perpetual sermonising on the moral character of Burns, let us quote a sentence or two from others. Burns himself writes, "My passions, when once lighted up, raged like so many devils till they got vent in rhyme." His brother Gilbert, a quiet, deliberate man it seems: "The symptoms of his passion were often such as nearly to rival those of the celebrated Sappho. I never, indeed, knew that he *fainted, sunk, and died away*; but the agitation of his mind and body exceeded anything of the kind I ever knew in real life." Carlyle, in 1828: "We are far from regarding him as guilty before the world, as guiltier than the average; nay, from doubting that he is less guilty than one of ten thousand. . . . Granted, the ship comes into harbour with shrouds and tackle damaged, and the pilot is therefore blameworthy, for he has not been all-wise and all-powerful; but to know *how* blameworthy, tell us first whether his voyage has been round the Globe, or only to Ramsgate and the Isle of Dogs."

And now we bid a glad farewell to pious Principal Shairp, with the expression of a hope and a wish. We hope that young Oxford enjoys its Professor of Poetry by laughing at him even unto a *smascellamento*; for if it takes him seriously, young Oxford is likely to mature into an insufferable sanctimonious prig. We wish it were possible for the publishers to suppress this book (which, unfortunately, will be kept in circulation by the Series to which it belongs and the position of the writer); so that the subject Burns could be entrusted to a man with some insight, some discernment of character, some poetic sympathy, and, above all, some human nature.

Review: Anthony Trollope, *Thackeray*

[*This review, here reprinted for the first time, appeared in the "Smoke Room Table" column of* Cope's Tobacco Plant *in July, 1880. It is one of Thomson's last, and surely most colorful, reviews.*]

THIS LITTLE BOOK more than fulfils our expectations: we expected to find it considerably poor, and we find it considerably poorer. Disgusted by some fulsome biography, as well he might be in an age wherein it is "the custom to publish two volumes upon every man or woman whose name has appeared on a title page," Thackeray charged his daughters not to publish any Life of him; so it is not Mr. Trollope's fault that his Memoir is very meagre. But it *is* Mr. Trollope's fault that the biographical chapter, containing about enough matter for a readable magazine article, is swelled out to sixty pages, or two-sevenths of the book, by details that are quite trivial, explanations that are superfluous, and reflections that are easy twaddle. As to the remaining five-sevenths, occupied with descriptions and criticisms of Thackeray's works, we find them on the whole of somewhat less than no value; the descriptions void of illumination, the criticisms always shallow, and often mean or perverse or both. And the style is as poor as the matter, lax throughout, and frequently incorrect. So that, as we have said, the booklet even surpasses our expectations, and may be briefly characterised as shoddy and slipshoddy. Being thus, it has, of course, in itself no claim to our notice; and we only give it, grudgingly, a portion of our valuable space on account of the position of its writer, and in deference to the Series of which it is another unworthy member.

We find it pervaded by a misconception, so gross as to be ludicrous, of the relative magnitude and importance of its writer and his subject, of Trollope and Thackeray. Mr. Trollope appears to feel, without, perhaps, thinking it out clearly: The other T. is a popular novelist, so am I; my popularity was much more readily acquired, and my popular novels are much more numerous than his; therefore any difference between us is in my favour; and I can sit in judgment upon him with an easy equality, as foreman of the jury of his peers; or, rather, indeed, with a benign and familiar superiority, as somewhat above him in station, and free from the indiscretions which brought him into court. In fact, Mr. Trollope seems quite unaware of Douglas Jerrold's pregnant distinction, that two men may row in the same boat with very different sculls. He begins, "I will give such incidents," "I will tell how," "Then I will tell how"; in the tone of a Macaulay opening a History of England, or a Gibbon that of the Decline and Fall of the Roman Empire; all by way of preface to a magazine sketch twaddled out to fill sixty pages. He graciously allows, p. 3, that Thackeray did a good life's work; but again and again denounces his laziness, as p. 7, "He was always idle," &c., and p. 19, "Unsteadfast, idle, changeable of purpose . . . no man ever failed more generally than he to put his best foot foremost." This, by-the-bye, occurs in a contrast of Thackeray and Dickens, of whom we are told, p. 18, "I will make no comparison between two such rivals, who were so distinctly different from *each*"; so that Dickens was distinctly different from Dickens as well as from Thackeray, and Thackeray distinctly different from Thackeray as well as from Dickens: a truly remarkable pair of rivals. Also, by-the-bye, we are told, p. 8: "Dickens has informed us that he first met Thackeray in 1835," when T. "'proposed to become the illustrator of my earliest book.' . . . We may presume that the offer was rejected." There is no need to presume; T. also has informed us of the offer, and, further, of its rejection. Again, p. 7, scanty as are his biographical materials, Mr. Trollope don't think it worth while to mention Goethe in connection with T.'s sojourn in Weimar, though T. favoured Mr. Lewes with a longish reminiscent letter for the Life of Goethe, and though Mr. Trollope was writing an In Memoriam of Lewes not long ago. But he does think it worth while to give us three and a-half pages, 10–13, of platitude on the fascinations and uncertainties of literature as a profession. Of three daughters, p. 20, the first is indeed the eldest, but the last is only the younger.

Concerning Thackeray's lecturing; and with reference to Forster's argument in disuasion of Dickens, pp. 43–5, "that to become publicly a reader must alter, without improving, his position publicly as a writer, and that it was a change to be justified only when the higher calling should have failed of the old success"; Mr. Trollope delivers judgment with characteristic spirit and logic: "When such discussions arise, money generally carries the day—and should do so. When convinced that money may be earned without disgrace, we ought to allow money to carry the day. When we talk of sordid gain and filthy lucre, we are generally hypocrites. (Speak for yourself only, Mr. A. T.) If gains be sordid and lucre filthy, where is the priest, the lawyer, the doctor, or the man of literature, who does not wish for dirty hands?" We think T. would have pleaded somewhat differently for his lecturing, and even D. for his public reading. We thought the very point in dispute was whether money *could* be thus earned without disgrace; Forster seeing a descent, only to be justified by necessity. We have also only been wont to term gain sordid when acquired sordidly, and lucre filthy when grubbed up filthily; attributing neither sordidness nor filthiness to the profits of any honourable profession exercised honourably. To meet Mr. Forster's case, the question should have been put somewhat thus: "Do the priest, the lawyer, the doctor, the literary man, who, not failing of success each in his own profession, respectively for greater profit turn crammer, pettifogger, apothecary, reporter, lower themselves or not? Are their extra gains thus secured sordid or not?" However, we quite appreciate the forcibleness, from the pen of Mr. Trollope, of that "money generally carries the day—and should do so." The one impassioned and poetical outburst we have remarked in the book gushed from the same aureate inspiration: that, p. 12, in which he chants of the literary novice "who succeeds in earning a few halcyon, but, ah! so dangerous guineas." Halcyon guineas; oh, the gorgeous dithyrambic! the "liberal phrases of his golden tongue"! as another lyrist sings. There is, indeed, further on a passage of a similar strain, though in a somewhat less elevated key; wherein we are saluted, to borrow his own wonderful poetic diction (p. 8), by "the continued note of triumph which is still heard in the final voices of the spoilt child of literature, even when they are losing their music"; though how this child becomes possessed of these final voices surpasses our prosaic comprehension. This passage may be found, by those who think it worth finding, on pp. 51–2. It relates how, about two months before the *Cornhill* came out, the big T. asked the little t. whether he could go to work at once on a long novel, so that it might begin with the first number. Little t. carries on his continued note of triumph through text and note: "At the same time I heard from the publisher, who suggested some interesting little details as to honorarium. The little details were very interesting, but absolutely no time was allowed to me. . . . Now, it was my theory—and ever since this occurrence has been my practice—to see the end of my own work before the public should see the commencement. If I did this thing I must not only abandon my theory, but instantly contrive a story, or begin to write it before it was contrived. That was what I did, urged by the interesting nature of the details. . . . I hesitated, but allowed myself to be allured to what I felt to be wrong." Little t. does himself injustice inconsistent with his former wise dictum, "we ought to allow money to carry the day." The continued note of triumph of the final voices of the spoilt child of literature swells into a note thus concluding: "Could I not begin a new one [story]—English—and if possible about clergymen? The details were so interesting that had a couple of archbishops been demanded, I should have produced them." A mere couple of archbishops! we should think so, indeed! and if those dear little details were interesting enough, would have doubtless thrown in, if required, a batch of cardinals, a Pope, a Patriarch of Constantinople, a Sheikh-al-Islam, and a Grand Lama. How the pleasant humour of the little aureate poet chuckles over the delicious refrain of those interesting little details; mouthing them over and over lingeringly, sweetest morsels on his golden tongue! He is not like that great idle, unsteadfast Thackeray; not he. Has he not informed the world that he can turn out morning after morning his regular amount of copy, with some insignificant variation allowed for a cigar or glass of wine more or less the previous night? just as a machine can be depended upon to turn out its regular amount of work day by day, with some very slight variance for fouling or lubrication. Little t. has thus over big T. all the eminent commercial advantages which a steady-going machine possesses over a mutable man; with the additional advantage of being comfortably conscious of them!

We would cite much more set to Mr. Trollope's favourite tune of "His bags of chink he chunk"; but pass on to some high-toned moral criticism of Thackeray's "Four Georges," which proves that our little aureate poet is likewise a little poet laureate. He tells us, pp. 46–8: "There arose the question whether too much freedom had not been taken with an office which, though it be no longer considered to be founded on divine right, is still as sacred as can be anything that is human. If there is to remain among us a sovereign, that sovereign, even though divested of political power, should be endowed with all that personal respect can give." The idea of divesting sovereignty, which is sacred, of political power, which is its very essence! "And this should not depend altogether on personal character. . . . The respect of which we [I] speak should, in the strongest degree, be a possession of the immediate occupant . . . and the throne of which we wish to preserve the dignity seems to be assailed when unmeasured evil is said of one who has sat there within our own memory." His Most Gracious Majesty George the Fourth, to wit. "He [Thackeray] was one who revered modesty and innocence rather than power, against which he had in the bottom of his heart something of a republican tendency." A dangerous fellow! — but it must have been a tendency against nothing in this case, for your sovereign is divested of power. Little t. returns to the charge, like the valiant illogical Royalist he is, pp. 155–7. Thus: "It is difficult to speak fittingly of a sovereign, either living or not, [*dele* comma] long since gone. You can hardly praise such a one without flattery." What! the D. T. flatter our Queen! Theodore Martin, C.B., flatter Prince Albert! Infelix Whitehurst or Blanchard Jerrold flatter Napoleon III.! * Cancel this in your next edition, Mr. T. "You can hardly censure him without injustice." This is right; as we see in Thackeray on George IV., or Victor Hugo on Napoleon III. "We are either ignorant of his personal doings or we know them as secrets, which have been divulged for the most part either falsely or treacherously, — often both falsely and treacherously." This is truly exquisite. "It is better, perhaps, that we should not deal with the personalities of princes." This is simply damnable; for we should thus be bereft of all those lofty panegyrics on their superemiment private virtues which kindle our loyal enthusiasm. Prob-

*The "D. T." was the *Daily Telegraph*; Theodore Martin (1816–1909), poet, translator, man of letters, wrote at the Queen's request the five-volume *Life of His Royal Highness the Prince Consort*; Felix M. Whitehurst and William Blanchard Jerrold both wrote in defense of the regime of Napoleon III.

ably, however, Mr. Trollope, when he has filled Mudie's to bursting-point with novels and settled Cæsar and Cicero once for all, will run us off a History of the British Empire under the House of Brunswick, wherein the personalities of the sovereigns shall be reverently ignored. He has the distinction of agreeing with that illustrious monarch James I., who, when asked why he did not like Sir Walter Raleigh's "History of the World," shrewdly replied, "It is too saucy in censuring the acts of princes." But then, James was a king, while Mr. Trollope is only a superior postman.

The literary criticism is nearly as high-toned, but we have not space for more than the smallest sample. Mr. Trollope is pleased to think the lectures on the English Humourists better than those on the Four Georges; but he cannot quite approve the list, pp. 157, &c. "Pope we [I] should hardly define as a humourist"; but may he not be this, as well as much else? "Nor should we [I] have included Fielding or Smollett, in spite of Parson Adams and Tabitha Bramble, unless anxious to fill a good company." Trollope on Swift is of course beyond notice. "I almost question Prior's right to be in the list." As for Sterne, he is indeed a humourist, but "the less often he is taken down the better." Just so; leave Sterne on the shelf (and take down Trollope), in contempt of that nuisance "the intelligent foreigner,"—not more intelligent, after all, than a mere Goethe, or Heine, or Balzac!

So much, and too much, for the shoddy; a few specimens must serve for the abundance of slipshoddy. P. 3, "His very notes would be delightful to read, partaking of the nature of pearls when prepared for his own use"; 58, neither of them give; 13, it is to that *which* he is brought; 46, the second series were; 197, neither easy or lucid; 155, the lecturer had not time enough or room enough for real history; 84, requirements demanded of them; 106, the reader will have found that every page will have been; 119, sad tragedies; 122, "as a chain is not stronger than its weakest link, so is a . . . novelist to be placed in no lower level than that which he has attained by his highest sustained flight,"—a muddle of direct analogy and inverse proportion. Such scribbling may do well enough for the circulating libraries, but decidedly does not befit a series of books on English Men of Letters by English literary men.

IV. Phantasies

A Lady of Sorrow

[*"A Lady of Sorrow," the longest and most important of Thomson's phantasies, was begun in 1861–62 while he was still in the army; it was completed in London in 1864, and was published in the* National Reformer *in 1867 (in eight installments, July 14–September 1). In 1891 T. B. Mosher reprinted it as a separate volume, the first and, up to now, the only prose work of Thomson's to be published in America. In his "Introductory Note" Thomson employs the device of pretending to edit the papers of his friend Vane, whom he had used earlier as the "speaker" in his 1864 satiric poem, "Vane's Story." Thomson once told Dobell that he chose the name "Vane" because it suggested something vain or unreal, but it seems even more likely that "Vane" is derived from his famous pseudonym, "Bysshe Vanolis" (a combination of Shelley's middle name and an anagram of Novalis). "Vanolis" is highly significant here, for, perhaps even more so than De Quincey's phantasies, Novalis'* Hymns to the Night, *from which Thomson had translated passages very similar to the "Angel" section of "A Lady of Sorrow," exerted an important influence on this work. Thomson published two other phantasies, in addition to those included in the present edition — "A Walk Abroad"* (National Reformer, *April 21, 1867) and "The Fair of St. Sylvester"* (Cope's Tobacco Plant, *January, 1876); he reprinted all four in* Essays and Phantasies, *but it was "A Lady of Sorrow" that he chose to place first in the only collection of prose published in his lifetime.*]

INTRODUCTORY NOTE

About three years before his death I received from my friend Vane certain manuscripts with the somewhat fierce *Envoy:* —

From the midst of the fire I fling
  These arrows of fire to you:
If they sing, and burn, and sting,
  You feel how I burn too;
But if they reach you there
  Speed-spent, charred black and cold,
The fire burns out in the air,
  The Passion will not be told.

From these papers I have selected and now edit the following piece, which embodies the ideas then supreme in his mind with relation to the question of the immortality of the human soul. He was at that time wont to declare that he believed in the soul's immortality as a Materialist believes in the immortality of matter: he believed that the universal soul subsists for ever, just as a Materialist believes that universal matter subsists for ever, without increase or decrease, growth or decay; he no more believed in the immortality of any particular soul than the Materialist believes in the immortality of any particular body. The one substance is eternal, the various forms are ever varying.

That this composition is true in relation to the author, that it is genuine, I have no doubt; for the poor fellow had large gifts for being unhappy. But is it true in relation to the world and general life? I think true, but not the whole truth. There is truth of winter and black night, there is truth of summer and dazzling noonday. On the one side of the great medal are stamped the glory and triumph of life, on the other side are stamped the glory and triumph of death; but which is the obverse and which the reverse none of us surely knows. It is certain that both are inseparably united in every coin doled out to us from the universal mintage. The night-side of nature has been the theme of literature more often than the day-side, simply because literature, as a rule, is the refuge of the miserable; I mean genuine, thoughtful, and earnest literature; literature as an end in and for itself, not merely as a weapon to fight with, a ware to sell, a luxury to enjoy. The happy seldom write for writing's sake; they are fully employed in living. "Were a God asked to recite his life, he would do so in two words," is a grand truth in *Le Centaure* of Maurice de Guérin. For health is simple, always one and the same, while the forms and variations of disease are innumerable and complex.

> He lives full life who never thinks of life;
> He is half dead who ponders life and death.

Mystery is but misery dissolved in thought, the intolerable concrete rendered abstract and vague.

The triune Lady of Sorrow must have derived from De Quincey, whose influence is obvious in other respects. But why did the author take such a roundabout way of expressing his ideas? Some men see truth and express truth best in imagery and symbol, others in syllogism and formula. Both modes are good done well, both bad done ill. And they are constitutional. The artist will adhere to his pencil, the anatomist to his scalpel, remonstrate and exhort we ever so much.

I.—THE ANGEL

Come as thou cam'st a thousand times,
A visitant from radiant climes,
And smooth my hair and kiss my brow,
And ask: My love, why sufferest thou? *

Come down for a moment, O come! come serious and mild
And pale, as thou wert on this earth, thou adorable child!
Or come as thou art, with thy sanctitude, triumph and bliss
For a garment of glory about thee; and give me one kiss,
One tender and pitying look of those pure loving eyes,
One word of solemn assurance and truth that the soul with its
love never dies!†

I LIVED in London, and alone. For although I had many work-fellow acquaintances, and of these a few were very friendly, I had no intimate relatives near me and no bosom friend. No bosom friend, were it not one whom I scarcely knew whether to call friend or enemy; she who came suddenly (though indeed her advent had been long before announced) in the brilliant morning of a joyous summer holiday, to dwell with me and possess me; permitting no rivals nor any approach to rivalry, absorbing every thought and feeling to her devotion, and compelling even the dreams and visions of both day and night to worship her; the darkly beautiful Queen, the disinherited Titaness, the Pythia of an abandoned and ruined shrine, the wild, passionate, tender-hearted, desolate, sorcery-smitten Sorceress; Sorrow, the daughter of Love and Death. I call her queen, for queen in truth at first she was, royal as Persephone herself, and not one of the many ladies of her court. For Death

*Matthew Arnold, "Longing," ll. 5–6, 11–12.
†Thomson's own "Mater Tenebrarum," ll. 5–10.

is a great rival, magnanimous in the instant of his cruelest triumph; sending ever to companion those whom he has bereaved of their darlings no menial, but this his own beloved daughter. She is mournful, she is desolate, she is stern, she is often insane; in her queenliest beauty she is terrible, "as an army with banners" defeated, as a noonday in eclipse; but she is always great-hearted, always high-minded: pique, malice, querulousness, perversity, and all the meaner emotions of loss, are far beneath *her*. And now with her I was to live alone; in the heart of London, yet mysteriously alone with her who is "Grief wound up to a mysteriousness." She annihilated from me the huge city and all its inhabitants; they, with their thoughts, passions, labours, struggles, victories, defeats, were nothing to me; I was nothing to them. As I passed daily through the streets, my eyes must have pictured the buildings and the people, my ears must have vibrated to the roar of the vehicles; but my inward vision was fixed the while on her, my inward ear was attentive to her voice alone. Scarcely at night, when I went up with her to the solitude of my room, or wandered with her through deserted thoroughfares and environs, were we more perfectly alone than amidst the noise and glare of the populous day. Indeed we were often by day the most inviolably alone, when the besieging armies of the perceptions of the outward world had driven us to take refuge in the far security of the innermost citadel of my soul. She annihilated so utterly from me the mighty metropolis, whose citizens are counted by millions, that the whole did not even form a dark background for the spiritual scenes and personages her spells continually evoked.

She is a mighty enchantress, herself the victim of enchantments mightier than her own; and, in obedience to subtle inward impulses, or perhaps to imperious agencies from without, which she can neither resist nor control, is perpetually suffering transformation. Usually, vague and slight changes affect her every moment, decided and obvious changes—in form, and feature, and expression—almost every hour. These I attempt not to describe; as who, for instance, would attempt to describe the momentary or even the hourly changes affecting any landscape in the course of one diurnal revolution of the earth? But as we speak of morning and noon and evening in the day; of the four seasons in the year; of childhood, youth, maturity, and old age in life; of a few tones and semitones in sound, and a few colours in the reflection of light; among the infinitely fine gradations of all seizing certain points definitively different even to perceptions and judgments so gross as are ours; so I, from her multitudinous and still evolving variations, catch at three which are conspicuously distinct and representative, and try to give them expression.

I speak not of her, I cannot speak of her, as she came at first; when my spirit was stunned and lay as dead in the body mechanically alive; lay in swoon with but the dimmest consciousness of her presence, sitting down black-veiled beside me many days and nights, speaking not a word, as the friends of Job sat silent at first, for they saw that his grief was very great.

In the next period of our intimacy, when I was again aroused, there was but one phase of her being to which she could be constant for hours together, to which she persistently recurred day after day, week after week, month after month; and that phase was the most sublime and beautiful in the whole series of her metamorphoses; it was her Transfiguration.

When she blessed me by assuming this glorious mask, whether by day or night, whether in storm or calm, whether in solitude or amidst many people, instantly I beheld deep midnight tranced in perfect summer peace; the full moon was shining, the heavens were crowded with stars: we were alone. And always the earth was at least so far away under us that I saw it, when I saw it at all, with catholic vision comprehending in one glance a vast concave of mountains, woods, fields, cities and rivers and seas. Yet she, my companion, was by no means new or strange to me in this new and strange relation, nor would she have appeared strange to many thousands now alive. For she was simply the image in beatitude of her who died so young. The pure girl was become the angel; the sheathed wings had unfolded in the favourable clime, the vesture was radiantly white with the whiteness of her soul, the long hair was a dazzling golden glory round the ever-young head, the blue eyes had absorbed celestial light in the cloudless empyrean: but still, thus developed and beatified, she was only the more intensely and supremely herself; more perfectly revealed to me, more intimately known and more passionately loved by me, than when she had walked the earth in the guise of a mortal. She would take me by the hand, sometimes impressing a kiss, which was an ample anodyne, upon my world-weary brow, and lead me away floating calmly through the infinite highth and depth and breadth, from galaxy to galaxy, from silver star to star. We ever floated in still peace, our flight never stirring against itself a rush of the surrounding æther; yet I could remark how swiftly worlds strewn broad behind us gathered themselves into constellations, and constellations crowded before us dispersed into unrelated stars. Our approach never divested the worlds of their pure spheric beauty, never discovered them rugged with mountains, blotted with storms, varicoloured with day and night, and land and sea; they remained always to us bright throbbing stars, that grew in size and glory as we neared them. Choirs of bright seraphs floated vague in their ambient brightness. And though the life-roar of their mortal or immortal habitants was unheard by us, they ever rolled enveloped with music which was divine. And as we thus wandered, like two children, sister and brother, straying in delight solemnised by awe through the palace and the measureless domains of Our Father, our beings were ever in most intimate communion. Our lips scarcely moved, our hands never gestured save in startled rapture, our eyes rarely expressed aught save reverence and gratitude and love of Him and to Him through whose realms we were thus enfranchised to wander as in our own heritage; yet spirit into spirit, and specially (as I felt) her spirit into mine, poured itself fully without any material or symbolic medium: then first was I taught beyond all after forgetting that there is a perfect interfusion of soul with soul, when the pure fire of love has utterly consumed matter and space and time.

With what, then, was my spirit overfilled from hers? With love too infinite for language, faith too solemn for the world, hope too glorious for mortality. I who have fallen and still grovel in the dust, with wine-lees clotting my garments and wild-rose thorns tormenting my brow, how should *I* dare to usurp the office of expounding the mysteries of holiness and love? I have forgotten the wordless language she spake; I remember only that I would have listened for ever. I cannot recall the music's tune; I am only certain that it ravished my soul. I cannot even, alas! retrace her features and form; I know only that her beauty was divine. One sentence of that language I seem to remember; then it meant eternal union, now it interprets into everlasting farewell. One cadence of that music I seem to recall; then it chanted, *Gloria in excelsis Deo,* now it knells a *De Profundis.* One spark of that radiant beauty seems still to burn within me; then it lamped my spirit as a star of heaven, now it tortures me with fire of hell. For she revealed to me (if in this, also, I do not dream, as mainly in my life I have dreamed) that she was resting in a sphere divine and tranquil; she and many, many others who, like her, could not continue their infinite ascension until rejoined by the twin-souls left beneath them on earth, and who also like her were permitted to visit their twin-souls with heavenly consolations until death's consummate beatitude should remove all need and possibility of consolation. The sphere was so glorious that in its light and heat all their earth-stains were washed and consumed away, and so inviolably calm that in its constant perfect summer their souls developed all the potential beauty and virtue of this life-phase—as in our brief and troubled earthly summer one generation of roses out-bloom to their prime, then the rose-tree endures patiently through the winter and the spring, growing strong and broad for a richer efflorescence when the succeeding summer arrives. Their lives were praise and thanksgiving to God, intercommunion of the holy mysteries of love, and angelic visits to the dear ones bereaved of their mortal presence. And therefore, month by month and year by year, until also released by beneficent death from the prison-house of this lower world, I was to grow wiser, purer, braver, in faith and hope and love, unto the Supreme Sacrament of our union in Heaven.

> Fratelli, a un tempo stesso, Amore e Morte
> Ingenerò la sorte.
> Cose quaggiù sì belle
> Altre il mondo non ha, non han le stelle.*

II.—THE SIREN

> All the wide world beside us
> Show like multitudinous
> Puppets passing from a scene:
> What but mockery can they mean
> Where *I am*—where *thou hast been?*†

*Leopardi, "Amore e Morte," Canto xxvii, ll. 1–4.
†Final stanza of Shelley's "Invocation to Misery."

> Draining the wine of that voluptuous sin,
> Which heaven and earth seem both well lost to win.

The earth's time passed over me unperceived, unregarded; but the true time, which is change, wrought within me. The natural world refused to be wholly shut out; and its countless objects, besieging persistently the gateways of the senses, began gradually to penetrate into my soul. But still I perceived them merely as phantasmagoria, fleeting bubbles and cloud-shadows on the hurrying river of time. The unutterable want, wretchedness, ignorance, folly, the unfathomable crime and sin of the awful metropolis would have intolerably crushed my spirit with the oppression of their substantial reality—my spirit already faint to the verge of death in its own dearth of love-sustenance; but the fever of its famine transmuted them all, with the shapes in which they were embodied, into fantastic delirious dreams. The world was a great theatre; life but a carnival masquerade and drama, with irony for the secret of its plot; the passions were all mimetic, none of the personages were what they appeared, all was illusion and mockery. And the irony culminated in the grand fact that the masquers went about their masquerading, the actors went through their parts, soberly, seriously, and often with tragic earnestness; not one in ten thousand being permitted to suspect that he and all his fellows were indeed only playing mad mime-tricks for the inextinguishable laughter of that supreme Fate, beneath whom in secret they cowered with awe and terror; beholding deep down in the dark abysses of contemplation an enormous stone idol, dumb, blind, dead, pitiless, passionless, eternal; and beside it the laws of doom and destiny graven on tables of stone; as if the God and His ordinances had been petrified into immutability in the instant of cosmic creation.

Such was the enchantment now wrought upon me by my spell-bound Enchantress. For she was always with me, though she assumed now rarely, and ever more rarely until never, the holy guise of an angel. When fresh from the consecration of bereavement, I was found worthy to be comforted with angelic communion; but as in the course of time the virtue of that consecration from without was exhausted, while yet I had not by its blessing attained inward self-consecration, my ignoble heart found ignobler companionship. When the mouthful of Eucharistic wine inspires us no more, we may gulp down the wine of the tavern; when the temple-incense is mystical no more, we may drug ourselves with opium and hasheesh. Thus Sorrow, my intimate, now chiefly swayed me in her character of Siren. And this Siren Sorrow was the saddest I have ever known; for she affected—nay, frantically endeavoured—to renounce, to defy, to ignore her own essential sorrowfulness, expressing a wine of mad intoxication from the berries of her deadly nightshade.

In the workshop, in the streets, in my room, she would suddenly gesture to me with gesture imperiously alluring; and instantly we were away, down, down, down, through serene solitudes of water. Sometimes the sun was burning in the far heavens, sometimes it was moonless and starless night; generally the season was of fervid summer, and a drowsy dreamy warmth and tempered unsparkling light pervaded the abysses wherein we wandered; the hour and the season being seldom the same as those of the world whence we fled. And there were occasions when it was polar winter; when the moon shone sharp, bitter, naked, like an intense icy crystal, radiating positive arrowy cold as the sun radiates heat; when the waters cut my limbs like steel, and the stars glittered down barbed and piercing frost-points, and the sky hung like a petrified sea or the stony vault of a sepulchral world. She would lead me adown the beds of great rivers and over the desert floors of the ocean, amidst the unstartled shoals of their strange inhabitants, amidst the wrecks and remnants of ships and the drowned crews of ships. Ever and anon, at the suggestions of a wild caprice, she broke out into fragmentary singing, terrible yet sweet, magical with weird phantasy and mocking mirth. But two or three times she abandoned herself to a melody of such overwhelming sorrow and desolate despair, that I knew Love, her mother, was dying.

In the vast sea-crystal above us she would make flit before me in carnival processions all the scenes and peoples of the upper earth, flinging jeers of gesture and voice, irony, sarcasm, scornful pity, irresistible laughter, against them as they went by. The churches dwindled before her into whitened sepulchres, the palaces were seen as dungeons populous with vermin; she showed the fire raging under the earth's thin vesture of green grass broidered with flowers, and the skeleton padded with raw flesh beneath the skin of the beautiful; her finger-point seared the hidden folly of the wise and the secret terror of the brave; her glance transfixed the foul lust in the lover, and the core of sublimated selfishness in the holy ones; all the noble and mighty and reverend of the kingdoms she transformed into gibbering apes. She laughed back the world into chaos.

Then she would lead me into labyrinthic caverns, shut in from the waters with marble doors, tapestried with mossy growths and long slender sea-blooms purple and crimson and amber; floored with golden sand and iridescent shells, walled with emerald, roofed with crystal, lit with gleaming pearls and flashing precious stones. In the innermost chambers couches of soft and fragrant weeds were strewn around low tables of coral and jasper, on which were heaped sumptuous banquets. When King Harald first touched the hand of the Lapland witch-girl Snæfrid, "immediately it was as if a hot fire ran through his body"; and this same hot fire ran through me as we reclined to the banquet. Then the walls waved like green waters, the sands quivered as through flowing streams, the gems shot out fiery sparkles, the cavern-chamber was all athrob and full of murmurous sounds like the throbbing and the murmuring of the sea. She clothed herself with a fiercer beauty, haughty, passionate, intoxicating, irresistible. Lithe as a panther, she arose and moved restlessly; her green hair wreathed in snaky fascinations, her eyes burned with humid fires, her moods varied incalculably. From beakers that perchance were the spoils of imperial argosies sea-entombed for millenniums, she poured forth wines more imperial, fragrant as morning, glowing as sunset, fervent as noontide. Her restless movements harmonised into miraculous dancing, in the pauses and whirls of which her voice rang forth a music growing wilder and ever wilder, the phantasy more astounding, the melody more ravishing, the mirth more riant, the mockery more terrible, the passion more overwhelming; until drunken, dazed, electrified, frenzied, I reciprocated upon her the spell; and we two masquers in the universal carnival, the maddest and most lawless in a world all mad and lawless, revelled for a while with triumphant delirium in the recesses of our ocean-guarded solitude.

The Siren, even more terrible than beautiful! From the

voluptuous swoon I started suddenly and lo! the feast was vanished; the coral and emerald and jasper were no more, the wine was black blood, and its jewelled golden beakers were human skulls; the gleaming sand was a loathsome slime whereon and wherein crawled shapes of clammy hideousness. Then amorphous monsters of the unfathomed sea came heaving in by thousands, by myriads; and the flat was a Golgotha of human bones, the bones of men and women and children devoured by the insatiate sea; with inexpressible loathing and agony, I was compelled to "see things that ought not to be seen, sights that are abominable, and secrets that are unutterable." And worst of all, the most beautiful was become the most hideous, the Siren was a foul wrinkled hag, who kissed me with intolerable kisses, and pointed out bone by bone the huddled wrecks of my kind, and embraced me with her withered arms, as if taking me into everlasting possession; so that the conviction was seared into me, that I, though still breathing, was drowned as utterly as the skeletons, separated for ever to this death-in-life by the whole impassable ocean-firmament, from God in heaven and from man on earth. And when I wrenched myself loose and fled away, not with any definite hope, but simply rapt by an ecstasy of abhorrence, she pursued me with her train of hungry monsters, and clung to me with mocking endearments; and I again escaped, again to be pursued and overtaken; and so again and again; and hours were prolonged into immeasurable ages; and thoughts of horror and feelings of putrefaction crawled writhing in my brain and heart like the swarming of palpable worms; while weary with an unimaginable weariness I implored and imprecated rest, unconsciousness, annihilation; until at length, exhausted, sick, trembling, I awoke into the blessed natural world and found myself once more a man among men, and vowed—alas, how vainly!—never to harbour *her* more.

III.—THE SHADOW

Yes, dark, dark is my secret bower,
   And lown the midnicht may be;
For there is none waking in a' this tower,
   But you my truelove and me.

The dead are sleeping in their sepulchres;
And mouldering as they sleep: a thrilling sound,
Half sense, half thought, among the darkness stirs,
Breathed from their wormy beds all living things around;
   And mingling with the still night and mute sky
   Its awful hush is felt inaudibly.*

Victors or vanquished from the fearful strife,
What matters? — Ah, within our Mother's breast,
From toil and tumult, sin and sorrow free,
Sphered beyond hope and dread, divinely calm,
They lie all gathered into perfect rest:
And o'er the trance of their Eternity
The cypress waves, more holy than the palm.

Still the earth's time passed over me, unperceived, unregarded: but the true time, which is change, wrought within me. Besieging persistently the gateways of my senses, gradually the whole outer world — the innumerable armies of woes, sins, fears, despairs, — the dreadful legions of all the realities — poured in upon and overwhelmed my spirit. The earth was become massy, substantial, intolerably oppressive, a waking Nightmare; its inhabitants were no shadows; their lives were woven into no fantastic mime, but into a vast tragedy ruthlessly real; their passions were how far from merely scenic! With awe and secret shuddering terror, I felt crushing me down the omnipotence of Fate; Fate the Sphynx in the desert of Life, whose enigma is destruction to all who cannot interpret, and a doom more horrible before destruction to him who does interpret; Fate which weaves lives only too real in the loom of destiny so mysterious, uncompassionate of their agonies in the process; Fate, God petrified; the dumb, blind, soulless deification of Matter. And still I felt myself no nearer to a union of sympathy and common thought with my fellow-men.

And I wandered about the City, the vast Metropolis which was become as a vast Necropolis, desolate as a Pariah; burdened in all places and at all times with the vision of wrath and hatred that might dye the green earth blood-red, lust that might pollute all the seas, ignorance and guilt and despair that might shroud the noonday sun with eclipse. Desolate indeed I was, although ever and anon, here and there, in wan haggard faces,

*Shelley's "A Summer Evening Churchyard: Lechlade, Gloucestershire," ll. 19–24.

in wrinkled brows, in thin compressed lips, in drooping frames, in tremulous gestures, in glassy hopeless eyes, I detected the tokens of brotherhood, I recognised my brethren in the great Freemasonry of Sorrow. And she, the sombre patroness of our unassociative fraternity, the veiled goddess of our lonely midnight mysteries, the dreadful Baphomet in whose worship we all alike perished,—she never left me; nay, if so it could be, she interwrought herself yet more completely with my being. Never more an Angel, seldom more a Siren; but now a formless Shadow, pervading my soul as the darkness of night pervades the air. I do well to write *now,* for still she is with me, and still this is her dominant metamorphosis; and whether it will be the last, lasting until death, or will have successor or successors, I cannot pretend to judge. But as she is now thus with me—be it for ever, be it only for a time—I will speak of the Shadow in the present tense. Ah, how well I know her! yet my affection toward her I cannot define: it may be awe, fear, love, distrust, almost hate and contempt; but whichever of these, or whatsoever strange compound of them, it is of mystical potency, and I am thoroughly the slave of her enchantments.

At first she used to lead me, and still she often leads me, hour after hour of dusk and night through the interminable streets of this great and terrible city. The ever-streaming multitudes of men and women and children, mysterious fellow-creatures of whom I know only that they *are* my fellow-creatures—and even this knowledge is sometimes darkened and dubious—overtake and pass me, meet and pass me; the inexhaustible processions of vehicles rattle and roar in the midst; lamp beyond lamp and far clusters of lamps burn yellow above the paler cross shimmer from brilliant shops, or funereally measure the long vistas of still streets, or portentously surround the black gulphs of squares and graveyards silent; lofty churches uplift themselves, blank, soulless, sepulchral, the pyramids of this mournful desert, each conserving the Mummy of a Great King in its heart; the sky overhead lowers vague and obscure; the moon and stars when visible shine with alien coldness, or are as wan earthly spectres, not radiant rejoicing spheres whose home is in the heavens beyond the firmament. The continuous thunders, swelling, subsiding, resurgent, the innumerable processions, confound and overwhelm my spirit, until as of old I cannot believe myself walking awake in a substantial city amongst real persons. Then she, the Shadow, interweaves herself more wonderfully about me and within me; so that seeing I may see not and hearing I may hear not, so that not seeing I may see and not hearing I may hear. As my eyes fix and dilate into vision more entranced of the supreme and awful mystery, the browbrain upon my eyes expands and protends into a vast shadowy theatre for processions more multitudinous and solemn. The lamps withdraw and ascend, and become wayward meteors of the night; the night itself grows very dark, yet wherever I gaze I can discern, seeing by darkness as commonly we see by light; the houses recede and swell into black rock-walls and shapeless mounds of gloom; the long street is a broad road levelled forthright from world's end to world's end. All of human kind that have ever lived, with all that are now living and all that are being born into life, all the members of the æon of humanity, compose the solemn procession. Far, far in advance gleam stately figures in ample Oriental robes, "dusk faces with white silken turbans wreathed," from whose midst sway the long necks of high-backed camels; then follow mediæval knights on noble horses splendidly caparisoned; kings dark-bearded and queens most lovely trailing brilliant retinues; hooded monks in sombre gowns; barbarians fantastically arrayed or unarrayed, the limbs and features weirdly tattooed; nomad tribes moving with their flocks as they move in the deserts of Central Asia; legions on legions countless of all history's soldiery, from the heroes who fought around Troy to the warriors of Waterloo; the chariots and the spoils of a Capitolian triumph; "elephants endorsed with towers"; the silent flash of Mænads who run as they ran upon the Thracian mountains; dim crowds in the garb of our own time and country: and, as upon an unseen river flowing down the mid-stream of the swollen river of the peoples, glide forward galleys and galleons and ships of all seas and centuries: all come sweeping by, thronged and intermingled yet unconfused, in ghostly silence; and their trampling does not shake the earth beneath their feet: not more silent is the procession of the stars. I introvert my vision yet more intensely, and see the great flood far, far behind, emerging from the underworld, heaving up steadily wave on wave, each billow a mass of countless human lives, dark against the background of a serenest golden dawn. Oh, what an affluent dayspring! how it floods there the world with light! But where I stand reviewing the spectral march—so incalculable is the length of the procession—it is not daybreak, it is not morning; the noontide may be thousands of leagues remote, the twilight and the evening are immemorially overpassed; it is deep perfect night. Where I stand, absorbed, astonied, dismayed, overwhelmed, the legions are traversing a vast desert moorland, above which hover gross yellow meteors, upon which swell endless ranges of rock-wall and immense gloomy mounds, athwart which the broad road protends straight and level from world's end to world's end.

I have said that there is no sound or stir from the multitudinous trampling; but is there no music at all to time the spectral march? Music there is, or the vague echo of music from some sphere remote; music like the rhythm of a tide beating upon far-off shores; music which now interprets into that Dead March heard by Handel, full of pomp and majestic lamentation; now into that Dead March to which Beethoven listened, with its fitful bursts of desolate keening; now into that Russian Hymn March of Life-in-Death, with its sublimity of yearning pathos: such and so vague is the music to which the armies march. But are the symphonies all orchestral? is there no vocal psalm or anthem, no pæan or dirge articulate? One anthem there is, though I had again and again watched the multitudes defile as it seemed through the hours of many ages, before I apprehended its language. But at length, suddenly, on an autumn night very dark and still, in an huddled dimness of sad autumn night, it was given me both to see and to hear. Right opposite to where I stood, a league beyond the farther bank of the silent everflowing river of the peoples, towered a vast black shape dwarfing the Cyclopean rock-wall behind it; an image colossal, like to that which the king of Babylon set up in the plain of Dura, that all men might bow down and worship it; a colossal image of black marble, the Image and the concentration of the whole blackness of Night, as of a Woman seated, veiled from head to foot; and the ranks as they pass it bow down all with one impulse, like ranks of corn before a steady blowing wind. And from where this statue sits throned, a voice of innumerable voices, like the voice of a sea which is the voice of innumerable waves, or rather like the voice of a forest in calm which is the murmur of innumerable leaves, but dim and faint to extremity, is for ever intoning with unwearied monotony of recurrence certain simple childish words, a chant such as may be sadly chanted among dusky aboriginal tribes: —

All must move to live, and their moving
    Moves on and on to Death;
Wherever they pause in their moving,
    There awaiteth them Death;
Let them move as they will, their moving
    Soon brings them unto Death;
Let them move where they will, their moving
    So surely leads to Death:
All Life's continual moving
    Moveth only for Death.

No other chant than this have I ever heard while watching the procession. No war-song from the soldiery, no psalm from the monks, no love-lay from the gallant knights; and never has the faintest whisper reached me from the newly-emerged pilgrims whose background is the golden dawn, — the daybeams which struck music from the marble Memnon thrill no sounding chords in these. A vague pulsing of slow march-music full of the solemn sadness of death, a vague breathing of choral singing full of the sombre triumph of death; save for these, unearthly silence while the infinite march sweeps on.

Whence do the countless armies emerge? From the unknown chasm between the earth and the golden dawn. Where do they march? Along the broad road level through a vast wilderness of rock-strewn billowy moorland, above which hover vaporous yellow meteors. Whither do they immerge? Into the unknown chasm between the earth and the illimitable black night. Into an unknown chasm which may be a sea, for the rhythm of the vague march-music is like the rhythm of waters moaning upon the far, far forward shore. The broad road sweeps straight to this chasm, but also detaches narrow defiles and tortuous ravines thereto. And a bewildering mist as well as the great darkness broods over the horizon; and the moon there hangs spectral and beamless, and the stars there are as unclosed eyes of the dead.

Into that chasm all immerge. But do not all or some re-emerge on the side of the golden dawn? The dull meteor-gleams on the misty gloom unshroud none of its secrets, are altogether ineffectual save for half-revealing weird suggestions of ghostly imagery in the mist itself; and the moon hangs spectral and beamless, and the stars are blind as the unshut eyes of the dead. The chasm may be a bottomless void, or a desert ocean without farther shore, or a sea whereon hidden barks await the pilgrims, or a narrow Lethe-stream. Singly or by thousands they plunge; none is from the hither side ever seen again; no voice or sound is ever heard from them after the plunging. And not all the torches and lamps of the earth gathered together, not the sun and the moon and the stars of heaven conjoined into one glory, not the whole world itself burning in clear conflagration, could light up and disinter the secrets of that aboriginal gloom.

But often when I have been gazing through timeless hours upon the innumerable legions marching, marching, marching, in unintermitted march, to the rhythm of a far-booming tide; bowing down with one impulse before the colossal Image, which is as the concentration of the whole blackness of Night, to the monotonous breathing of a slow sad wind; disappearing into the black mist-shrouded gulph, while ever-new multitudes appeared emergent on the background of the golden dawn; often then have I pondered: — Are not these who now ascend the same who there descended? Is not the appearance a reappearance? May not the whole circle be fulfilled in the under world; above here in the day a march from dawn to dark, below there in the night a march through dark to dawn? Are not the innumerable multitudes now visible, together with equal multitudes now invisible, adequate for the continuous, never-pausing procession, without constant destruction and constant creation? If the sun which arises in the east is the same sun that set in the west; if the moon which is seen crescent is the same moon that dwindled down from the full until, for a time, her place in heaven was void; if the armies of the stars which circle the heavens are ever almost all the same stars; if the populations which arouse in the morning are, with very few exceptions, those that sank to sleep at night; — are not also these legions of human beings phantasmal, these millions on millions numberless commencing their march, the same who aforetime, and, perchance, many hundreds of times, traversed the earth-wilderness and disappeared?

And then She, the Shadow, beholding me that I am utterly aweary and forworn with the burthen of the vigil and the vision she has imposed, will murmur to me ere she suffers me to sleep — "Peradventure the new are also the old, but never shall any mortal be sure. The resources of Nature are infinite; the mysteries of Destiny are eternally unrevealed. It is as easy to bring forth new as to reproduce the old, and the thrift of the universe may be human lavishness and waste. Stars fall through the night; the affluent heavens are not careful of their stars. Every prodigal æon squanders broadcast myriads of its lives, and the hours of every cycle are squandered by myriads; yet not one monad, not one moment, to the universe has ever been lost. Know this only, that you can never know; of this only be assured, that you shall never be assured; doubt not that you must doubt to the end—if ever end there be. . . . But hearken yet again to the iterations and reiterations of the triumphant threnody, streaming evermore from where the veiled Image is enthroned: to that lulling you also shall soon sink in sleep, O my poor, desolate, weary child!"

All must move to live, and their moving
    Moves on and on to Death;
Wherever they pause in their moving,
    There awaiteth them Death;
Let them move as they will, their moving
    Soon brings them unto Death;
Let them move where they will, their moving
    So surely leads to Death:
All Life's continual moving
    Moveth only for Death.

So I knew her chiefly at first, but thus I chiefly know her now. In the workshop, in the streets, in my own room, she suddenly envelopes me; and forthwith, be it day or night with the outer world, it is for me dense night, moonless and starless, infinite, amorphous, solitary, silent. I have said that she pervades my soul as night's darkness fills the air; yet also I am conscious of her projected by my side, a vague womanly shadow, as it were the dark sun whence is radiated the darkness. We float not through the ethereal abysses, we glide not to the floors of the sea; we wander slowly yet unobstructed a little beneath the surface of the earth, passing as only spirits and spectral shades can pass through the solid ground. The Angel spake not with sounding speech—her soul immediately informed mine; the Siren articulated no earthly language—pure melody sufficed her for consummate enthralling expression; but the Shadow speaks to me in a terrene tongue, though in unworldly tones. Her words are the words of men and nature, but her voice is preterhuman and preternatural; murmurous, yet thin, never hurried, scarcely modulated, as it were the phantom of a living voice; and it gives to her simplest words weird significance. She leads me just beneath the surface of the earth, through sepulchral vaults, catacombs, cemeteries, graveyards, through the confusion of cities buried by time and sea and earthquake and volcanic bombardment, through all mortuary relics from the primæval fossil to the corpse inhumed yesterday. And ever as we wander she murmurs to me; and I have long since discovered that much of the dust wherewith she is cloudily enveloped, and which tempers to my spiritual vision the intensity of her innate gloom, has been gathered from mouldered and mouldering libraries. Solemn and even appalling is her low thin voice in the utter obscurity and silence, in the untravelled labyrinthic vastitude of these "camps and cities of the ancient dead."—"Cycle after cycle hath given me countless votaries," she murmurs; "age after age hath added liberally to my empire; year by year the world with its children bows to the sway of Oblivion. All must move to live, and their moving moves on and on to death; all life's continual moving moveth only for death. For Love, my own mother, is she not long since dead? But my father, who is Death himself, still exists, and shall exist for æons beyond number before he sinks exhausted, for lack of prey, upon my bosom, and is shrouded and sepulchred for ever with all the already sepulchred world by my loving hands. Until then, I to him—who is now my sole parent—and he to me—his eldest and dearest and mightiest daughter—must we be mutually devoted. . . . Surely all things by their nature, and all thoughtful beings by their nature and their reason, join with him who in his epitaph '*implora pace*.'"

Sometimes in speaking of this her dead mother, but never on any subject else, she loses her wonderful calmness, and expresses herself with a wild lyrical fervour of passion; her voice grows hurried and agitated, and swells sealike with the ominous mutter and roar of echoes from other worlds, and rings with every resonant note, and thrills with every modulation of love and grief and despair; and she herself, the Shadow, is swollen and agitated tempestuously, and lurid lightning-flashes leap from the heart of her gloom. But now only at long intervals and for briefest periods is she swayed by this impassioned mood.

Commonly after some short prelude she commences what I may call the rites of her self-worship. The liturgy and the hymns are from men, the homily is her own. As for her theme, it is in fact always the same, one which includes all themes possible to man; a subject by us variously named as it is contemplated in various relations and moods, and which she with her mystic insight seems to call indifferently by any one or more of the names we have thus bestowed — World, Life, Birth, Death, Time, Eternity, Oblivion, Cosmos, Chaos, Heaven, Hell, Matter, Spirit, Happiness, Misery, Health, Disease, Growth, Decay, Vanity, Reality, Illusion, Truth, God, Fate, All, Nothing; for under all these titles she sees the sole Substance itself always essentially one and the same, "itself by itself, solely, one everlastingly, and single." But as one of these names is supreme in the poetry of solemn suggestivness, is itself for us mortals (who are dazed from clear vision of *Life*) the profoundest poem ever written, and is very grand in our English mother-tongue, I choose this name to entitle her theme, and say that the text of all her homilies is *Death.*

But before the sermon and during its intermissions come the reading and the chanting. And for reading, besides all human scriptures, she has two mighty Books of Chronicles; the one azure and black-purple leaved, with white and golden and crimson illustrations, the commas and period-points in whose vast-flowing sentences are planets and comets and suns; the other an autobiography in this Universal History, wherein the generations of the earth have written down their own lives, so that every stratum-leaf holds the fragmentary archives of an æon of innumerable thousands of years. Volumes too vast for piecemeal citation or epitome, even if one had conquered their lore. But a few of the briefer human anthem-words and collects which she adopts in her burial service for all death — adopts for the sake of me, her human auditor — a very few of these I will cite; for these mournful echoes from hearts vacant of all hope, these *suspiria de profundis* of world-weary spirits, these perpetual moans and murmurs of the restless waters of Time beating against the barren shores of the World, ever exercise upon me a strangely powerful fascination. They sigh forth timid and tremulous, they leap forth like swift arrows of fire piercing and burning with passionate anguish, from hearts that have mouldered for centuries, from hearts that have not yet reached the grave toward which they yearn. Hush! for her voice is very faint and low and slender, as she chants and recites these melancholy spells.*

> And deth, allas! ne wil not have my lif,
> Thus walk I lik a resteless caytif,
> And on the ground, which is my modres gate,
> I knokke with my staf, erly and late,
> And saye, "Leeve moder, let me in.
> Lo, how I wane, fleisch, and blood, and skyn.
> Allas! whan schuln my boones ben at rest?
> Moder with yow wil I chaunge my chest,
> That in my chamber longe tyme hath be,

*The following passages, with Thomson's text followed throughout, are identified in the order in which they appear: "Pardoner's Tale," ll. 727–738; *Faerie Queene,* I.ix.40; *Macbeth,* V.v.19–28; *Tempest,* IV.i.156–158; Beaumont and Fletcher, *Thierry and Theodoret,* IV.i; Thomson, "Castle of Indolence," I.xii; Byron, *Cain,* I.i.287–289; Shelley, "Invocation to Misery," St. IX; Shelley, "Julian and Maddalo," ll. 505–510; Keats, "Ode to a Nightingale," ll. 21–30; Emily Brontë, "The Philosopher," ll. 7–10, 53–56; Anna Brownell Jameson, "Take Me, Mother Earth" (in *A Commonplace Book of Thoughts*), st. 3; Elizabeth Barrett Browning, "De Profundis," sts. 6, 7, 12; Arnold, "Requiescat," ll. 1–4; Browning, *Paracelsus,* V.363–365; Job, iii.13–15, 17–22, x.21–22, xvii.14; Ecclesiastes, ii.17, iii.19–21, iv.2, ix.10, xii.8; Jeremiah, xx.14–18; Plato, "Apology of Socrates," pars. 17, 32; Raleigh, *History of the World,* Bk. V, ch. 6, penultimate par.; Mornay, *A Discourse of Life and Death,* trans. Mary Sidney, Countess of Pembroke, par. 1; "An Essay on Death," in *The Remaines of the Right Honorable Francis, Lord Verulam,* spurious work ascribed to Bacon, pars. 1, 2, 3; John Eliot, MS of "Monarchy of Man"; Sir Thomas Browne, *Hydriotaphia,* Ch. V, par. 1, plus spurious passage attributed to Browne; De Quincey, *Suspiria de Profundis,* "Levana and Our Ladies of Sorrow," last par.; G. W. Curtis, *Nile Notes of a Howadji,* ch. 19, pars. 3, 14, 15; Carlyle, *French Revolution,* Bk. I, ch. 2, par. 5; Bk. V, ch. 5, par. 12.

When the phantasy originally appeared in the *National Reformer,* Thomson included almost twice as many quotations, and had identified the authors of each passage; when reprinting it in *Essays and Phantasies,* the text herein followed, he omitted identifications, eliminated roughly a third of the prose quotations by omitting parts of what had been longer passages from Job, Ecclesiastes, Mary Sidney, Bacon, Eliot, Browne, and Curtis, and entirely eliminated the following passages from the poetry section: two stanzas from Scottish ballads, "The Marchioness of Douglass" and "Marie Hamilton"; *Tempest,* IV.i.152–156; *Duchess of Malfi,* IV.ii.179–186; Chidick Tichborne, "Elegy," sts. 1, 3; Byron, "Euthanasia," last st.; Shelley, "Invocation to Misery," St. X; Shelley, "Adonais," St. LII; Ebenezer Elliott, "Lyrics for My Daughter," sts. 3, 4, 5; James Montgomery, "The Grave," sts. 1, 3, 5; Poe, "For Annie," sts. 5, 6, 8; Anna Brownell Jameson, "Take Me, Mother Earth," st. 2; Tennyson, "The Lotos-Eaters," ll. 88–98; and Arnold, "Requiescat," sts. 3, 4.

Ye, for an haine clout to wrap in me."
But yet to me sche wol not do that grace,
For which ful pale and welkid is my face.

He there does now enjoy eternal rest,
And happy ease, which thou dost want and crave,
And farther from it daily wanderest.
What if some little pain the passage have,
Which makes frail flesh to fear the bitter wave?
Is not short pain well borne that brings long ease,
And lays the soul to sleep in quiet grave?
Sleep after toil, port after stormy seas,
Ease after war, death after life, does greatly please.

To-morrow, and to-morrow, and to-morrow,
Creeps in this petty pace from day to day,
To the last syllable of recorded time:
And all our yesterdays have lighted fools
The way to dusty death. Out, out, brief candle!
Life's but a walking shadow; a poor player
That struts and frets his hour upon the stage,
And then is heard no more: it is a tale
Told by an idiot, full of sound and fury,
Signifying nothing.

We are such stuff
As dreams are made of, and our little life
Is rounded by a sleep.

Nothing is heard,
Nor nothing is, but all oblivion,
Dust, and an endless darkness.

Come ye! who still the cumbrous load of life
Push hard up hill; but as the farthest steep
You trust to gain, and put an end to strife,
Down thunders back the stone with mighty sweep,
And hurls your labours to the valley deep,
For ever vain; come, and withouten fee,
I in oblivion will your sorrows steep,
Your cares, your toils; will steep you in a sea
Of full delight; O come, ye weary wights! to me.

Were I quiet earth,
That were no evil: would I ne'er had been
Aught else but dust!

Hasten to the bridal bed—
Underneath the grave 'tis spread;

In darkness shall our love be hid,
Oblivion be our coverlid:
We may rest and none forbid.

Quick and dark
The grave is yawning: as its roof shall cover
My limbs with dust and worms under and over,
So let oblivion hide my grief. . . . The air
Closes upon my accents, as despair
Upon my heart: – let death upon my care!

Fade far away, dissolve, and quite forget
What thou amongst the leaves hast never known;
The weariness, the fever, and the fret,
Here where men sit and hear each other groan;
Where palsy shakes a few sad last grey hairs,
Where youth grows pale and spectre-thin and dies,
Where but to think is to be full of sorrow
And leaden-eyed despairs;
Where beauty cannot keep her lustrous eyes,
Nor new love pine for them beyond to-morrow.

Oh, for the time when I shall sleep
Without identity;
And never care how rain may steep,
Or snow may cover me!
Oh, let me die – that power and will
Their cruel strife may close;
And conquered good and conquering ill
Be lost in one repose!

To thy dark chamber, mother earth, I come;
Prepare my dreamless bed for my last home;
Shut down the marble door,
And leave me – let me sleep;
But deep, deep,
Never to waken more.

The past rolls forward on the sun
And makes all night. O dreams begun,
Not to be ended! Ended bliss,
And life that will not end in this!
My days go on, my days go on.

Breath freezes on my lips to moan:
As one alone, once not alone,
I sit and knock at Nature's door,
Heart-bare, heart-hungry, very poor,
Whose desolated days go on . . .

Only to lift the turf unmown
From out the earth where it has grown,
Some cubit-space, and say, "Behold,
Creep in, poor heart, beneath that fold,
Forgetting how the days go on."

Strew on her roses, roses,
  And never a spray of yew;
In quiet she reposes —
  I would that I did too.

I give the fight up! let there be an end,
A privacy, an obscure nook for me:
I want to be forgotten even by God!

"Now should I have lain still and been quiet, I should have slept; then had I been at rest. With kings and counsellors of the earth, which built desolate places for themselves; or with princes that had gold, who filled their houses with silver. There the wicked cease from troubling, there the weary be at rest. There the prisoners rest together; they hear not the voice of the oppressor. The small and great are there; and the servant is free from his master. Wherefore is light given to him that is in misery, and light unto the bitter in soul? Which long for death, and it cometh not; and dig for it more than for hid treasures. Which rejoice exceedingly and are glad when they can find the grave? . . . Before I go whence I shall not return, even to the land of darkness and the shadow of death. A land of darkness, as darkness itself; and of the shadow of death; without any order, and where the light is as darkness. . . . I have said to corruption, Thou art my Father, and to the worm, Thou art my Mother and my Sister."

"Therefore I hated life: because the work which is wrought under the sun is grievous unto me: for all is vanity and vexation of spirit. . . . For that which befalleth the sons of men, befalleth beasts; even one thing befalleth them: as the one dieth, so dieth the other; yea, they have all one breath; so that a man hath no pre-eminence above a beast: for all is vanity. All go unto one place; all are of the dust, and all turn to dust again. Who knoweth the spirit of man that goeth upward, and the spirit of the beast that goeth downward upon the earth? . . . Wherefore I praised the dead which are already dead more than the living which are yet alive. . . . For there is no work, nor device, nor knowledge, nor wisdom, in the grave whither thou goest. . . . Vanity of vanities, saith the preacher, all is vanity."

"Cursed be the day wherein I was born: let not the day wherein my mother bare me be blessed. Cursed be the man who brought tidings to my father, saying, A man-child is born unto thee: making him very glad. And let that man be as the cities which the Lord overthrew and repented not; and let him hear the cry in the morning, and the shouting at noontide: because he slew me not from the womb; or that my mother might have been my grave, and her womb to be always great with me. Wherefore came I forth out of the womb to see labour and sorrow, that my days should be consumed with shame?"

"For to fear death, O Athenians, is nothing else than to appear to be wise, without being so: for it is to appear to know what one does not know. For no one knows but that death is the greatest of all goods to man; but men fear it as if they well knew that it is the greatest of evils. . . . And if it is a privation of all sensation, as it were a sleep in which the sleeper has no dream, death will be a wonderful gain. For I think that if any one, having selected a night in which he slept so soundly as not to have had a dream, and having compared this night with all the other nights and days of his life, should be required on consideration to say how many days and nights he had passed better and more pleasantly than this night throughout his life; I think that not only a private person, but even the great king himself, would find them easy to number in comparison with other days and nights."

"O eloquent, just, and mighty Death! whom none could advise, thou hast persuaded; what none hath dared, thou hast done; and whom all the world hath flattered, thou only hast cast out of the world and despised; thou hast drawn together all the far-fetched greatness, all the pride, cruelty, and ambition of man, and covered all over with these two narrow words, *Hic jacet.*"

"It seems to me strange, and a thing much to be marveilled, that the laborer to repose himself hasteneth as it were the course of the sun; that the mariner rowes with all force to attaine the port, and with a joyful crie salutes the descried land; that the traveller is never quiet nor content till he be at the end of his voyage; and that we in the meanewhile, tied in this world to a perpetuall taske, tossed with continuall tempest, tyred with a rough and cumbersome way; yet cannot see the end of our labour but with griefe, nor behold our port but with teares, nor approach our home and quiet abode but with horrour and trembling."

"I have often thought upon death, and I find it the least of all evils. All that which is past is a dream; and he that hopes or depends upon time coming, dreams waking. . . . Physicians in the name of death include all sorrow, anguish, disease, calamity, or whatsoever can fall in this life of man either grievous or unwelcome; but these things are familiar unto us, and we suffer them every hour, therefore we die daily. I know many wise men that fear to die; for the change is bitter, and flesh would refuse to prove it: besides, the expectation brings terror, and that exceeds the evil. *But I do not believe that any man fears to be dead, but only the stroke of death.*"

"Death has its consideration but in terror; and what is assumed from that is like the imagination of children in the dark, a mere fancy and opinion. . . . It has been slandered, most untruly, most unjustly slandered. For either happiness it contains, or it repels calamity, or gives satiety and weariness an end, or does prevent the hardness of old age. . . . Death only is the haven to receive us, where there is calmness and tranquillity, where there is rest from all these storms and tempests. In that port all fluctuations of our life are quieted and composed; nor winds nor seas have power upon us there; fortune and time are excluded from that road; there we anchor in security, without the distractions of new troubles; there without danger or hazard do we ride."

"If we begin to die when we live, and long life be but a prolongation of death, our life is a sad composition; we live with death, and die not in a moment. . . . Time sadly overcometh all things, and is now dominant, and sitteth upon a sphynx, and looketh to Memphis and old Thebes; while his sister Oblivion reclineth semi-somnous on a pyramid, making puzzles of Titanian erections, and turning old glories into dreams. History sinketh beneath her cloud. The traveller as he paceth amazedly through these deserts, asketh of her who builded them, and she mumbleth something, but what it is he heareth not."

"Through me did he become idolatrous; and through me it was by languishing desires that he worshipped the worm, and prayed to the wormy grave. Holy was the grave to him; lovely was its darkness; saintly its corruption."

"After acute agony, death is like sleep after toil. After long decay, it is as natural as sunset. . . . Nature adorns death, even sets in smiles the face that shall smile no more. But you group around it hideous associations, and of the pale phantom make an appalling apparition. . . . Why should you not conspire with Nature to keep death beautiful?"

"Sovereigns die and sovereignties: how all dies, and is for a time only, is a 'Time-phantasm, yet reckons itself real!' . . . They are all gone, sunk, down, down, with the tumult they made: and the rolling and the trampling of ever new generations passes over them; and they hear it not any more for ever. . . . O poor mortals, how ye make this earth bitter for each other, this fearful and wonderful Life fearful and horrible; and Satan has his place in all hearts! Such agonies and ragings and wailings ye have, and have had, in all times: to be buried all in so deep a silence; and the salt sea is not swoln with your tears."

These, and such as these, are the anthem-words and hymns, the lessons and litanies and ejaculations, which she intones and recites in her wonderful self-worship: these and such as these are the incantations of the spell wherewith she so utterly subdues me. Whatever faith in immortality or hope of resurrection their context may avow, she ignores with solemn disdain. She murmurs them at intervals, rhythmically, she croons them over and over again, in her weird remote voice, while leading me on and on, through "the wide-winding caves of the peopled tomb." And between them, around them, past them, lapses slowly the full dark flood of her own monotonous eloquence; as Lethe may lapse for ever unrippled and unhurried, between its banks of pallid poppies, beneath the broad still leaves of its black lotus, past the crumbling islet grave-mounds which are as stepping-stones for sad Imagination when she would explore to the dimmest end, where the stream so nearly stagnant is swallowed in Chaos and aboriginal Night.

"Am I not kind?" she asks me, "am I not kinder far than all the gaudy Patronesses of Life? They bring agitation, I give rest; they bring the hopes which ever deceive, I give consummate fruition; they bring Memory, the sad, the grievous, the remorseful, I give Lethean absolution from the Past; they bring Time, I give timeless Eternity. All their woes, wants, sins, despairs, I translate into the beatitude of unconsciousness. This bone moulders forgetful that it slew a brother man; this skull decays unremembering that it harboured schemes of monstrous wickedness; these lips wither untormented by the cruel lies they have framed; these empty sockets crumble unaware of what hell-fire once burned in them. The limbs are weary no more; the heart-throb and the brain-throb are quiet for ever. Better the worms fretting that heart than the lusts and passions which fretted it of old; better the worms winding through that brain than the thoughts which used to possess it. I admit that the evil once conceived or done is indeed everlastingly existent (as it was indeed everlastingly pre-existent), still pulsing on apparent or unapparent, poison circulating with the life-blood of the world, until the world itself shall be exhausted; but the evil-doer is no more; the poison glass is shattered with the glass that held the wine; his personality is dissolved, his responsibility is diffused throughout the whole world; he is safe in the sanctuary of Oblivion. His crimes and sins (which you brand with harshest emphasis, in your unfraternal cruelty and injustice to each other), are indeed recorded as debts in the great Account Book, the infallible Ledger of the Universe: but in vain would the debtor be cited, for he is not; his very name will in a few brief years be illegible. For myriads and myriads and myriads of talents lost or misapplied, Nature seems continually pleading against an unknown number of debtors unknown; for they are all surely shielded and hidden by Nature herself, by Me the divine Oblivion, in the depths of the inviolable grave. For She, who is the sole head of the house, alone knows the profit and the loss of all the intricate commerce; and takes upon herself the liabilities as she takes to herself the acquisitions of all her agent children—salaried so poorly with golden joy and paper hope for their hard life-service.

"But you murmur that if the evil thus elude the punishment of their evil, the good must be defrauded of the recompense of their good. For those who have in this life been afflicted with the worst of all afflictions, an evil nature, ought to be punished after death for that supreme misery of their life! and those who in this life have been blessed with the richest of all blessings, a virtuous nature, ought to be rewarded after death for that supreme happiness of their life! And if the evil have no resurrection, the good can have no resurrection: though evil is the essence of nothingness and death, and good is the essence of being and life! It is hard indeed to teach aught of natural and simple truth to the children of men. The vulture, the tiger, the serpent, the lamb, the dove, the butterfly, have life's lesson perfectly by instinct; but man, weaving and ravelling it through the convolutions of his superior brain, still spells it for the most part backwards, and distorts the prayer of thanksgiving into a blasphemous curse.

"You complain, my poor child, on account of the good; but the good themselves, be assured, complain *not*. It is true that the evil suffer in life, and are blessed when here in their mother's bosom they are safe from life's suffering; but it is not true that the good rejoice in life, and are injured here by privation of life's joy. Unconsciousness, which is the sole perfect anodyne, can never be a harmful poison. Nor are the good on earth the happy any more than the evil, though these are truly cursed and those are truly blessed. The only men and women happy in life are such as not even you can imagine in a glorious life hereafter. Very sad, overwhelmingly sad, 'with great heaviness and continual sorrow in his heart,' lives a holy loving man. Look abroad over your sin-ulcered earth, and say how shall such a one dare to rejoice! Jesus must be a man of sorrows and acquainted with grief; and tradition shall record of him that he was known to weep but never known to laugh: how could he laugh, while his brethren throughout the whole world were in horrible bondage of ignorance, wretchedness and sin? I say unto you that your God Himself, the God whom your seers have beheld in vision, throned omnipotent and eternal in the Heaven of Heavens, veiled with burning glory, amidst countless legions of quiring seraphim and adoring saints, *He* could not be what you call happy while one cry of suffering ascended from His earth or one spark of evil glowed in His hell.

"Sin ought to be punished and virtue rewarded! And the sins of your race are so voluntary and Satanic, that no limited time can contain their retributions; the virtues of your race are so inherent and divine, that no period less than Evermore has capacity for their recompense! When will you be persuaded and possessed by the truth which you heard chanted long ago, the truth that there is no punishment and no reward, that every being by its own nature weaves every thread of the web of relations connecting it with the world around?

"You cannot but trust that the pure, and the brave, and the wise, really merit an after-death recompense, that their noble faculties really claim after-death spheres of exercise and continual growth. Whomsoever Faith hath dowered with purity, valour, or wisdom, to him in that one gift Fate hath been unusually bountiful; and he may well be content, however adverse seem the circumstances of his lot. Let the impure have high rank, and the coward lavish wealth, and the fool princely sway: the rank and the wealth and the sway are even to human judgments miserably inadequate compensations for inherent vileness, are generally even to human judgments miserable aggravations of the inherent vileness. But, after death? Oh, believe me, there is not one among you whom his fellows justly account saint, or sage, or hero (being really an Excelsior, like the monarch of Lilliput, some nailbreadth taller than those around him, striking awe into the beholders), who would if it were permitted him go alone to the great Demiurgos to whom is intrusted the management of this mysterious World-Drama, and plead: I have performed the part allotted to me in this short life-scene so magnificently well, and have enjoyed it so thoroughly, that I must be allotted another and a higher part in the scene which is to follow. Still less would or could he plead: I must be allotted parts ever higher and higher in all the successive scenes until the Farce-Tragedy shall end with Time; and when the Drama and Time are ended, I must be glorified with apotheosis and be a little god for ever with the one great God in Eternity.

"Were Fate ever thus tender of individuals, thus dotingly fond of the rare beings in the world that seem perfect in their kind, very few men and women in comparison with what men and women call the inferior creatures and lifeless things would be found worthy of enduring existence. Some rose might proffer a valid claim; some rose which has blushed beauty and exhaled perfume to the uttermost sweetness of its nature; some rose which is as the microcosm of golden dawns and crimson sunsets; the rose by which Sharon is divine and Schiraz dream-lovely; the rose on whose petals Dante in fire-dew enamelled the names and marshalled the hierarchies of your supreme Heaven:* or a lamb without spot or blemish, type of Him who is there worshipped for ever and ever: or a dove, in whose form the Paraclete descended on the only Son of your only God. But a man! In the

*In forma dunque di candida rosa
Mi si mostrava la milizia santa,
Che nel suo sangue Cristo fece sposa.
— *Del Paradiso:* Canto xxxi. (Thomson's note.)

whole long masquerade of History, how many men, how many women, can be found whom even you would think white enough for the candidature? In the abundant treasures of your language, many, many names appear which are in themselves poems, and which therefore participate in the lasting life of beauty, but few of these class human kind. Gold, wine, lily, rose, dove, eagle, lion, panther, moon, star, dawn, dusk, river, meadow, each of these is in itself idyl, or lyric, or ode; but not man, not woman, not child, not infant, perhaps of all the terms that class humanity, only youth and maiden, mother and babe.

"Ah, I catch your murmur: *God created man in his own image, in the image of God created he him!* Yes; and the whole world is the image of God; for every creature and thing and circumstance in it is an uttered thought, a developed volition, of the universal life you term God. But when I led you so long through the streets of the great city, that vast crowded encampment of what you call Life, whose gloom is more appalling than the gloom of these subterranean sepulchres of Death; when you gazed into the eyes of all who passed, myriads on myriads innumerable; in how many among them did you recognise the image of God? Oh, the mean stupid faces, the mean dull eyes, the mean puckered foreheads, the mean formless eyebrows, the mean loose or pinched lips, the mean gross or withered bodies, the mean slouching gate, of the mass of them! And what were the chief variations from the prevalent meanness? Despair, ferocity, life-weariness, cunning, starved misery, immense greed or lust. If ever anything of divine began incarnation in those forms, it must have long ago shrunk away from the pollutions. So far are they now from any trace of the divine, that the very manhood and womanhood have long been crushed out of them. If one in a thousand was comely to the first glance, he was coarse or imbecile to the second; if one in ten thousand was lovely to the first glance, she was mindless or soulless to the second. The haughty capital out of its thousands of thousands can scarcely show a hundred men and women. What used to startle you into common life when the periods of the visions I gave you power to see were fulfilled? Some painted girl soliciting to impurity, some child in colourless rags begging for bread, some reeling drunkard hoarsely singing or blaspheming. For such goodness and comfort as you have among you never accost strangers, but go about carefully shut up in themselves. If one whom you know not ventures to address you, your first feeling is of distrust and defiance: this is your instinctive judgment of each other. Poor men, and women more wretched! I could weep for you bitter tears, even I the Shadow, were I not consoled by the knowledge that so soon ye shall all sink into my bosom, so soon be gathered tenderly from loathsome, shameful, miserable life into the beautiful and innocent sleep of death: and the sleep shall be everlasting.

"Still you urge that it is not because of perfection here, but of imperfection here, that Man claims a developing Hereafter: his aspirations announce their own fulfilment; his life should be a continuous indefinite ascension toward the unapproached Highest, ascending evermore because never attaining. Why his life alone, and not that of the worm, of the oyster? And do your aspirations, whose result you know, your aspirations limited to the things of this life, do you find that these generally announce their own fulfilment, or do you find that in fact they are never really fulfilled? And, if the development should prove a development of decay and corruption, not of healthy growth? If the tendency already in the little lifetime has curved round from upwards to downwards? Shall man ascend for ever and ever, and the poor toad and sponge never climb a grade? And what of the roses that are blighted in the bud, the lambs that are never sheep, the little unfledged things that never have their bird-life, the saplings, the acorns, that never grow into trees, the number-confounding spawn-germs that never attain definite individual existence? Shall all these, likewise, be granted a compensatory resurrection, that they may live up to the maturity of which here they were defrauded, and then grow more strong and beautiful for ever? For all these have certainly not much less capacity for indefinite ascension than has man. I have studied him now for many ages, and I find that his capacity is very limited; his *could* and *might* are scarcely larger than his *can*. He always gets drunken already on much strong truth; he always gets insane with much pure holiness.

"Why are you so unwilling to acknowledge your relationship with all the rest of the world and its creatures? Being so weak, and therefore so miserable, why would you disown the great family alliance? Succumbing inevitably to the least weighty strokes of Doom, you will yet rather bear them yourselves than be solaced and tended by the kindly earth that bore you. So you glut your perversity at the expense of your happiness like so many sulking children: —and, after all, the denial of kindred destroys not the fact of kinship. Of what use to sneer: This is not, this shall not be my brother! when you both issued from the same womb? Let no atom in the world be proud; it is now in the heart of a hero, it may soon be in a serpent's fang. Let no atom in the world be ashamed; it is now in the refuse of a dung-hill, it may soon be in the loveliest leaf of a rose. Each monad in its time plays many parts, and perhaps in the course of the world's existence plays all; and in spite of yourselves your being is expanded beyond its own miserable limits into fellowship and affiance and mysterious identity with the being of all the universe.

"When will you freely and gladly own the truth that whatever is born in Time must decay and perish in Time? As your race studies fossil relics of plant and shell and gigantic animal, so shall future existences (to you in their kind inconceivable) study fossil relics of your race. For every kind has its own æon, and when its æon is fulfilled becomes extinct: while your earth is by many signs so young in its æon; and you by your pruriency, your unbounded self-esteem, your pugnacity, your brutality, your ignorance, your weakness, are so plainly among the less noble thoughts and imaginations of its youth (closely succeeding the wild childish extravagances of mammoth, pterodactyl, ichthyosaurus, and the convulsive infant rages of flood and fire); that many much higher races than yours must surely be brought forth ere it reaches its prime and commences to decay. The races flourish and die out, and Demiurgos has no care for individuals. The coral insects swarm in the sea, of which they know a fraction more than equivalent to that which man knows of this visible universe; and they are distinct in their individualities and generations as are the children of men; and each dies having wrought its cell; and one cell is so much vaster (even to the thousandth of a line) than any of those around it, that it may well be long famed amongst them far and wide as a stupendous work; so the coral-reef grows by imperceptible increments until it almost reaches the surface of the sea; then the æon of the brood is finished, the life-period is fulfilled with the life-task, they cannot exist in the upper air; and the reef which is their stupendous self-wrought catacomb and mausoleum becomes an island, nourishing and sheltering quite new forms of life. The ancient

Egyptians have left a few tombs, columns, pyramids; these insects leave behind them hundreds of leagues of reef well-founded from the floors of the deep sea: which, Egyptians or insects, are more serviceable to the after-world? You have visited a great library, which is a species of human coral-reef; and you have beheld thousands upon thousands of volumes closely ranged around: these are the painfully elaborated sepulchral *exuviæ* of once living human intellects; and each contributed in some infinitesimal manner to the growth of knowledge; but how few of all do even you insects of the same race now distinguish and examine, though many were accounted great and wonderful works in their time; and those which to you are still great and wonderful, what are they to any other race? What are they even to such of you as dwell in another spot of this earth-grain and babble in a different tongue? They advanced a little what you pleasantly call science, they carried up the intellect to reach beyond themselves into new levels of thought; their work was then done; they are but names, the Library is a myriad-coffined sepulchre of dead minds.

"Nature has no care for individuals; and races and times are but individuals in broader genera and longer times, and these again in yet broader and longer; and Oblivion must cover all. Yet you poor mortals agonise for fame, and lavish much of your really finest bombast concerning 'immortal renown,' while the greatest and the noblest, together with the worst and the meanest, can but last as names for a few generations among a very few of their own kind, on a speck of this mottled dust-grain in the universe of space and time, which itself may be a dust-grain invisible amidst universes *not* of space and time, known by senses more and infinitely more vivid than yours, cognised by intellects whose laws and powers are indefinitely grander than those with which you are endowed. Ah, you endeavour to persuade yourselves that your minute glowworm soul-sparks lamp Infinity and Eternity; you have been generous enough to create a God who certainly never created you; you dissect him, every bone, nerve, and tissue; chemically analyse him into ultimate substances or substance; you exhibit him set up as an anatomical specimen, or elaborated into algebraical formulae, and designed in geometrical diagrams, in your metaphysical and theological discourses, your Athanasian creeds and the like: and yet you cannot say why the grass grows; you cannot prove whether the world and your own selves do or do not really exist; and the few of you who have reflected a little are conscious that

> The deep enormous Night unfurls
> Its bannered darkness left and right
> In solemn mockery of such light.

"I am just, though you conceive me so unscrupulous: I the sexton of the whole world-graveyard, the architect of the all-housing tomb, the weaver of the all-enveloping shroud, the planter of the all-shading cypress, the voice of the everlasting *Requiescant*—that dirge which is indeed a solemn triumphal hymn; I am just as Fate, impartial as Destiny; and the laws of my dealings are strict as that covenant in accordance with which the earth wheels round the sun. Here a fire smoulders out under the oppression of its fuel, there one expires for lack of fuel; here a fire burns steadfastly in calm, there one flares fiercely in storm; but all alike in subjection to the same universal laws; and all alike must at length be extinct, when all the fuel of each is devoured. There is one glory of the sun, and another of the moon, and another of the stars, and yet another of the household lamp; and for each its own lustre and its own æon is meted out by itself, by what itself is; its own nature gives its own vitality and destiny. No being can receive more than its capacity will hold; a finite being can no more receive eternal life than a desert-well-shaft can hold the ocean.

"Fire, the pure, the spiritual, the absolute, fire whose heat is love, and light is truth, *this* indeed subsists for ever in eternity; but all the material atoms and bulks upon which it feeds (and some of which account themselves living beings and immortal spirits during the process of the burning) must be sooner or later consumed. None lives in itself; its life is that without itself, though penetrating and informing it, which consumes it away; its being is the being dissolved into nothingness. For apart from the infinite eternal empyrean there is no self-subsisting fire. Go in to your chamber and seal up all its outlets, so that the air which it contains be quite cut off and shut in from the world's universal atmosphere; and very soon you will not respire but expire therein; it will be for you not the breath of life, but the miasma of death. Even so must what you call your individual spirit perish could it be cut off from the universal spirit; and the nearest approach you can make to this, intense and long-continued self-absorption, is recognised among yourselves as madness.

"I am just, as I am indeed gracious. As cold comes not, but heat departs; as darkness grows not, but light fades; so the black pall and the wan shroud with which I cover up the dead, are but the smoke and the ashes of their own burnt-out fires. The burning of the fire, the writhing of the flames, are torture and restless longing; I am the eventual coolness and repose. That which you call the World with its creatures—this gross multiform mass of matter consuming in the fervency of the one spirit—shall indeed at last be utterly annihilated. The law flames before your eyes in material analogies, the doom stamps itself into your consciousness by material symbols. Behold how the nebulous continuity of your sun-system has parted and congealed into separate calcined orbs hollow and centrally candent; and all are dwindling in the millennial cycles, and shall dwindle until the last fire-sustaining atom is exhausted, and remnant there is none of the worlds opaque in the infinite unadulterate empyrean. But now 'in the midst of life you are in death': not merely *liable* to death, as so shallowly you are wont to interpret the great truth into a truism; but *in* death; you and your transitory phantasmal Universe of matter floating in the midst of the eternal Divine Life which alone is Reality. The life surrounds you, clasps you, supports you, penetrates you, informs you, consumes you; but you are not the life any more than the submerged sponge is the ocean or the vanishing cloud is the air. The more intense your so-called life, the more of ecstatic and swiftly consuming torture do you suffer; the pure fire pierces you through and through; when the pure fire pervades and possesses you wholly, you are no more; in the instant of your attaining the perfect, the only true life, you are utterly annihilated. Of two men only is this divine consummation recorded in your very astonishing Holy Writings; and it is certain that you are wont to die now not by utter consumption of your materiality, but for want of the informing fire; so you perish from separate organisation, leaving abundant carcass to swell the earth's general stock and be worked up and consumed in other forms.

"I am generous, as I am indeed just. With me you shall sleep perfect sleep, dreamless shall be your slumber: the darkness is infinite, the repose is ineffable, the silence is divine. You dream that they who have sunken wearily into my arms, and have been hushed to sleep on my bosom, and have been laid away and covered up in the bed which I prepare for all, often arise from the rapturous rest, and steal out of the undisturbed dormitory, and wander the upper earth tortured and goaded by evil memories; and you affright yourselves with visions of them thus restlessly wandering. Most strange and calamitous delusion! The bed is too soft, the embrace too maternally dear, the trance is too profound, the oblivion too beatifically perfect for them ever to dream (if dream they could) of arising and revisiting that cold naked storm-beaten upper world of the 'Life which is a disease.' Could any who now lie here, quietly resolving into quiet earth, which again is dissolving and surely perishing into nothingness; could any of these awake for a moment, and remember, and have power to contrast their perfect sleep in my bosom under the folds of my vesture (whose shadow is holy and blessed as the shadow where *Sheckinah* dwelt, under the wings of the cherubim over the mercy-seat), with their ever-troubled wakefulness on earth, with the

> Famine, and bloodless Fear, and bloody War,
> Want, and the want of knowledge how to use
> Abundance—

how would they shrink with horror from the suggestion of returning, how would they smile triumphantly compassionate at your fearful hints of evil memories, how would they nestle back into the slumber-place athirst for the suckling nepenthe!

"If you really lived; knowing, and gladly accepting, and bravely working out your little part in the sublime economy of the universe; ever conscious of your insignificance as an isolated creature, but no less conscious of your lofty and even divine significance as one flame of the universal fire, one note in the infinite harmony; without arrogance, selfishness, delusion, disdain; without hope, or fear, or self-contradictory longing, yet burning with pure aspiration; then I would not preach to you thus, then not the Shadow but the Splendour would instruct you: for dying more and more daily by intensity of life into the impersonal and infinite and unconditioned, by supreme consuming domination and dominion of the spirit over matter, you would love death as the crowning glory of life, and reverence life as the *via sacra* of the triumph of death. But you have no hope, scarcely a dream, of thus living and dying. Yet you cling to your death-in-life, which you call life, while you never dare to really live; you, children afraid to go into the dark, although therein is your sole bed of rest. You dare not live up to even your own low thoughts of life: the mass of your works, ceremonies, laws, pleasures, are houses built to keep out the natural air, and blinds woven to temper the universal light. The sage studies a new science to escape an overwhelming sorrow, 'or haply by abstruse research to steal from his own nature all the natural man'; the soldier plunges into battle-blood-drunkenness to forget an unavailing love; the statesman weaves his mind into subtle webs of policy that so he may stifle some fierce passion; the poet chants victories he cannot fight to win, and beautiful happiness that can never be his lot; those most lavishly endowed by nature and by fortune are exactly those who suffer most from life-weariness. Who lives, who exercises and develops his whole nature joyously in his career? There is the cup of the wine of life; and scarcely one dares a deep draught of its fiery intoxication, though scarcely one is willing to have the unemptied and not-to-be-emptied cup withdrawn. One short, trembling, rapturous sip in the flushed fervour of youth; then you draw back, frightened at your own rash hardihood, and seek stupid safety in soulless business and pleasureless pleasure. Again and again you wish to be dead for a time, to sleep unconscious until some wished-for moment, to be relieved from the tedious burthen of uneventful hours and days; and when the wished-for moment has come and gone, and you are once more disappointed, you would die again for another period; and so again and again; wishing for sleep and unconsciousness for a limited time, that is, wishing for short and imperfect death; and yet with the miraculous and incredible inconsistency of man, abhoring with wild fear the one true and perfect death. And you complain of the narrowness and poverty of life, though it lavishes upon you such wealth of hours and opportunities more than you can use or enjoy! And this in youth and health; but you would even rather cling to old age, weak and sick, without the power while yet with the desire to enjoy, than sink into death, which takes away the desire in removing the power: you would rather be Tantalus with his thirst, than without it.

"O my poor homeless weary children, return at least unaffrighted, since return is inevitable, unto the embrace of me, your mother! Have at least the courage and the candour to own that you dare not live true life, that you infinitely prefer dreamless rest to this weary wandering without a goal. Leave your alien wretchedness, and the famine which is fain to devour the husks that the swine do eat, and come home to the banquet of joyous rest, ye poor helpless prodigals; be not ashamed to acknowledge your yearning to have part in the glorious promise, 'He giveth his beloved sleep'; and fear not to come unto me for this beatitude of sinless sleep; unto me the divine Oblivion dwelling ever throned in the realm whence you shall not return, even in the land of darkness and the shadow of death; a land of darkness as darkness itself, and of the shadow of death; without any order, and where the light is as darkness; where, O ye weary, sinful, desolate, orphan ones, where the wicked cease from troubling, where the weary be at rest!"

And the thin weird voice of the Shadow dies away remote in the dense blackness subterranean, as a star-speck dwindles in the formless night; and the gloom, so deep and crushing in the revelation of her voice, grows deeper still and yet more awful in the following utter silence.

In Our Forest of the Past

[*This phantasy appeared in the* Secularist *(February 17, 1877); Thomson chose to reprint it as the final piece in* Essays and Phantasies, *which would indicate that he intended it to serve as an important statement of his pessimistic philosophy.*]

A MILD pleasant day after weeks of wind and rain, a clear moonlit night heralding storm and flood; the last day of the Old Year and the eve of the New. About ten the bells began ringing for the "watch-night" services, wherein the few still faithful and the many merely curious solemnise the annual death and birth with confessions and litanies and chanting. And while the air rang with the bells, I thought: I have seen so many old years die, so many new years born; but when has the new proved better than the old? and where is omen or hope that the year yet unborn shall prove better than the year now dying? Have I any tender grief for the departure? Have I any joyous welcome for the advent? Let me pass in sleep that narrowest moment of midnight wherein ere a man can cry Now! the one has given place to the other. So I lay down and slept. But though St. Sylvester rules no more, and the weird ghostly masquerades are abolished, the night which was his remains for us mortals potent with sleeping visions as with waking reveries; a night that looks back to the past and forward to the future, a night pregnant with phantasy. Wherefore though I slept, my mind was not at peace, but carried me in sad dream to a forest immense and obscure, even the forest of the past which is dead; and it was full of moanings and wailings, vague yet more articulate than the moaning of winds or waters; and One moved beside me who was tall and stately and muffled in darkness. And when we had walked long, silent, under the thick leafage, among the massy boles, the wailings grew keener and more piteous; and we came upon an open space where was gathered a vast multitude of infants and young children, whose desolate cries and pining faces made my heart sore. And he my companion and leader murmured softly: Scarcely had they blossomed into the world of life than they withered away out of it; and for too early death they have no rest: they wail their frustrate lives. We left the poor little ones and walked on silent; and as their wailing sank, a sound of saddest moaning grew upon our ears; and in a broad glade we discerned a multitude of youths and maidens, wan or fever-flushed; all restless, though drooping with weakness and languor; and their tears were as tears of the very heart's blood, and all hope of comfort expired in their sighs. And when we had gazed long, my companion murmured: Young Love tendered them the apple of his Mother, golden and rose-red from her divine warm hand, but it turned to dust and ashes on their lips; for the bitterness of death they can never find peace: they moan their frustrate lives. We went onward through the gloom from moaning unto moaning; and beheld a multitude of men and women, halt, maimed, twisted, bent, blind, dumb, convulsed, leprous; hoarsely groaning or gesturing anguish; dreadful to hear and to see. And my guide murmured: The wine of existence was brought to them in goblets broken or leaking; for the full sweet draught they had but a scanty sip: they lament their frustrate lives. And as we walked on we heard wild shrieks and gibbering laughter; and we came to a rugged ravine, on whose banks clustered cowering idiots, many with a large tumour at the throat, and whose floor was full of a restless multitude, haggard and dishevelled, swift and abrupt in movement, furious in gesticulation; horrible to hearing and to sight. And my companion murmured as I turned away shuddering: The wine of existence passed to them was drugged or poisoned, and they drank stupor or madness; death has no nepenthe for these whose wine of love was as a philter of hate: they curse and mock their frustrate lives. Then we crossed a space of upland heath, and I saw the stars shining, cold and supreme in the deep dark heavens, and I said to him at my side: Nature is very cruel to man. And he answered calmly: But how kind to all other creatures! and how kind is man to his brother, and to himself! Then we plunged again into the thick forest, as into a moaning midnight sea, and came upon an immense multitude, many shivering in thin rags, many nearly naked, all gaunt and haggard, with hollow eyes and famished faces; and some huddled together as for warmth, and some moved restlessly hither and thither, and in their moaning was eternal hunger. And my leader said: Rich men grew richer with their toil; kings and priests and great lords were fed fat with the flesh that fell away from their bones; they starved in body and in mind; their existence was a long need: they moan their frustrate lives. And we went forward continually from moaning unto moaning. And we came upon a multitude of whom some were chained together in long files, some were fettered or manacled singly; many nearly naked were scored livid or blood-red with the lash; others lay helpless or writhing on the ground as broken on the wheel or dislocated by the rack; others were clothed in garments of flames as ready for their own burning; others glared wildly bewildered through tangled locks as stupefied or maddened by years of the dungeon; and their moanings were lamentable with the bitterness or sullenness of despair. And my guide said: They were imprisoned and chained and lashed for their crimes by the rich who had kept them wretched and ignorant and vile; they were dungeoned or tortured by kings because they dared try to be free; they were tortured and burned alive by priests because they dared to think for themselves: they moan their frustrate lives. And we went onward continually from moaning unto moaning. And we reached an enormous multitude, the soldiery of all nations, and many were mangled and mutilated, gashed and bleeding, torn and shattered; others lay as starving, others as in fever, others as devoured by frost; and those who seemed unhurt paced erect with a stolid misery in the forthright regard. And my leader said: They were torn from their kindred, they were cut off from the sweet life of home; for love they were given lust, for the ploughshare that produces the sword that destroys; from men they were drilled into machines: for the pride of kings and nobles, for the enmities of priests, they went forth to kill or be killed by their fellows whom they knew not, against whom they had no cause of hatred, who had no cause of hatred against them; to ravage and burn and massacre; the cries of the homeless, the widows, the fatherless, are ever in their ears: they moan their worse than frustrate lives. And we went onward continually from moaning unto moaning. And we came to a vast multitude; cowled monks and veiled nuns moaning for ever a hopeless *Miserere*; cadaverous ascetics, self-starved, self-lashed, self-tortured, grovelling on the earth, staring spellbound on skulls, sobbing and weeping, supplicating with desperate despairing supplications the image of a wretched human figure nailed to a cross. And my guide said: For religion they renounced the sweetness of home, the healthful brotherhood and sisterhood of humanity, freedom and self-reliance; they renounced all the goodness and sweetness of the world, to gain the Heaven in which you see them here: they moan their frustrate lives. And we went onward continually from moaning unto moaning. And we came to a multitude, of whom some frail and languid were reclining on the earth, and others paced to and fro, while all were in profound dejection. And my guide said: Here are the dreamers who made no earnest effort to realise their dreams of goodness, or beauty, or truth; and here are the strong and strenuous minds baffled and vanquished by feeble bodies or adverse fate: they moan their frustrate lives. And we went onward continually from moaning unto moaning. And we came to an innumerable multitude of men and women, dull-eyed, bloated, sluggish, bewildered, moaning uneasily in their semi-torpor. And my guide said: Their lives were narrowed to their homes, they worshipped wealth, they cringed to the dust before rank, they aspired but to comfort and good repute, they were shut in and walled up from Nature and art and thought: they moan their frustrate lives. And we went onward continually from moaning unto moaning. And we came upon a multitude; great lords in rich furred robes, great prelates in purple and crimson; and they were drooping and broken and crushed down as if robed with lead, and coronet and mitre seemed of lead on their brain. And my guide said: They lived superb and luxurious as a race apart and above their kind, trampling on the necks of their fellows; they were fat with the insolence of unearned wealth; their choice wines were the blood of the poor, their choice meats were the flesh of those who toiled for them; they scorned and denied human brotherhood: they moan their worse than frustrate lives. And we went onward continually from moaning unto moaning. And in the deepest depth of gloom of the forest we passed among figures each wandering alone, and they were crowned monarchs, and the crowns seemed of fire burning ever through the brain; and in the regard of each I read the anguish and despair of a horrible isolation, and each pressed his right hand to his heart as if it were bursting with agony. And my guide said: They counted themselves as gods, looking down upon their kind, contemptuous, impassible, unbeneficent; moving them hither and thither at will, sacrificing thousands to a lust or a caprice, sending them forth by myriads to slay and be slain; before them was terror, and behind them death and desolation; for their glory and their sumptuousness millions toiled in want and misery: they moan their worse than frustrate lives. Then I paused and spoke to my leader: My heart is sick and sorrowful to death with this vision of the past of my kind; have all human lives, then, been frustrate, and not any fulfilled? And he answered: Come and see. And we turned to the right and went down through the wood, leaving the moanings behind us; and we came to a broad valley through which a calm stream rippled toward the moon, now risen on our left hand large and golden in a dim emerald sky, dim with transfusion of splendour; and her light fell and overflowed a level underledge of softest yellow cloud, and filled all the valley with a luminous mist warm as mild sunshine, and quivered golden on the far river-reaches; and elsewhere above us the immense sweep of pale azure sky throbbed with golden stars; and a wonderful mystical peace as of trance and enchantment possessed all the place. And in the meadows of deep grass where the perfume of violets mingled with the magical moonlight, by the river whose slow sway and lapse might lull their repose, we found tranquil sleepers, all with a light on their faces, all with a smile on their lips. And my leader said: Their wine was pure, and the goblet full; they drank it and were content: their day was serene,* every hour filled with work that was pleasure, or with equable pleasure itself; so when night came they lay down content: they had health and strength, they were simple, truthful and just, they were free-hearted and could give bountifully, they were free-minded and lived free, they were warm-hearted and had many friends, they loved and were beloved, they had no fear of life or death; wherefore when life was fulfilled they died content: and therefore they now sleep placidly the sleep that is eternal; and the smile upon their lips, and the light in shadow from beneath their eyelids, tell that they dream for ever some calm happy dream: they enjoy unremembering the fruit of their perfect lives. And as we lingered along the valley,

*A happy soul, that all the way
To Heaven rides in a summer's day.
— *Crashaw*. (Thomson's note.)

side by side with the river, and the moon from above the southern wooded slope gazed down as in trance on that entranced Elysium, the thought of the sombre and baleful forest through which we had come weighed heavily upon my heart, and I said: How few are these in their quiet bliss to all the countless moaning multitudes we have seen on our way! And my companion answered: They are very few. And I sighed: Must it be always so? And he responded: Did Nature destroy all those infants? Did Nature breed all those defects and deformities? Did Nature bring forth all those idiocies and lunacies? or, was not rather their chief destroyer and producer the ignorance of Man outraging Nature? And the poor, the prisoners, the soldiery, the ascetics, the priests, the nobles, the kings; were these the work of Nature, or of the perversity of Man? And I asked: Were not the very ignorance and perversity of Man also from Nature? And he replied: Yea; yet perchance, putting himself child-like to school, he may gradually learn from Nature herself to enlighten the one and control the other.—Then the dolorous moanings again filled my ears, even in the moonlit valley of peace; and I awoke in the moonlight and heard the moaning of the gale swelling to a storm.

Index

Index